Digital & Hybrid Scrapbooking & Card-Making

With Photoshop Elements

Patty Debowski

Finally a book that explains it all in plain English!

Digital and Hybrid Scrapbooking & Card-Making with Photoshop Elements
By Patty Debowski

Editor-In-Chief – Nancy Carter
Assistant Editor – Michael Adam

Trademarks
Products and trademark names are used for information purposes only with no intention of infringement upon those trademarks.

Photoshop & Photoshop Elements are registered trademarks of Adobe Systems, Inc.
All screen shots are from Adobe® Photoshop Elements® unless otherwise specified.
Adobe product screen shots reprinted with permission from Adobe Systems Incorporated.

Windows is a registered trademark of Microsoft Corporation
Microsoft product screen shots reprinted with permission from Microsoft Corporation.

Warning and Disclaimer
This book is designed to give information about scrapbooking and card-making with Photoshop Elements. All information is as accurate as possible and no warranty is implied. Patty Debowski and The Digital Scrapbook Teacher shall have no liability or responsibility to any person who suffers damage from the disc included with this book or information from this book. It is imperative that you always duplicate a photo before editing it, back up your files frequently, and run virus protection regularly.

All website addresses published were correct at the time of printing but may have changed due to reasons beyond our control.

Printing History:
August 2007 First Edition

ISBN-10: 0-9796959-0-2

ISBN-13: 978-0-9796959-0-2

Library of Congress Catalog Card Number: 2007904160

This publication is available for bulk purchase. For information contact the publisher:

The Digital Scrapbook Teacher
18837 Brookhurst Street Suite 201
Fountain Valley, CA 92708
USA
www.TheDigitalScrapbookTeacher.com

Printed in China

Acknowledgements

OK, I have to admit it; every time I read the Acknowledgements in the beginning of a book I always think that writing a book was probably a lot of work, but how much did those other people really help out. Then I wrote a book, now I know!

My biggest thank you goes to my husband Mike, who now jokes that he's my executive assistant. I could have never done it without your help. Thanks for doing everything yourself including dinner, dishes, laundry, life, shopping, errands, setting up my classes, etc., etc. Your support and positive attitude means the world to me, I love you.

Thank you to my children whose mother essentially abandoned them when she started this project. Kristin, thank you for the dinners, running errands for me, and putting up with me when I abandoned my grandmotherly duties. Ryan, thank you for insisting that if I started this project I would finish it, I admit there were times late at night when I really didn't like you too much! Thank you for always taking the time to explain the different aspects of web commerce to me. Chris thanks for picking up the slack at home and running my errands without complaining, even when there was no food in the house or dinner on the table. For my grandson Logan, and granddog Cooper, thanks for letting me have fun with the camera and you at the same time. Thank you to my son in law Gary, a very gifted artist whose input and help I greatly appreciate. Thank you all for being good sports about the photos I take, and always giving me something interesting to scrap about. I love you guys!

To Gayle Kelley my mom, whose artistic talents escaped me. Thank your for instilling your passion for creativity in me. While I can't compare to your artistic creations, the computer has given me a boost up. I wish I could have shared this adventure with you.

Nancy Carter, you are my hero in more ways than you know. Because of you, I will never look at a comma the same way again! Thank you for your support and encouragement always, and for stepping up in my moment of panic. First I got your photos out of the attic, next I'll get you digi-scrapping!

Nami Aoyagi, my digi-scrapping buddy, thanks for being there for the late night calls and IM's. I can always count on you to tell me where the scroll bars have gone. It's been a fun and sometimes exhausting journey. I can't believe how far we've come together.

Thank you to Dee Steger, Robbi Sanders, and Stephanie Blay who have supported me for many years with their great friendship. Thanks for your input, candid advice, and putting up with me on my cranky days! Andrea Bunnell, thank you for taking over my Grama duties and inventing the perfect broken rib wrap to allow me to keep on writing. Sherrie Lodge, Dash Cotter, and Pete Schultz thank you for being my biggest cheerleaders. Bonne and David Irvine your help, advice, and enthusiasm for this project has been incredible, thank you. John Shipp, and Glenn Grandis thank you for dropping everything numerous times to lend your support.

A special thank you to my teachers-Pat Jones who possesses more knowledge about Photoshop Elements than any person I've ever met. Thanks for always answering my questions no matter how far fetched they were. Amy Castro, thank you for your enthusiasm, knowledge, and belief in me and all your students. Tracy Foreman, thank you for your love of digi-scrapping and your support in teaching my first class. Thank you to the students in my classes who have helped me see digi-scrapping from a different point of view.

The support of the digi-scrapping community has been overwhelming! Clara Wallace of MatterofScrap.com, thank you for your advice, my digi-chick, and the book cover, now if I could just look like the digi-chick I'd be really happy! Ashley Smith of PolkaDotPotato.com, thank you for the classes, advice, support and always offering to help. Ro Paxman of Scrapgirls.com thank you for having the right words at the right time (several times). Cindy Wyckoff at Scrapbook Dimensions Magazine thank you for sharing with me your years of experience, suggestions, and advice. Thank you to all of the contributors to the DVD listed on the next page who have made this book a true success.

Tim Flynn and James Neal, thank you for your patience with a brand new author. Your enthusiasm and willingness to help me publish this book is greatly appreciated.

Thank you to Bobbie Christensen for a great self publishing class and to Orco Construction for the perfect sign they displayed on my way to class on the 55 Freeway in Santa Ana, CA on March 11, 2007. It truly is Never Too Late to Be What You Could Have Been!

About The DVD

Included with this book is a DVD with Digi-kits that contain more than 1,000 pieces of digital scrapbook elements contributed by more than 30 digital designers. Enjoy them and please follow the designer's Terms of Use (TOU).

I originally planned on providing a CD to accompany this book so you may find that term sprinkled through the book until editing changes can be made. Because of the tremendous response from the digi-scrapping community one CD grew into three which necessitated using a DVD instead. Please be sure to thank the digi-scrapping sites for their contributions by shopping at their online stores.

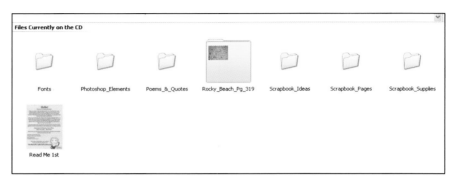

Some of the folders on the DVD are empty and are included as an organizational demonstration only. Please read the Organizing Your Photos, Digi-Kits, Ideas, Time, & Extras section to help you set up an organization system of your own.

Thank you to the following companies for their tremendous support of this project.

AtomicCupcake.com	Great Photoshop Elements Actions
CGEssentials.com	$1 off your first purchase coupon
ClassiqueDesigns.com	Kit & 25% off your first order coupon
CrazyUniverse.com	Kit
DecoPages.com	Kits & 25% off your Club Deco Membership coupon
DigitalScrapbookPages.com	Kits & 20% off your purchase coupon
DigitalPcrapbookPlace.com	Kit & 20% off your next order coupon
FreeDigitalScrapbooking.com	Kit & Buy 2 kits and get the 3rd one free coupon (lesser or equal value)
MatterOfScrap.com	Kit & 20% off one order coupon (not valid for custom stuff)
PeppermintCreative.com	Kit & 25% off your first purchase coupon
PingDesigns.com	Kit & $2 kits all the time
PolkaDotPotato.com	Kits & $3 off your order of $5 coupon
	25% off your first print order coupon
Scrapbook Dimensions Magazine	Kits & $2 off a one year subscription coupon
ScrapbookGraphics.com	Kit & Studio Doris 25% off coupon
ScrapGirls.com	Kit & Sign up for free six days a week newsletter
ScrapOutsideTheBox.com	Kit & 20% off your purchase coupon
ScrapStreet.com	Kits & 25% off your first purchase coupon
TheDigitalScrapbookTeacher.com	Alpha & Scrapbook Page Templates, Instant Organizer Tags*
Ztampf.com	Kits & 20% off your first purchase coupon

Please note coupons are valid for only a short period of time and may have expired by the time you purchased this book. If the coupon has expired contact the digi-scrapping website to see if they have extended the expiration date.

*To purchase all of the files on this DVD tagged please see the order form at the back of the book or our website at TheDigitalScrapbookTeacher.com. Purchase of this book is required to purchase the Organizer Back-up copy.

Table of Contents

Introduction

Why I'm Writing This Book

The first thought that truthfully comes to my mind is that I've gone completely bonkers. Then I think back on how difficult it was for me to learn digital scrapbooking, and I realize why I felt the need to write this book. I wish that someone else would have written a book like this years ago. Learning to digi-scrap, for me, was a very long and frustrating experience. I spent many hours surfing the web and reading anything on the subject I could get my hands on. If I would have had a book with complete instructions on how to use Photoshop Elements specifically to scrapbook sitting on my desk at all times, my scrapbooks would all be up to date (OK that's a lie!). Hence, the book you're now holding! This book is written in plain English so that a non-techie (like me) can use it. You will find that some things are repeated in different areas. There is a large index because nothing is more frustrating than trying to thumb through a book to find something you need especially at 2 a.m. If you are clueless like I was, or somewhere in between, this book is your opportunity to become competent without being committed!

I first became aware of digital scrapbooking in 2003. I liked the idea of simplifying my scrapbooking, even though I knew nothing about using my computer to scrapbook. I was working on a family scrapbook and a scrapbook for each one of my children, which was overwhelming. The next year I attended a class put on by Epson where they showed you how to scan your traditional page and print it out on a 12 x 12 printer. I bought the scanner and 12 x 12 printer, thinking I'd finally found the solution to my ever growing pile of supplies and photos. My plan was that I'd make one page traditionally, and then scan it and print 3 copies for my children's books. The printer and scanner were delivered and quickly began to collect dust, because it just wasn't as easy for me as the class made it appear. My computer skills, while adequate for my career with work specific applications, didn't come close to actually making a digital scrapbook page. I was completely clueless!

In 2004, my husband bought me a digital camera to take on trips across the country to photograph our son, who was playing college baseball. I kept it in my camera bag and used my regular film camera because I was terrified of a digital camera. When I dropped and broke my regular camera, I was forced to use the digital camera, but I fought it all the way! Now, with the digital images that my husband put on my computer, I would have to learn what to do with them. Of course I had no idea how to get them on or off my computer!

What I discovered was that when digital scrapbooking first began, many of the digi-scrappers were highly trained graphic designers and computer experts with expensive software programs. I had no idea what any of the terms like: pixel, RGB, CYMK, or rasterizing the vector shape meant-heck I was still perplexed as to why you press "start" to turn off your computer!

After buying every book available on Photoshop Elements, I finally found a Photoshop Elements Adult Education class. The books and class taught me how edit my photos and make slide shows, not how to make a scrapbook page or a card. I found some video tutorials online that I purchased, but I had difficulty watching and doing the work on the computer at the same time. I read and watched online tutorials and eventually learned how to use my computer to make scrapbook pages and cards the hard way! Next, with a friend I approached the Adult Education School about offering a digital scrapbook class using Photoshop Elements. During those ten weeks, of class I learned more than all of my students combined, probably because I spent many hours a week learning new things to teach them. My students loved my step by step instructional handouts. They could go home and follow, step by step and get the same results as they got in class. When I joked to my students that I should write a book, they all encouraged me and said it would make Oprah's Book Club. If anyone knows if Oprah is a scrapper, please let me know!

I hope that this book will help make your journey into digi-scrapping not only easier, but very enjoyable.

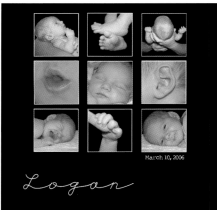

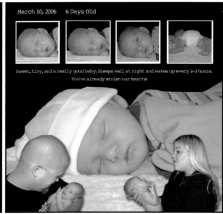

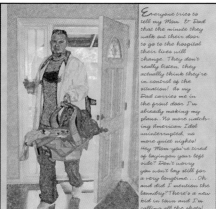

Questions Every New Digi-Scrapper Has

Why Photoshop Elements?

Photoshop Elements is the consumer version of the professional Photoshop program. The biggest reason to use Photoshop Elements over Photoshop is quite honestly, the price. Recently one of the large office supply chains ran an ad in my area offering Photoshop Elements 5 for $49.99, which makes it very affordable.

Photoshop and Photoshop Elements both use layers and Brushes, which is an advantage over many of their competitors. Using brushes gives your scrapbook pages and cards a professional artistic look. With Photoshop Elements you can even make your own brushes and I explain how to do it in this book.

Photoshop has many features that Photoshop Elements does not have but there is usually some kind of work around you can do with Photoshop Elements to get the same result. There are other programs available to download for free, like Grant's Tools that work with Photoshop Elements and will accomplish some of the same tasks that Photoshop does. Photoshop Elements does not take up as much room or require as much memory as its big brother, Photoshop. While Photoshop Elements doesn't have actions, there are some that you can install that will work great like the Chipboard Action from AtomicCupcake.com. This is on the CD that came with this book. If you are planning on submitting your work to a commercial printer, be aware that Photoshop Elements cannot produce CMYK images, but your printer may be able to convert your RGB images to CMYK for you.

Since I have been using Photoshop Elements, I have discovered only one thing that I couldn't do, which is make a text path. However, I can buy texts paths very inexpensively, so it's not a big deal. Someday I plan on checking out Photoshop, but for now I'm very happy with Photoshop Elements.

During the course of writing this book, an interesting trend occurred. I found as I talked to digital scrapbook designers, many told me that they use Photoshop to design their digi-kits and used Photoshop Elements to scrapbook with.

If you're new to digital scrapbooking and haven't purchased any software yet, most companies offer a free trial download. Try them out and decide which one you like the best. Visit Adobe.com to download a free trial version of Photoshop Elements or Photoshop. And, in answer to your question: No, Adobe has paid me nothing to write this book, I even paid for my own copy of the software!

What Should I Do If I Have An Older Version Of Photoshop Elements?

With every new version that Adobe introduces, they make changes that are usually well received. With Photoshop Elements 5 they removed the Undo button which almost caused a riot among users. I've found this to be a good thing, because it's forced me to use the Undo history, which works better by far. This will be the hardest thing to get used to if you upgrade to Photoshop Elements 5, but it's worth it. Most of what you read in this book will work for lower versions, and if it's a brand new feature not available in older versions, I've tried to make note of it.

If You're Using A Mac

I've read and heard from friends that when using graphic programs Apple makes a better computer than a PC. I have never tried a Mac so I don't know, but my PC works great. It is my understanding that if you use a Mac, you replace the commands that use the Ctrl key with the Command key, the Alt key with the Option key, the backspace with the Delete key and replace right click with Control click. Most of the commands should work the same for a Mac, however, since I use a PC, I make no guarantees that they will.

Scrapbooking or Card-Making - What's This Book About?

During the course of the book, I will usually use the term scrapbook page or scrapbooking; however all of the techniques apply to making a card or a scrapbook page. A card is nothing more than a scrapbook page folded, right? There is a section that shows the ins and outs of setting up a folded card and making a logo, but all of the other techniques shown can be used for either cards or scrapbooking.

Advantages Of Digital Scrapbooking

I should probably do a top ten list of why I like digi-scrapping but there's way too many things to list, but here's a few:

No Scissors. This written by a woman who once dropped a pair of razor sharp scissors right into her thigh while silhouetting a photo. After I pulled them out and visited the local ER, my husband and I were grilled by the ER doctor as to just how the scissors got in my thigh! Apparently this was the first scrapbooking injury they'd ever had. When our mothers told us not to run with scissors they forgot to tell us scrapbooking was dangerous too!

Save Time. Digital Scrapbooking is definitely faster, after you have learned how by completing a few pages. I can complete a nice page in 15 minutes or less. You can make a page for one child, and swap out the photos, and customize it for another child in minutes.

Save Money. Digital Scrapbook supplies are reusable and if you don't like the color or size, just change it. Your supplies don't dry up like pens, stamp pads, or glue sticks.

No Mess! I have no paper scraps on the floor or stuff sitting around. If I start a page and don't have time to finish it, I can put it away half done. Kids can't get into your stuff and make a mess because there's nothing out to mess up, there's also nothing to store. One ad for digital supplies shows a woman scrapping with a baby on her lap, which I guess is possible. Think of all the time you spend cleaning up and vacuuming after you scrap. All that time can be spent digi-scrapping. Learn to keep your computer files organized, and you have no mess and plenty of time to scrap.

I can shop 24 hours a day! For me this is a really good thing because I don't usually get creative until about 10 p.m. at night. Even though I have a lot of great scrapbook stores near me, none of them stay open that late! You don't need a car or have to pay for gas to visit digital scrapbooking sites!

Scrap anywhere! With a laptop anything is possible! Take your laptop to your kids soccer practice, camping, on an airplane; the possibilities are endless. I read an article about a woman who scrapped her entire cross country trip, as her husband drove. This would not be a good idea for people who get car sick obviously and somewhere there's probably a warning about digi-scrapping in a front seat in a car with airbags. I can take just my laptop by itself and scrap, or teach a class, even though the laptop's keyboard and touch pad drive me nuts.

Journaling is easier! If you made a mistake, just back up and type over the mistake, no need for liquid paper! It doesn't matter if my handwriting is messy. I can't drag my hand over fresh journaling and smear my ink either. I can even buy a font with my own handwriting so that it looks like I really did journal it by hand! I can print in white text, which means I can throw away my white ink pens that never worked properly anyway!

The Undo Command! Have you ever tried moving cardstock after your glued it down? That is, if you were able to find a glue stick that wasn't dried up. Enough said! Everything in digital scrapbooking can be fixed with the click of your mouse! I can ink the edges of my digital paper and if I don't like it, I can just undo it. I don't get the ink all over my hands, and who cares if my ink pad is dried up again!

Scrapbook stuff, what scrapbook stuff? No one (husbands, etc.) can see how much scrapbook stuff you have when it's neatly stored in folders in your computer. Gone are the boxes and organizers crammed full of overflowing supplies that you'll probably never use anyway.

More Options! I can change the colors of my supplies to exactly match colors in my photos or vice versa. I can blend my photos and papers together with blending modes to create new and different looks. Photos can be cropped digitally easily and better than with scissors, and there's no need for a corner rounder. Supplies are endless, you never run out of anything, expensive adhesives included! Digi-scrapping techniques allow you to produce a page that looks exactly like a traditional page or a fancy magazine spread or something in between.

No hammering or straining your hand setting brads and rivets! Digital brads and rivets are so easy and look so good! I have them in more colors and shapes than you've ever seen, and if I don't have the perfect one, I can make it easily.

Print Multiple Copies, or don't print them at all and share them by email. Make a slide show or burn them on a CD. I made a scrapbook for my Dad's 75th birthday, printed a copy for myself and gave a copy to my sisters, with no extra work.

Disadvantages Of Digital Scrapbooking

Once all of your friends and family find out about your new hobby, they'll be after you to fix a photo for them "really quick". Don't tell them how quick, easy and inexpensive your digital scrapbook page was to make or they'll want you to make them for their children too. They'll tell you they don't have time to learn how to digi-scrap. Take my advice and buy them a copy of this book now, because it will work out better for you in the long run!

If your children are on sports teams, soon you'll be asked to make their end of the season programs or sports cards. While this is a lot of work and responsibility it's good to practice on someone else's children. Usually the problem with doing projects like this is that you can never get all of the information you need by your printer's deadline. I solved this problem one year when one of my son's high school football coaches didn't get me the statistics I needed on time. I pasted his head on another person's body with a threat to print it in the team's program, and emailed it to him. I got exactly what I needed very quickly. The same coach is late with his statistics every year, but as soon as he finds out my successor knows my secret trick, he coughs up the statistics immediately.

Trying to share computer time with your family can be difficult. Setting up a time schedule for each user of your computer is sometimes helpful. Adjusting your children's bedtime to 5 p.m. so they can get up for their scheduled computer time from 3 a.m. to 6 a.m. before school starts, usually works out pretty well. Putting them to bed that early will also allow you to digi-scrap instead of making dinner. If this solution doesn't work for your household, start using your grocery coupons and buy yourself a new laptop. After all, you are scrapbooking for your family, right?

Digital, Hybrid, Bi-Scraptual, Tra-Digital, Traditional-What Does it all Mean?

Digital means using digital technology to scrapbook. If you own a digital camera you're already digital scrapbooking in a sense. Traditional scrapbooking, by definition, is not using any digital means at all, that's probably not too prevalent today. While I don't know for sure, I would bet that most scrappers today are using a digital camera. I was sad when I tried to recruit a friend into a digital class, and she asked me not to tell anyone that she didn't have a digital camera. She was embarrassed and said that she wasn't smart enough to use it. Using digital cameras or computers has nothing to do with being smart. All of us can do wonderful things that other people can't do. What I've experienced is that a younger person can pick up a digital camera, cell phone, or use a computer program that they've never used before because they were raised with that technology. Ask them to bake a pie, sew a dress, garden or especially make change, and watch what happens. For a really good laugh watch me try to put gas in my car!

Hybrid, Bi-Scraptual, Tra-Digitial are all terms which mean that you combine traditional and digital scrapbooking. To simplify things, I'm going to just use the term hybrid in this book. You are probably already hybrid scrapping and you didn't even know it.

How To Use Digital Techniques With Traditional Pages

The easiest way to incorporate digital techniques with your traditional pages is to edit your photos. Removing red eye, adjusting lighting, changing color photos to black and white, adding type, brushwork or a talk bubble to a photo can be done easily. Making these changes on your photos make a big difference on how your traditional scrapbook page looks.

Make a journaling text box in Photoshop Elements or in a program like Microsoft Word. There are thousands of fonts to choose from, and you can even buy a font in your own handwriting at several websites to make it look like you wrote the journaling yourself. Print page titles with word art and attach them to your page.

Print your digital supplies and use them on your traditional pages. Digital paper is just as beautiful as the paper you see in your local scrapbook store, but there are a few differences. The digital paper can be changed to any color you want, it can be downloaded instantly without a trip to the store, and it can be printed as many times as you want in any size your printer can print. Digital Alphas can be printed and cut out in any color and size you want. The big advantage with digital Alphas is that you'll never run out of any letters! Print clip art, journaling tags, and other embellishments to add to your traditional pages that you can size and change color to your liking.

Crop and print your photos in different sizes than the standard 4 x 6 and 5 x 7 sizes. Zoom in on a flower, baby's face, or butterfly and print your photo in a larger size and you'll be amazed at the difference it makes. When I have a photo printed 4 x 6, I can crop it down to a 2 x 2 myself with scissors and get the baby's head. By digitally cropping my photo to a 2 x 2 I get a completely different result as shown below, which is a little bit more impressive.

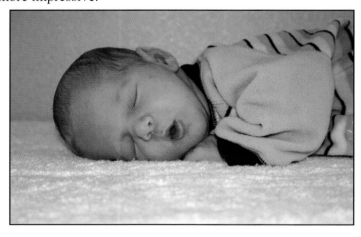  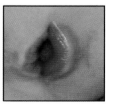

How To Use Traditional Supplies With Digital Pages

Anything that you fasten on to a traditional page can be fastened onto a digital page. Paper, embellishments, ribbon, tags, brads, etc. all can be fastened onto a digital page.

Several ways to use traditional scrapbook paper on a digital page include printing your digital page in a smaller size like 10 x 10 and gluing it onto a 12 x 12 piece of paper. Traditional paper can also be cut up and pasted to a digital page.

You can eyeball the traditional element or actually measure it to determine where you'll place it on your digital page. I measure my traditional elements and make a shape with the Shape Tool (U) similar to the shape of the element and put it on my digital page. I do this so I can get an idea of how it will look on the page. Before I print the page, I delete the shape so it doesn't print.

I have also measured a traditional element and made a stroke outline box on my page that I placed the item into. To make a Stroke Outline a specific size, activate the Marquee Tool (M) and choose Fixed Size Mode and enter in the size of the marquee you want to make. To move the selection border (marching ants), put your cursor inside the selection you've drawn. Make sure the New Selection button on the Marquee Tool (M) is activated and drag your marquee selection border to a new location with your mouse. Make a new layer with the new layer icon on the top of the Layers palette, and go to Edit>Stroke (Outline) Selection. Choose a width for your outline. I usually use 38 px because on a 300 resolution scrapbook page or card it's about 1/8 inch (300 ÷ 8 = 37.5).

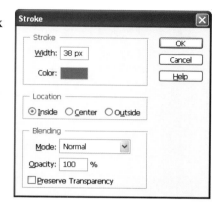

To get a square corner you will have to use Inside location because Center and Outside will slightly round the corners. Mode and Opacity can be changed at another time since you've made the stroke on its own layer. Do not check preserve transparency. Click OK, and you have a nice 1/8 inch outline to place your traditional scrapbook element on.

The example below is a 24 inch wide by 12 inch high double scrapbook page layout. I used the same 8 ½ x 11 scrapbook template and flipped it for a balanced effect. After I added my journaling, I printed this layout as two 12 x 12 pages on my home printer. I pre-measured my embellishments and made the white rectangle shapes with the Rectangle Tool (U) and added a Stroke Outline, as explained above. In those boxes, I added two packages of embellishments with red accents. Across the top, I added blue rick rack and blue gingham ribbon along with some buttons. On each side of the page, I added a package of balloon embellishments and cut a slit along the red Stroke Outline for the strings to go through the back of the paper. Everyone who's looked at the page was sure it was a traditional page.

Understanding The Terms Used in This Book

(T)	I have identified shortcuts in parenthesis. Make it a point to learn the shortcuts because you'll be able to work faster.
Shift>Ctrl>I	Press the Shift key then the Ctrl Key and then the letter "I" key. This is the format for the steps to take in this book.
Alt	Press the Alt key located on either side of your space bar.
Arrow keys	Use one of the 4 arrow keys on the bottom right part of your keyboard.
Backspace	Press the backspace key located on the upper right area of your keyboard.
Bracket keys	The Bracket keys are located to the right of the letter "P" Key. [&] are used to adjust brush size. Using the Bracket and Shift Keys adjusts brush hardness.
Ctrl	Press the Ctrl key located on the left bottom & right side of your keyboard.
Ctrl click	A method to select more than one non-consecutive item like a file, element or folder at a time. Click on the first item and then hold the Ctrl key and click on other items and they will all be selected. If the items are directly in a line use the Shift Click method. To select consecutive files see Shift Click.
Delete	Press the delete key.
Digi-kit	A digital scrapbook kit downloaded from a website or purchased on a CD. They usually consist of paper, embellishments, and sometimes alphas in matching colors and patterns.
Digi-scrapper	A digital scrapbooker.
Digital designer	A person who makes digital scrapbook kits.
Drag	Click the left button on your mouse, hold it, and move your mouse.
EHD	External hard drive. Used for back up purposes and when your internal hard drive in your computer gets too full of scrapbook supplies.
Elements	Parts of a digital kit, paper, ribbon, brads, etc. are elements.
Esc	Press the Esc key located on the upper left side of your keyboard. The Esc key is used to remove a selection border (marching ants).
Font	Different styles of type. Fonts can be easily installed on your computer. Many free fonts are available on various websites.
Freebie	Free scrapbook elements given away by digital scrapbook sites.
Marching ants	A selection border that surrounds your selection made with one of the selection tools.

Message Board	Similar to a traditional bulletin board, but on internet sites. Ask and answer questions that people need help with. A great way to get help quickly.
PS	Abbreviation used for Photoshop in magazines and message boards.
PSE	Abbreviation used for Photoshop Elements in magazines and message boards.
Scraplift	Using someone else's page design; digital and traditional scrappers look to others for inspiration, just be sure to credit the original designer.
Shift	Press either of your Shift keys.
Shift click	A method to select more than one consecutive item like a file, element, layer, or folder at a time. Left click on the first item, and then Shift click on the last item, in a line, and all of the items in between will be selected. To select non-consecutive items see Ctrl Click.
TOU	Terms of use. Terms of use are included in digital scrapbooking kits which specify what you are allowed to do with the elements of the kit. The designer tells you if you can use the elements for commercial use and usually tells you that it is a copyright infringement to share the contents of the kit with anyone.

What Do I Do Next?

First and foremost, I will tell you to resist the urge to download every freebie kit or font you can find everywhere and anywhere. What you'll end up with is a million files to unzip and organize (read the chapter about organization!). You can always spot a brand new digi-scrapper by their bleary eyes! If you ask them what they've learned, they'll tell you that they haven't had time to learn anything because they were up until 2 a.m. downloading freebies that they will probably never use. The CD that came with this book is filled with great digi-kits and templates. Use those to get some confidence, and figure out what you really like before you spend all your time surfing the web. We all only have so much time to devote to this wonderful hobby, I'd rather see your confidence and abilities increase, than your hard drive fill up with freebies.

Keep it simple, make a simple page and finish it. I start my classes out making a simple page that consists of a solid color background, a few photos with mats, and journaling. They are so excited because they actually accomplished something. Remember that you're scrapping to preserve your memories, not to win a contest; you'll get good enough for a contest with practice. Please do not open up a magazine and attempt to make the most complicated page for your first page; even if they have some instructions, you'll just end up frustrated.

I only wish I would have saved my first digital page to show my students. I couldn't figure out Photoshop Elements 3, so I made the page in Microsoft Word. I managed to make it and print it 12 x 12, which was a major accomplishment, and it was completely skewed, but I was excited because I accomplished something. You'll have much better luck because you have this book with step by step instructions, and your first page will look great!

If you're just getting started and you've got photos and digi-kits all over your computer, don't try to organize everything overnight. Make a plan to practice good file management now and begin by organizing a little bit at a time so that you have time to scrap too. Organizing seems like more work than scrapping, but once you see how much faster you can scrap if you're organized, you'll get excited about organizing too. Years ago I thought I was the only one who didn't understand good computer file management, but after attending many computer classes, I see that the majority of people don't understand it at all. I've tried to give good guidelines throughout the book to help you learn good file management.

The best advice I read somewhere was to scrap about something I was passionate about. This would motivate me to get better and learn more about digi-scrapping. I can tell you that this advice is true!

Practice, Practice, Practice, I can't say this enough! Because there are many ways to do the same thing in Photoshop Elements, sometimes I think it would be easier if there was just one way to do everything. Then you wouldn't have to remember so much. I've tried to show you the methods that I feel are the best and easiest to use. In addition, I've shown you ways to do things that you might think take too long. Be aware that there are shorter ways to do some things, but I've had you take an extra step or add another layer so you have more options to make changes. When you're first starting out, you need lots of options to make changes! You don't have to remember anything because it's all written down for you here in this book, in black and white. Write notes in your book to mark things you want to remember, fold the page corners, do whatever you can do to make this book work better for you because remember, it's yours, you bought it!

One of the best ways to get started is to take a computer class. I know you probably don't have a digital scrapbook class in your area (yet), but believe me they're coming! I flew half way across the country with two girlfriends to Dallas to attend a weekend of classes at PolkaDotPotato.com, and it was worth every penny I spent on the trip. For online classes, visit Photoshopelementsuser.com and EclecticAcademy.com (teacher Sara Froehlich) for some good inexpensive classes. I have a hard time with internet classes but when I print out my lesson and work from the printed lesson it's easier for me, so try that. Who knows, after taking a few classes you could end up being a teacher like I did! If you're in the Southern California area, check my website (TheDigitalScrapbookTeacher.com) to see if there is a class near you at a local community college. Maybe you have a Photoshop Elements class near you that will teach you to become familiar with the program, which is a great start. Any kind of computer class will improve your overall computer skills and introduce you to other people with your same interests. I often wish I had taken a basic computer class just to get started using the computer. People you meet in computer classes are very interesting. I was once in a class where in a five minute time period, I had the man in front of me screaming "I can't get it up" and the women next to me telling me her mother "Came out of the closet". Believe me, it's not at all what you're thinking, but it was interesting! Take a friend who's interested in digi-scrapping, or find a buddy in your computer class that also likes to stay up all hours of the night, and can take your phone calls and IM's (instant messages) when you get stuck.

Last but not least find a Digital Scrapbookers Anonymous in your neighborhood, because you're going to need it. Digital Scrapbooking is addicting!

Getting Started

How To Install Adobe Photoshop Elements 5

It's really easy to install the Photoshop Elements program. Follow the step by step instructions and you're all ready to go.

Close all programs on your computer, put the installation CD in your CD drive, you will hear the computer running.

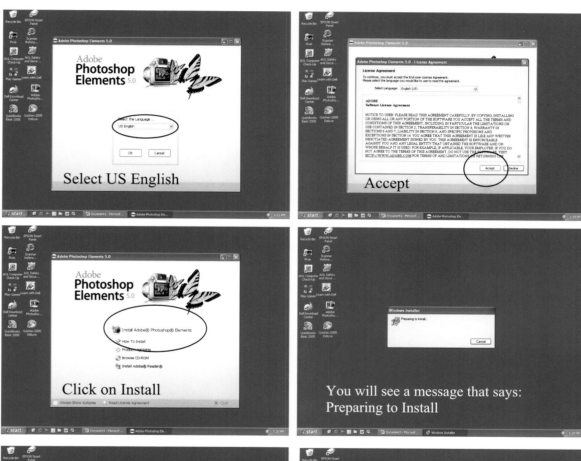

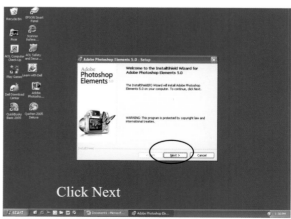

Click Next

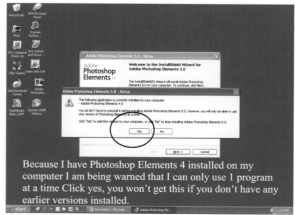

Because I have Photoshop Elements 4 installed on my computer I am being warned that I can only use 1 program at a time Click yes, you won't get this if you don't have any earlier versions installed.

I have Photoshop Elements 4 on my computer. I can use Photoshop Elements 4 in the future or I can use Photoshop Elements 5 but I can't open them both up at the same time. If I created something in Photoshop Elements 4 and saved it as a PSD file (Photoshop layered file) I can still open it up and work on it in Photoshop Elements 5.

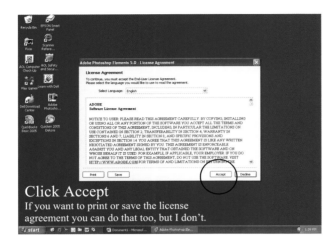

Click Accept
If you want to print or save the license agreement you can do that too, but I don't.

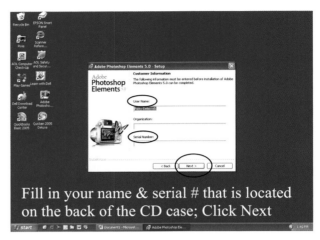

Fill in your name & serial # that is located on the back of the CD case; Click Next

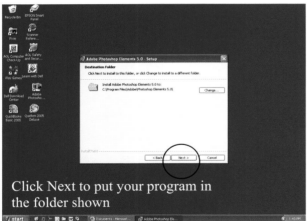

Click Next to put your program in the folder shown

The computer wants to install this program on my C Drive in the Program Files Folder in my Adobe Folder in a folder called PhotoShop Elements 5. This is exactly where I want it to go. If you want the program installed in another place, you can click "Browse" but normally this is where you want it to go.

You will get a screen with a progress bar that shows the program is installing and will take several minutes. Mine actually took 15 minutes before I got this screen that said the installation had been completed.

Click next and you will now notice a new icon on your screen for Photoshop Elements 5. Mine looks exactly the same as the Photoshop Elements 4 icon. For me to avoid confusion I deleted the icon for version 4 from my desk top by right clicking on the icon and choosing "Delete". Version 4 is still installed in my computer but the icon no longer shows on my desktop.

If you received a rebate offer with the purchase of this software don't forget to mail it in!

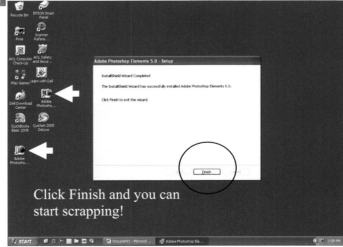

Click Finish and you can start scrapping!

Converting Your Organizer Catalog From An Earlier Version Of Photoshop Elements

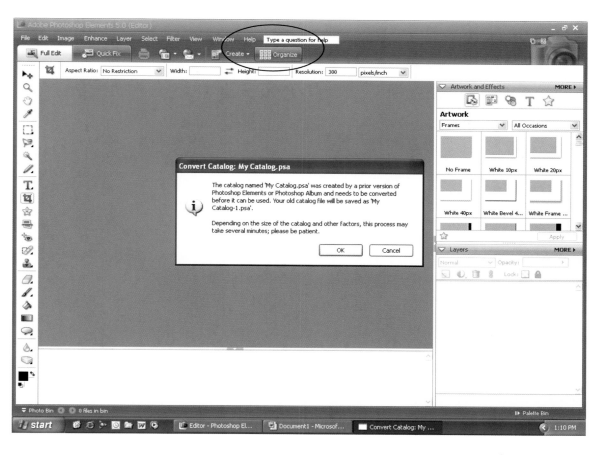

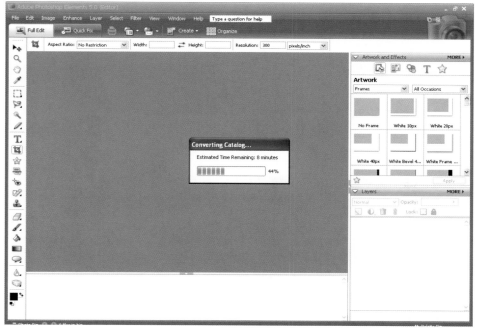

If you were using an earlier version of Photoshop Elements and imported images into the Organizer, you will need to convert your Catalog before it can be used in Photoshop Elements 5.

After you've installed Photoshop Elements 5, click on the Organize button in the Standard Editor (circled).

Click OK to convert the catalog. It may take several minutes if your Catalog is large.

If you get an error message restart the program and try it again.

What Did I Do Wrong?

Sitting in front of a computer screen that won't do what you want it to do is a frustrating experience. Even more frustrating is the fact that it's usually not the computer's fault. Believe me, I know from first hand experience which is why I'm writing this book.

When I first decided I wanted to learn digital scrapbooking, there was no place I could find to teach me. Digital scrapbook sites were just starting out and their tutorials left a lot to be desired. Books on Photoshop Elements only covered how to fix photos, so I learned in bits and pieces. This book includes all the bits and pieces that I learned, all combined into one place.

When you're first starting out with a new program, you will encounter problems. Even after you've used the program for several years, you'll get tired and encounter problems. When my friends and I make really foolish mistakes we call them ID 10 T errors. It's a very technical term used by IT people but if you read between the lines you'll figure it out!

These are a few things that hang me up even to this day if I'm not paying attention:

Where did my photos/scrapbook elements go?

Relax; if you dragged them onto a page they're still there. When you drag images onto a scrapbook page they all automatically land in the center of the page on top of each other. Check your Layers Palette to see if you have a layer for each item you're missing. If they are there, use the Move Tool (V) and move them around on your page.

Check to make sure that the layer is not hidden. If the eyeball icon is turned off, the layer is hidden; turn it back on and you should see the layer.

Is there a bigger layer on top of the layer you're missing? Check the Layers Palette and see. If it is, drag the missing layer above the larger layer.

Always make a point of being on the top layer when you drag on a new photo or element onto your page. This way, the new layer will always be the top layer. Otherwise, your new layer will be inserted directly above the layer that was active when you made the new layer.

Where's my text? I typed it but it's gone!

First, check the Layers Palette to see if you have a text layer to make sure that you really did type the text. Next, check to see if the text layer is underneath other layers that are covering your text. Is your text the same color as the layer you're typing on? If so, change the color of the text and you'll be able to see your text.

Why won't Photoshop Elements do anything?

Nine times out of ten you didn't check the checkmark for a crop or text changes. Look for the checkmark because they're located in different areas of the screen, and check it or try double clicking.

Why can't I edit my Stroke Outline or Brush work?

You didn't put your Stroke Outline or Brush work on its own separate layer. Always, always make a new layer for these items!

Where's my shape I just made?

If you've made a shape with the Shape Tool (U), check to se that it does not have a layer above it, covering it up. Also check to see if you made it in the same color as the background layer so it blends in with it.

I dragged my 12 x 12 digital scrapbook paper onto my new page but it's way too small, why?

If you made your page in 300 resolution, the digital scrapbook paper is probably a lower resolution. Check the resolution of the scrapbook paper file (not when it's dragged on the blank page) by going to Image>Resize>Image Size and see what it says. If the paper is 200 resolution or higher, it will probably be OK to size/transform it with the Move Tool (V) by dragging a corner sizing handle. All of my examples show you starting with a new document to avoid having a problem with lower resolution images.

I tried to size/transform an image and it's all out of whack, why?

In Photoshop Elements 5 you only need to pull a corner sizing handle to keep the aspect ratio the same. In earlier versions you had to use the Shift key, so if you're using the Shift key, stop. Pulling one of the side sizing handles will also cause the image to size incorrectly.

My cursor looks like a tiny + what did I do wrong?

You may have pressed the Caps Lock key in error. Try pressing the Caps Lock key again and see if the problem goes away. If you are using a tool that uses a brush, you may have a very small brush selected. Try tapping the right Bracket key to increase the brush size. To change the way your cursor displays, go to Edit>Preferences>Display and Cursor and change it there.

When I try to move something with the Move Tool (V) I get a rectangle of marching ants. Why?

Usually marching ants appear with small scrapbook elements or elements with a transparency in them. You are clicking in the transparency area and not on a solid part of the element. Zoom way in with the Zoom Tool (Z) so you can grab the element with your cursor. If you're still having trouble, turn off the Auto Select Layer option on the Move Tool (V). Holding the Ctrl key when the Move Tool (V) is activated toggles Auto Select on/off.

My baby turned off my computer and now my scrapbook page is gone!

Always save your page as soon as you make a new document and continue to save as you complete each step. This is a very good habit to get into.

Why do I have grid lines on my screen?

Your grid lines are turned on; go to View>Grid and turn them off if you don't need them. Grid Lines will not print on your project. Grid Lines are very helpful to help you lay out your card or scrapbook page. Changing your Grid preferences allows you to divide your project in half, thirds, etc. To change your Grid Preferences go to Edit>Preferences>Grid

The computer repair guy says my hard drive is fried, how do I get my pictures out of it?

You probably can't, or at least without paying a lot of money and then you still might not be able to get them out of your hard drive. Hopefully you've made a back up copy of all of your photos and scrapbook supplies as explained in the Organization chapter. Make a back up to keep at a friend's house too in case you have a fire, or someone steals your computer.

Why do I have a checkerboard on my screen?

The area with the checkerboard area is transparent; it will not print on your screen. If you want to change the appearance of the transparency go to Edit>Preferences>Transparency, and change the color and/or pattern.

I cropped a photo on my scrapbook page and my whole page is gone!

Don't use the Crop Tool (C) or Cookie Cutter Tool (Q) on a multi-layered document. Undo the crop and either crop the photo before you drag it onto your page, or use the Marquee Tool (M) to make a selection of the area you want to crop. Press the delete key to crop off the selected area.

I made changes to a photo that I saved how do I change it back to the original?

If you saved and closed the photo you can't get back to the original. Hopefully you made a duplicate, as I've stressed through the entire book!

My computer is running really slow, why?

Turn off other programs to help your computer focus on Photoshop Elements. Check to see if your hard drive is full. A good rule of thumb is to keep a minimum of 10% of your hard drive space empty. Installing lots of fonts, textures, brushes, actions, etc. will slow your program down too. If you've been working a long time with the program, clear your Undo History by going to Edit>Clear>Undo History. If your computer is still running slow, you should probably perform regular computer maintenance like running a disc check or defragging your computer which are not covered in this book.

I saved my pictures/scrapbook elements/scrapbook page but I can't find them.

When you saved your images, the computer asked you to verify that you wanted them saved in a certain place. If you're confused about computer organization, be sure to read the whole chapter about organization. If you recently worked on this file, you may be able to reopen it from Photoshop Elements by going to the file menu and choosing Open Recently Edited File. The last 10 files you worked on will show on the drop down list.

My wrist, neck, shoulders, eyes, swollen feet, etc. hurt!

Get off the computer and take a chocolate break. Use the good posture your mother taught you, and think about getting a tablet to work with. Set a timer, and make it a game to get something finished in that time period, this helps when you get addicted to looking for freebies.

People always run their finger over my card/scrapbook page, what did I do wrong?

You didn't do anything wrong! Your finished project looks so good that people think it's a traditional page!

I printed my page but cut my text and elements off the edges, why?

This shouldn't happen, but sometimes it does. I always try to keep text and elements ¼ inch from the edges of my projects. After you use your own printer or photo lab a few times, you'll know if you're going to have this problem or not.

My computer screen doesn't look the same as yours, why?

I always use the Maximize Mode when using Photoshop Elements. I like to see only one open image at a time in the Image Window, and the remainder of my open images in the Photo Bin. Maximize, Tile, and Cascade are the three choices you can choose from. To change your settings you can click on one of the icons on the top right corner of your screen. Hover your mouse over the icons for a second, and it will display the name of the settings. You can also go to Window>Images and make your change there.

The layer thumbnails in my Layers palette look different than your examples, why?

I changed the settings for my layer thumbnails, because when working with small items like brads I couldn't see what was on the layer thumbnail. Step by step instructions for changing this are located in the Layers section. To change how the layer contents are displayed in the thumbnail, click the More button on the top of the Layers palette. Choose Palette Options, and choose Layer Bounds for Thumbnail Contents. Now when you have a brad on your project, you'll be able to see the whole brad on the thumbnail. I've found I don't have to rename as many of my layers since I can now see what they are.

How can I tell what a specific font will look like without printing something out, The font drop down list shows them all as a plain looking font, why?

One of Photoshop Elements new features allows you to preview how your font will look. Granted, you only get to see how the word "Sample" will look in the font, but that is better than nothing. I think this feature became available with Photoshop Elements 4 but I may be wrong. To check and see if you can add this feature, go to Edit>Preferences>Type and make sure there is a ✓ in front of the Font Preview box. While you're at it, change the size to Large so you don't have the next problem.

When I select a font, the drop down list is so small I can't see the font examples, why?

My examples show my Font drop down list in the largest size available, which I still think is too small. Yours is probably set at the default setting. To change the font display size, go to Edit>Preferences>Type. Choose Font Preview Size Large. Make sure the ✓ is in front of the Font Preview box.

Places To Get Help

Use this book! If you need the information, it's probably in here somewhere. Check the index for a specific topic. Make notes and highlight in your book, so you remember where things are later on.

Check Adobe Help. The F1 key on the top of your keyboard will automatically bring up Adobe Help. Type in the term you're searching for, press the search button, and Adobe Help will search for related topics. I've had very good luck with Adobe Help, although in my version it still shows the Undo button, which might be enough to drive a brand new Photoshop Elements 5 user who's already cranky about losing their Undo button over the edge. The F6 key will bring up the How To Palette, where you can read tips on how to do things and you can even click on buttons that say "do this for me". Click on the printer icon, and the tip is printed for you so you can read it on a piece of paper rather than trying to read it and work on your computer screen at the same time.

Call your buddy. One of the best things you can do is get a buddy, preferably a buddy who is up very late at night and very early in the morning. This way you can call or instant message them at all hours of the day. Get a buddy who is excited about starting a new hobby and learning new things. I dragged my buddy Nami into digital scrapbooking against her will, and now she's a fabulous digi-scrapper and she also teaches. Fortunately for us we both think differently, so we each absorb different information. Usually when one of us is stuck, the other one can easily solve the problem….usually.

Ask one of your children; they're probably waiting for you to get off the computer so they can do their homework anyway. Because they're been raised with a computer, children and younger adults are more comfortable around them and have a knack for figuring out computer issues. It can't hurt to try.

Check a message board. The thought of visiting a message board was terrifying to me until one day I got so stuck, I had no where else to turn. Message boards are a wealth of information, and very easy to use.

My very favorite message board is www.photoshopelementsuser.com/forum. Everyone on this site is so knowledgeable and nice, it's unbelievable. There are people from all over the world on this site and some of them have posted 30,000 replies (no that is not a typo-thirty thousand). Post a question here and check the box to ask for instant email notification that someone has responded to your question. You could have an answer in minutes. Always do a search for your problem first and you may discover that you don't even have to post your question, because it's probably already been answered on this site. After I've performed a search, I always try to write a very specific title instead of just typing something like "Help". This way, someone who knows my answer will have an easier way of spotting my question. You will need to sign up to post on any board, but they're free. Photoshop Elements User publishes a newsletter that is fabulous, and entitles you to view many tutorials on their website for free. They also offer training courses online that are very good and inexpensive. If you are new to Photoshop Elements, I would suggest that you start with their Layers class.

Other digital scrapbook websites have message boards that you can visit. Just be sure to visit their program specific areas or you may get an answer from someone with a different program than you use. ScrappersGuide.com and ScrapGirls.com have message boards that I've participated in.

The Yahoo group of digital scrappers can be found at: http://groups.yahoo.com/group/computerscrapbooking. This is also a great group of people, but it is not Photoshop Elements specific, so be sure to state what program you're using when asking for help.

Don't be intimidated. Remember your computer is not the boss of you! Don't be afraid to just try something new. Always make a duplicate of your image and then try it; what do you have to lose? If you really get mad at your computer, you can always unplug it to show him (computers must be men don't you think?) who's boss. If you want to go that far, I'd recommend turning him off before you unplug him.

Take a break. Sometimes you just need to walk away and clear your mind for a little while. Take a walk around your neighborhood, talk to your family (if they still remember who you are), make dinner, or just relax. When you go back to your computer, and as long as you saved it, it will still be there waiting for you.

Equipment

To digi-scrap all you need is Photoshop Elements installed on your computer. If you don't have a digital camera, you can have your film put on a CD at your local photo lab for a nominal fee. If you don't have a printer, you can keep your scrapbook pages on your computer or send them to your photo lab to be printed. To share them with friends and family, upload to a digital scrapbook site's gallery, a service like Snapfish or make a slide show.

If you're hoping that I'll tell you exactly the perfect equipment to buy for your needs, I'm sorry to disappoint you. Beyond not being qualified as an electronics salesperson I have no idea what your needs are. Everyone has different things they want to do with their equipment. There are many books available that discuss equipment, but by the time they're printed, they're probably obsolete. To compare different models of equipment, I would suggest you visit several electronics stores and pick up a few magazines. Check with your friends and family to find out what they like and dislike about their equipment. I'll give you some hints to look for and tell you how I use my equipment.

Cameras

Digital cameras offer us instant gratification, especially for those of us who were used to buying film, and waiting a few days to see if we actually took any good photos or not. Buying a good camera is an investment in your future. What other purchase can you make that will provide you with years of entertainment long after it's gone? The photos you take today could possibly be around for hundreds of years. With the introduction of digital photography, cameras have changed so dramatically in the past ten years that a digital camera you bought five years ago is now obsolete.

I have two digital cameras, both made by Canon. I've always had good luck with Canon cameras so I've stuck with them for many years. I have friends that swear by their Nikons, Minoltas, and every other brand out there and all take wonderful photos.

My Canon Digital Rebel has automatic and manual settings and I can also change the lens. This camera does more than I will ever use or understand. It takes beautiful pictures with little help from me. One disadvantage of the Rebel is its size. Many times, when I'm traveling by air and have a lot of carry on items, I bring my tiny camera because it's easier than taking the big camera bag with all of the lens in it. I'll also bring the tiny camera if I'm taking pictures where I don't want something big hanging around my neck for a long period of time.

When I want a camera I can shove in the pocket of my jeans, I bring my Canon Digital Elph This little camera takes good pictures, but not of the quality of the Rebel, which stands to reason because it costs a fraction of what the Rebel does. We were lucky to find a small padded camera case that fits the camera, extra media cards, and the battery charger that can be worn right on your belt, This is great for traveling. My boys have borrowed this camera to take on trips because it's so easy to take with you.

Camera Tips

Set your camera setting on the highest quality setting available. Yes, it increases the file size, but it's worth it. When I digi-scrap now with my photos I don't worry about checking my resolution. I know from experience that it's very good, and I can print my photos poster size and they look great.

Set the correct date on your camera. This may sound like a no brainer, but so many of my students have the wrong date on their photos. Turn off the date setting that prints it on your photos. If you really want a date on the photo, you can type it more attractively with the Type Tool (T) or have it printed on the back at some photo labs.

Buy an extra battery. This is something my husband and I didn't think of until we were in the middle of a city tour of New York City when our new digital camera died on us. Don't let your battery get too cold because it won't take as many pictures.

Buy extra and larger media cards to hold your photos and keep it in your camera bag. Nothing is more aggravating than filling up a small media card and having to swap out another one when something exciting is happening.

Shop at a real camera store. Compare the prices to the larger electronic stores, usually they'll match the price or be just a little bit higher. The difference is that at the camera store they know how to use the camera and may offer classes too.

Read your manual (I know it's scary!). My manuals are very small with tiny print. I recently bought a book about my camera which, for me is much more user friendly to read and use. It has color photos and explains different ways to use the camera.

Write your name and phone number on your media card. In the event you leave your card stuck in a card reader at a photo lab, or drop it at a football game, you may have a chance of getting it back if someone can call you. Without a name no one knows who it belongs to, you might even add the word "reward" to it.

Write your name on your camera too; definitely add the word "Reward".

Make sure your media card is in the camera and not at home in your card reader; don't even ask me about my grandson's first birthday party. Some cameras have a setting that will not allow the camera to work if the media card is not installed. This is helpful especially if you can't read the writing on the display screen that says "no media card" without glasses.

Encourage other people to pick up and use your camera if it's sitting at a gathering because this is the only way you'll end up in any photos. My friends all know that it's OK to take pictures with my camera. If you're hosting an event, ask a friend to take lots of photos with your camera or their own. It's amazing the different types of photos you'll end up with when other people take them for you.

If your camera has a strap, wear it around your neck so you don't drop it.

Learn how to set the camera to take a photo itself so you can get some pictures of you in the group. If that's not possible ask a stranger, to take your group photo and offer to return the favor. If you feel funny about asking, take a look around and see how many people are taking photos that they're being left out of, and offer to take their photo first.

Take lot of photos, remember, they're free! If you've got too many photos, just delete the ones you don't want.

Photography Tips

I am not a professional photographer, and I don't pretend to be one. I take a lot of pictures at a time and I'm lucky when I get some really good ones. Several years ago before I went digital, I took a photography course offered by my local community college. I learned a few tricks but was a failure in the darkroom. Some of the tips I've learned over the years are:

Fill The Frame With People! When taking a group shot of people, get as close as you can to them. Usually what ever is in the foreground isn't important. Try this out yourself and you'll see a big difference. You also won't have to use the Crop Tool (C) very much.

Take photos from different vantage points. I've taken some great baby shots lying on the floor along the side of a crawling baby. Standing up high on a chair also gives a different perspective to the photo.

Use your photos to tell a story. I am not a big fan of posed photos where everyone is dressed up in their Sunday best, posed in front of the camera. These types of photos do serve a purpose sometimes but not usually for the type of projects I work on. When my mother passed away, my father wanted to use a posed photo of her from their church directory. I chose a photo of her on a camping trip where she had on a big straw hat and a huge smile. I remember telling him the photo he chose was canned and mine was real, but I don't think he really understood. People remarked to me how they loved the photo of her because it showed who she really was.

Frame the photo with some of the foreground, if you're on the ground shooting a photo of a toddler get some of the grass in your viewfinder and take a few photos to see if you like them.

Practice taking photos with different setting on your camera. One of the best hours I've spent on my photography skills was taking many pictures in my backyard trying different settings. I wrote down the settings I was using and then downloaded the photos on my computer. It was amazing what a difference the settings made especially on the close up shots of insects and flowers. I've learned from personal experience at sporting events that the sports setting must be used or I'll just end up with blurred images.

Follow the rules of thirds. Divide your camera view finder into thirds horizontally and vertically. Placing the focal point of your photo at the areas where the lines intersect (indicated by the circles in the example) creates a more pleasing photo. Take a photo where you've centered your focal point in the photo and then take another one based on this theory. I'll bet you like the second photo more.

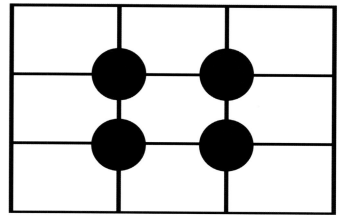

How to Move The Photos From Your Camera To Your Computer

The easiest way to get photos into your computer is with a card reader. Many newer computers now come with a built in card reader. Card readers used to be fairly expensive but in the last few years they have become affordable. Using a card reader doesn't deplete your camera battery which is also a plus. When I first got my digital camera, I had a cable that came with it. I hooked it up to the camera and to the computer and downloaded my photos that way. Either way works, it just depends on the equipment you have available. Unless you have a built in card reader, your camera cable or external card reader will need to be plugged into one of the USB ports on your computer.

Photoshop Elements has a Photo Downloader that will automatically make a new subfolder for your photos, rename them, and import them into your Organizer. If you want to use this feature, in order for it to work correctly, you must make sure that your Organizer was last opened in your Photo Catalog. Otherwise your photos will be imported into your Scrapbook Supplies Catalog (read more about this in the Organizing Chapter).

To download your photos, plug your media card into your card reader and by default the Adobe Photoshop Elements Photo Downloader will take over.

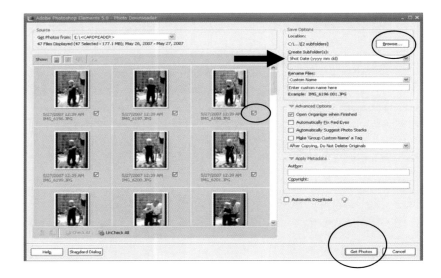

Click on the Browse button to decide where you want your photos to download I chose my folder named 2007 which is a sub-folder of My Pictures.

A subfolder will be automatically created for your photos, and you need to choose what you want the name of the subfolder to be. I like to store my photos by the date they were taken in a month, day, and year format (Shot Date mm dd yy), so I am going to choose that option. Your choice in subfolder names will become your default, and won't change unless you change it. Notice that all of the photos are automatically selected as indicated by the ✓ on the bottom right side of each picture (circled).

Under Advanced Options, I do not select Automatically Fix Red Eyes because I'd rather individually fix them myself. It also takes much longer for the computer to download your photos if it checks each image for red eye. I also select "After Copying Do Not Delete Originals" because I'd rather do that myself too. After checking my downloaded images, I go to My Computer and locate the photos on my card reader and delete them.

If you would like to rename your files, click on the drop down arrow. Choose a custom name which is the date the photos were shot in different formats, and a blank field that you can fill in yourself. For instance, if I shot my photos on January 1, 2007, I could choose Shot Date (mm dd yy) + Custom Name, and type in the field New Years Day.

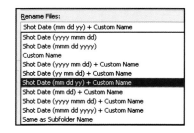

All of my image names would be named 01-01-07 New Years Day 001, etc. instead of the normal image name that is assigned by the camera like IMG 6200.

If you want to add any Metadata information like the name of the photographer or digital designer (in the case of scrapbook elements) or copyright information, you can add it here and it will be stored with the image.

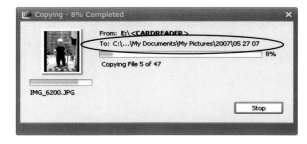

Once you set up where you want your files downloaded and how you want them named, click the "Get Photos" button (circled in the preceding example). A status box will show you the folder where your photos are being downloaded, and which file it is currently downloading.

Once all of your files are downloaded you will get a message showing that the download is complete. The next time you open the Organizer, the images will be automatically imported.

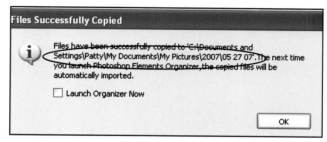

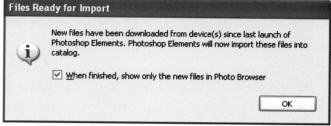

If you don't like the Photo Downloader, you can go to the Organizer Preferences and choose Edit>Preferences>Camera or Card Reader, and turn it off by deselecting the Auto Launch box.

If you delete your images from your media card by mistake and haven't made a copy, there are several websites that offer programs to help you recover lost images. I myself have never used them, nor do I know anyone who has ever used them. If you're in this situation, Ultimaterecovery.com offers a free trial download of their program. If your photos are gone, you might as well try it for free!

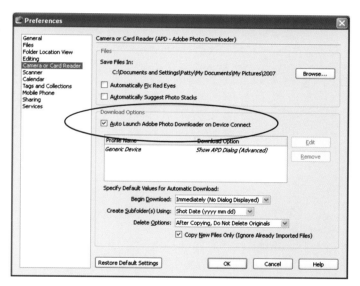

Computers

Once again, I'm no expert here either. I'm told by people in the graphics field that you have to use a Mac to be effective with programs like Photoshop Elements. I've always used a PC and I don't have any problems. If you're in the market for a new computer, try out both kinds and see what you like the best.

The best advice I can give you is to buy the fastest computer, with the biggest hard drive that you can afford, and then some. High quality digital photos and scrapbook elements take up a lot of hard drive space. It would be ideal for me if I could store them all on my computer's hard drive, but I outgrew it long ago and now I depend on an external hard drive (EHD).

Just like a camera, the minute you bought your computer, it was probably obsolete! I am not a laptop fan, but I use a laptop attached to a docking bar with a wide format monitor. I've got a regular keyboard, mouse, and Wacom tablet. I admit I haven't used the tablet as much as I'd like to but I'm working on it. In my real life job, I do accounting work in my home office, so I rarely move my computer around. I can't get used to the laptop keyboard and touch pad, so I stick with my old standbys. When I travel, I struggle with the keyboard and touch pad, but I'm getting better. My friends love their laptop with touch pads, so it's just a personal choice.

Adobe lists the minimum system requirements to run the Windows version of Adobe Photoshop Elements 5 right on their website. If you have a computer that was manufactured before 2006 you should probably check to see if your computer can handle this program. The majority of the information can be found by going to Start>Control Panel>System, and Start>Control Panel>Display>Settings. The amount of hard drive space that's available on your computer, which is very important to check frequently, can be found by going to Start>My Computer and looking where it says free space. This requirement of 1.5 GB hard drive space is only the amount of space required for the program, not any images (photos or digital scrapbook supplies) that you will be storing on your computer to work with.

Home / Products / Photoshop Elements for Windows /

Adobe **Photoshop Elements** 5.0 WINDOWS

System requirements

Windows

- Intel® Pentium® 4 or Intel Celeron® (or compatible) 1.3GHz processor (dual-core processors and those with Hyper-Threading Technology supported)
- Microsoft® Windows Vista™ (32-bit only), Windows® XP, or Windows Media Center Edition (XP and MCE require Service Pack 2)
- Windows XP: 256MB of RAM (512MB recommended)
- Windows Vista: 512MB of RAM (1GB recommended)
- 1.5GB of available hard-disk space
- Color monitor with 16-bit color video card
- 1,024x768 monitor resolution at 96dpi or less
- Display driver compatible with Microsoft DirectX 9 or later
- CD-ROM drive

Do not overload your hard drive or your computer will crash. A minimum rule of thumb is to leave 10% of your hard drive's space free. For example I have a 90 GB hard drive on my computer so I should always leave at least 9GB of free space to keep it running smoothly. I can tell you from experience that when I deviate from this rule, I have problems. Because hard drives fail, you need to be diligent about backing them up regularly.

If your computer crashes, you may possibly (very small possibility) be able to recover some or all of your files. My son, who owns his own EBay business, was fortunate that he was able to take his computer to one of the large electronic stores and have them retrieve his files, but he was lucky.

External Hard Drive (EHD)

A hard drive stores files and programs for your computer. The internal hard drive on your computer is probably named the "C" drive. An external hard drive is an additional hard drive that you plug into one of your computers USB ports. Adding an external hard drive is like adding an extra file cabinet or desk to your scrapbooking area to store more photos and scrapbook stuff. If you are reading a message board, it will probably be referred to by it's abbreviation of EHD because a lot of digi-scrappers are using them. External Hard Drives need to be plugged into an electrical outlet, unless you purchase a portable one. Office supply stores, electronic stores, and places like Costco all sell EHDs at affordable prices, often with coupons or rebates. Installing an EHD is easy because all you do is plug it into one of the USB ports in your computer and into the electrical outlet.

If you run out of USB ports to plug in your EHD, printer, scanner, etc., you can purchase a USB Hub. A USB Hub is kind of like an electrical extension cord with extra receptacles, only it's for your computer. My USB Hub is a lifesaver! It's made by Belkin, but I'm sure there are other companies that manufacture these too.

If you are taking any computer classes, it's nice to take a portable external hard drive to class with you. This enables you to bring your photos or scrapbooking supplies with you so you can work on them in class and bring home whatever you created. I use two separate EHDs as backups for all of my files. I store one of them at my work office and keep the other one in a different location than my home office. I also burn my photos on DVD's. Utilizing this system keeps me protected, not only from a computer problem, but also from a fire or theft. External Hard Drives will also fail, just like the hard drive on your computer, so you need to back up any files you store on it just like your computer's internal hard drive. Many scrappers buy 500 GB external hard drives and store their friends and families photos for each other as a back up measure, which is a great idea.

Internet Connection

Get the fastest internet connection you can afford! No beating around the bush when it comes to this. You can spend hours, day, or weeks surfing the web to shop for digital scrapbooking supplies, it's extremely addicting. Files to download are large and take time, even with a fast internet connection. Some of the digi-scrapping websites understand this and offer a choice of one big file or multiple small files to download a kit. Other websites offer a million small files, which drives me crazy and takes forever. If you live in a rural area and only have a dial-up connection available, you may want to consider having the site burn a CD and mail it to you. Many of the sites offer this service for about $5 for each CD. If you hate downloading and don't mind waiting for your kits to be mailed, you might want to think about purchasing a CD because this way your back up copy is already done for you.

I really shouldn't have to say this but-you must install and set your computer to update virus protection software regularly or you're asking for trouble.

Scanners

A scanner is just like a digital camera taking a photo of what you placed on the glass. My scanner is almost four years old; an antique in electronics age but it works great and does everything I need it to do. Since I bought my scanner, Digital Ice Technology has been introduced and possibly more features have become available. If you regularly scan photos that have been damaged, Digital Ice may be something you're interested in. Review the models in the stores and read magazines to find the type of scanner you're looking for. If you plan on scanning negatives or slides, look for a scanner that also has this ability, but be aware that scanning slides and negatives takes a long time. There is also an attachment you can add to your camera to take digital photos of slides and negatives, which may be faster than scanning them.

Originally I bought my scanner so I could scan a traditional scrapbook page and print out copies for my children's scrapbooks. This way, I only had to make one original page and print three exact copies with my 12 x 12 printer. Since that time I've scanned all kinds of things for different projects.

One thing I learned the hard way was to be sure to duplicate an image that I scanned before I edited it, because when I messed it up, I had to take the time to rescan the item.

Read your scanner manual for cleaning information. Don't spray glass cleaner or any other liquid on the scanner glass to clean it. Use a soft damp cloth to wipe any dust off the glass and if you have any large particles on it, blow it off before you wipe it clean to keep from scratching the glass. If you are putting food or something that will scratch the glass on it, put down clear plastic wrap or a clear piece of plastic like an inkjet overlay to protect the glass.

Your scanner will ask you what you want to scan (photo, text, negative, slide, etc.), choose the correct item.

Be sure to select color even if you are scanning black and white photos because it will give you more options in editing them.

Your destination will usually be a printer.

Most important is the resolution you want to scan at in DPI which is dots per inch which is not the same as PPI (pixels per inch). If you are going to use the image in the same size, choose 300. If you are going to enlarge it, you'll need to increase the DPI. By choosing target size, you let the scanner figure out the correct DPI.

Scanning Tips

Scan anything to use for a background paper or embellishments such as: clothing, toys, food, candy (chocolate not recommended, eat it instead), children's artwork, medals, awards, degrees, invitations, birth certificates, just to name a few.

If you're scanning something large and bulky, put it on the scanner bed and put the lid down, cover with a black or dark blue cloth or towel, turn the lights off and scan it. If it doesn't come out like you planned, photograph it.

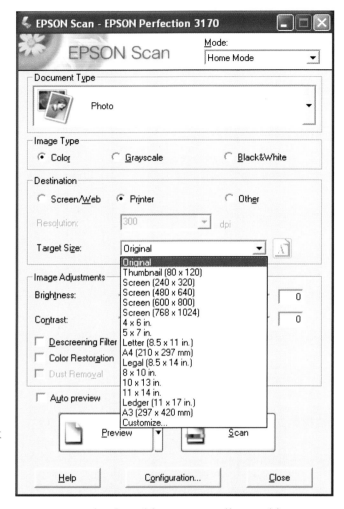

Stamp your rubber stamps using black ink and scan them so you can make them bigger or smaller, and in any color on your scrapbook pages and cards. Rubber stamps that you've scanned can also be turned into brushes.

Clip and scan newspaper articles on top of black paper to make quality images.

If you scan something and you get a funny pattern, rotate it 90° and try it again to see if the pattern goes away. The scanner light sometimes reflects on printed material and causes a pattern. Rotating the item on the scanner glass helps stop the reflection.

Scan doodles, handwriting, and almost anything to make brushes or copy and paste them onto your page or card. Writing with a black felt tip pen like a Sharpie marker on white paper seems to work the best for things you want to scan. If you're not happy with the scan, you can adjust it by adjusting the levels (Ctrl>L or Enhance>Adjust Lighting>Levels), move the sliders until you like how it looks. Select the black image with the Magic Wand Tool (W) and Ctrl>C to copy and go to your scrapbook page and Ctrl>V to paste. To make a brush from a scanned image, follow the instructions in the Brush Tool (B) section.

When you've got memorabilia piling up that you want to save in your scrapbook, scan it and use it on your scrapbook pages. At least it will be seen because no one is going to see it in a box in your closet, or attic.

How To Scan Multiple Photos At One Time And Divide Them Easily

After I scanned 600 photos in a 24 hour period, I discovered that I could have scanned many photos at a time and divided them quickly and easily.

Begin by placing your photos on the scanner bed. My example shows scanning four photos at one time. They do not have to be straight but it's best if they're not touching each other. Sometimes the computer thinks that two photos touching each other are one photo.

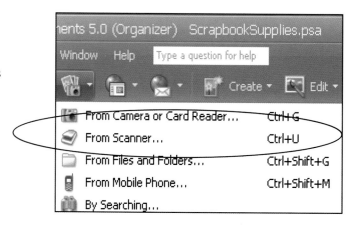

Go to the Organizer and choose Get Photos from Scanner (Ctrl>U). Choose a file where you want your photos saved by clicking on the browse button. Choose the quality and if you want to automatically fix red eyes. Click OK and the photos are scanned directly into the Organizer. Select the scanned photos and go to the Editor by clicking on the Full Edit button or Ctrl>I.

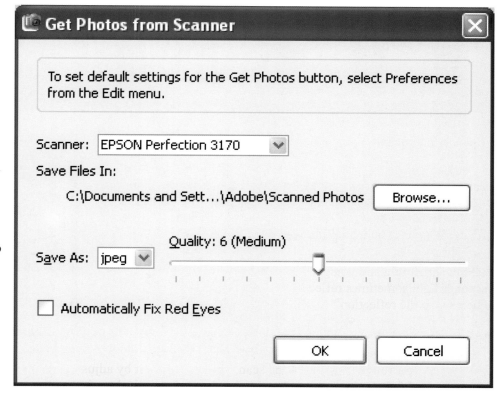

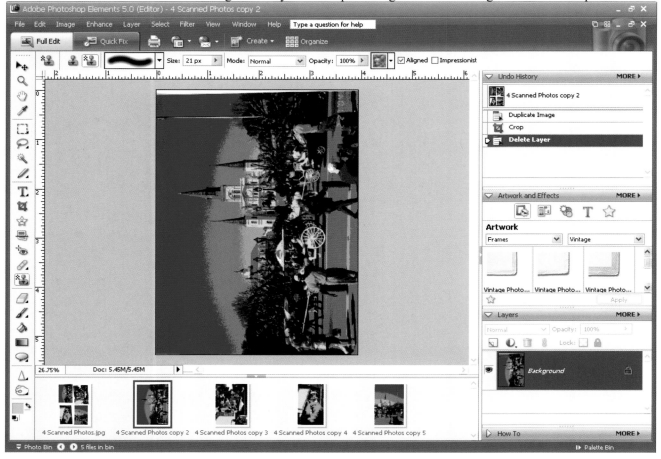

In the Editor go to Image>Divide Scanned Photos.

Like magic, my four photos are divided perfectly in seconds. Notice in the Photo Bin, my original scan is on the left and the four photos are to the right of it. My original file name was "4 Scanned Photos" and each individual photo has that name followed by Copy 2, 3, 4, 5.

It's a good idea to scan like type photos together, meaning don't scan black and white along with color photos.

The Divide Scanned Photos command can also be used to divide

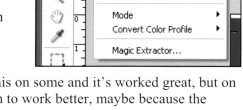

scrapbook elements that are all on one layer like Alphas. I've tried this on some and it's worked great, but on others it doesn't work as well. The rectangular shaped elements seem to work better, maybe because the program thinks they're photos.

How To Scan A 12 x 12 Scrapbook Page On A Standard Size Scanner

This is the whole reason I got into digital scrapbooking in the first place. My original plan was to make one traditional page and scan and print a copy of it for each of my children's books. My plan has evolved a little bit!

Put your scrapbook page face down on the scanner glass, pushed way into the top left corner. Go to the Organizer and choose File>Get Photos>From Scanner (Ctrl>U). Choose a file where you want your photos saved by clicking on the browse button. Choose the highest quality and do not select automatically fix red eyes. Click OK and half of the page is scanned directly into the Organizer.

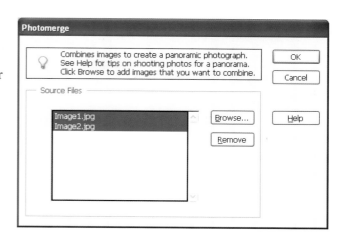

Put the other corner of the page snug into the upper right corner of the scanner bed and scan this too. There are now 2 partial copies of your scrapbook page in the Organizer. Select both of the scanned pages and go to the Editor by clicking on the Full Edit button or Ctrl>I.

Go to File>New>Panorama Photomerge, select the two files that you want to merge and click OK. Your computer screen goes wild for a few seconds.

I do not check the "Keep As Layers" box because the program does such a good job blending the two images that I don't need to fool with them.

Check the image size by going to Image>Resize>Image Size to make sure that your page measures 12 x 12. Go to the Crop Tool (C) and crop it 12 x 12 at 300 resolution and then you can print it.

If your files are merged perfectly, Click OK and you're done. Every time I've tried this with two sides of a scrapbook page, it works perfectly.

If your scrapbook page is bulky you may want to scan all four corners instead of scanning each side.

When I try to make a panorama of several photos, I don't usually get great results because I didn't take the photos from the same spot. Using a tripod would help with this problem.

Printers

The major expense you'll have when digi-scrapping is printing your pages. My advice to you is that if you're new to this hobby, wait awhile before you buy a printer. Find out what you really like and don't like in printers, or if you even like digi-scrapping. Try printing your pages at different places in your neighborhood or at Costco. The best pages I've ever printed have been printed at PolkaDotPotato.com. The prints were shipped to me, but they're worth the wait. While Polkadotpotato.com prices are a little bit more expensive than Costco, their prints are worth it.

Buying a printer will depend on a lot of things, the biggest consideration when buying a printer is what size you like to scrap. For a die hard 8 ½ x 11 scrapper you have a huge choice of printers. If you scrap 12 x 12 your choices are narrowed down considerably. You can always print your pages 8 x 8 on a regular printer.

I've owned an Epson Stylus Photo 2200 for several years, and it works fabulously even though it leaves a white border by design. My friend bought a new Epson Stylus Photo R1800 that prints borderless. Even though she has the new borderless model, she prefers to print with borders the way my older printer does. Something we discovered is that the 2200 allows you to change an ink cartridge in the middle of a printing job with no problem, while the 1800 spits the page out if it runs out of ink. One of my students owned a Canon that printed 12 x 12 pages beautifully. When we both printed the same page, we couldn't tell which printer printed which page.

Once again, my advice is to go shopping and read some trade magazines to find out what you really want. One thing that I do recommend is a printer that has different color ink cartridges. I used to own a color printer that only had one color cartridge. When I printed out photos of my son's football team in their blue uniforms, my cartridge quickly ran out even though I hadn't used any of the red or other colors in it.

Matching like brand photo papers with their respective printer makes a huge difference in the quality of the prints. I used to think that this was a big sales gimmick, but I personally have found it's true. I never refill my cartridges because it just isn't worth saving a few dollars to have it break inside my printer. Make sure that your ink is archival because if you're spending a lot of time on your pages, you don't want them quickly fading.

If you really want to find out how your ink and paper stand up go to www.wilhelm-research.com and check them out.

Wacom Tablets

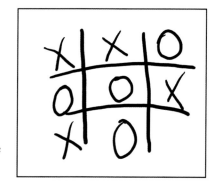

A Wacom Tablet is the electronic version of a note pad (tablet) and pen (stylus). For me using a tablet keeps my wrist and hand much happier than when I use my mouse all the time. It's also much easier to paint and make selections with the tablet than a mouse. Remember the difference a mouse made over using a keyboard (OK I'm dating myself here!), that's the difference between using a mouse and a tablet. The key to learning how to use the tablet is lots of practice. Practice painting and making selections with the stylus. Play tic tac toe and when you get tired of that, play Solitaire without using your mouse. Watch your monitor instead of your hand when using the tablet.

There are different models of tablets available, but the model I'm most familiar with is the Wacom Intuous. My tablet came with a mouse that I've never used. I'm not alone on this, when I've seen posts on message boards where someone is contemplating buying a tablet, the responses are usually: "Don't buy a mouse if you don't have to". Don't put the mouse and the stylus on the tablet at the same time or it will cause a problem. As a matter of fact, keep the mouse away from the tablet if you're only going to use the stylus. Don't leave the stylus on the tablet and attempt to use your regular mouse because your screen goes haywire. Keep the stylus in its stand where it belongs!

Wacom includes a great manual with the installation CD that comes with your tablet. The manual is written in plain English with lots of photographs to fully explain everything. If you've installed a tablet and have no idea where the manual is, go to Start>All Program Files>Wacom Tablet>User's Manual. Your tablet can be customized to your individual specifications. I've changed my tablet's Expresskeys to enable me to size my brushes and Undo by clicking on an Expresskey. To adjust the settings of your tablet, go to Start>Control Panel>Wacom Tablet Properties.

The Stylus tip is also called a nib and it does the same thing as your mouse, depending on the tool that's selected in the Editor. Nibs are replaceable. With the Move Tool (V) selected, you can move layers around by tapping on the tablet (same as clicking with a mouse) with the stylus and dragging the layer. You do not have to touch the stylus to the tablet to drag, but must be within ¼ inch for it to work. Paint with the Brush Tool (B) or make a selection with any of the selection tools the same way you would with a mouse but with better control. Tapping twice on the tablet is the same as double clicking with your mouse, or you can click on the top button on the stylus. Click on the bottom button on the stylus will be the same as right clicking your mouse. These settings along with Tip Sensitivity, Tip Feel, and Tip Double Click Distance can be changed to suit your individual requirements by sliding one of the sliders or clicking on the drop down box and choosing a different option.

If you are left handed be sure to change Handedness to Left. Side Switch Expert Mode requires you to hold the side button on the stylus and then click.

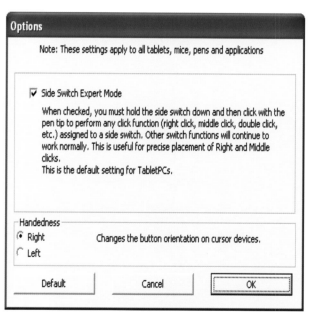

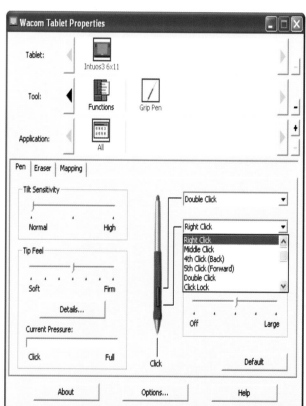

Use the eraser end of the stylus to erase an area on an image. If you would rather use the eraser end to do something rather than erase, chose something else from the drop down list. Change the sensitivity and feel of the eraser by sliding the sliders.

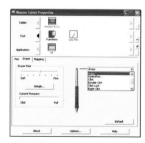

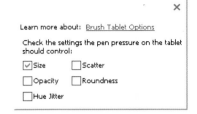

By using pressure on the tablet you can control size, opacity, roundness, hue jitter, and scatter of the brush. The Intuous has more than 1,000 levels of pressure sensitivity. Adjust these settings on the Brush Tool (B) Options Bar under Tablet Options.

Expresskeys are meant to be used by your non dominate hand while you hold the stylus with your dominate hand. I tend to use both my hand and stylus on the Expresskeys. To customize your Expresskeys, click on the dropdown box for the one you want to modify as shown below. I chose to make my bottom right Expresskey an Undo key. To do this, choose Keystroke from the drop down list and then type the keystroke you want to use, in my case Ctrl Z. If you make a mistake don't press the delete or backspace key, because the tablet will think that's the key you want to use. Press the delete key on the bottom of the dialog box instead. Type the name of the Keystroke you want to appear on the Menu, which is Undo for me. Now every time I want to Undo instead of typing Ctrl>Z all I have to do is click on the Expresskey with my stylus or finger. I have also changed two other Expresskeys to the right and left Bracket keys to quickly size my brush. This trick is a real timesaver!

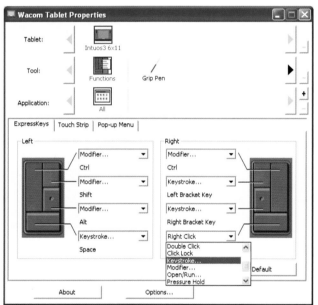

The touch strip allows you to scroll your screen. On my left touch strip I've customized it to fit my image to the screen (Ctrl 0) because I use this shortcut all the time.

The only way to learn to use the tablet is to play around with it and practice but, in the end it's really worth it.

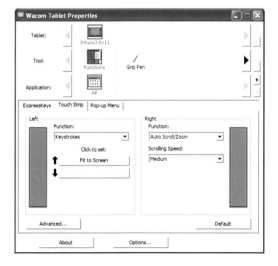

Organizing Your Photos, Digi-Kits, Ideas, Time & Extras

This is the most important chapter in this book, simply said but true. Notice how this chapter comes before all of the other chapters that tell you how to use Photoshop Elements and make projects.

If you know how to use Photoshop Elements like a pro, but can't find your photos or digital elements what's the point? If your computer is organized, you'll save time, money, and most of all frustration. Who wants to finally sit down with an hour to scrapbook and not be able to find the photos, papers and embellishments that you want to use?

Do you know where to find everything in your computer? Have you set up an organizational system that you can remember and use? Can you find the perfect blue paper with yellow stars that you downloaded two years ago? You want to make a scrapbook for your son's best friend. Can you find every digital photo of them together that you've ever taken? Would you believe me if I told you that you could find anything you need in about 15 seconds, if you follow my advice?

One of the biggest questions on the digital scrapbook message boards is; How do I organize all this stuff I've downloaded? Many of the scrappers who use Photoshop Elements post some pretty elaborate organizational systems. Their method usually consists of downloading their kits into a file with the name of the website where they purchased it. After downloading the kit into the website file, they make a folder with the designer's name and put a copy of the kit in that file. Next, they take the paper from a kit and copy it into a folder named "Paper". They've got folders named Ribbons, Brads, Rivets, Alpha, Journaling Tags, etc. Some even go so far as to make individual folders for colors, copy their items again and place them in more folders they've made up. Some really organized scrappers will print out a page of each kit and put it in a binder so they can see the kit. This system at first sounds pretty good, and hey, at least they have a system! However, this takes up too much time and hard drive space! Their system, as good as it sounds, will quickly have you overwhelmed. Copying everything over and over again will fill up your hard drive overnight. For example, a piece of red, white, and blue scrapbook paper will have at least six copies on your computer in different folders (Site, Designer, Paper, Red, White, and Blue) if you follow this system. I've met a lot of people who just download their digi-kits all over their computer and don't really know how or where to find them.

When these organized scrappers duplicate their digi-kit files they are also doubling (or more) the amount of storage space required to store them on their computer. My digi-kits take up about 30GB of space; if I duplicated them just once and then split up the duplicated kit into different element type files I'd have 60 GB of digi-kits. I myself, would rather use the "extra" 30 GB of storage space to buy more digi-kits (don't tell my husband, because he thinks they're all free!). Some scrappers have posted that they're using different organizational programs that they have purchased, and that they love. I haven't evaluated any of these programs so I don't know if they are wonderful or not. I myself use the Organizer that's included with Photoshop Elements for FREE! Instead of buying an additional organizational program I bought more digi-kits!

I used something similar to the "duplicate the kit and split it into a million different files method" explained above when I first started digi-scrapping, until it got completely out of hand. Even though I used the Organizer to organize my photos, it never occurred to me that I could use the Organizer for digital scrapbooking supplies. The default categories in the Organizer are geared towards photos (People, Places, and Events), however, you can easily add new categories of your choosing. Using the Organizer to organize my digital supplies has been a life saver! Any kind of organizational system takes time to set up, but I think you'll find that mine can be done easily and without any extra expense. If you don't use my method, set up your own system that you can remember and use faithfully.

Visualize your scrapping area after you've been on a major shopping spree at all of your favorite scrapbook stores. You've also just picked up a few months worth of photo prints at your local photo lab. Do you just let them sit all in one big pile and try to muddle through (O.K., I know the answer is Yes, sometimes)! Hopefully you'll organize everything in some kind of order. If you're like the majority of scrappers you've bought supplies that you know will be perfect for some project that you'll tackle in the future. If you're like me and my friends, you have enough supplies for all those future projects stored all over your house to open your own scrapbook store!

The key to working quickly in traditional or digital scrapbooking is to have all of your supplies and tools available at your finger tips. I've bought every kind of traditional scrapbooking organizational system out there and I am pretty organized but it is still a lot of stuff to store. My goal is to work towards being like a lady I met at a weekend crop. She only scrapped in her local store or at an organized crop. She had no supplies at home nor did she ever scrap at home. She carried her sewing machine and computer with her along with her scrapbook tools. She did beautiful work and was always caught up. I can't even imagine how much money I would have saved over the years if I was like her! I'm not going to cover organizational systems for traditional supplies now but hopefully the computer organizational ideas will get you started organizing those supplies too.

Getting Organized With Windows XP

A computer uses folders, just like manila file folders, in which to store items. Think about making a few manila folders and putting all your stuff in them. Make folders for photos, paper, ribbon, buttons, etc. and write the folder name on the tab. When you get around to scrapping, you just pick up the right folder and life is good. The reality is that in traditional supplies, your 12 x 12 paper isn't going to fit in a standard folder. Your buttons and brads will fall out, and your file cabinet won't be able to store everything you have, because it only handles standard size folders and one file cabinet probably won't be enough. Sure you can go out and buy the special expensive scrapbook furniture to fit it all, but all of that costs money. Computer folders are FREE!

Making New Folders In Windows XP

See the screen shot example on the next page for help with this. Turn on your computer, press the green Start Button, and choose My Documents Go to File>New>Folder. Underneath the folder it will say "New Folder" highlighted in blue. No not touch your mouse, immediately type !Scrapbooking Supplies and press enter. By using the ! Windows XP will automatically put this folder at the beginning of your folders; the same thing can be accomplished by using numbers. If you want your folder listed in alphabetical order leave the (!) off. However, because you'll be using this folder a lot, it would be helpful to have it first in your list of folders. If you made a mistake, right click with your mouse on the name under the file and choose "Rename" and type in the name for your file. You've now made a new folder.

Double click on the !Scrapbook Supplies folder to open and repeat this step to make folders for all of the Digital Scrapbook sites you have downloaded supplies from. Make an "Unknown" file because you probably have some digital scrapbooking supplies that you don't know where you got them from. Reading the Terms of use (TOU) file that came with the file will probably give you this information. Windows XP will automatically put the folders into alphabetical order inside the !Scrapbook Supplies folder. When making another folder, be sure to click off the folder you just made or you won't be given the option to make a New Folder. To delete a folder you don't need, right click on the folder and choose delete. Be aware that when you delete a folder, you delete all of the sub-folders and files in that folder.

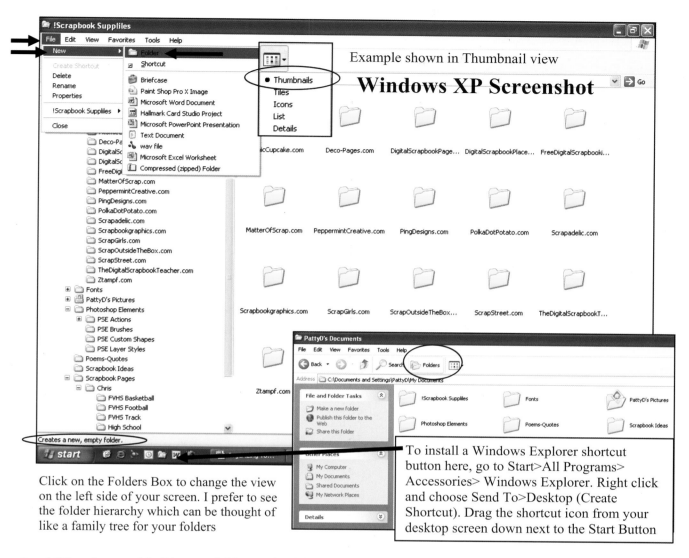

Click on the Folders Box to change the view on the left side of your screen. I prefer to see the folder hierarchy which can be thought of like a family tree for your folders

To install a Windows Explorer shortcut button here, go to Start>All Programs> Accessories> Windows Explorer. Right click and choose Send To>Desktop (Create Shortcut). Drag the shortcut icon from your desktop screen down next to the Start Button

In addition, in your My Pictures folder, make folders for 2007, 2006, 2005, and for any other years that you have digital photos (either scanned or taken with a digital camera).

Included on the CD that came with this book are a variety of digital gifts from many very talented, generous digital designers that you'll need to make folders for.

If you're brand new to digital scrapbooking, I've saved you a few steps! All of the free kits on the CD are already in a folder with the name of !Scrapbook Supplies. Inside this folder are all of the individual site folders. All you need to do is open the CD, right click on the !Scrapbook Supplies folder and choose copy. Go to your My Documents folder and right click again and choose Paste. It may take a few minutes to copy everything to your computer because there's a lot of great stuff on the CD! I've also made folders for: Photoshop Elements (Actions, Brushes, Custom Shapes, & Layer Styles), Fonts, Poems & Quotes, Scrapbook Ideas, and Scrapbook Pages. Be sure to look inside the Actions Folder for the AtomicCupcake.com Chipboard and other free actions.

Starting today, as you download from the internet, make it a point to download directly into the correct folder. Soon you'll be on your way to always being organized. For tips on downloading files, be sure to read the Shopping, Downloading, & Installing chapter. If you have photos, fonts, and digi-kits that are floating around in your computer start spending a little bit of time every day to get them into the correct folders. To move your digi-kit files and folders, drag and drop them into your new folders. Another method to use it to go to Edit>Move to Folder and then select the folder you want to move to in the list. If you have a large amount of files that need to be organized, don't get overwhelmed! Do a little bit at a time and reward yourself when you get the whole project done by buying more digi-kits! It might be helpful to print your computer screen on a piece of paper and mark off each file that's organized as you complete it. To do this press the "Print Screen" button located at the upper right area of your keyboard. This copies your computer screen like my screen shots. Go to a word processing program like Microsoft Word and open a new document and type Ctrl>V (or Edit>Paste) and you'll paste your computer screen shot onto your new document. Print out the screen shot and mark off the folders as you organize them. This method works very well for me.

By now you're questioning this method because you're thinking that you don't really care where you got the supplies; you just care about where all of your soccer kits are. After all, you volunteered to make the team scrapbook and you need to find your supplies pronto! I should have made a chapter that tells you how to keep your new hobby a secret!

I keep the kits by site for several reasons:

Sometimes I forget if I bought a kit. I can quickly check in my folder, which is quicker than trying to check my account file on the site. PCCrafter.com, a great website for clip art says right on the item "You already own me" if you're signed in to their site, which is really nice. They also have a wish list. My wish is that more of the sites would add these features.

If I have a file that has a problem I can email the site and get it replaced. I bought a kit from ScrapGirls.com and, against all my own advice, only unzipped the paper that I wanted to use right away. When I went to use the Alphas that I hadn't unzipped, I realized that I didn't download them correctly and I had a corrupted zip file. I emailed ScrapGirls.com and they promptly sent me a link to download the alphas again.

Before you proceed be sure that you've copied the folder !Scrapbook Supplies from the CD that came with this book to your My Documents folder.

Backing Up Your Folders

To copy a folder right click on the folder and select copy, go to your External Hard Drive (EHD) or CD/DVD (disc) drive and paste it. Don't forget to burn the CD/DVD.

If you use an EHD, it's easy enough to delete the old folders and replace them with a new updated folder when it comes time to back-up again. If you're backing up on a disc, this method is not feasible because you'll be burning new discs constantly.

To make a back-up copy of your folders, copy and burn your files to a disc and write the date on the disc. Set up a schedule to back-up all of the files that you've modified since your last back-up. To view your modified files, open the folder that you are going to back-up. My example shows my 2006 folder that's located in my My Pictures folder. I have my folders displayed in detail view which can be accessed by going to View>Details or clicking on the icon that looks like a waffle and choosing Details. Normally I keep my view setting at Thumbnails so that I can see a Thumbnail view of my image. When you're doing the back-up, switch to Details and then switch back to Thumbnails.

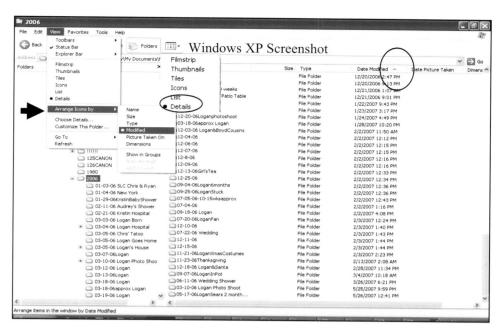

When you select Modified, your folders are arranged according to the last date they were modified. Folders will be listed in order of date with either the newest or oldest folder on top. To change the order that your folders are displayed, click on the triangle next to Date Modified (circled in my example). Copy and burn the files and folders to CD/DVD that have been modified since the last time you backed up. Write the date on the disc so you don't forget when you did the back-up. Keep a copy of the discs away from your home.

Don't forget to return your Folders View back to Thumbnails when you're done.

Getting Organized With The Photoshop Elements Organizer

There are a couple of ways to get to the Organizer in Photoshop Elements 5. If your program opens in the Welcome Screen, click on "View and Organize Photos" and the Organizer will open.

If you would like to skip the Welcome screen (which I do), click on Welcome Screen drop down arrow at the bottom left of the screen and choose Editor or Organizer. Your program will open to whichever one you choose. This speeds up opening your program by eliminating one step. If you want to change your mind later, go to Window>Welcome and the Welcome screen will once again open up first.

The Organizer does not store the actual images, it stores links to the image and information about the image. One important thing to note is that you do not want to move your images after you've imported them into the Organizer, so get your folders set in your My Documents folder first.

Importing Your Photos and Digital Scrapbook Supplies Into The Organizer

If you're in the Editor in Full Edit or Quick Fix mode, click on the Organize Button on the right under Help. In earlier Photoshop Elements versions, the Organizer

was sometimes referred to as the Photo Browser; if you see this term know that it refers to the Organizer. In my version of Photoshop Elements 5, Adobe Help has many topics for the Browser, If you need help for the Organizer and you don't have any luck, type "Browser" in the search field.

I've found that it's better to have a separate Catalog for my photos and scrapbook supplies. To make a new Catalog go to File>Catalog (shortcut is Ctrl>Shift>C). Click on New and then type in the file name Scrapbook Supplies. Because I already have a catalog with this name, I'm using Scrapbook Supplies 1 in my example.

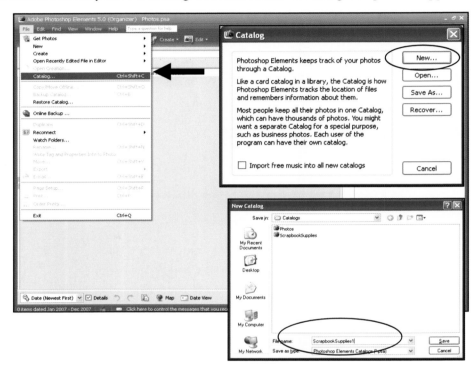

After you type in the name of your new catalog, the Organizer will open into the new catalog. To make sure you are in the correct catalog, look at the very top of your screen to the right of the words Adobe Photoshop Elements 5.0 (Organizer), and it will list your catalog name followed by PSA.
Bringing photos or digital scrapbook supplies into the Organizer is accomplished the same way because the program considers all images photos. Click on the camera icon at the top of the Organizer screen and choose where you want to get your images from. In this example I'm going to import a scrapbook kit from the Scrapbook Supplies folder in the My Documents folder.

From the Get Photos drop down list, click "From Files and Folders" or type the shortcut Ctrl>Shift>G.

Locate the folder where your images are stored in your !Scrapbook Supplies folder, which is in your My Documents folder.

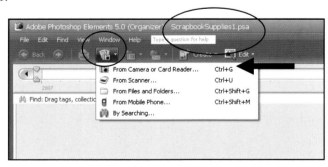

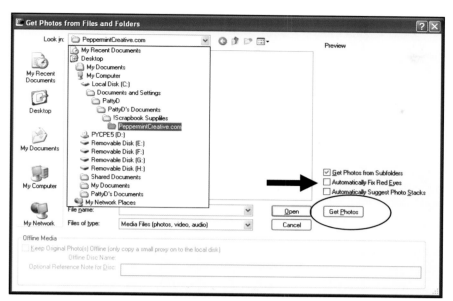

This example shows the Miss Mint Coordinated Kit from PeppermintCreative.com that is included on the CD that came with your book.

Click on the kit folder so that it's highlighted.

Some kits, like the ScrapGirls.com Refresh kit, have different folders for paper, embellishments, alphas, etc. It's much faster to import each folder separately and tag it, because you can tag all of your paper at once instead of trying to tag paper and alphas all together.

I purposely left the "Automatically Fix Red Eyes" button unchecked because it slows the import time. I also prefer to fix my own red eyes on my photos. Scrapbook supplies don't have red eyes, but remember it's an image, so Photoshop Elements will look for red eyes and try to fix them anyway, so keep it turned off.

Click the Get Photos Button. Don't panic when you get a message like this. The media they are talking about is the TOU (terms of use) file that comes with the kit. The TOU spells out what you can and can't do with the kit like using it for commerical use, giving it to your friends, etc. Click OK.

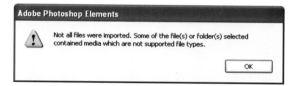

The only items that you see now are what you just imported from the Miss Mint kit. If you want to see everything else in your Organizer, you can press the back button. All you want to see right now is what you just imported because it's easier to tag small groups of files than a million at a time.

Check the box "Don't Show Again" if you don't want to see this warning each time you import images.

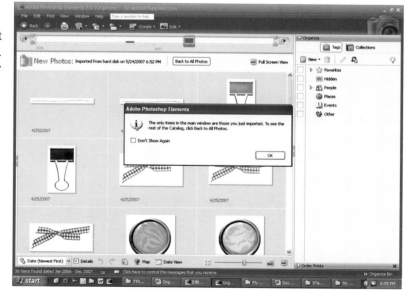

Now that you have all of the kit in your Organizer, you can highlight one or more images and then click on the Editor drop down menu and choose Quick Fix or Standard Edit (shortcut Ctrl I) to edit them. To select more than one image, click on an image and Ctrl click on the other images if they're not directly next to each other.

To select images all in a row, click on one and Shift click on the last image and all images in between will be selected (highlighted).

Having the images in the Organizer is nice because you can see them much better than the tiny thumbnail view in your folder. Tagging your images is what makes the Organizer really wonderful.

Installing My Instant Tag File To Save You Hours of Work

Adding tags to your digital scrapbook supplies allows you to find a blue, white, and yellow striped paper with stars on it in about five seconds. Adding tags to your photos will locate photos just as fast. The key is that you have to take the time to set up a set of categories and tags, and actually tag your images. I can promise you that every minute you spend tagging your images will pay off in time saved looking for things.

Because I file my photos by date and event in my My Pictures folder, I have put more emphasis on keeping up to date on organizing my scrapbook supplies. Not to say that I don't plan on getting caught up soon on my photos. If you have a choice of what to tag first, I'd tag the scrapbook supplies while keeping your photos in chronological order.

By purchasing this book you have made a giant step forward in getting organized, whether you realize it or not! Included on the CD that came with your book is a file called "Organizer Tags". This file will save you hours and hours of work making your own tags and categories. This file alone is worth every penny you paid for this book. There are probably more tags and categories than you need in this set, but I figured it was easier for you to delete tags than make new ones. The really cool thing is that I've inserted images on all of the tags for you already. The red tag is red, the alpha tags shows an alpha, etc. Installation of the tags is almost instant which seems too good to be true, but it is!

Installing the tags file is simple. Click on the "New" drop down arrow and choose From File. Open the Organizer Tags folder on the CD, select the Tags file and click Open.

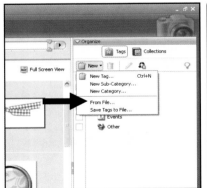 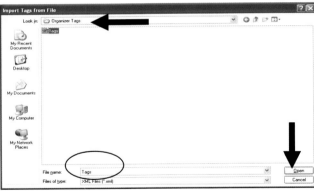

The installation of your tags is lightening fast! At first you're not too impressed by what you see; that is until you click on one of the drop down arrows on Color, Designers, Elements, or Theme.

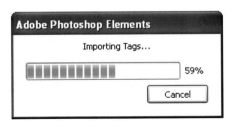 

I told you this is worth every penny you paid for this book! The only problem is that you now have no excuse for being unorganized!

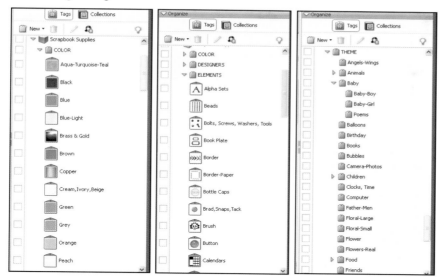

In addition to the other categories shown, the Designers Category has sub-categories for every designer that contributed a kit in support of this book.

```
<tagset-item-value-name>
  <![CDATA[ Scrapbook Supplies ]]>
</tagset-item-value-name>
<tagset-item-value-icon>
  <![CDATA
  [ 89504e470d0a1a0a0000000d4948445200000
  >
</tagset-item-value-icon>
<tagset-item-value-frame-color>
  <![CDATA[ 52aaaa ]]>
</tagset-item-value-frame-color>
<tagset-item>
  <tagset-item-value-container-flag>1</tagset
- <tagset-item-value-name>
    <![CDATA[ COLOR ]]>
  </tagset-item-value-name>
```

Almost every person that has received the Tags file has decided that they didn't need to follow the step by step easy instructions to install them. I end up getting emails that say "Help! I don't understand what I'm supposed to do with this, I can't understand any of the writing!" Guess what? I don't understand it either because it's written in code! If you see something like this you didn't follow my instructions. Go back and follow the instructions exactly and you'll have all your tags perfectly installed.

Making Your Own Categories, Sub-Categories & Tags

Follow these instructions to make other tags and categories for this Catalog and for your photo catalog.

Go to Tags>New>Create New Category

The big difference between Category, Sub-Category and Tag is the icons that identify them. A Category uses one of the cartoon like icons, and a Sub-Category uses a plain looking tag. A Tag uses an actual Tag icon that is filled with the first image you tag, which can be changed. I've chosen to use Sub-Categories for some items only because they take up less space. If you later decide you want a Sub-Category to be a Tag or vice-versa, right click on it and change it.

Type a Category Name and choose an Icon. The Choose Color box will take you to the Adobe Color Picker, but the only color that will change is the thin tag outline around the icon. Click OK when you've changed the color.

With the Scrapbook Supplies Category highlighted, click on Tags>New Sub-Category and make Sub Categories for Color, Elements, Designers, and Theme. Make sure each time you make a new Sub Category that Scrapbook Supplies is highlighted. The Sub-Categories are automatically placed in alphabetical order by default. If you want to change the order you can put a number in front of the name, or change to manual sorting by changing it in the Tags and Collections Preferences as shown later in this section.

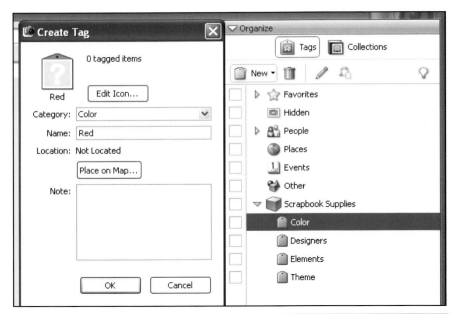

Next highlight the Color Sub-Category and go to New>New Tag or Ctrl N and make tags for all of the colors you want to make. The icon is currently blank. You can click on the Edit Icon button to put inside the icon however, the first time you tag a file that file will become the icon so I wouldn't spend my time doing this now.

Continue making tags and categories until you have them set up the way you want. If you want to remove some of the default categories, right click and choose delete. You can't delete the Favorite and Hidden Category, which is fine because I use them for scrapbooking. When I've taken many similar photos, I mark the photos I want to use on my pages with a 5 star tag from the Favorite category.

To edit a tag or category, right click on it and choose one of the options.

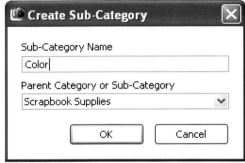

When making tags for your photos try to think of how you'll want to use the tagging system you set up. At the very least set up individual tags for every family member and pet. From there you'll want to add tags for friends and possibly places you've been, etc. The possibilities are endless.

Because I've used this system for a few years, I've made some changes to my system. Most of this concerns the Designer tags. I've discovered that Designers don't always stay at the same site. Hey, regular people change jobs too! What I do is make a sub-category for the Designer's Name and then add a hyphen and type the site name. Next I create a sub-category with the name of the kit. This way I can pull up all of the images from just one kit or all of the elements the designer has made that I own.

This is an example of how I would make sub-categories for the Candy Fairway kit by Miss Mint at Peppermint Creative.

Changing The Image in Your Tag Icon

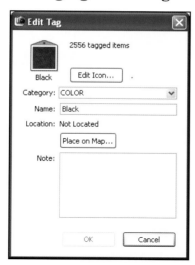

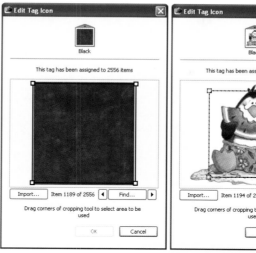

To edit the image that shows in your tag, right click on the tag and choose "Edit (name of your tag) Tag". The Edit Tag dialog box will appear. Click on the "Edit Icon" button.

When the Edit Icon dialog box appears, you are given the option to import an image or to scroll through your tagged images and choose another image to display. Once you find the image you want, drag the corner sizing handles in, out, or to another location on the image to crop the part of the image that will appear in the tag.

Click OK when you're finished and your tag will now display the image you chose.

How To Tag Your Photos & Digital Scrapbook Supplies

To apply the tags and sub-categories to your images, click and drag the tag or sub-category to your image.

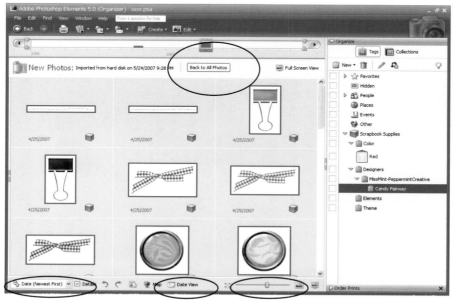

For example, I want to tag all of the images from the Candy Fairway kit with a tag for that kit. I click on one of the images and then type Ctrl>A to select them all. Drag the Candy Fairway sub-category tag over, and they are all tagged at once as shown by the little icon on the lower right side of the image. Continue tagging by color, theme, and element type, selecting similar items and tagging all at one time works best. In this example, select all of the brads and drag over the Brads tag. Select all the paper and drag over the Paper tag, etc. This kit came with all of the elements in one folder, but some sites split their kits into different folders according to element type. If you have folders of the same type of elements (paper, alphas, etc.), import them separately because the tagging will go much quicker that way.

As seen in the preceding example, on the bottom left side of the screen is the Photo Browser arrangement drop down list. You can choose if you want your Organizer to display your images according to the Newest First, Oldest First, Import Batch, or Folder Location. Click on one and the order of your images will change.

Click Back to All Photos to return to all of your images in the Organizer. Currently, the Organizer is showing only the images that were imported from the Candy Fairway kit, which is how you want it until you're done tagging the kit.

The size of the image thumbnail is adjustable by sliding the "Adjust size of thumbnail" slider on the bottom right side of the screen. The slider can be adjusted to show only one image at a time, or up to almost thirty at a time in very small thumbnails. To view your image in full screen view, which gives you a close up view, go to View>View Photos in Full Screen view or press the F11 key. To go back to the Organizer press the Esc key.

Clicking on the Date View button on the bottom near the size slider will display your images on a calendar according to the date they were created. With photos, this is great, but for scrapbooking supplies it doesn't do you much good. To get back to the Photo Browser, click the Photo Browser button in the same location.

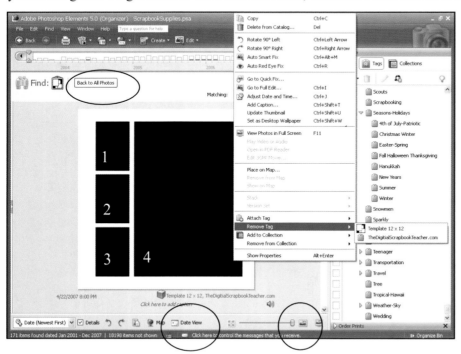

If you can't remember if you tagged a certain image, double click on the image or slide the size slider all the way to the right to get a full screen view of the image. All of the tags that are attached to the file are listed below the image. Right clicking on the image gives you many options including: Copy, Delete from Catalog, Rotate, Auto Smart Fix & Red Eye Fix, Quick Fix, Full Edit, Adjust Date and Time, Add Caption, Attach Tag, Remove Tag, Add to Collection and Remove from Collection.

Collections are similar to tags, except that you can change the order of the images when you view them, which is helpful when doing some things like making a slide show or to make an instant scrapbook from the Create Menu. Sorry, slides shows aren't covered in this book.

Changing Tag Preferences

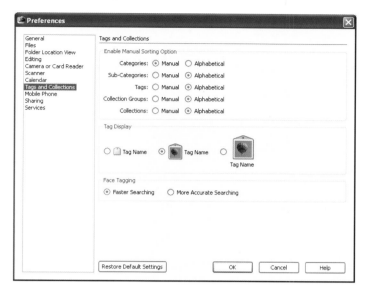

To change the size of your tags, go to Edit>Preferences in the Organizer and click on the size tag you want. The large tag looks inviting at first, but it takes up a lot of room in the palette. Using large tags requires a lot of scrolling through the tags list to find what you're looking for, so be aware of that.

To change your Categories, Sub-Categories, Tags, Collections & Collections Group to Manual Sort rather than the default of Alphabetical, click on the appropriate button.

Face Tagging can be accessed by going to Find>Face Tagging. I'd rather tag my photos by myself without Photoshop Elements helping finding the faces.

Searching With The Organizer

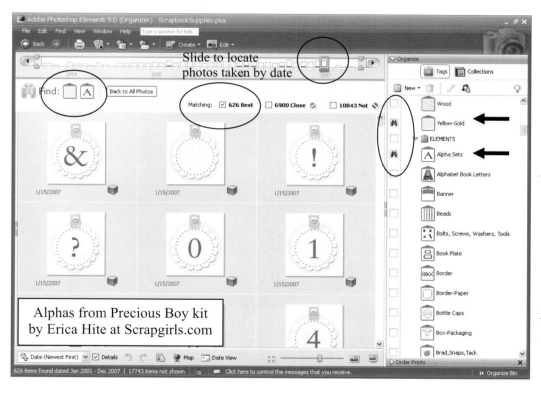

The true beauty of the Organizer is finding what you need quickly. In this example I want to find all of my yellow alpha sets, so I click in the box next to Yellow and Alpha Sets as indicated by the binoculars.

I currently have 626 matching images that are yellow alphas of some kind. Notice the tags are shown in the upper left of the screen too.

Another way to search is to drag your tags to the Find Bar marked by the binoculars. If you haven't tagged your items, dragging an image to the Find bar will find other images that match the color or appearance of your image.

To go back to all files, either click on both binoculars to deselect, or click on the Back to All Photos button. By using the Organizer to organize your photos, you can find the photos that you have of an individual or of a group of people as long as you've tagged your photos correctly.

Located at the top of the Organizer is a date slider that you can use to locate photos taken during a certain time frame. Slide the bar to December to find Christmas photos etc. This works well in your Photo Catalog but you probably won't use it in your Scrapbook Supplies Catalog.

Image Properties

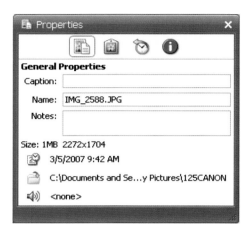

To show the properties of an image, right click on the image and choose Properties or click on the image and type Alt>Enter. In the Properties dialog box, you can see when the photo was taken (as long as the date is right on the camera), the size of the image, the image name, and where it's located on your computer. If you are looking at the properties of a scrapbook element, the date will be the date the file was created. Captions and notes can be added. Captions are used when you use the Photoshop Elements Create menu to make scrapbook pages and other items. Add notes to your photos to use for journaling when you finally get around to scrapbooking, or to list the supplies you used when making a scrapbook page.

Clicking on the icons across the top of the dialog box will also show any tags that are attached to the file, and information regarding the history of the file, when it was imported, modified, etc.

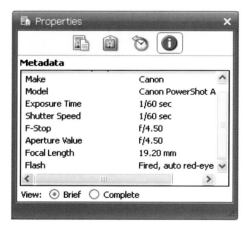

The Metadata information can be displayed in a brief or complete format, and has more information than you will probably ever need. The camera that took the photo is shown along with the exposure and shutter speed, whether you used red eye reduction, or if your flash fired. In addition, file sizes are listed along with resolution and much, much more.

Information for a Digimarc watermark used to deter copying Copyrighted images will be listed in the Metadata. Also check Filter>Digimarc in the Editor. I was unable to find a photo that was marked with a Digimarc watermark, even though I have several digital photos taken by professional photographers.

Safeguarding Your Organizer Catalogs

You've spent hours and hours organizing and tagging your photos and digital scrapbook supplies. If your computer crashed, was stolen, or you had a fire in your home, you would be pretty upset if you lost everything. Obviously a computer issue is your first concern, but I can tell you after working in the insurance industry for more than twenty years, you should be concerned about other issues too. Make back-up copies of your photos and scrapbook supply images and your Organizer Catalog and keep one at home but also store one at another location. I keep an external hard drive backed up with everything in my home and also at my office. Trade with a friend, or send it to work with your husband if you work at home. Storing in a safety deposit box at a bank would be nice but would also be a hassle. I am a firm believer that you need to set up a regular system of backing up your Organizer and your images folders. If you have not made a copy of your digital photos, do it before you do anything else, because they can never be replaced. Make your buddy do it too and trade copies.

Write Tag Info To Files

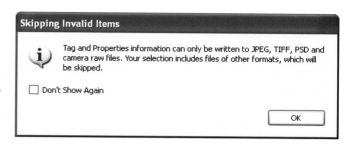

Writing the tag to my images is one safeguard I use which also has other benefits. When you write the tag info to the file, it becomes attached to the image. This information can only be written to JPEG, TIFF, PSD, and camera raw files. PNG files that scrappers use a lot do not allow tags to be attached to their file at this time.

Before you Write Tag Info to Files, it's a good idea to check and see if you have any untagged files. To view your untagged files go to Find>Untagged Files (Shortcut is Ctrl>Shift>Q) and all of your untagged files will be displayed. Try to work on getting everything tagged. When you tag a group of files, use Write Tag Info to Files. The only way the tags will be attached to your files is to do this step, even backing up doesn't write the tags to the file.

When I write tags to my files, the tags are already attached and you don't have to tag them yourself. You're thinking you'd never use that feature right? All of the templates from TheDigitalScrapbookTeacher.com in PSD & JPEG format are already tagged for you so when you import them into your Organizer, they're tagged, and it saves you the work. Sorry but you'll have to tag the PNG templates yourself. If you regularly share photos with a friend and you tag your photos by writing the tag to the file, your friend doesn't have to tag them herself.

When you import your images into the Organizer and they are tagged, you will be asked if you want to import the tags. If you don't already have that tag, it will be added to your list of tags. To import the tags, even if you have a tag by the same name as listed on the dialog box, you need to check that box or choose select all. What this box means is that it will bring in the tags that are listed. Students in my classes get confused and think that since they already have a tag by that name they don't have to select them. They're disappointed when their images aren't tagged.

You may have to place the tags in another order if you receive them from someone else, such as changing them to a sub-category in your tags if your friend uses different tags. This can be done by right clicking on the tag and choosing the correct option, which is much faster than retagging everything yourself. If you've installed my tags, and are also installing TheDigitalScrapbookTeacher.com products, they will match up perfectly.

Writing the tags to your files protects you in the event your Catalog crashes. Of course, you will also have a back-up copy of your Catalog because you're following my instructions to the letter. If for some reason you don't follow my instructions and have a back-up of your Catalog, all of the tags will be written to your images except for the PNG files. Simply import all of your images back into the Catalog, and they're tagged except for the PNG files as long as you have a back-up of your Scrapbook Supplies and My Pictures folders.

Splitting Up Catalogs

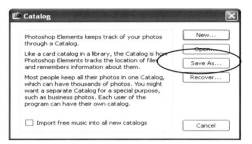

If you started out with one Catalog and would like to split your Catalog up into two different Catalogs like I do, it's pretty easy. Before you try this be sure to: Write Tag Info to Files and Back-up all of your image folders and your Organizer. Open the Catalog that you want to duplicate and Go to File>Catalog and choose File>Save As.

Type a new name for your catalog and choose Save.

You now have two Organizer catalogs with the same exact contents. Say for example, you had an Organizer catalog for photos and scrapbook supplies and now you decided to split it up. Rename your new Organizer Scrapbook Supplies and go into that Organizer and begin deleting all of the photos by selecting them and right clicking and choosing Delete, or tapping the Delete key. Hopefully, if you've got them tagged well, this is easy because you can click on a tag and bring up all of your photos. If not click on each photo tag and they'll pop up.

Delete your photo tags by right clicking on the tag and deleting them. It sounds like a lot of work, but it goes very quickly.

When you delete images from the Organizer, be sure that you are not deleting the whole file from your computer! If you want to get rid of an image like a photo with no hope of being edited, click in the box to delete from the hard disk too.

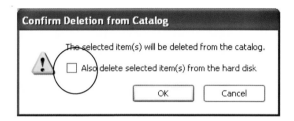

When I first started out with the Organizer, I used the default catalog and then renamed it later. When my Organizer got so large that it was difficult to scroll through all of my photo and Scrapbook Supplies tags, I decided that I needed to split it up. I copied my Organizer and renamed it Scrapbook Supplies and deleted all of the photos and photo tags. Next, I renamed my original catalog Photos. Because I had my entire scrapbook supplies tagged with a Scrapbook Supplies category tag, I selected it and all of my Scrapbook Supplies were displayed. I selected them all by Ctrl>A (Select>All), right clicked, and selected Delete from Catalog. I did not delete anything from my hard drive.

Working between two different Catalogs is easy. To switch back and forth just go to File>Catalog (Shortcut Ctrl>Shift>C), click Open, and choose the catalog you want to open. When you open the Organizer, the last catalog you used will open. You cannot search more than one catalog at a time. To use two catalogs when scrapbooking, choose your photos and then go to your Scrapbook Supplies catalog and choose your elements. If you need another photo go back to the Photo catalog. It's easy, it just sounds like more work than it is.

Moving Image Files Around Using the Organizer

To move image files so that the Organizer knows where they are, go to File>Move, choose a new destination folder, and click OK.

Another way to move a folder is to display your Organizer images in Folder View and to drag and drop the files inside the folder pane, but I prefer going to File>Move.

Moving your files this way will avoid having any missing files.

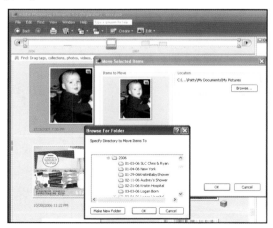

To rename files in your catalog so that the Organizer can find them, go to File>Rename and type the new file name or use the shortcut Ctrl>Shift>N.

Missing Files In The Organizer

If you move your images from one folder to another outside of the Organizer, your Organizer will not be able to find them. A missing file will be marked with a tiny red icon that looks like a photo ripped in two. Once you click on the image to edit it, the Organizer will automatically begin searching for the missing file image, which is a little bit scary when it first happens.

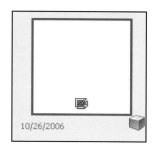

If you know where you moved the file, click on Browse and find the folder for the Organizer and this usually speeds up the search. If you've deleted the item from your hard drive, you'll need to delete it from the Organizer too. Right click on the image and choose Delete from Organizer.

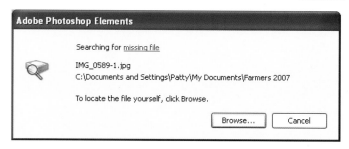

If you've moved things around on your computer in an effort to get organized and you've got several missing files, go to File>Reconnect and choose All Missing Files. Depending on how big your hard drive is and how many missing files you have, it may take a while to find them all. It might be a good idea to set this up when you won't need to use your computer for awhile. The Organizer will go through all of your folders to locate the image that you previously imported. The Organizer will locate some files and will not locate other files. Once it's done searching if there are images that are classified as missing that you've deleted from your hard drive, delete them from your Organizer too. If you still have images that the Organizer cannot locate, it may be a possibility that you've changed the file name or you didn't search in the proper places. Try searching for these again yourself if you know where you moved them. If you still can't find the images, delete them from the Organizer because you can't use them anyway.

Backing Up Your Organizer Catalogs

It's important to back-up your Organizer Catalog in case you should have a computer problem. Keep at least one copy of the back-up file in a safe place, preferably at another location other than your home. Maybe, if I keep repeating this, you'll listen!

The Organizer will automatically remind you to back-up your Catalog unless you click on the "Don't Show Again" box. When you get this reminder, you can back-up directly from here by clicking on the box or go to File>Back-up Catalog (Shortcut Ctrl>B). I always choose Full Back-up because it doesn't take that much longer to do.

Choose Next, and you may get the warning screen that says you have Missing Files. If so, you will need to Reconnect at this time. Hopefully you reconnected your files and Wrote Tag Info to File before you tried to back-up.

Choose a place to back-up your Organizer Catalogs. I have an Organizer Back-up Folder inside my Photoshop Elements Folder. This is located on my C drive inside the My Documents folder. After I back it up here, I copy it to my external hard drives that I keep at home and at my office for safe keeping.

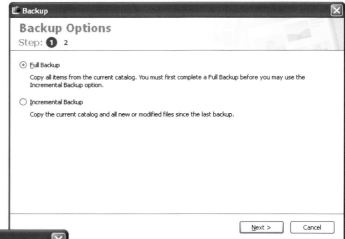

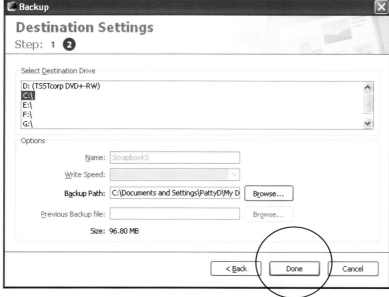

The Organizer will advise you how far along it is in the back-up process. As soon as it's done backing-up, it will tell you it's done. Backing up your Organizer may take awhile especially if it's large so you may want to do this when you won't need your computer for awhile, like when you go to bed at night.

When you back-up your Organizer, you are not only copying the Catalog with all of your tags but also your photographs. If you have any creations, or video and audio files, they will also be backed up.

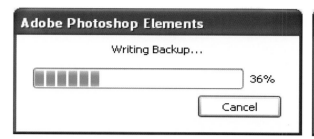 

Backing Up Your Organizer Online

Go to File>Online Back-up and you will be directed to an electronic file storage company that Adobe uses for online back-up. This sounded pretty exciting to me, because with just a quick glance, it looks like you can schedule the back-up of your Organizer. It would be a no brainer, and I wouldn't have to worry about backing-up to my external hard drive and DVDs. My excitement was short lived when I came to the pricing section. The largest size storage plan they showed, which is classified as "Professional", was $32.50 a month or $349.95 a year. This is a little bit out of my price range, especially since I have at least 40 GB of photos and digital scrapbook supplies. I will check into other options for online storage in the future.

There are other options available for online back-up, which relieves you of the time and responsibility to do it all yourself. There are several programs on the market that will automatically back-up your computer as you work. I am not using one of these programs at the moment, but plan to as soon as I can find the one that works the best for me. All of these companies advertise very attractive pricing; most of them at less than $50 a year. If you are using an external hard drive, be sure to find a program that will also back-up the external hard drive too. Three sites that scrappers mention on message boards that they say work well are Mozy.com, Carbonite.com, and Acronis.com.

If you do not choose to back-up on-line, PLEASE back-up on DVDs or another external hard drive, and keep it out of your home. Mozy.com says it best where they list the alternative to using their program: "Do nothing and don't worry about backing-up. We suggest closing your eyes, plugging your ears and repeating "I'm in my happy place, I'm in my happy place."

Organizer Problems

Occasionally your Organizer may experience a hiccup and needs to be calmed down. The best fix is to Recover your Catalog by going to File>Catalog and choosing the Recover Catalog button. My Organizer has close to 20,000 images in it, and it works like a dream until I save a large multi-layered scrapbook page in the Organizer. It slows down, and doesn't respond quickly. I thought maybe it was just me, until I read that another scrapper on a message board had the same issue. For this reason I no longer save my scrapbook pages in my Organizer. Instead, I save them in a folder called Scrapbook Pages that has sub-folders for every book I'm working on and this method works great for me. If your Organizer is running slow, try this to see if it works for you.

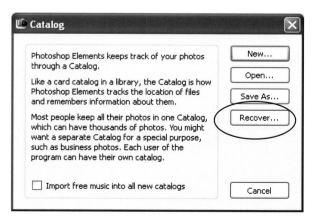

To Recover your Catalog, click OK and the Organizer will Recover your catalog. I do not check the "Reindex Visual Similarity Data" box. If you normally drag items to the Find Bar to find matching images, you will want to check this box.

A status bar will advise you how far along you are in the process, but don't be alarmed if it seems to get stuck at 33% and 66% for awhile because for some reason it likes to stop there. When I've had trouble with my Organizer running sluggishly, this always fixes whatever the problem is.

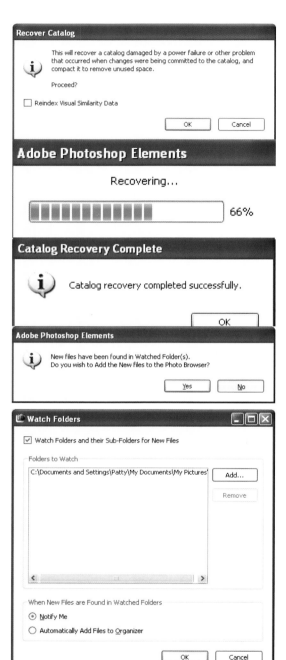

When you back-up your catalog the Catalog Recovery is also done, but I prefer to do it before I back-up to avoid any problems.

Watched Folders

The Organizer can be your own personal spy to find out if you've downloaded new photos or scrapbook supplies. It will remind you that you have new files in any folder you specify, and ask if you want to add the files to the Photo Browser (Organizer). Your My Pictures Folder is probably set as a default folder for the Watched Folders to check. If you have photos you have not imported into the Organizer, you'll get the message that says there are new files in a Watched Folder. If you want the Organizer to import these files right now, you can click on the "Yes" button and they'll be imported to the last catalog you used. You can customize the Watched Folders setting to automatically import your images from different folders.

To change the settings for Watch Folders, go to File>Watch Folders in the Organizer.

To turn this setting off, uncheck the box that says "Watch Folders and their Sub-Folders for New Files". I do this to eliminate one more program running on my computer.

To add other folders, click "Add" and locate the folders you want on your computer. My Pictures and Scrapbook Supplies would be good folders to Watch. If you want to remove a folder, click on the folder to highlight it, and then choose "Remove".

If you want your files to be automatically imported into your Organizer, choose "Automatically Add Files to Organizer". If you choose this option you would have to be diligent about checking your untagged files by going to Find>Untagged Items (Shortcut Ctrl>Shift>Q) to keep up on your tagging.

How to Restore A Catalog

If you've had a computer problem or you purchased a new computer, you may need to Restore your Catalog from a Back-up Copy. To Restore a Catalog go to: File>Restore Catalog.

Choose from where you want to restore the Catalog, which in my case was on my hard drive. Choose where you want the Catalog restored to, and then choose Restore.

Depending on the size of the Catalog, this may take awhile.

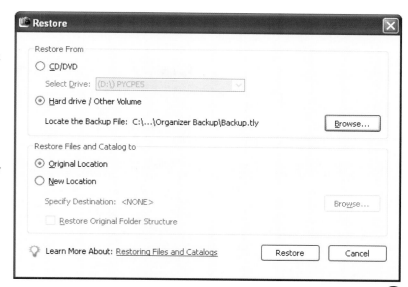

Stacking Photos In The Organizer

When I take photos, I normally take a lot at a time of the same thing. Trying to photograph my young grandson is an exercise in futility because, as soon as I think I've got a great shot, he moves. Some of the duplicates I discard, and others I keep, but I don't really want to have to scroll through all of them when I'm looking at my photos in the Organizer.

The Organizer gives you the ability to stack the photos on top of each other, just like you'd do with a paper stack of photos. To stack a set of photos, select the photos you want in a stack, and then go to Edit>Stack>Stack Selected photos, or right click. The shortcut to stack photos is Ctrl>Alt>5. A stacked photo icon appears at the top right corner of the photo, however, isn't that easy to see.

To show all of the photos in the stack, go to Edit>Stack>Expand Photos in Stack (shortcut is Ctrl>Alt>K), and they are all shown.

To Unstack photos, go to Edit>Stack>Unstack Photos, and they're all back to their individual thumbnails.

To change the top photo to a different photo, expand the photos first and then choose the photo you want on top, and go to Edit>Stacked>Set as Top Photo.

If you would like the Organizer to automatically suggest photo stacks of visually similar images, you can choose this option, but it will want to stack up all of your digital scrapbook supplies too. The shortcut to automatically stack images is Ctrl>Alt>K.

Collapsing photos in a stack shows only the top image thumbnail, the shortcut to collapse the stack is Ctrl>Alt>Shift>R. Flattening the stack will remove all thumbnails from the Organizer but the top one, however the images will not be removed from your hard drive.

To find all Stacked sets of images, go to Find>All Stacks or Ctrl>Alt>Shift>S.

Version Sets In The Organizer

When you save a file, you are asked if you want to save the image in the Organizer. I don't always want to save my file in the Organizer and I get a little bit aggravated that I can't seem to figure out how to turn it off permanently. As I've stated before, I no longer save my multi-layered PSD scrapbook pages in my Organizer because it seems to slow it down.

When you save images in a version set, you are saving the same image with changes that you've made to it. You must be using File>Save As and not File>Save. They are grouped together very similar to being stacked. If you don't save in a version set, your images will appear in your Organizer side by side, as long as you did not change the file name.

When you apply a tag to a version set, all of the images in the set are tagged. To make changes to a version set, go to the Edit menu and choose Version set or right click and choose one of the options.

Edit>Version Set>Expand Version Set (Shortcut Ctrl>Alt>E) will expand a version set.

Edit>Version Set>Remove Item from Version Set will remove images from the version set after you've expanded the set.

Edit>Version Set>Collapse Items in Version Set (shortcut Ctrl>Alt>Shift>E) will collapse images from the version set after you've expanded the set

Edit>Version Set>Flatten Version Set will delete all of the images in the version set with the exception of the most recently edited image.

Edit>Version Set>Convert Version Set to Individual Items will split apart the version set.

Edit>Version Set>Revert to Original will delete all images except for the original image.

Edit>Version Set>Remove Items from Version Set will remove an item from the version set after you've expanded the set.

Edit>Version Set>Set as Top Item will set the image as the top one in the version set after you've expanded the set.

How To Edit A Photo In The Organizer?

Simple editing can be done right in the Organizer. Rotate 90° Left (Ctrl>Left Arrow Key), Rotate 90° Right (Ctrl>Right Arrow Key), Auto Smart Fix (Ctrl>Alt>M), and Auto Red Eye Fix (Ctrl>R), are available in the Edit menu of the Organizer (circled below). To go to Quick Fix Mode or Full Edit Mode, click on the Edit button marked with an arrow in the example below. When your image is in Quick Fix, or Full Edit Mode, you will see the Edit in Progress Marker across your image. You will be unable to perform any of the editing functions of the Organizer, until you close the image in the Editor.

To open an image and import it into the Editor so you can use it on a scrapbook page, click on the image and then Ctrl>I (or click on the Edit button and choose Go to Full Edit). To select more than one image at a time, adjust the image thumbnails so you can see more than one image at a time by sliding the slider bar marked below. Click on one image, and then Ctrl Click on the other images so they are all selected (highlighted) and then. Ctrl>I. Images all in a row can be selected by clicking, and then Shift clicking on the last photo in a row.

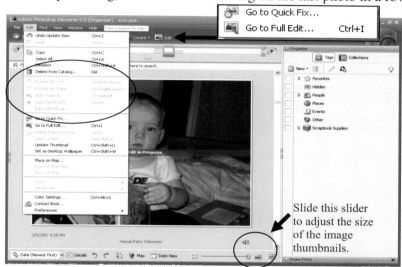

Edit In Progress Marker

If your image in the Organizer displays a red line across it with a lock, along with the wording "Edit In Progress" as seen in this example; this means that the image is currently open in the Editor. Go to the Editor and close the file and the red line will disappear.

Making An Idea File

When I first started subscribing to traditional scrapbook magazines, I kept my magazines in standing magazine racks on a bookshelf. After a few years I discovered that I had no way of finding anything unless I thumbed through all my magazines, which was not an easy task. With about five years of magazines neatly displayed, I decided that I would rip (gasp!) the pages out that I wanted. I put them in binders and passed the remainder of the magazines off to a friend with different interests than mine. Not only do I save copies of scrapbook pages, I save ads and any other design that catches my eye. I once saved an ad for a Kelly Clarkson concert. My husband told me if I really wanted to go, he'd try to get tickets. I didn't know what he was talking about until he showed me the ad I'd had sitting on the kitchen table for a few days. I tried to explain what I was saving it for, but I don't think he understood.

My binder system worked pretty well until I went digital. When I would see a great digital page on the internet, I would copy (click on picture and Ctrl>C) and paste it onto a blank Word document (Ctrl>V to paste the picture) and print it out to put in my binder. This took time, used up paper and ink, along with valuable storage space.

I've perfected my system a little bit. Since there aren't many digital magazines around yet, I keep those magazines in their entirety. Because the traditional magazines hardly offered any digital tips or examples, I stopped renewing my subscription, so I no longer have those to contend with. When I find a page or card that I like on the internet, I copy and paste it to a Word document and save it in my Scrapbook Ideas Folder in my My Documents folder. This way when I need an idea, it's very easy to find.

I also go one step further if I purchased a digi-kit because I liked the example they displayed. I copy and paste the page to a blank Word document, and then I save it along with the kit files and name the file (Scrapbook kit name) Idea. This way when I get ready to use the kit, I can see the page that originally inspired me to purchase the kit in the first place.

Don't get so involved in saving copies of ideas that you don't do anything yourself. If you scraplift be sure to give the original designer the credit. Usually, when I try to scraplift, I end up with something that looks completely different than the original design I started with, which is OK too.

Organizing Your Time

Unfortunately, we only have 24 hours in a day and even though on many nights I try to stretch it out, I still come up short. I've been known to say that if I just had one more day while the rest of the world stopped I'd be all caught up. I've come to the conclusion I'll never be caught up, probably because I've constantly got too much on my plate. I've found that if I'm organized, I can accomplish much more and I don't easily get stressed out.

If you follow my tips in this chapter on how to organize your photos and scrapbooking supplies, you'll be a happier scrapper because you won't be pulling your hair out looking for things. When you have some free time, you will actually be able to turn on your computer and scrap instead of searching through your computer and websites frantically wondering if you downloaded your photos or if you really did buy a certain kit.

One of the best things about digi-scrapping is that unlike traditional scrapping, you can break up your scrapping into small time segments and don't have to put everything away in between sessions. Each one of the following steps can be done at any time and stopped until you have time to move on to the next step.

I've found that foe me, the most efficient way to scrap is to begin with my photos. Normally I take a lot of photos because after all, they're free. After I download the photos, I go through them and delete the obviously bad ones. If I have a photo I like but the quality is bad, I may be able to repair it, or use it as a background at a lower opacity, or blur it. I tag my photos in my Organizer and for the ones that I want to scrap, I use the 5 star tag from the Favorites category. If it's a "maybe" I'll use a 4 star tag.

Next, I fix my photos that I'm going to use by adjusting the lighting, color, etc. and cropping out obviously unwanted areas. Sometimes, it's best not to crop before you bring the photo onto the scrapbook page because you may end up needing part of the photo.

Make a new blank page and drag your photos onto it if you need to stop at this point, and when you come back to it everything will be in one file waiting for you.

Choose your kit and embellishments by searching with your Tags, arrange them on your page and you're done.

The best part of all is there is no clean up, and even if you had to stop during the process of making your page, you didn't have to move it or put away so it wouldn't get messed up.

The Really Technical Stuff

Resolution

I can use a whole chapter to describe resolution but the bottom line is, the higher your resolution, the better the print quality will be for images you print including photos, cards, and scrapbook pages. A digital image can be printed in any size but, when you enlarge the pixels, you reduce the printed quality.

OK, I admit it right off the bat, I'm really lax about checking the resolution of my images. However, because I use the same camera and buy my digital scrapbook supplies from sites that only sell 300 PPI (pixels per inch) resolution items, I usually don't have to worry about resolution…usually. Every once in awhile I'll drag an element onto a scrapbook page and for a minute I'll be confused as to why it's so tiny and then I remember that it's probably a freebie that I picked up that's in a lower resolution.

The preferred resolution to use when digital scrapbooking, card-making, or any other craft is 300 pixels per inch. Some tutorials will tell you it's OK to use 150 or 200 PPI, but why would you spend your time creating a scrapbook page and gamble on how well it will print out? All of the instructions in this book tell you to make your projects with 300 PPI resolution, so if you stick with my directions, you'll be fine.

72 PPI should be used for any images that will be displayed on the internet or they won't display correctly.

I promise not to get too technical but keep reading, because you'll learn some very interesting things that will impress your friends.

What's A Pixel?

Digital images are made up of pixels. A pixel is a unit of measure, just like an inch, a centimeter, or a point, only pixels are used to measure digital images. In this example, I zoomed in as far as I could on a photo. Each individual square is a pixel. Many of the Photoshop Elements tools search for pixels based on their color like the Magic Wand Tool (W).

A megapixel is 1 million pixels; the camera I use is a 6 megapixel camera so that means in every photo my camera takes the image has 6 million pixels.

How Big Are My Images?

To see how big your images are, open an image in the Editor. Go to Image>Resize>Image Size. Your image dimensions will be shown similar to this example.

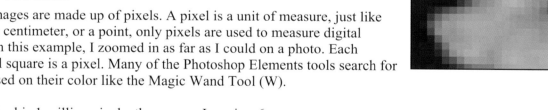

The photos my camera takes are 3072 pixels wide and 2048 pixels high. When you multiply 3072 x 2048 you have 6,291,456 pixels or 6.29 megapixels.

To find out how big this photo can be printed at very high quality, just divide the dimensions by 300. 3072 wide/300 = 10.24 wide and 2048 high/300 = 6.83. I can print this image 10.24 wide by 6.83 high in very high quality.

If I wanted to print it in 180 PPI, my image would be 17.07 wide by 11.38 high. The larger I print this photo, the lower the quality of the print. The print will look pixilated, which means you can actually see the pixels and it will be fuzzy if you go below 150 PPI.

Printing your photos at 200-250 PPI will probably be fine.

If you have ever tried to use a photo from the internet on a scrapbook page and it looked bad, that's because images on the web are 72 ppi resolution. An opposite example would be if someone sent you a photo by email with high resolution, and when you opened it, and it was so big you couldn't tell what you were looking at.

Common Resolution Problems For Digi-Scrappers

When you move a photo or scrapbook element onto a new scrapbook page, it will take on the resolution of the scrapbook page. This is a common problem for new scrappers who post questions on message boards. Some freebies are 200 resolution whereas their page is 300 resolution and they can't figure out why when they drag their 12 x 12 digital scrapbook paper onto their 12 x 12 new blank scrapbook page they've made it's smaller.

A 12 x 12 element at 200 resolution will be 8 x 8 when dragged onto a 300 resolution scrapbook page. A 12 x 12 element at 150 resolution will be 6 x 6 when dragged onto a 300 resolution scrapbook page.

With a lower resolution digital scrapbook paper or other element, sometimes you can drag the corner sizing handle by activating the Move Tool (V) and size (transform) it larger and it will look OK, and sometimes it won't. If it doesn't look OK stretched, use it for a photo mat, journaling block, or other embellishment in a smaller size.

This is one of the reasons all my tutorials start with a new blank file at 300 resolution, and ask you to drag your digital elements on to it with the Move Tool (V). If you open a digital scrapbooking paper and "Save As" with a different file name and then drag your elements onto it, you will probably run in to problems with resolution. Starting with a brand new page that you've set the size and resolution for puts you in control.

If the photo resolution is larger than the scrapbook page the photo will grow larger once you drag it onto your page.

DPI Or PPI What's The Difference?

DPI is dots per inch, PPI is pixels per inch. Dots per inch are how many dots (round) are actually printed per inch and the space around them. Pixels (square) per inch is the amount of pixels per inch in a digital image, they have no space around them. As my printing friend explained to me, when your image is printed the pixels are changed into dots and a 300 PPI image will become a 150 DPI printed photo. Many people use the terms interchangeably.

How Do I Resize A Scrapbook Page To Upload To A Online Gallery?

Almost every Digital Scrapbook Site has their own gallery for people to post their newest creations. Browsing these sites can be fun and a great source of ideas. Some sites have rules that you can only post pages made of items that are sold on their site. You will be asked to identify the source of your supplies, the name of the fonts you used, and any special techniques you used. This is where it's important to keep track of the elements you used, and the best way I know how to do this, is to drag your supplies up from the Photo Bin with the Move Tool (V) on to your scrapbook page so the layer name is the actual file name.

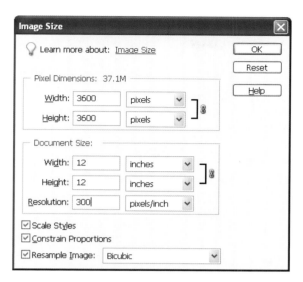 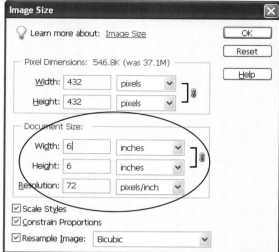

First you will need to read the file size requirements for the site you are going to send your scrapbook page to. Once you have the file requirements, make a duplicate copy of your scrapbook page and go to Image>Resize>Image Size. My original scrapbook page is shown on the left in the example.

Change the resolution to 72, and the width and height if required by the site. Notice how the width and height in pixels also changed automatically.

Save this image with a new name like Scrapbookpagelowres so you'll remember that it's a low resolution copy for posting on the web and should not be printed.

How To Resize An Image Larger

You can drag a sizing handle of an image to make it a little bit larger, but it's not the best way to do it if you want a great print. If you have an image that you want to make into a larger print or poster you can try this method. This can take a long time if you want to increase the size dramatically, but it usually works pretty well.

Duplicate the image. Go to Image>Resize>Image Size.
In the example my original image is shown on the left. On the drop down box shown, change inches to percent and type in 110 in the width box, the height box will automatically change to 110 percent. Click OK. Go back to Image>Resize>Image size and the size of your image will be increased 110% as shown in the example on the right. Repeat this until your image is the size you want.

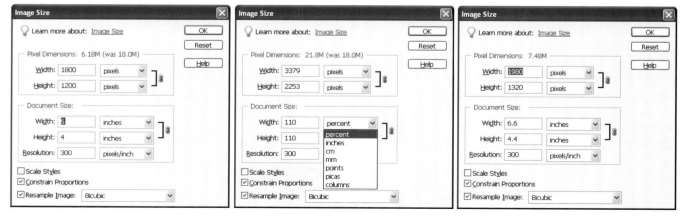

File Types

As a digital scrapper, you'll be using different kinds of files. This is just a little bit of information about the type of files you will probably encounter. I usually only use three file formats: JPEG, PNG, and PSD. I save each one of my scrapbook pages as a PSD file to preserve all of the layers and, as a JPEG, if I am having it printed at a photo lab.

JPEG

Joint Photographic Experts Group
JPEGs or JPGs are the most common file type you will encounter. Photos are JPEGs as are most of the digital scrapbook paper files. Every time you save a JPEG file it loses a little bit of its data. However, just opening a JPEG does not harm it. JPEGs cannot have transparent areas. If you try to save an image with a transparent area, it will automatically be filled with white. To have a photo printed at a photo lab it will need to be in JPEG format.

PNG

Portable Network Graphic
PNGs are used by designers to make elements such as brads, rivets, and doodles, etc. because they can have a transparent background.

GIF

Graphics Interchange Format
CompuServe Gif
GIFs can also have transparent areas and are a file used a lot on the internet. GIFs only store 256 colors. Text looks sharper in a GIF format. If you want to edit a GIF file in Photoshop Elements, you will first have to change it's mode from Indexed Color to RGB. To do this go to Image>Mode and choose RGB.

TIFF

Tagged Image File Format
TIFF files can be color, grayscale, or black and white. Sometimes when you use a scanner, your image will be saved in a TIFF format. TIFF files do not lose any data when they're saved.

BMP

Bit Map Image
Bitmapped graphics also known as raster graphics are made up of bits, which are dots. These graphics do not size well and don't work well for web graphics or photos.

PSD

Photoshop Document
PSDs store your image with layers, masks, text, etc. so that you can open the file and go back to work where you left off. Always save your scrapbook pages in PSD format so that you can go back and make changes later on. You cannot upload a PSD file to a photo lab for printing, it must be converted to a JPEG first.

PSE

Photo Creation Format
This is a new file format that is essentially a folder with Photoshop Document (PSD) files inside it. PSE files are created when you make a Photo Creation using the Create Menu like Adobe's photo book. You can still individually edit each PSD and convert them to a JPEG if you want to upload them to a photo lab.

PSB

Photoshop Big
This is a Photoshop file that is used for files 2GB and larger. I have never come close to having one file that big but, never say never!

PDD

PhotoDeluxe Document
Photo Deluxe is an Adobe program that was replaced by Photoshop Elements. PDDs were a type of a Photoshop Document file supported by Photo Deluxe.

Changing The Default Program To Open A File

Two of the most asked questions I get are: "Why when I click on a PNG file does it open up an advertisement for Paint Shop Pro X?", or "Why when I try to open a photo, Photoshop Elements opens up and it takes forever?".

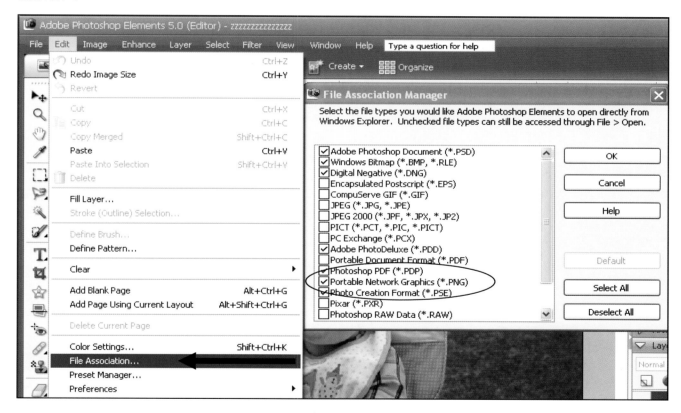

This is a really easy fix which will solve a lot of your frustration.

To change which type of files Photoshop Elements opens up, go to Edit>File Association. Mark the file types you want Photoshop Elements to open. For example, if you want PNG files to open in Photoshop Elements automatically click in that box. After you put a checkmark in the box for Portable Network Graphics (*.PNG), it will open up in Photoshop Elements instead of giving you the Corel Paint Shop Pro X advertisement.
If JPEG is checked, remove the checkmark and you will no longer have to view your photos in Photoshop Elements.

Modes-Color And Image

Image Modes are a way to describe color. Before you change the mode of any image, always make a duplicate copy.

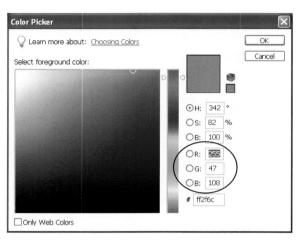

The image modes supported by Photoshop Elements are:

RGB

RGB (Red-Green-Blue) is the default mode for any new image like a scrapbook page you make or image you import from your camera. Televisions and computer monitors display images in RGB color. Each color is assigned an intensity from 0 to 255. Black is 0 and White is 255. RGB mode can display 16 million colors. This example displays the RGB values circled.

Images that are printed by professional print shops should be in CMYK mode which Photoshop Elements does not support, however a printer should be able to convert it for you.

Bitmap

A Bitmap image is black and white only. To convert a color image to a Bitmap image you must first convert it to a Grayscale image.

Grayscale

A Grayscale image is gray only but in 256 shades. Grayscale images have a brightness value from 0-255. Black is 0 and White is 255 just like in the RGB mode.

Indexed Color

Indexed Color images can have up to 256 colors. To edit an Indexed Color Image you will need to temporarily change it RGB mode.

CMYK

CMYK (Cyan, Magenta, Yellow, Black) is used by traditional 4 color professional presses and is not supported by Photoshop Elements. If you try to open a CMYK image you will get a warning asking you to convert the mode. When you view a CMYK image on a computer monitor you are viewing it in RGB mode. A professional printer should be able to convert a RGB file to CMYK.

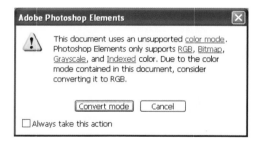

The Photoshop Elements Editor

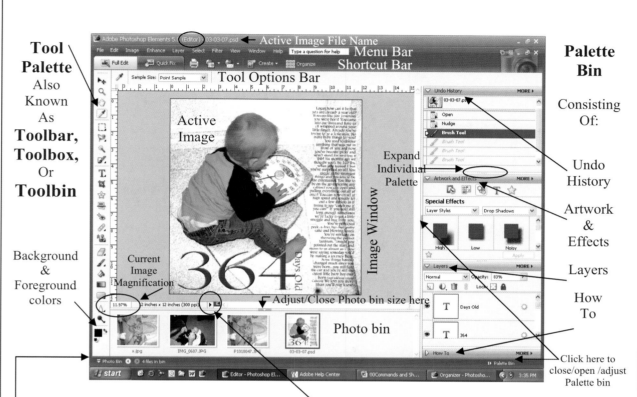

To collapse or expand a palette, click on the downward facing triangle to the left of the palette name. To expand a palette, drag the dotted area up or down. To add it to the Palette bin, drag it by title bar into the Palette bin. To change its location in the Palette bin, drag it by its title bar to the new location.

To remove a palette from the Palette bin, drag it out by its title bar. Palettes can be moved anywhere on your screen. To size a palette not docked in the Palette bin, drag on the lower right dotted corner. Press Tab to show/hide all palettes not docked in the Palette bin. Window>Reset Palette Locations will return all palettes to their default positions.

Click on a photo in the Photo Bin and it becomes the active image. If you accidentally hid your Photo Bin you either right clicked in the Photo Bin or clicked the adjustment button. Go to Window>Photo Bin to re-open and also check Edit>Preferences>General to make sure Photo Bin Auto-Hide is disabled.

Commands and Shortcuts

Learning to use the proper commands in Photoshop Elements is essential to being successful. Learning the shortcuts for those commands makes digi-scrapping so much easier. Don't try to learn them all at once because you'll drive yourself crazy. Memorize the ones you use a lot and then make it a game to learn one a week and you'll be surprised how many you remember. There are many shortcuts but I've only listed the ones that I use on a regular basis.

Put a paperclip or a bookmark on this page because you'll be referring to it a lot.

Editor Commands and Shortcuts

Command	Shortcut	Description
File>New	Ctrl>N	Creates a new blank document
None	Alt>Ctrl>N	Creates a new blank document with the same specifications as the last one you made
File>Open	Ctrl>O	Opens a file like a photo, element, scrapbook page
File>Save	Ctrl>S	Saves a file to the same place that it was originally saved
File>Save As	Shift>Ctrl>S	Saves a file with a name and you are asked to specify a folder you want to save it to
File>Duplicate	None	Duplicates a file so you don't have to worry about ruining your original
Select>All	Ctrl>A	Selects the entire layer
Select>DeSelect	Esc or Ctrl>D	Deselects your selection-removes marching ants
Select>Inverse	Shift>Ctrl>I	Inverses your selection
File>Close	Ctrl>W	Closes your active (displayed) file only
File>Close All	Alt>Ctrl>W	Closes all open files. You will be asked if you want to accept changes on each file individually
File>Exit	Ctrl>Q	Closes all open files. You will be asked if you want to accept changes on each file individually AND closes the program. QUIT
None	Ctrl>Tab	Cycles through open files in your Photo Bin
File>Print	Ctrl>P	Prints your active image
Edit>Undo	Ctrl>Z	Undoes the last thing you did
Edit>Redo	Ctrl>Y	If you Undo and decided you liked it you can Redo
Edit>Cut	Ctrl>X	Copies and removes selection so you can paste somewhere else, this is easier than Copy and Pasting and then going back and deleting what you copied
Edit>Copy	Ctrl>C	Copies selection
Edit>Paste	Ctrl>V	Pastes your copied selection (to remember, think Velcro)
Edit>Paste Into	Shift>Ctrl>V	Pastes into a selection, this is very helpful when using single layered templates
Edit>Preferences	Ctrl>K	Changes your Preferences settings
Layer>New>Layer Via Copy	Ctrl>J	Creates a duplicate layer of the selection or layer, this will be one of your most used commands
Layer>New >Layer Via Cut	Shift>Ctrl>J	Makes a new layer from the selection and cuts it from the layer
Layer>Merge Layers	Ctrl>E	Merges the selected layers
Layer>Group With Previous	Ctrl>G	Groups two layers together, sort of like cutting out a layer into the shape or text below it and pasting them together

Command	Shortcut	Description
None	Hold Ctrl key	Temporarily activates the Move Tool (V) (with some tools)
None	Hold Alt key	Temporarily activates the Eyedropper Tool (I) (with some tools)
Filter>Last Filter	Ctrl>F	Applies the last filter used with the same settings again
None	Ctrl>Alt>F	Selects the last filter used and allows you to change settings
View>Fit on Screen	Ctrl>0	Show Full Screen Image
Help	F1	Adobe Help
How to Palette	F6	Step by step instructions on how to perform certain tasks
None	Press Caps Lock Key	Changes regular cursor to a crosshair
None	Ctrl Click Layer Thumbnail	Selects the contents of the active layer
None	Bracket keys [&]	Right Bracket] key increases brush size, Left Bracket [key decreases brush size. Tap to increase slowly or hold down key to quickly size brush.
None	Shift & Bracket keys [&]	Right Bracket key]Hardens brush tip Left Bracket key [Softens brush tip
None	Hold Shift Key & Drag	Draws a straight line, or a perfect square or circle.
None	Alt Drag	Draws selection or shape from the center point outward
Edit>Fill Layer	Alt>Backspace	Fills layer or selection with Foreground color
Edit>Fill Layer add ✓	Alt>Shift>Backspace	Fill with Foreground color and preserves transparency
Edit>Fill Layer add ✓	Ctrl>Shift>Backspace	Fill:With Background color and preserves transparency
Edit>Fill Layer	Ctrl>Backspace	Fills layer or selection with Background color
Enhance>Auto Smart Fix	Alt>Ctrl>M	Automatically corrects photo, you may or may not like it! Shortcut is the same in the Organizer

Organizer Commands and Shortcuts

Command	Shortcut	Description
Edit>Go to Full Edit	Ctrl>I	Brings image into the Standard Editor
Find>Untagged Items	Ctrl>Shift>Q	Find any images that are not tagged
View>Compare Photos Side by Side	F12	View photos side by side, Press Esc to return to Organizer
View>Photos in Full Screen	F11	View selected photo in full screen, Press Esc to return to Organizer
File>Get Photos from Camera or Card Reader	Ctrl>G	Get photos from your camera or card reader
File>Get Photos from Files and Folders	Ctrl>Shift>G	Get photos from your files and folders
File>Get Photos from Scanner	Ctrl>U	Get photos from your scanner
File>Catalog	Ctrl>Shift>C	Opens Catalog dialog box to make a new catalog or switch between catalogs
File>Exit	Ctrl>Q	Closes (quit) the program
File>Backup	Ctrl>B	Backs up your current catalog
Windows/Properties	Alt>Enter	Displays general properties, tags, metadata & history
Edit>Rotate	Ctrl>Left or right arrow	Rotate 90° right Ctrl> → Rotate 90° left Ctrl> ← to rotate images in the Organizer

Tool Shortcuts

Tool (listed in order on the Toolbar)	Shortcut	Description
Move Tool	V	Moves layers from one file to another or within a file
Zoom Tool	Z	Zooms in and out so you can see your image
Hand Tool	H	Moves your view of an image
Eyedropper Tool	I	Samples color from an image
Rectangular Marquee Tool	M	Makes a rectangular or square selection
Elliptical Marquee Tool	M	Makes an oval or round selection
Lasso Tool	L	Makes a selection wherever you click
Magnetic Lasso Tool	L	Makes a selection by sticking to edges
Polygonal Lasso Tool	L	Makes a selection with straight lines
Magic Wand Tool	W	Makes a selection based on color
Magic Selection Brush Tool	F	Makes a selection of similar colors
Selection Brush Tool	A	Makes a selection wherever you paint
Horizontal Type Tool	T	Types text horizontally
Vertical Type Tool	T	Types text vertically
Horizontal Type Mask Tool	T	Types a mask horizontally(make text from photos, etc)
Vertical Type Mask Tool	T	Types a mask vertically (make text from photos, etc)
Crop Tool	C	Crops photos in standard sizes or freehand
Cookie Cutter Tool	Q	Crops photos into shapes
Straighten Tool	P	Straightens photos
Red Eye Tool	Y	Removes Red Eyes
Spot Healing Brush Tool	J	Fixes small areas of your image
Healing Brush Tool	J	Fixes large areas of your image
Clone Stamp Tool	S	Copies area of an image to another area
Pattern Stamp Tool	S	Copies a pattern to an image
Eraser Tool	E	Erases an image
Background Eraser	E	Erases the background area of an image
Magic Eraser	E	Erases an image based on color
Pencil Tool	N	Draws a thin, hard edged line
Brush Tool	B	Paints different brush strokes wherever you paint
Impressionist Brush	B	Changes color & details to look like a painting
Color Replacement Brush	B	Replaces color in your image with another color
Paint Bucket Tool	K	Fills an area with color or a pattern
Gradient Tool	G	Fills a layer or selection with a gradient
Rectangle Tool	U	Makes rectangle or square shapes
Rounded Rectangle Tool	U	Makes rectangles or squares with rounded edges
Ellipse Tool	U	Makes oval or round shapes
Polygon Tool	U	Makes multi-sided shapes
Line Tool	U	Makes lines and arrows
Custom Shape Tool	U	Makes shapes you choose from drop down list
Shape Selection Tool	U	Moves shapes that have not been simplified
Blur Tool	R	Blurs area you drag over
Sharpen Tool	R	Sharpens area you drag over
Sponge Tool	R	Removes/adds color in area you drag over
Smudge Tool	O	Smudges area you drag over like finger painting
Burn Tool	O	Darkens area you drag over
Dodge Tool	O	Lightens area you drag over
Default Foreground/ Background colors	D	Foreground Black-Background White
Switch Foreground/ Background colors	X	Swaps your Foreground and Background colors

Tools, Commands, & Tips

The Toolbar is located on the left side of your Image Window. It is sometimes called the Tool Bin, Toolbox or Tool palette. There are tools that you'll probably never use on the Toolbar and there are others you'll use over and over again. Each tool is explained in detail in this chapter including how to change the Option Bar settings and what you can use the tool for. Learning all about the different tools will help you make beautiful projects quickly.

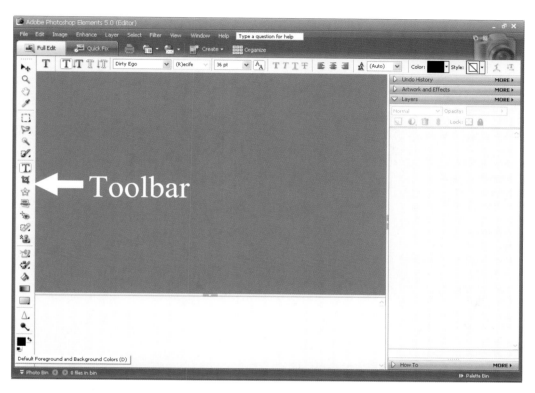

If there are several tools nested in one tool like the Eraser Tool (E). If your Preferences are set to "Use Shift key For Tool Switch" when you hold the Shift key and type the shortcut key and you will toggle through all three Eraser Tools. This will work regardless of what tool you currently have selected

Holding the Alt key and clicking the tool icon on the Toolbar will toggle through all of the hidden tools.

One of my favorite tricks is to hold the Ctrl key to temporarily activate the Move Tool (V). You can't do this if the Hand (H) or Shape Tool (U) is active.

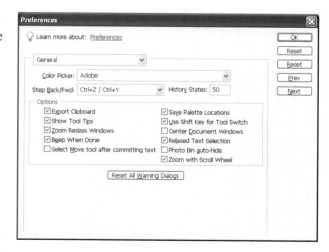

The Standard Editor Toolbar

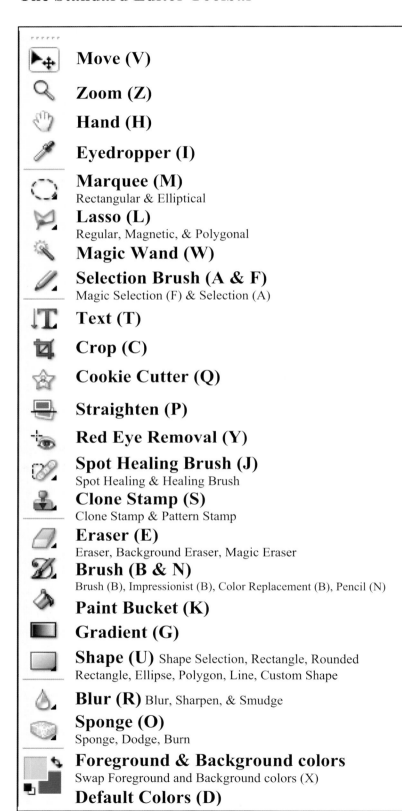

Move (V)

Zoom (Z)

Hand (H)

Eyedropper (I)

Marquee (M)
Rectangular & Elliptical

Lasso (L)
Regular, Magnetic, & Polygonal

Magic Wand (W)

Selection Brush (A & F)
Magic Selection (F) & Selection (A)

Text (T)

Crop (C)

Cookie Cutter (Q)

Straighten (P)

Red Eye Removal (Y)

Spot Healing Brush (J)
Spot Healing & Healing Brush

Clone Stamp (S)
Clone Stamp & Pattern Stamp

Eraser (E)
Eraser, Background Eraser, Magic Eraser

Brush (B & N)
Brush (B), Impressionist (B), Color Replacement (B), Pencil (N)

Paint Bucket (K)

Gradient (G)

Shape (U) Shape Selection, Rectangle, Rounded
Rectangle, Ellipse, Polygon, Line, Custom Shape

Blur (R) Blur, Sharpen, & Smudge

Sponge (O)
Sponge, Dodge, Burn

Foreground & Background colors
Swap Foreground and Background colors (X)

Default Colors (D)

To select a tool, click a tool on the Toolbar/Tool Bin/Tool Palette or type the shortcut unless you are currently using the Type Tool (T). The Move Tool (V) is currently selected in this example.

If there is a tiny black triangle in the lower right corner of the tool icon, click and hold your mouse to see the hidden tools. The little black square (circled) means the Magnetic Lasso Tool (L) is the active Lasso. Pick the tool you want.

When you select a tool with Hidden Tools, all of the tools will show on the Tool Options Bar after the tool is selected.

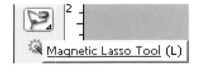

Hover your mouse over a tool and you can access Adobe Help for this particular tool. Click on the blue underlined word. To turn this on or off go to:
Edit>Preferences>General>
Show Tool Tips

If you would prefer to have your Toolbar displayed two columns wide, drag it from the very top of the toolbar and drop it in the Image Window. To put it back to a single wide column, drag it back to its original spot.

Undo (Ctrl Z) & Redo (Ctrl Y)

Imagine you're making a traditional scrapbook page or card and you cut your paper the wrong size, smear your journaling, or set an eyelet in the wrong spot. If you have extra supplies and time maybe you can fix your mistake. Imagine clicking an Undo button and you're back where you were before you made your mistake, INSTANTLY! Welcome to one of the advantages of digital scrapbooking!

Undo will no doubt be your best friend when you are using Photoshop Elements. For earlier version users of Photoshop Elements you are probably aggravated because they've removed the Undo and Redo buttons. Trust me after you use the program for a day or two you won't miss it.

The most important shortcut you can learn is Ctrl Z for Undo. Otherwise to Undo something you've done you will have to go to Edit>Undo each time you want to Undo something.

The shortcut for Redo is Ctrl Y but you won't be using this one as much. You can go to Edit>Redo if you don't learn the shortcut. If you Undo something and then decide you didn't want to Undo it you can Redo (Crtl Y).

One of the best ways to use the Undo command is with the help of the Undo History Palette. You can access this by going to Window>Undo History or by pressing F10 on the top of your keyboard. Clicking next to Undo History will make it show up on your screen. You can leave the Palette floating or install it in the Palette bin by dragging it by the folder tab where it says "Undo History" and dropping it into the Palette bin. If you want to get rid of the Undo History Palette pull it out of the Palette bin by the folder tab and click on the red x in the top right corner.

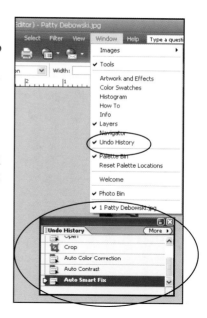

The example to the right shows that I opened a photo cropped it, applied auto color correction, auto contrast, and finally auto smart fix. If I didn't like any of the changes I made, I can click back on the top line that says Open or I can go to one of the other changes to see if maybe one of them was OK. Be aware that as soon as I click on the line that says Open, the lower changes are grayed out. If I do something else, all of the previous changes will now disappear.

My recommendation is to install the Undo Palette in your Palette bin and use it that way because it's easier than clicking Ctrl Z several times. Once installed in your Palette bin you can open and close the Undo History by tapping F10. In my examples I show you the Undo History as a way for you to see the steps I've taken.

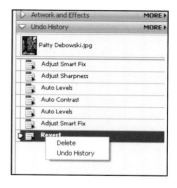

Be aware that when you close your file even if you save it as a PSD file (Photoshop file that saves with all layers) you will lose your Undo History and the ability to Undo anything you've done. Be sure that if you have created something you might not be happy with, use Undo or fix it before you close the file. When you save the file but don't close it you will still have your Undo History.

If you are working on a large project that has a long Undo History your program may slow down. You can clear your Undo History a couple of ways. Close your file as a PSD file and reopen it or go to Edit>Clear>Undo History. Once you do this, either way your Undo History is gone and cannot be retrieved.

To change the command for Undo & Redo or the number of actions it will keep track of, you can go to Edit>Preferences>General. Here you are given two other options to change, Step Backward/Step Forward-the formal name for Undo/Redo. My computer was set to track 50 History States, (the formal name for steps or actions). If you enter that you want to track 1001 changes it will tell you that the maximum available is 1000. Be aware that if you change this to a higher number, your program will probably slow down and you may want to drop it down a little bit from the default of 50.

If you want to go back to the last time you saved your file you can go to Edit>Revert. When you do this, Revert will show in the Undo Palette but so will all of the changes made before it. If you then decide that you don't want to revert to the last time you saved, you can right click and then click on delete, and it will ask you to confirm or you can do Ctrl Z.

To stop an operation in progress, like a filter being applied, hold the Esc key until it's stopped.

Tools That Move You Around

The Move Tool (V)

This is the tool you will probably use the most for digital scrapbooking, other than the Undo command. Make it a point to learn the shortcut. While using another tool hold down the Ctrl key and the Move Tool (V) is activated until you release the Ctrl key (this won't work if you're using the Hand or Shape Tools.)

What you can do with the Move Tool (V):

Move/Copy photos or digital scrapbook elements onto a scrapbook page, card or other photo.
Move/Copy a selection to another location (this is helpful for putting your head on the body of a beauty queen).
Transform/Resize photos & scrapbook elements.
Rotate photos or scrapbook elements.
Copy photos and elements-even in a straight line if you know the special trick.
Move your layers up and down in the Layers palette.
Align and space photos & scrapbook elements perfectly with the click of your mouse.

Auto Select Layer

If you are working on a multi-layer file like a scrapbook page or card, this option is usually helpful. Click on an item on your page and the layer in your Layers palette is selected so that you can make changes to that layer. Sometimes this doesn't work well for various reasons. If you are working with very small items like brads and eyelets it's almost impossible to select them on your page unless you zoom in by either using the Zoom Tool (Z) or the wheel on your mouse. You'll end up selecting another layer so zoom way in to grab the center circle move/rotation point. If you're working with layers that have transparent backgrounds (checkerboard) make sure you're clicking on the image itself and not the transparency. If you're still having trouble you can turn this off. If you turn it off, you will have to individually select each layer in the Layers palette which is aggravating!

To toggle the Auto Select Layer feature on and off press the Ctrl key when the Move Tool is activated.

Show Bounding Box

The Bounding Box is shown at the right. If you don't like working with it, you can turn it off. If you are working with tiny items like brads or rivets it's sometimes helpful to turn it off. To move your item click on the image and drag it. If you're not right on the image when you click and drag you'll end up drawing a rectangle of marching ants. You'll also need to turn on the Bounding Box if you want to resize with the sizing handles. Otherwise you'll need to go to Image>Transform>Free Transform which is the long way to turning on the Bounding Box.

Note:

If you turn off both the Auto Select Layer and Show Bounding Box while your layer is selected in the Layers palette, you can click anywhere and move it. You do not have to be right on the image.

Show Highlight on Rollover

This is new for Photoshop Elements 5. Auto Select Layer must be turned on for this to work. When you hover over a layer this Tool surrounds it with a bright blue rectangle UNLESS it's the selected layer. In this example the top left image is the selected layer and I'm hovering over the middle image. I can now click on the middle image and it will be my selected layer. I do not use this Tool because I find it very distracting.

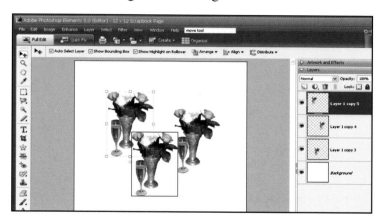

Arrange

This is also new for Photoshop Elements 5. When working with a multi-layer file such as a scrapbook page you can change the location of a selected layer. Click on the down facing triangle to bring up your choices or right click on the image you want to arrange. If Bring to Front is grayed out that means the layer you've selected is already at the front (top) of your file. Bring Forward will bring it up one layer. You can do the same thing by dragging your layers in the Layers palette.

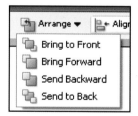

Align

This is a fabulous new tool for Photoshop Elements 5 that they must have designed with scrapbookers in mind! This aligns all selected layers to the same edge. The key to getting this is to work correctly is to highlight all of the layers you want to align in the Layers palette and knowing that Photoshop Elements will chose the "most" image to Align to. For example using Bottom Edges it will align all of the leaves below with the Bottom "most" shape. It's not proper English but the easiest way to explain it! Each item must be on its own layer or this won't work. Once all of the layers are highlighted click on one of the Align choices and like magic everything is perfectly in line. I normally use "Bottom Edges" to line up clip art, brads, etc. to make borders.

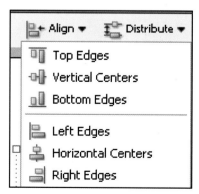

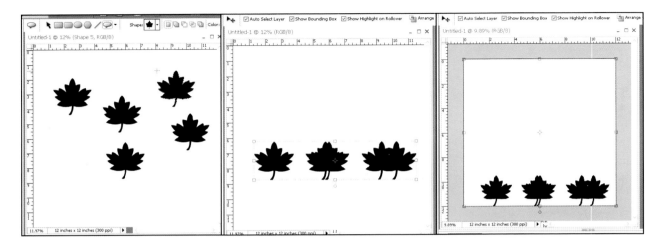

The first image on the left shows five leaves that I drew with the shape Tool at a fixed size. The middle image shows Align> Bottom Edges with only the five leaf layers selected. The right image shows Align>Bottom Edges with all five leaf layers selected <u>and</u> the Background layer. Note that only the bottom edges are aligned so now some of the images are overlapping each other but their bottom edges are perfectly aligned.

Distribute

Another new Tool for Photoshop Elements 5 that's fabulous for scrapbookers! This evenly spaces the selected layers apart. The key once again, just like Align is to make sure that all of the layers that you want to Distribute are selected. All items must be on their own layer. You have the option to Distribute from the Top Edges, Vertical Centers, Bottom Edges, Left Edges, Horizontal Centers, or Right Edges.

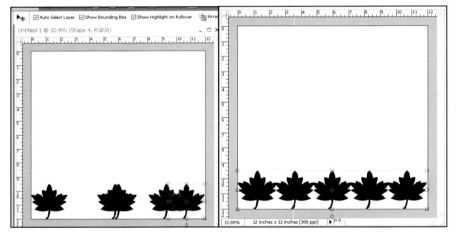

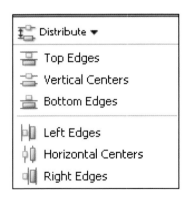

Because I wanted to Distribute my leaves across the entire bottom of my page I used the Move Tool (V) to drag the leaves on the far right and far left all the way to the edge of the page.

Notice in the left example that there are 2 sets of leaves that are still overlapping each other. I selected all of the leaves layers but not the Background layer and selected Horizontal Centers and they were spaced evenly across the bottom of my page on the example on the right.

If you use different shapes and sizes you will get different effects and you need to experiment with this to get the look you want. Align seems to be easier to use and understand than Distribute.

A note for Photoshop Elements 3 & 4 users if you want to use a Tool like the Align and Distribute but don't want to upgrade yet, Grants Tools will do something similar for free. Do an internet search for "Grants Tools" and install it per his directions.

Move/Copy A Photo Or Scrapbook Element To Another File

There are several ways to move images from one file to another. These two methods show what I consider to be the easiest ways. The only difference in using method #2 is that to move some layers it takes a little bit longer. The benefit is that your layer is identified with the file name of the digital element you used. Knowing the digital supplies you used is important if you want to submit your page to a magazine for publication which requires you to list your supplies and where you purchased them. If you post your page on a digital scrapbook site gallery for others to see, you are also asked for your source of supplies. This helps other scrappers locate the supplies you've used and it's been very helpful to me when I see a digital element I just can't live without!

Method #1

1. Click on the photo/element and activate the Move Tool (V)by either clicking on the icon on the Toolbar or just typing "V".

2. When the Move Tool (V) is activated and you click on the photo you want to move you will see the Move Tool (V) symbol.

3. Click on the photo and drag it down to your new scrapbook page in the Photo bin as shown above. Once you click on the photo you will only see the pointer arrow not the four headed arrow.

Possible Problems

If you get this message just click OK. This means you clicked on the photo/element layer but let go before you dragged it down to your page below in the Photo Bin. Click and drag again but don't let go until you get to the scrapbook page

When trying to move an item with a transparent background (checkerboard) you get a rectangle shape of marching ants. In this example I did not click right on the brad but to the side of it. If you're working with small items like brads and staples this is sometimes difficult. One of the best ways to avoid this problem is to zoom way in to see the element so that you can grab the circle in the middle of the bounding box. Grab the center circle when you move the element to avoid this problem. Use the wheel on the top of your mouse to do this or use the Zoom Tool (Z). Also read the sections on turning off Auto Select Layer & Bounding Box that follow in this section.

When you are working with a multi-layer file and you are moving a new image on to it, be sure that you have the top layer selected. By doing this the new item you move will become the new top layer. If you have your Background layer selected and move a new image on your page, the new image will be placed right above the Background layer. If you've got several layers that are the same size on your page you probably won't be able to see it!

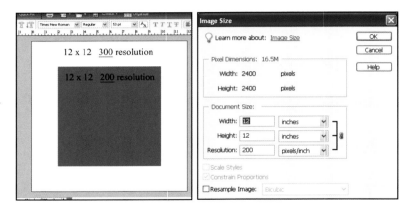

If you are moving a higher or lower resolution image onto your scrapbook page you may be surprised to see the size it transfers onto your page. For example, you've set up your new scrapbook page as 12 x 12 - 300 resolution and you drag on a piece of digital scrapbook paper that is 12 x 12. The paper you've dragged onto your page doesn't cover your new page as you expected or in the case of a brad or rivet it's microscopic. Your scrapbook paper/element is probably 200 resolution or less.

A lot of free sites give away lower resolution images. You can size it bigger by dragging on a corner handle but be aware that it may not print well because of the lower resolution. To check the size and resolution of your supplies before you drag them onto your page first go to Image>Resize>Image size and see what the height and width and resolution is. The majority of the supplies you buy now are 300 resolution.

When cropping photos before bringing them onto your page, be sure that you've selected 300 resolution on the Crop Tool (C) Option Bar.

4. When you drag down to the scrapbook page as soon as you cross into the Photo Bin you will see a white arrow with 2 rectangles. One of the rectangles has a + in it Release and your image will be dropped in the middle of your page. Notice you have 2 layers on your Layers palette now. When you use the Move Tool (V) to drag a photo onto your scrapbook page a new layer is automatically created. The photo is on top of your white 12 x 12 scrapbook page. The photo shown is a 2 inch square. You can use this method to drag several photos or digital elements on your page, remember that they are all going to be placed in the middle of your page. You may not see them all because they'll be stacked on top of each other on different layers.

If you were moving a 12 x 12 piece of scrapbook paper onto this scrapbook page, you would have 2 similar items in your Photo Bin. It's important to name your scrapbook page since you can easily get confused.

If you are moving items between two scrapbook pages that are both 300 resolution, using the Shift key with the Move Tool (V) activated will move the item to the same spot on the new page. Dragging and dropping without the Shift key will drop the item right in the middle of your page. If you are moving between two images that do not have the same resolution, using the Shift key will allow you to drop everything right in the middle of your page.

Note:
You can accomplish the same thing by starting with the photo and selecting, copying and pasting it to your scrapbook page using the Edit Menu Bar. With the photo as your Active Image go to Select>All (Ctrl A) and then Edit>Copy (or Ctrl C), click on the scrapbook page in the Photo Bin and it becomes the Active Image and go to Edit>Paste (or Ctrl>V). This method utilizes your Clipboard which will slow down your computer especially after you copy several things. To speed up your computer clear your Clipboard by going to Edit>Clear>Clipboard Contents. A warning will tell you "This cannot be undone. Continue?" click OK. You can see that using the Move Tool (V) is a much faster and efficient way to scrap!

Method #2

Photoshop Elements 5 has now added the option of dragging up from the Photo Bin to your Image Window. When you first try this it doesn't seem like there is much difference in the two methods; other than dragging up seems to take longer with some images (usually 12 x 12 digital paper or large high resolution photos). However, there is a big difference between the two methods! When you drag up to your Image Window from the Photo Bin your new layer is named with the image's file name instead of something like: Layer 1, Layer 2, etc. This is a big timesaver if you routinely submit your pages to magazines or digital scrapbook sites for posting in their galleries because you won't have to rename your layers to keep track of your supplies. You will always know where your supplies came from as long as you keep the file in a PSD format. If you save this file as a JPEG, your image will be flattened and all of your layers and information stored there will be gone.

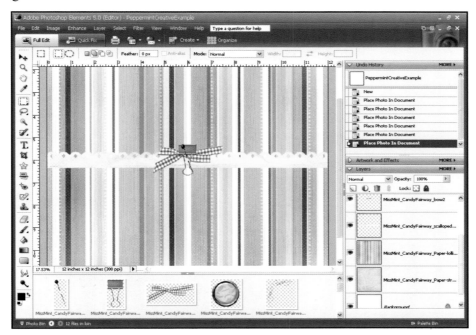

To drag up, click on the image in the Photo Bin you want to drag to your scrapbook page. It doesn't matter which Tool you have activated to do this. Click (without releasing) on the image and drag up to the scrapbook page. When you get to the scrapbook page release it and the image will be placed in the middle of your page.

If you click and release on an image in the Photo Bin before you drag it onto your scrapbook page the new image will show in the Active Image Window. If this happens just click back on your scrapbook page so that it is the Active Image and then start over.

Notice in my example I have two pieces of paper on top of my Background layer but only the top paper shows right now. All of the layers are named with the file name. Just by looking at my layer name I can see that the bottom paper is from Miss Mint's Candy Fairway Kit. Since the name is so long, if I double click on the layer name I can see that the name of the paper is Strawberry Pop. Miss Mint at PeppermintCreative.com was very generous to allow me to include this kit on your CD that came with the book. While it might seem like this is a feminine kit she has a wonderful example of a boy's page made with this kit on her website at www.CreativeMint.com that is absolutely darling.

Move/Copy A Selection From One File To Another

In this photo I've made a selection (marching ants) around the flowers, vase and champagne glass using the Lasso (L)and Selection Brush (A) Tools. You could also select your head to place it on the body of a swimsuit model using this same method!

I clicked on the Move Tool (V) and now I am going to drag it by the center circle move point down to my scrapbook page down in the Photo bin.

My champagne glass & vase full of roses is now in the center of my scrapbook page. Since I don't really want it there I'm going to move it.

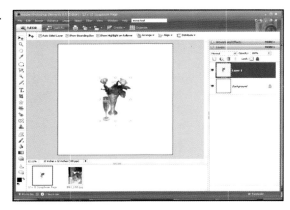

How to Move An Image On A Scrapbook Page

With the Move Tool (V) still activated (you can see the Bounding Box around the image), click and drag the center circle move/rotation point to another area of the scrapbook page or use the Arrow keys to nudge it where you want it. Every time you hit the Arrow key once, the selection moves one pixel. When you hold the Shift and hit the Arrow key, it moves ten pixels. Many times you use both methods to move an image.

Moving a Selection Border

If you only want to move your selection border (marching ants), keep your selection Tool activated. When you click inside the selection you will see a white arrowhead and box for your curser. Click and drag to move the selection or use your Arrow Keys. For example, you are using the Rectangular Marquee Tool and you want to move the rectangle of marching ants over a little bit; with the Marquee Tool (M) still selected, click inside the rectangle of marching ants and drag. If you forget and switch to your Move Tool (V) you will get a result like the photo below.

Possible Problems

If you end up with something that looks like this, you let go of your mouse before you got to your scrapbook page. You have only moved your selection on your original image and the black hole is a hole you've cut in your image with your Background color showing through. If you do this Undo, (Ctrl Z) and do it again.

You can move several layers from one file to another by highlighting all of the layers you want to move and dragging them to the new file. The layers do not have to be linked. If you like to work in the Cascade or Tile View you can drag multiple layers from the Layers palette onto your new file. If you work in the Maximize Mode as I do it doesn't work.

Resize-Transform Photos & Scrapbook Elements On Your Scrapbook Page

My flowers are moved to the right corner of my page but I want the image to be bigger or smaller. There's a couple of ways to do this but I'll tell you the easiest way first! Click on one of the 4 corner sizing handles, (notice that the pointer has now turned into a 2 headed arrow). You can click and drag and reduce or enlarge the size. Notice that when you click on one of these handles the options bar changes to this:

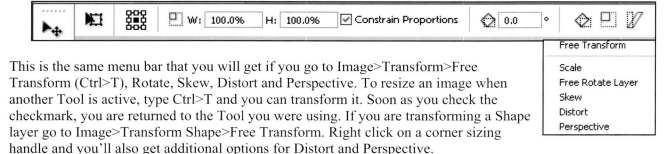

This is the same menu bar that you will get if you go to Image>Transform>Free Transform (Ctrl>T), Rotate, Skew, Distort and Perspective. To resize an image when another Tool is active, type Ctrl>T and you can transform it. Soon as you check the checkmark, you are returned to the Tool you were using. If you are transforming a Shape layer go to Image>Transform Shape>Free Transform. Right click on a corner sizing handle and you'll also get additional options for Distort and Perspective.

As long as the ✓ is in front of Constrain Proportions **and you are dragging from one of the corner sizing handles,** the image that you're resizing, whether it be a photo or scrapbook element will keep the right aspect ratio, also known as proportions. Your width & height numbers will change together proportionately.

To size from the center, hold the Alt key as you drag the corner and your image resizes from the center outward or inward depending if you're enlarging or reducing it.

A special note to Photoshop Elements 3 & 4 users
Previously you had to use the Shift key when resizing to keep the proportions correct-if you can't get used to this change, you can always uncheck Constrain Proportions and go back to using the Shift key. Using the Shift key now will remove Constrain Properties and do the opposite of what it used to do. Yes, I know they're trying to drive you nuts! Yes, I know you thought removing the Undo button was the worst that could happen and now this, but it's nice when you get used to this change!

If you drag from one of the middle sizing handles your image will stretch out and the ✓ will be automatically removed from the Constrain Proportions area. By dragging from your top middle sizing handle, your flower vase will end up tall and skinny (this does have some advantages for people) and you will see that while your width stays at 100% your height number will increase.

 Once you click on any of the sizing handles whether you sized an image or not, you will need to commit your changes. **This is one of the biggest places people get stuck because they try to go on to something else and the program just sits and waits for them!**
If you want to accept your change you can either click on the ✓ , tap your enter key once, or double click in the Bounding Box. If you don't want the change click on the ⊘ or hit your Esc button once.

If you select all layers in the Layers palette so that they are all active, or link the layers together by linking them in the Layers palette, you can size and or rotate several items on a scrapbook page at the same time.

Rotate Photos Or Scrapbook Elements On A Page

Many times you want to rotate a photo because your subject is facing the wrong direction to create a pleasing scrapbook page. Rotating images is easy, the key is to pay attention if you're working on a single image or a scrapbook page with multiple layers. When you go to Image>Rotate you need to read each option and make sure that you pick the correct one. Choosing one of the top six rotate items will rotate everything on your page. Usually you only want to rotate one layer on your page. If you make a mistake and your whole page flips around in some wild way that you don't want, you probably picked the wrong rotate option, remember there's always Undo (Ctrl Z).

Rotate Scale

Rotate handle

The current example shows how easy it is to use the rotate handle while the Move Tool (V) is still active. Remember, this image is the <u>active</u> layer on a scrapbook page. If you're on the Background layer this won't work. We've used the corner and middle handles and the middle circle point to move and resize the image. Notice the circle located under the center bottom sizing handle. When you hover your mouse over this you'll see a circle comprised of rounded lines and arrows. Hovering your mouse over any of the square sizing arrows produces a two headed curved arrow. Any of these can be used to rotate the image. Notice that as you rotate the image, the center move/rotation circle point stays stuck in the same place.

I rotated this image with the handles after I sized it. Notice that the width and height are both 118.6%. They started out at 100% before I made the image bigger. The image is rotated 26.6°. Not that I'd ever know I wanted to rotate something to that exact degree but I'd probably know if I wanted to rotate something to 90°. If I wanted to rotate to 90° I would just type 90 or -90 in this box depending on if I wanted to rotate the image right or left.

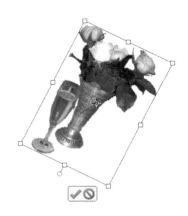

You can also flip this image using the middle sizing handles. Make sure your image is near the top of your scrapbook page and click and drag the middle top sizing handle down over the image. The Constrain Proportions is automatically turned off. Check your width and height numbers and try it until you get it right. Unfortunately typing in the numbers or rechecking Constrain Proportions just brings you back to the original image, but it can be rotated this way. It's easier to go to Image>Rotate>Flip Layer Vertical.

If you want to rotate your item from a certain point, click in one of the nine boxes on the Reference Point Box. By selecting the lower left corner box in this example, when I rotate my photo it's almost like there's a thumbtack holding it in place on the lower left corner. The photo spins around in a circle from the lower left corner. The Reference Point Box tells the Transform Commands where to anchor.

By default the center of the selection or layer is the rotation point. The small circle in the middle of the Bounding Box is the rotation point. Every time you rotate and click the check mark the rotation point is returned to the center default location.

Note:

You can also accomplish the same thing by Image>Rotate>Free Rotate Layer.

Image>Rotate>Layer 90° right (or left) will rotate your image 90°.

Image>Rotate>Flip Layer Horizontal will flip your layer completely horizontal which is sometimes helpful if you want an image facing a different way on your page (instead of a child looking off the edge of the page flip him horizontally and he'll be looking in to the center of your page).

Image>Rotate>Flip Layer Vertical will flip your layer vertically which in the case of our roses and champagne glass they would be upside down.

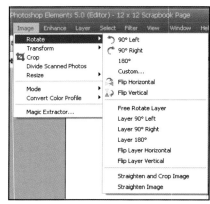

Rotate a Single Image

Oftentimes you want to rotate a single photo or a scrapbook element before you put it on your page. If you use one of these commands on a multi-layer scrapbook page the whole page will rotate. To do this go to Image>Rotate> 90° Left (Counterclockwise, ¼ turn) 90° Right (Clockwise, ¼ turn) 180° (1/2 turn) Custom (you specify amount to rotate

Custom will ask you for an angle and right or left.

Flip Horizontal
Flip Vertical

Just remember to read if you are choosing to rotate your whole file or just a layer and you won't have any problems!

Flip can only be applied to a regular layer not a Background layer - click OK

Rotating a Scrapbook Template

If you want to rotate a multi-layer file like a template and the layers are linked you can flip it or rotate it using any of the settings as long as you have one of the linked layers selected.

Scale

Scale is another way to resize. Photos, layers, selections or shapes can be resized by using the Scale command. Show Bounding Box will be activated if it's turned off.
Click on the sizing handle so that you get a two sided arrow and then right click and choose Scale or go to Image>Resize>Scale.
Scale can only be applied to a layer. If you want to scale an image that's a Background layer you must change it to a layer first, the program will give you this option.
To keep the image in proportion make sure that constrain proportions is checked and then enter a percentage in the first box for the width and it will automatically be entered in the second box for height. If you don't want to keep the original proportions uncheck the constrain proportions box and enter two different numbers for the width and height percentages. This is one opportunity to make a person a little bit taller and thinner. When you are happy with your results click the checkmark or double click.

Left - Original   Middle-Skew pulling on lower right corner   Right-Distort pulling on lower right corner

Skew

Skew slants your image/shape vertically or horizontally and almost makes them look like they're coming off the page. Show Bounding Box will be automatically activated if it's turned off. Click on the sizing handle so that you get a two sided arrow and then right click and choose Skew or go to Image>Transform (Transform Shape if skewing a Shape Layer)>Skew. Using the Ctrl>Shift keys and dragging a corner will also Skew the image.
Skew can only be applied to a layer. If you want to Skew an image that is a Background layer you must change it to a layer first. The program will give you this option. Click the checkmark or double click to accept the change.

Distort

Distort twists and stretches the image/shape. Show Bounding Box will be automatically activated if it's turned off. Click on the sizing handle so that you get a two sided straight arrow and then right click and choose distort or go to Image>Transform (Shape if Distorting a Shape Layer)>Distort. Holding the Ctrl key and dragging a sizing handle will also Distort your image.

Distort can only be applied to a layer. If you want to distort an image that is a Background layer you must change it to a layer first. The program will give you this option. Click the checkmark or double click to accept the change.

Perspective

Perspective makes the image/shape appear to have three dimensions. Show Bounding Box will be automatically activated if it's turned off.

Click on the sizing handle so that you get a two sided straight arrow and then right click and choose Perspective or go to Image>Transform (Transform Shape if applying Perspective to a Shape Layer)>Perspective. Ctrl>Alt>Shift and dragging a sizing handle will also activate Perspective.

Perspective can only be applied to a layer. If you want to give perspective to an image that is a Background layer you must change it to a layer first, the program will give you this option. Click the checkmark or double click to accept the change.

Copy Photos And Elements
(Even in a straight line if you know the special trick)

This trick is most useful when using scrapbook elements such as eyelets, brads, and buttons but you can use it to copy anything.
x
We'll use our roses in the vase example again on a blank scrapbook page just so I really get my money's worth out of my daughter's wedding!

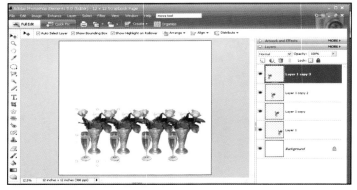

Click on the center of the flower vase and also press on the Alt key. Now Drag and let go of the mouse and you'll see that you now have a copy of your flower vase, don't let go of the Alt key and click and drag again. If you also press on the Shift key at the same time, (Yes! I know you only have 2 hands!) you'll get the vases in a straight line which is really nice for brads and eyelets.

Notice that in your Layers palette you now have Layer 1, Layer 1 copy, Layer 1 copy 2, & Layer 1 copy 3. Because I used the Shift key they're straight. If I didn't use the Shift key, I can line them up using the Distribute & Align menu previously explained in this section.

To copy the image and move it over one pixel so that you have a blur type effect, press the Alt key and one of the Arrow Keys depending on which way you want the image to move. If you merely tap the Arrow Key, you'll end up with one copy. If you hold it down for a very short time you'll end up with about 80 copies and something that looks like this. This effect would be much better on a race car or sports figure but it's interesting. If you've tried this, don't think that Undo (Ctrl Z) is going to work too well because you'll have to do it about 80 times. Instead, click on the top layer and then Shift Click on the Layer 1 Copy layer and drag them to the trashcan. To get the same type of effect but move it over ten pixels Press Alt, Shift and an Arrow Key.

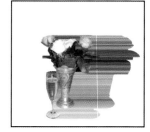

Adjusting Layer Opacity With The Move Tool

The short cut to adjust the Opacity for an active layer is to activate the Move Tool (V) and type 9 for 90%, 8 for 80% etc. To set the opacity to 35 % type 35 quickly, type 0 for 100%.

Changing Blending Modes With The Move Tool (V)

With the Move Tool (V) activated press Shift>+ to cycle down through the different Blending Modes. Shift>- will cycle up through the list.

The Zoom Tool (Z   )

To be completely honest I don't use this tool this way. I use the Zoom Tool (Z) all the time but when I want to zoom into an image I use the wheel on the top of my mouse. I roll away from me to zoom in and roll back towards me to zoom back out. Zooming with your mouse wheel will only work if it is set up in your Preferences. Go to Edit>Preferences>General>and make sure that Zoom with Scroll Wheel has a checkmark by it. If you don't like zooming with your mouse wheel you can uncheck it and turn it off. The Zoom Tool (Z) is more accurate than rolling the mouse because it zooms in on the area where you're clicking your mouse. When I want to bring my image back to the full screen view after zooming in I use the short cut Ctrl 0 instead of switching to the zoom out tool and clicking my mouse.

To activate the Zoom Tool (Z) when you're using another Tool, Ctrl + zooms in and Ctrl – zooms out. Using the zoom this way is very similar to rolling the mouse wheel and not as precise as actually clicking in the image. When another Tool is active and you want to be more precise, hold the Ctrl key and Space Bar and drag out a window with your mouse to zoom into the area in the window.

What you can do with the Zoom Tool (Z):

Zoom in to look at an active image just like a magnifying glass to help you make selections, erase items, check for spelling errors, etc.
Always zoom in and check your page completely before you print it because you'll always find one little thing (and maybe 10 big things) that you're not happy with.
When working in Cascade or Tile view you can zoom in the same percentage of magnification on all windows at the same time. You can also zoom into the same area of the photos.

Zoom Toolbar Options

Resize Windows to Fit

When checked, the window size changes when you zoom in or out. When not checked, the window size remains the same. This is more noticeable when in Cascade or Tile View.

I keep Zoom Resizes Window checked in my Preferences. Go to Edit>Preferences>Zoom Resizes Window and check it, then click OK.

Ignore Palettes

This allows the image to resize under the Palette bin but Resize Windows to Fit must be checked for this to work.

Actual Pixels

If your image is on the Web this is the size it would be.
You can also go to View>Actual Pixels or Alt Ctrl 0

Fit On Screen (Ctrl 0)

Your image fits your screen. This is the view I use the most while working in Photoshop Elements. It can also be found at View>Fit on Screen but learn the shortcut Ctrl 0 because you'll use it a lot.

Print Size

This shows the size your image will print. Most digital cameras will take pictures that are much bigger than your screen. Because I have a large wide screen monitor this view is not very accurate. You can also find this at View>Print Size.

Zoom All Windows

If you work in a multi window view (Cascade or Tile) all of the images will zoom but not at the same percentage. If you want them to zoom in at the same percentage select Window>Images>Match Zoom. When working in a Cascade or Tile View only the top image will Fit on Screen.

Why Would You Want To Work With The Zoom Tool In Cascade Or Tile View?

When I have taken several photos of the same thing and want to compare them in order to pick the best one, I will usually look at them in tile view. You can also use this to compare scrapbook elements. Using the next two settings makes it really easy.

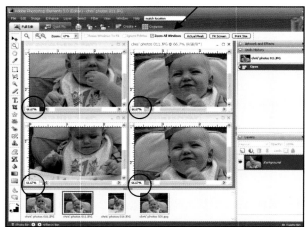

Match Zoom

Window>Images>Match Zoom will match the magnification in all of your open images to your Active Image as long as Zoom All Windows is checked. Remember your Active Image will show in the Layers palette and will have a blue rectangle around it in the Photo Bin.

Match Location

Window>Images>Match Location will match the magnification in all of your open images to your Active Image in the same location as long as Zoom All Windows is checked. For example, click in the center of your photo and it becomes your Active Image. When you select Window>Images>Match Location all of the other photos are now showing in the center.

How To Use The Zoom Tool (Z):

To Zoom in, click on the magnifying glass with the + and then click on the area of the image that you want to magnify and your screen will zoom in. Every time you click your mouse the zoom % increases. Mine finally stopped when I hit 1600% - by that time I couldn't even tell what the original image was. You can enter your own zoom % in this box if you want to, as soon as you click on the triangle, a slider box opens that you can slide to get the amount of magnification that you want.

To zoom out, click on the magnifying glass with the – (minus) and then click on your image and you'll zoom back out. If you have the + (plus) Tool activated and want to use the – (minus) Tool, just press on the Alt and you can switch back and forth without changing Tools.

To zoom into a specific area of your image, click and drag a rectangle and you will zoom into just that area. If you need to move your rectangle before you let go of the mouse button, hold down the space bar and you can move it around just like the crop Tool. If you use the Zoom Tool (Z) like this a lot you should probably check out the Navigator also explained in this chapter.

Double clicking on the Hand Tool (H) icon on the Toolbar when zoomed into an image will fit the image to the screen.

Ctrl>+ will make your document window larger, Ctrl>- will make your document window smaller.

View>New View

Open a photo and go to View>New Window for (Your image name). By opening a new window for your photo you have the ability to have one photo zoomed way in to edit it and the other copy can be at full screen view. You can make several new windows for your photo if you want to.

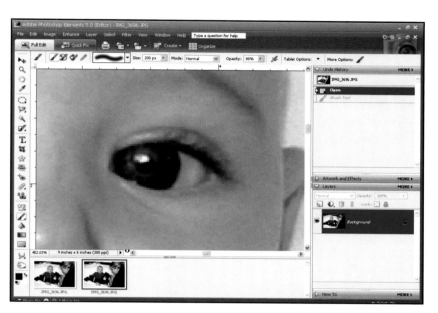

This example shows the same photo open in two different windows. The photo on the left hand side of the Photo Bin shows in my image window in full screen size and the photo on the right in the Photo Bin is currently shown in my image window at 452% magnification so I can fix a red eye problem. When I make changes to one image they both are changed at the same time. Notice that the image name is exactly the same. Use this when you're editing a scrapbook page or photo and don't want to be constantly zooming in and out, this is a good trick to use.

The Hand Tool (H)

Normally I don't use this Tool a lot unless I'm working with images where I've zoomed in very close and need to pan the image. I use the Navigator instead because it combines the Zoom (Z) and the Hand Tool (H)

What you can do with the Hand Tool:

Move (pan) around an image that is larger than the image window, instead of using the scroll bars.

Double clicking on the Hand Tool (H) icon in the Toolbar when zoomed into an image will fit the image to the screen.

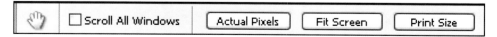

Hand Toolbar Options

Scroll All Windows

You can activate Scroll All Windows by clicking the box or pressing the Shift key when the Hand Tool (H) is activated. When in Tile or Cascade View you can pan across all images similar to Zoom All Windows.

Actual Pixels

If your image is on the Web this is the size it would be.
You can also go to View>Actual Pixels or Alt Ctrl 0

Fit On Screen

Your image fits your screen. This is the view I use the most while working in Photoshop Elements. It can also be found at View>Fit on Screen but learn the shortcut Ctrl 0 because you'll use it a lot.

Print Size

This shows the size your image will print. Most digital cameras will take pictures that are much bigger than your screen. If you have a large wide screen monitor, this view is not very accurate. You can also find this at View>Print Size.

When you activate the Hand Tool (H) your cursor changes into the Hand symbol.

To activate the Hand Tool (H) when doing something else, hold down the space bar and you will see the curser temporarily change to the hand symbol. When you release the space bar you are automatically returned to your previously selected Tool. This works really well when you're using the Lasso Tool (L) to make a selection and you are zoomed in to see the edges and come to the end of your screen. Hold the space bar and the Hand Tool (H) allows you to move the image so you can continue on with the Lasso Tool (L).

When using the Hand Tool (H) you can temporarily switch to Zoom In by holding down the Ctrl key or Zoom Out by pressing Ctrl Alt.

To fit an image on the screen double click on the Hand Tool (H) icon on the Toolbar.

The Navigator

The Navigator is like using the Zoom (Z) and Hand (H) Tools at the same time. The Navigator is located under the Window menu bar, not on the Toolbar like the Hand (H) and Zoom (Z) Tools are.

What you can do with the Navigator

Zoom and move your image without switching between the Zoom (Z) and Hand (H) Tools. Using the Navigator makes zooming in to edit photos easy. The Navigator works well when you want to view all the tiny details of your scrapbook page before you print it.

To open the Navigator Palette, go to Window>Navigator, or press F12 at the top of your keyboard. The Navigator will be floating on your photo. If you plan on using this all the time, you can drag it by the folder tab that says Navigator and drop it into your Palette bin and it will be there every time you open Photoshop Elements. If you only use it occasionally, you can close it by clicking the red X or removing the ✓ at Window>Navigator. To remove it from your Palette bin, go to Window>Navigator and remove the ✓.

When you first open the Navigator you may not notice the red rectangle around your photo because it's at the edges of the photo. Move the zoom slider up and down and your cursor is an arrow. The Navigator's red rectangle will enlarge and reduce your active image view to only what's inside the Navigator's rectangle. If you want to change the location on your image, click inside the red rectangle and move it to another location. When you click inside the red rectangle your cursor becomes a hand.

The default color for the Navigator rectangle is red. If you want to change this color (possibly because you're working on images with a lot of red in them), click the More button on the top right corner of the Navigator Palette, and then Palette Options. This is your only option. Click the dropdown arrow for the default colors, or if you click in the big color block you can pick your own custom color.

Color-How To Pick It, Use It, & Save It

The Eyedropper Tool (I)

This is a great Tool to use for scrapbooking that helps you match all of your colors exactly.

While using the following Tools hold down the Alt key and the Eyedropper Tool (I) is activated to change your Foreground color, but only until you release the Alt key.

Cookie Cutter (Q)	Color Replacement Brush (B)	Paint Bucket (K)
Straighten (P)	Pencil (N)	Shape (U)
Brush (B)	Gradient (G)	

What you can do with the Eyedropper Tool (I):

Copy/Sample a color from a photo or scrapbook element that is active or another one that is currently open in your Photo Bin.

Copy/Sample a color from your computer's desktop (internet, another program etc.)

Create your own Custom Color Swatches

Copy/Sample a color from a photo or scrapbook element that is active

How many times have you tried to match your photos to paper, embellishments, and journaling ink with traditional scrapbooking supplies? It usually doesn't work very well and it's a lot of work!

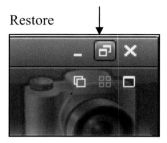

Now with one click of your mouse you've got an exact match! Click on the eyedropper Tool to activate it and click on your active photo or scrapbook element. Your Foreground color now changes to the color you selected. In my example, I am copying/sampling the green of the leaf. It is helpful to zoom way in with your mouse when using the Eyedropper Tool (I), because in my example, the leaf is going to have many different colors of green and some may be in a shadow. If you click and drag over the color you want to sample you can see the Foreground color change as you move.

If you want to change your Background color in the above example, press on the Alt key. If you're using the Straighten Tool (P), Brush Tool (B), Paint Bucket Tool (K), Gradient Tool (G), or Shape Tool (U) and have pressed Alt to temporarily activate the Eyedropper Tool (I), this won't work. Just activate the Eyedropper Tool (I).

Sample Size

You can change your Sample Size by clicking the drop down box or by right clicking on your image when the Eyedropper Tool (I) is active. The default setting of the Eyedropper Tool (I) is Point Sample. Zoom way in with your mouse wheel, you can see the individual pixels and you can pick one. I work in a 3 by 3 Average which means that it selects a block of pixels 3 wide by 3 high and averages the color of those 9 pixels (3 x 3 = 9). By setting my point average to 3 by 3, color selection works better. The 5 by 5 Average would select a block of pixels 5 wide by 5 high and average the color of those 25 pixels.

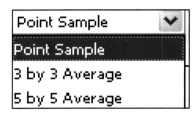

Copy/Sample a color from a photo that is open in your Photo Bin

With the Eyedropper Tool (I) activated, click anywhere in the Active Image and drag it down into the Photo Bin to the image you want to sample. Let go of the mouse and your Foreground color (or your Background color if you were using the Alt key) will change. Because it is difficult to get a good color sample from small images in the Photo Bin you will probably get better results if you click on the photo in the Photo Bin and make it the Active Image. Sample the color, and then go back to the Photo Bin and click on the photo you were originally working on.

Copy/Sample a color from another location on your computer screen (internet or another program

To sample color from a program other than Photoshop Elements, you will need to have both programs showing on your screen. There are several ways to do this but I will show you the way I do it.

If you are going to sample from the internet, go to the site that you want to sample from-my example is the website for Photoshop Elements. On your internet screen click on the top right corner to Restore or Restore Down. On the top right corner of your Photoshop Elements screen click on Restore. This will shrink the display down.

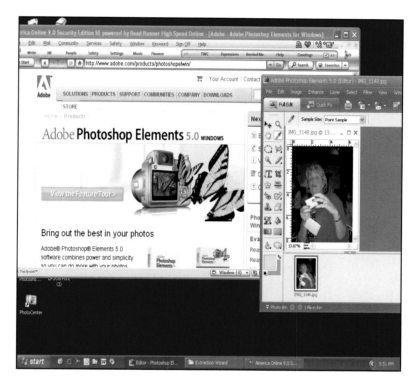

Your two screens will be side by side. In my example, if I click on the internet page it will be on top. You can also drag and move the pages up and down or side to side by grabbing the top menu bar. Click on the Editor so that it shows on top like my example. Click on the Eyedropper Tool (I) and click in the photo to activate the Eyedropper then move across to the butterfly and click and your Foreground color will change to yellow. If you want the butterfly yellow as your Background color hold down the Alt key. After you've got the color you want click back on same button that earlier said Restore but now says Maximize and your Photoshop Elements screen will fill your entire monitor screen again.

Possible Problems- You must have a photo or even an empty transparent file open in the Editor for this to work. You must click the eyedropper on the photo in the Editor and don't let go until you get to the color you want to sample on the webpage.

Imagine the possibilities of being able to copy a color from a website. Do you have a favorite card stock manufacturer, paint company, or traditional scrapbook company that you'd love to borrow a color to match something you've bought? The color you get from the web will probably not be an exact match but it will be much closer than if you tried to match it by trial and error.

Bazzill Basics Paper recently introduced a new book called "Chemistry (of) Color 2007 Inside this book they list the RGB, CYMK, & Pantone codes for their 2007 paper line so that you can match their card stock.

Bazzill is also offering their Chemistry of Color Designer Kit which includes more than 500 3x5 cardstock samples with their codes, along with a book and CD. This kit is for the professional designer who is working to match exact Bazzill color codes and it's listed at a professional price of $399. Check out www.ChemistryofColor.com or www.BazzillBasics.com.

Copy color As HTML

Locate this option by right clicking on your image when the Eyedropper Tool (I) is activated.
You can then either paste (Edit>Paste or Ctrl V) this information onto your page using the Text Tool (T) or onto a word document. This is the hexadecimal color formula that you would use for Web projects. An example of exactly what it prints out is: color="#85898c".

Foreground & Background Color Swatch

The Foreground and Background color Swatch is located at the very bottom of the Toolbar.
The top larger square is your Foreground color. Black is the default Foreground color. The bottom larger square is the Background color. White is the default Background color. The two tiny black and white squares on the lower left corner are your Default colors.

To swap your Foreground and Background colors, type the letter "X" (except when you have the Text Tool (T) active) or click on the rounded two headed arrow located to the right of the Foreground color. To set your Foreground and Background colors back to the default colors, type the letter "D" (except when you have the Text Tool (T) active) or click on the tiny black and white boxes to the bottom left of the Foreground color.

By using the Eyedropper Tool (I) Color Picker or Color Swatches you can change the Foreground and Background colors.

Foreground Color

The Foreground color sets the color for your Text (T), Brush (B), Color Replacement Brush (B) Pencil (N), Paint Bucket (K), and Shape (U)Tools. The Gradient Tool (G) set to default setting uses the Foreground and Background colors. To fill a layer or selection with your Foreground color use Alt Backspace.

Background Color

The Background color is shown when you use the Eraser Tool (E) on a Background layer and is the default for increasing your canvas size by going to Image>Resize>Canvas Size. The Gradient Tool (G) set to the default setting uses the Foreground and Background colors. To fill with your Background color use Ctrl>Backspace.

Using The Color Picker

Check to make sure that your Color Picker is set to the Adobe Color Picker by going to Edit>Preferences>General (Ctrl>K). Your only other choice is the Windows Color Picker.

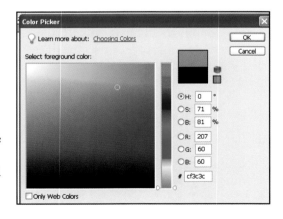

To use the Color Picker to change the Foreground color click inside the Foreground color and the Color Picker box appears. Click in the color you want. If it's not shown, click on the tall skinny rainbow type box and you'll be directed toward that hue or you can drag the two white slider arrows shown at the bottom. Double click on the color you want and two colors will show in the box to the left of OK. The top color is your new Foreground color and the bottom one is the old Foreground color.

To change the Background color click inside the Background color box on the Toolbar.

You can also manually enter numbers which are called Hexadecimal Numbers or Hex # to get an exact color. Designers use them and if you're working on a joint project with someone it would be helpful to use them. If you were working on a high school sports program with a partner and wanted to make sure that the royal blue you were both using was an exact match you would decide on the hexadecimal number and both make sure you keyed that number in at the bottom of all the numbers where it says #.

HSB Color

HSB stands for Hue, Saturation, Brightness. Saturation and Brightness are entered as percentages (%). Hue is entered as an angle degree (°) that matches a spot on the color wheel. This is sometimes referred to as Hue, Saturation, Intensity (HSI).

RGB Color

RGB stands for Red, Green, Blue. Values from 0 to 255 are entered in the appropriate boxes.
The lower the number, the less of that color, the higher the number means there's more of that color. For example, a true red would have the following settings Red 255, Green 0, Blue 0. The settings for white are Red 255, Green 255, Blue 255. The settings for black are Red 0, Green 0, Blue 0. If all of the settings are the same number between 1 and 254 you will get varying shades of gray. The higher the number, the lighter the gray, the lower the number the darker the gray.

Hexadecimal Values

This is a color number that is used to identify an exact color. Using the example of the color white: the RGB settings are Red 255, Green 255, and Blue 255. The Hexadecimal Value for White is ffffff. The Hexadecimal Value for Black is 000000.

If you are taking a class, your instructor may refer to a color as Hexadecimal #, Hex #, or just #. This is the number they are referring to. If you have a Hex # you can enter it in by typing the number in the circled box in my example.

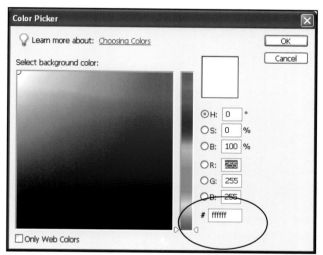

You don't need to understand how they come up with the numbers, (because I sure don't) but just understand that if you want to match a color with someone you're working with on a joint project, use the same Hexadecimal Values for the predominant colors in your project. Use the same printer and your colors will match. Because all printers print a little bit differently, even though you use the same Hexadecimal Values, your colors may not match exactly because they were printed on two different printers, even if they are the same model.

Web Safe Color

If the color you picked is not safe for the Web, you will see a multi-colored box that when you hover your mouse over it says "Warning not a web safe color." Hover your mouse over the bottom box and it says "Click to select web safe color". If you check Only Web Colors, you won't have to worry about this!

Viewing Color Values with the Info Palette

The Info Palette can be activated by going to Window>Info. If you want to install this palette into your Palette bin drag it by the top tab to your Palette bin.

I don't use this Palette but you may find some use for it.

Once you have the Info Palette displayed with any Tool selected, drag your cursor over the paper and the RGB numbers will change in both readouts.

Paper shown is:
Shabby Princess Festival Kit
Dotty Paper

In my Info Palette Options menu my options are set as RGB Color Readout for the first box and Web Color for the Second Color Readout. If you want to change these you can click on the drop down arrow and pick another one.

In the box on the area with the (+) this indicates the x and y coordinates of the cursor. My example shows X 5.958 and Y 6.014. In plain English what this means is this: X is the distance from the right edge, currently I am 5.958 inches from the right edge of the paper. Y is the distance from the top edge, currently I'm 6.014 inches from the right edge. In this example I'm almost in the exact center of the 12 x 12 paper. I know my measurement is in inches because in the options I've chosen my Mouse Coordinates Ruler Unit as Inches.

The box with the W & H shows the size of a selection drawn with the Marquee Tool (M). Read about the Marquee Tool (M) in the Selections Section.

Color Swatches

To View the Color Swatch Palette, go to Window>Color Swatches and the palette will appear on your screen. To install it into your Palette bin, drag it by the folder tab that says Color Swatches and deposit it in the bin. To remove it, drag it out of the bin by the same tab and click on the red X in the top right corner

Clicking in a color box will change the Foreground color.
Ctrl click in a color box will change the Background color.

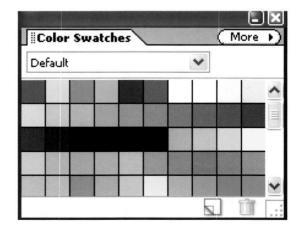

Clicking on the drop down arrow next to Default will show the other Color Swatches that are preloaded.

Click on the More button and you can change the view of your Color Swatches from the default of Small Thumbnail to Large Thumbnail shown to the right. You can also change it to Small List or Large List.

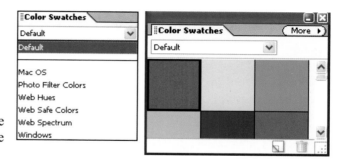

How to Make Your Own Color Swatch

I've found that if you're going to make your own swatches it's easier to view the swatch palette in the large list view. This way you can name them as you make them and you don't have to hover over the color square to see what the name is.

Open the Color Swatch Palette and click the More button on the Color Swatch Palette and change it to large list. Open the image that you want to use for your color swatch.

Activate the Eyedropper Tool by typing "I" or by clicking on the Toolbar. Click once on the color that you want to add to your swatch palette. Notice that the Foreground color changes to the color you just sampled. Click on the Create new Color Swatch from Foreground button on the bottom right of the Color Swatch Palette. A new Color Swatch is added at the bottom of the list.

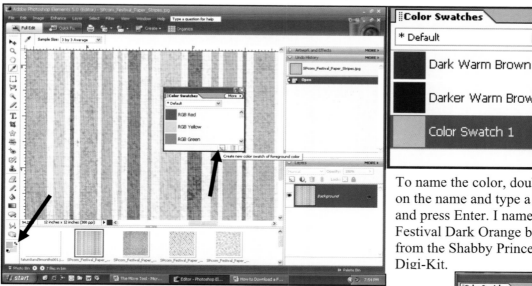

To name the color, double click on the name and type a new name and press Enter. I named this: SP Festival Dark Orange because it's from the Shabby Princess Festival Digi-Kit.

Other ways to make a New Swatch are to go to the More button and select New Swatch and you are immediately given the option to name your New Swatch.

If you have the large or small thumbnail view showing, you can click on an empty area in the last row and a new swatch is made and you're immediately given the option to name the swatch. When you use this method your Eyedropper Tool (I) turns into the paint bucket when you click in the empty area.

How to Save Your Custom Set of Color Swatches

You're probably asking yourself why would I ever want to go through the work of making my own set of Custom Color Swatches? If you've gone through the trouble of making the swatches to begin with you should save them because you'll probably need them again. It only takes a minute to save the set. I've saved sets of Color Swatches for use in a baby album because I used the same colors throughout and for my son's high school scrapbook because I used his school colors in his album and always wanted them to match.

Go to the More button and select Preset Manager.

When you first open the Preset Manager, "Save Set" is grayed out and that's OK. Click on the first swatch you made that you want to save which will be at the bottom of the list. The color you clicked on will have a dark outline around it which is pretty difficult to see. Shift Click on the last color you want to save in the set and all of the color boxes will have the dark outline. Click on Save Set.

Decide on a name for your Color Swatches that you will remember when you need them. In this case I chose SP Festival Colors. SP is the Designer, and Festival is the name of the kit. If you don't give your swatch set a name, the program will automatically name it Untitled Color Swatches and then you'll really be confused when you try to find it again!

Click on Save and you are returned to the Preset Manager.

Click Done.

You will need to restart Photoshop Elements for your custom SP Festival Color Swatch to show in the drop

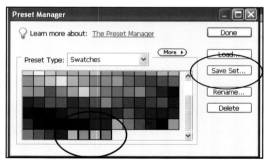

down list.

Please note that the colors that you originally placed in the default swatch list have been removed.

When you upgrade to a future version of Photoshop Elements, get a new computer, or you're working on a project with a partner and you want to use the same Color Swatch you can copy the swatch by going to:

C:\Program Files\Adobe\Photoshop Elements 5.0\Presets\Color Swatches

It would be a good idea to back up these files regularly.

Make a Fast and Easy Color Swatch of 256 Colors in Your Photo or Digital Paper

With a multi colored image active go to: Image>Mode>Indexed Color

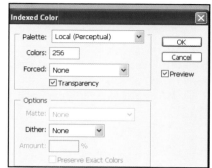

Note this example shows how to get a color swatch with 256 colors if you want a smaller swatch type in a lower number than 256

Change your settings to match the ones to the right.

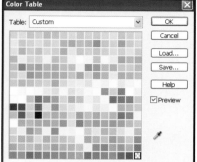

Palette-Local (Perceptual)-Colors 256-Forced None Transparency checked-Matte None-Dither None. Click OK

Go to Image>Mode>Color Table

If you chose 256 you have a MEGA swatch of more colors than you would probably ever use!

Click Save.

For consistency save all your Color Swatches in the same place:

C:\Program Files\Adobe\Photoshop Elements 5.0\Presets\Color Swatches

Your new color table will be saved as a Color Table ACT file.

Click Save

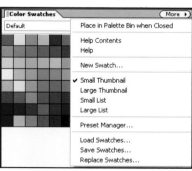

You will be brought back to the Color Table and click OK

Important-close the photo or paper that you were using to make the color swatch because you were working in Image Mode and we want to work in RGB Mode. <u>Say "No" to save changes</u>. Open it again and double check by going to Image>Mode and make sure RGB is checked.

Go to Window>Color Swatches and click the More button and then select Replace Swatches

At the bottom of the screen click the files of type dropdown box.
Choose Color Table (*.ACT)

Click on the ACT file that you want to load.

Click on Load.

Adobe does not allow you to save a Color Table (.ACT file) directly to the swatches files (ACO files). What this means is that if you switch to another Color Swatch set this one disappears and you will have to go through the replace swatches scenario again to display the SPFestivalColorsMany Swatch set (or your file name).

To avoid this you can save it as a Swatch File. (screen shots are shown at "How to Save Your Custom Set of Color Swatches". Click on the More button, Preset Manager>Click in the first color square and Shift Click in the last Color square so all the squares are selected.

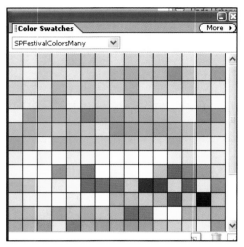

Click Save Set and type in a name for your Color Swatch set-notice that Photoshop Elements is now saving this as an .ACO file.
Click Done.
Close Photoshop Elements.
Re-open Photoshop Elements and your Swatch is now listed in the drop down box.

Great Color Swatches on the Web

www.steeldolphin.com/color_scheme.html
www.njit.edu/~walsh/rgb.html
www.htmlhelp.com/cgi-bin/color.cgi
www.colorschemer.com/online.html
www.wellstyled.com/Tools/colorscheme2/index-en.html
www.colourlovers.com
www.behr.com/behr/workbook/indes.jsp (you must create a free account to use this but it's worth it!)

Remove a Color Swatch

To remove a single Color Swatch you can Alt Click on the swatch and a pair of scissors appears to cut it out of the swatch. If you look fast enough you can see the trash can in the lower right corner light up every time you cut a swatch out. Dragging to the trash can also works, but you get a warning box for each swatch that you have to click OK for, so it's easier to use the Alt Click method.

To remove a color swatch set go to:
C:\Program Files\Adobe\Photoshop Elements 5.0\Presets\Color Swatches, highlight the color you want to delete and press the delete key.

Selections And The Tools That Make Them

What Is A Selection?

A selection is an area you select with one or more of the selection Tools which is surrounded by a selection border. How's that for confusing?

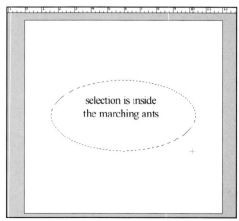

selection is inside
the marching ants

When you make a selection you select only the pixels (part of the image) that you want to work with. Normally any changes you make are applied to the whole layer but with a selection you can make changes to just your selection while the rest of the layer remains unchanged. This is because the selection is the active area of the layer. You can add a filter, duplicate, rotate, size, change the color, paint, lighten or darken, etc. a selection.

In this example the Brush Tool (B) was stamped on the scrapbook page but only the part that was inside the selection actually was stamped because the selection is the active area.

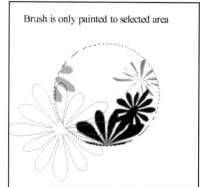

Brush is only painted to selected area

Surrounding your selection is a selection border which is most commonly called marching ants. Other names for a selection border are selection boundary, outline marquee, flashing border of black and white lines, and dancing ants. In the first example you can see a simple oval selection made with the Elliptical Marquee Tool (M). The area inside the dotted line is the selection.

Different Selection Tools work better for some selections. I use the Marquee Tool (M) if I need to make a rectangular selection to add a Stroke Outline which is a frame type effect; this is the easiest type of selection to make. When I want to move my head to the body of a beauty queen, I need to make an exact selection so that I only select my head and none of my body. In this case I'd probably use the Lasso Tool (L). The Magic Wand Tool (W) or Magic Selection Brush Tool (F) works well if there is a big difference in color between what I want to select and the background, like a golf ball sitting on green grass. The Selection Brush Tool (A) can be used to make selections, but normally I use it to clean up selections made with the other Selection Tools.

Good accurate selections take time and practice. With practice you'll learn which Selection Tools work better to make a particular selection. As you get more experienced in making selections you'll learn to take your photographs differently. If I am truly going to put my head on the body of a beauty queen I want to be able to select my head reasonably easy. Taking my picture in front of a white wall would make more sense than taking my picture in a group of people at a party. The white wall would be very easy to select with the Magic Wand Tool (W), otherwise it's going to take some time with the Lasso Tool (L) selecting my head from a busy background filled with people.

In cases like the white wall example, it's easier to select the part of the layer that you don't want and then invert your selection. In the preceding example, my selection is the oval area inside of the marching ants. If I were to inverse it I would be selecting the area around the oval. The marching ants would still be around the oval and they'd also be around the edge of my scrapbook page.

To make a soft edged selection use Anti-Alias, Feather, or use a soft brush with the Selection Brush Tool (A).

Once you make a selection, you can save it forever as long as you save your image as a PSD file. You can also temporarily hide your selection in the event you find it distracting.

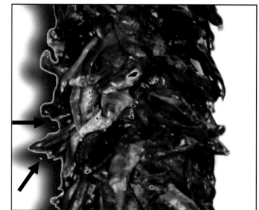

Stray pixels often show up after you thought you made a nice clean selection. There are several ways to check for stray pixels. Depending on the colors of your selection, putting the selection on top of a black or white background temporarily can show stray pixels that need to be erased. Another way to spot stray pixels is to apply a High Drop Shadow to the selection.

This is a photo of a string of dried peppers from a Mexican restaurant. When I put them on a white background they looked fine, but when I added the High Drop Shadow stray pixels became visible. After I erase these I will need to rotate the image, or change the drop shadow angle so the drop shadow shows on the other edges of my peppers.

Select items from photos to use as embellishments on your scrapbook pages. This will save you money on supplies and make extra special pages at the same time.

Selection Commands, Shortcuts, And Tips

Cropping With A Selection Tool

Once you drag a photo onto a scrapbook page, you're not able to crop it with the Crop Tool (C) because the Crop Tool (C) will crop off the whole scrapbook page. You'll be left with your cropped photo and all the other layers cropped to the same exact size. It's usually easier to crop your photos before you drag them onto your scrapbook page however you don't always know exactly how big you want your photo when you're first starting your page.

With the selection Tools you can select an area that you don't want and press the Delete Key and the selected area will be deleted.

In this example with the Rectangular Marquee Tool (M) I selected an area on the right side of the photo to crop off. Pressing the Delete Key or Edit>Cut will remove the selection. If I chose Image>Crop the only part remaining would be the area selected inside the rectangle which I don't want.

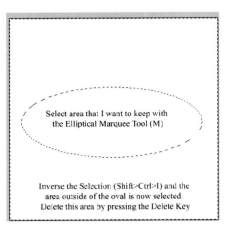

Select area that I want to keep with the Elliptical Marquee Tool (M)

Inverse the Selection (Shift>Ctrl>I) and the area outside of the oval is now selected. Delete this area by pressing the Delete Key

To keep only part of the photo, make a selection around the part that you want to keep and then inverse the selection Shift>Ctrl>I and delete it. Just be sure that you're on the right layer in the Layers palette when you are doing this on a scrapbook page.

Another way to crop a photo using a selection is to make a selection on your photo using one of the selection Tools. Ctrl J (duplicate layer/selection) to make a copy of just the selection. Hide (turn off the eyeball icon) or delete your original photo and you're left with your photo cropped to your selection outline.

Select All

Use this when you want to select everything on a layer like the entire photo. To Select All: Ctrl>A, Select>All, or Ctrl Click on the Layer Thumbnail

Deselect

Once you have a selection with marching ants and no longer want the selection, you Deselect. To Deselect: Esc, Ctrl D, Select>Deselect, or right click on the selection and choose Deselect.

Reselect

If you Deselect your selection and then decide you still want, it you can reselect it by:
Select>Reselect, or Shift>Ctrl>D. You can also Undo Ctrl>Z if you Deselected recently.

Inverse

When you Inverse a selection,
you swap the selected area
with the unselected area.
To Inverse a selection:
Shift>Ctrl>I, Select>Inverse,
or right click on the selection
and choose Select Inverse.

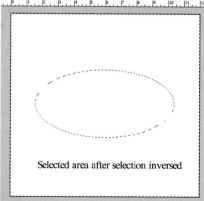

Selecting Layers

To select the contents of a
single layer, Ctrl click the
layer thumbnail.

To add to your current selection Ctrl>Shift>click the other layer thumbnail.
To subtract from your current selection Ctrl>Alt click on layer thumbnail.
To Intersect with your current selection Ctrl>Shift>Alt click on layer thumbnail.

Select All Layers

This command selects all layers but the Background layer. To select all layers go to Select>All Layers. You can also click on one layer in the Layers palette and shift click on the last layer to select them all. Select All Layers is nice when you want to drag everything to the trashcan icon and start over!

Deselect Layers

This command deselects all layers. To deselect all layers go to Select>Deselect Layers and no layer will be selected in the Layers palette.

Select Similar Layers

This command selects all layers that are similar. To select similar layers select a layer in the Layers palette and go to Select>Similar Layers and all of the similar layers will be selected. For example, if you click on a Text Layer all of the Text Layers will be selected.

Feather

Feathering softens, fades, and blurs the
edge of a selection. A selection can be
feathered 0.2-250 pixels.

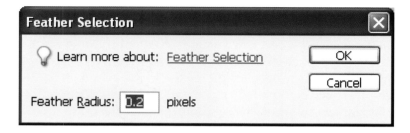

The next example shows that if you Feather a selection 0.2 pixels it will look like it was cut with a pair of scissors. Whereas, if you Feather it 250 px, it is very faded at the edges like in a vignette. Adding a feathered edge makes the selection blend into where ever you move it-try about 2 pixels for this effect. Adding a feather can be done automatically on the Marquee (M) and Lasso (L) Tools Option Bars otherwise: go to

Select>Feather, Alt Ctrl D, or right click on the selection and choose Feather. In all instances a dialog box will pop up requesting the amount of pixels to Feather your Selection.

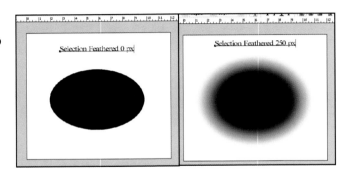

Defringing a Selection

If you are left with a fringe or halo around the edges of your selection after you move it to another location you might want to try defringing your selection. Select the width in pixels that you want to smooth out.

Defringing does not remove pixels from your selection but changes their color so that they blend better with the image you've placed them on top of. If you selected a white golf ball from a green lawn you may have some extra green pixels attached to your golf ball. If you were to place this selection of the golf ball on a photo of a blue sky, you would see the green around the edge of the ball. Defringing will take the green around the white golf ball and blend it to match the sky better.

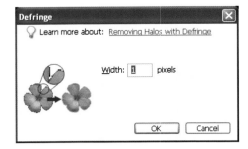

To Defringe, go to Enhance>Adjust Color>Defringe Layer. Experiment with the width but I usually use 2 pixels.

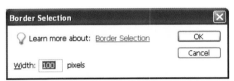

Modify Border

To add a soft edged border that gently fades into your image, select the edge of the image. To select the edge of your image it's usually easiest to Ctrl Click on the image layer thumbnail. Go to Select>Modify>Border and choose a width for the border size from the dialog box. Copy the selection to a new layer Ctrl>J to give you more options in editing it at a later time. With the new selection layer active, go to Edit>Fill>Layer and choose a color or pattern you want for your border. Click OK. Since you put your border on its own layer you can adjust the opacity and add blending modes and filters to it and not affect the image.

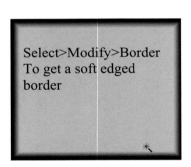

Select>Modify>Border
To get a soft edged border

Marquee Border

To draw a border that does not have a faded edge, use the Marquee Tool (M) to draw a border around the outside edge of a photo or scrapbook page. Hold the Alt key or choose Subtract from selection and drag out an area that you want removed from your selection to make the frame/border. Make a new layer using the New Layer icon on the Layers palette. Choose a new Foreground color by clicking in the Foreground color box at the bottom of the Toolbar. Alt>Backspace to fill your frame/border with color. Hit the Esc key to get rid of the marching ants. You have no limit on how big you make your frame, unlike the Stroke Outline or Modify>Border command.

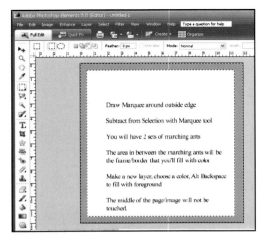

Stroke Outline

To put a solid outline around a selection or layer, first make a selection around the edge of what you want to outline. Usually the fastest method to do this if you are outlining a layer is to Ctrl Click on the Layer Thumbnail (this won't work on a Background layer). Make a new layer by clicking on the new layer icon so you will have the opportunity to make changes to the stroke outline. Go to Edit>Stroke Outline.

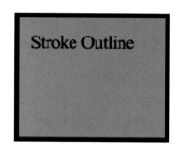

If you are outlining a rectangular corner and wish to maintain a crisp corner, you will need to choose Inside Location as Center and Outside Location will slightly round the corner. Any location works for a rounded shape. Inside Location puts the stroke on the inside of the selection which may cover up part of your image. Center puts the stroke centered on the selection border (marching ants) and Outside puts the stroke on the outside of the selection. The Stroke Outline follows the outline of your selection border (marching ants) exactly.

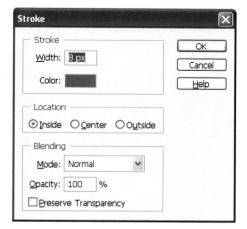

You have the opportunity to change the Blending Mode and Opacity on this dialog box but since you're putting the Stroke Outline on its own layer, you can change that later. Uncheck preserve transparency because it will put a stroke only on opaque pixels on a layer.Make sure this is not checked when you're putting the stroke selection on its own layer because there are no opaque pixels on a blank layer.

Click OK and your Stroke Outline is placed on its own layer. If you want to add an inside stroke selection as a border on a Background layer, Preserve Transparency is not available because there are no transparent pixels.

It is a good idea to link the Stroke Outline layer with the layer that you're outlining by selecting both layers and linking them by clicking on the link icon in the Layers palette.

If you are working on a scrapbook page with 300 resolution and want to add a Stroke Outline of about 1/8 inch around a photo as a mat, try using 38 pixels and see how it looks. To add a ½ inch border around the edge of a scrapbook page, use 150 pixels inside location.

To put a Stroke Outline under a photo, text, or shape for a mat, you can choose Outside Location. Drag the Stroke Outline layer below the layer you're outlining and then add your drop shadows. This works if the edges you're outlining are rounded otherwise your Stroke Outline is rounded when you choose Outside Location.

A work around would be to choose Inside Location for your rectangle shape and make it a little bit larger than you normally would. Drag the Stroke Outline layer under the original layer and activate the Move Tool (V) to transform (size) it. Hold the Alt key as you drag a corner sizing handle and it will size from the center. Add your Drop Shadows and you have a perfect mat.

To add a feather to your Stroke Outline after you have made your selection, go to Select>Feather and choose an amount of feather. Next make a new layer and go to Edit>Stroke Outline and choose a color and size. This feathers the selection which in turn will feather the Stroke Outline. Using a feathered black stroke outline adds an inked edge type of effect.

To add a white edge around your photos like photo labs offer, open the photo and go to Edit>Stroke Outline choose inside location and add a white (or other color) 50 px border.

If you want to use a border that fades from the photo outward choose Select>Modify>Border.

Modify Smooth

This is a good way to clean up jagged edges on selections made by the Magic Wand Tool (W). It smoothes out edges by finding similar colored pixels by the number of pixels you entered in the dialog box. If it doesn't work you may have better luck using the Selection Brush Tool (A).

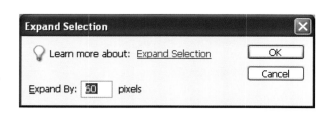

Modify Expand

Select/Modify/Expand increases the size of your selection by an amount of pixels that you enter. If you have a selection with rounded edges it keeps the same shape which makes this a good choice for making photo mats. If your selection has rectangular corners Expand rounds the corners of your selection.

Modify Contract

Select/Modify/Contract contracts the size of your selection by an amount of pixels that you enter. When you contract a square cornered selection the corners stay square unlike the expand command. Contracting your selection by 1 pixel will sometimes smooth out a rough selection that you've made with a Tool like the Magic Wand (W) or Magic Lasso (L).

Grow

Select/Grow adds to your selection to include more of the same contiguous colors. When you use Grow your selection might not keep the same shape depending on the image you're working on. You do not get a dialog box after you select Grow. Photoshop Elements selects all the same colored contiguous pixels.

Similar

Select/Similar adds to your selection by finding all pixels of the same color not just the contiguous ones. When you use Similar your selection might not keep the same shape depending on the image you're working on. You do not get a dialog box after you select Similar. Photoshop Elements selects all the similar pixels.

Save Selection

Saving a selection gives you the opportunity to use the selection at another time. Your selection is saved only if you save your file as a PSD file. Make a selection with one of the selection Tools, go to Select>Save Selection and choose a name for your selection and click OK. More than one selection can be saved for an image and you can also Add to, Subtract from, or Intersect with a selection.

Load Selection

To Load a Selection that you previously saved, open the image and go to Select>Load Selection. Click on the drop down list if you have more than one selection saved for this image. You are also given the opportunity to Invert the selection. If you want to Add, Subtract, or Intersect with the previously saved selection you can draw a new one and then Load your selection and choose one of those options.

Delete Selection

If you no longer need the selection you saved, open the image and go to Select>Delete Selection and click OK.

Fill Selection/Fill Layer

If you have a selection as your active image, you will be filling a selection instead of layer.

To Fill a Selection/Layer with Foreground color, Background color, Color (from Color Picker), Pattern, Black, 50 % Gray, or White, go to: Edit>Fill Selection or Layer. If you have an active selection and it says Fill Selection, the dialog box will still say Fill Layer. I suggest using a new layer for everything to help with editing along the way so, if you do this, you will need to uncheck Preserve Transparency if you are filling a selection on a blank layer.

The shortcut to Fill a selection/layer with the Foreground color is Alt>Backspace. To Fill a selection/layer with the Background color, use Ctrl>Backspace. Remember the A in Alt for foreground comes before the C in Ctrl for the background.

Paste into Selection

Normally you drag a photo onto your scrapbook page or template by using the Move Tool (V) or you Copy (Ctrl C) and Paste (Ctrl V) them. When you use these methods, your selections end up in the center of your scrapbook page or template and you have to move them around. If you want to paste your image directly into a selection, especially if you're using a Template that is in a PNG format with overlapping openings, it's much easier to use Paste into Selection. The shortcut for Paste into Selection is Shift>Ctrl>V or Edit>Paste into Selection.

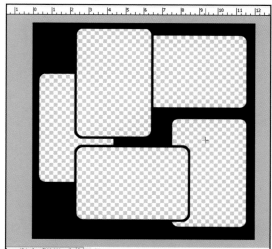

To Paste into a Selection:
Make a selection on the scrapbook page or other image. In this example of a PNG scrapbook page template, click once in the opening with the Magic Wand Tool (W). Make a new layer on the scrapbook page or other image. Select the photo or other image that you want to paste by Ctrl>A to Select All, and then Copy Ctrl>C. Go back to your scrapbook page and Shift>Ctrl>V to paste the image into your selection or Edit>Paste into Selection.

Hide Selection

Sometimes it's helpful to turn off your selection and hide it but still keep it active. This command is a little bit quirky. The key is to remember to hide it and not to switch to another Tool that cancels your selection. I was able to hide/unhide my selection and use other Tools except for the Text Tool (T). If you are using another Tool and have problems making changes to an image check to see if you have a hidden selection that you forgot about which may be causing your problems. To hide/unhide your selection Ctrl>H.

Moving a Selection

To Move a selection border (marching ants) 1 pixel at a time, use the Right, Left, Up, Down Arrow keys. Hold the Shift key to move 10 pixels each click. This moves only the marching ants, not the image you've selected.

To drag the selection border, put your cursor inside the selection you've drawn. Click on the New Selection button on the Lasso (L), Marquee (M), or Magic Wand (W) Tools. Drag your selection border to a new location with your mouse.

To Move a Selection 1 pixel at a time, activate the Move Tool (V) and use the Right, Left, Up, Down Arrow Keys. Hold the Shift key to move 10 pixels each click, or drag it with the cursor. This moves the marching ants and the image you've selected. If you only want to move the marching ants to reposition your selected area, go to any of the Tools other than the Move Tool (V).

The Marquee Tool (M)

The Marquee Tool consists of two different Tools: The Rectangular Marquee Tool (M) and the Elliptical Marquee Tool (M). To toggle between the Rectangle and Elliptical Marquee Tool, hold the Shift key and type the letter M. This works for all Tools that have hidden Tools as long as "Use Shift key for Tool switch" is checked in General Preferences (Ctrl K).

The Marquee Tool (M) is the easiest selection Tool to use, which is probably why it's the one used most often.

What you can do with the Marquee Tool (M):

The Rectangular Marquee Tool (M) is used to drag out rectangular selections and can also drag a square selection by holding the Shift key as you drag.

The Elliptical Marquee Tool is used to drag out oval selections and can also drag a circle selection by holding the Shift key as you drag. When making a square or circle selection be sure you let go of the mouse before you let go of the Shift key.

New Selection

Every time you click and drag with the mouse you create a new selection. If you have already made a selection it is deleted as soon as you start a new one. With New Selection activated, drag a selection from the center outward and hold the Alt key as you drag. To drag a perfect square or circle from the center, hold the Alt and Shift key as you drag with the correct Marquee Tool (T) selected.

Add to Selection

Use Add to selection when you have already made a selection and you want to add to it. You must be outside the first selection to add to it, but they do not have to touch. After you have drawn a selection, hold the Shift key to Add to the Selection or click on the Add to Selection button on the Options Bar. The cursor will have a (+) sign next to it.

Subtract From Selection

Use Subtract from Selection when you want to remove from the current selection. You must be inside the selection to click and drag and remove some of it. After you have drawn a selection, hold the Alt to Subtract from a Selection or click on the Subtract From Selection button on the Options Bar. The cursor will have a (-) sign next to it. To make a frame around an image, select the outside edge of an image and then subtract from that selection to form an outline around the image, and then fill it with color. See Marquee Border for more detailed instructions.

Intersect with Selection

Use Intersect with Selection when you want to select an area that intersects between two selections as shown on the button above. In the example of the menu button, the selection you would be left with after you release your mouse would be the shaded square where the two squares intersect. After you have drawn a selection, hold the Shift>Alt keys when you drag to Intersect with Selection or click on the Intersect with Selection button on the Options Bar. The cursor will have a (x) sign next to it.

Feather

Feathering softens, fades, and blurs the edge of a selection. A selection can be feathered 0.2-250 pixels. If you Feather a selection 0.2 pixels it will look like a straight cut. Whereas if you Feather it 250 px it is very faded at the edges like in a vignette. There are examples of feathering in the Selection Commands and Shortcuts Section. Adding a feathered edge makes the selection blend into where ever you move it-try about 2 pixels for this effect. If you forget to add a feather here while your selection is active, you can add it by going to Select>Feather, Alt Ctrl D, or right click on the selection and choose Feather. In all instances a dialog box will pop up requesting the amount of pixels to Feather your Selection.

Anti-Alias

Anti-Alias is used to smooth the edges of curved selections so they aren't jagged. It is not needed for rectangular selections so it is grayed out when the Rectangular Marquee is active.
I keep Anti-Alias turned on.

Mode-Normal

With Normal selected, you can click and drag a selection of any size with your mouse.

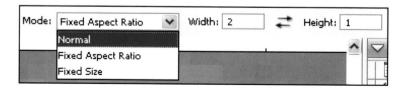

Mode-Fixed Aspect Ratio

Fixed Aspect Ratio lets you click and drag out a selection with a perfect ratio. In the example shown my width will be two times as big as the height. Entering width and height as the same number will produce a square or circle depending on which Marquee Tool (M) is activated. If you know the exact size you want, choose Fixed Size.

Mode-Fixed Size

Enter the size of the selection you want to make and, with a click of the mouse, it's done. Right click in the width or height boxes and there is a drop down box that lets you specify if you want inches, pixels, etc.

How to Use the Marquee Tool:

Select the Marquee Tool (M) (Rectangular or Elliptical) you want and click and drag the cursor over the area that you want to select. As you drag with the mouse you will see the marching ants indicating where your selection is. Hold the Shift key if you want to drag a perfect square or circle. Holding the Alt key draws your selection from a center point.

If you don't get the selection border exactly where you want it, to reposition the marquee while the Marquee Tool (M) is still active, hold the spacebar as you drag. If you're not happy with the size or location of the Marquee after you've released the mouse, hit Esc and start over.

Once you have your selection made you can do different things with it:

To move it to a scrapbook page, activate the Move Tool (V) and move the selection onto your scrapbook page by dragging it up or down to the page in your Photo Bin.

To save your selection for later use, go to Select>Save Selection and name it. As long as you save the file as a PSD file, you will be able to re-use the selection.

To save your selected image by itself on a transparent background, you will need to delete the unselected areas. Make sure your layer is not a Background layer. If it is, make a new layer by Ctrl J and delete the original Background layer. Inverse your selection Shift>Ctrl>I or Select>Inverse, and then hit the Delete Key. Save your file as a PSD or PNG file to keep the transparent background.

The Lasso Tool (L)

The Lasso Tool (L) cursor looks like a lasso that you would use to rope a bull at a rodeo! There are three different Lasso Tools: Lasso Tool (Regular) (L), Magnetic Lasso (L), and the Polygonal Lasso (L). All three Lasso Tools make selections by clicking and dragging around the area you want to select. Use your mouse or a Wacom Tablet to make a more precise selection. The Lasso Tools work best with well defined edges and color definitions. Remember good selections take practice! Using the Lasso Tool takes a lot of practice because sometimes it's hard to control.

What you can do with the Lasso Tool (L):

Hand draw selections so that you can use parts of your images for scrapbook photos, decorations, etc.

New Selection

Every time you complete the loop with the lasso you create a new selection. If you have already made a selection, it is deleted as soon as you start a new one.

Add to Selection

Use Add to Selection when you have already made a selection and you want to add to it. You must be outside the first selection to add to it, but they do not have to touch. After you have made a selection hold the Shift to Add to the Selection or click on the Add to Selection button on the Options Bar. The Lasso Cursor will have a (+) sign next to it.

Subtract From Selection

Use Subtract from Selection when you want to remove from the current selection. You must be inside the selection to click and remove some of it. After you have drawn a selection, hold the Alt to Subtract from a Selection or click on the Subtract from Selection button on the Options Bar. The Lasso Cursor will have a (-) sign next to it.

Intersect with Selection

Use Intersect with Selection when you want to select an area that intersects between two selections as shown on the button above. In the example of the menu button, the selection you would be left with after you click your mouse would be the shaded square where the two squares intersect. After you have drawn a selection, hold the Shift>Alt keys when you drag to Intersect with Selection or click on the Intersect with Selection button on the Options Bar. The Lasso Cursor will have a (x) sign next to it.

Feather

Feathering softens, fades, and blurs the edge of a selection. A selection can be feathered 0.2-250 pixels. If you Feather a selection 0.2 pixels, it will look like a straight cut. Whereas if you Feather it 250 px, it is very faded at the edges like in a vignette. There are examples of feathering in the Selection Commands and Shortcuts Section. Adding a feathered edge makes the selection blend into where ever you move it-try about 2 pixels for this effect. If you forget to add a feather here while your selection is active, you can add it by going to Select>Feather, Alt Ctrl D, or right click on the selection and choose Feather. In all instances a dialog box will pop up requesting the amount of pixels to Feather your Selection.

Anti-Alias

Anti-Alias is used to smooth the edges of curved selections so they aren't jagged. I keep Anti-Alias turned on.

Width-Magnetic Lasso Only

Enter a number between 1 and 256 pixels. The Magnetic Lasso (L) detects edges in your image only this far from the pointer. Pressing the Caps Lock Key enables you to see exactly how far away this distance is. Your cursor changes from the Lasso symbol to a circle with a + inside it as shown in this example. The default setting is 10 pixels.

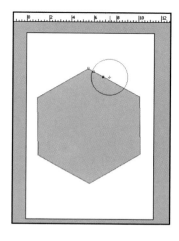

Edge Contrast-Magnetic Lasso Only

Enter a percentage between 1% and 100%. This specifies the Magnetic Lasso Tool's (L) sensitivity to edges in your image. A higher number is for edges that contrast a lot from the area around them, a lower number is for edges that don't contrast as much. The default setting is 10%.

Frequency-Magnetic Lasso Only

Enter a number between 0 and 100. This number sets how far apart the anchor/fastening points are automatically set. The lower the number, the farther apart the anchor/fastening points are. The higher the number, the closer they are to each other. Anchor/fastening points are marked by small squares either solid or open where the Magnetic Lasso Tool (L) has been. A solid black anchor/fastening point is the last one that's been set either manually by you or automatically, depending on the frequency setting. The default setting is 57.

Use Tablet Pressure to Change Pen Width-Magnetic Lasso Only

This controls how far the Magnetic Lasso Tool (L) searches for edges. To decrease the edge width, press harder. I use the Magnetic Lasso Tool (L) with my Wacom Tablet.

Lasso Tips

Zoom in to help make a good selection, it's best to have your image in full screen. If you come to the edge of your screen and can't see where to go from there, hold the space bar so the Hand Tool (H) is temporarily selected and you can move your image around in the screen. Let go of the space bar and the Lasso Tool (L) is automatically activated again.

To toggle your cursor on/off to a crosshair instead of the Lasso Tool (L), press the Caps Lock Key (Lasso & Polygonal Lasso (L) only). On the Magnetic Lasso (L), pressing Caps Lock Key will change the cursor to a circle with a + in the center that shows the area of edge detection.

Press the Backspace Key to remove an anchor point. Click the mouse to add an anchor point (Magnetic & Polygonal Lasso Only).

Ctrl Click or double click to close a Magnetic or Polygonal selection border without clicking on the starting point.

Use the Selection Brush (A) to fine tune your selections. The Esc Key will delete any full or partially drawn selection.

If you are working with items like alpha tags or other embellishments that are all on one layer and want to select only one:

Make a selection around it with the Lasso Tool (L). In this example I used the Polygonal Lasso Tool (L). You should have marching ants now.

At this point you can activate the Move Tool (V) and move the embellishment onto your scrapbook page.

To make your selection conform to your element exactly:

Hold the Ctrl key and press the up arrow key (↑).

The embellishments shown are from the All Boy Kit by Dora Phillips graciously donated by ScrapStreet.com. This kit and others from ScrapStreet.com are on the CD that came with this book.

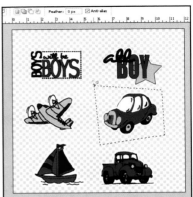

How to Use the (Regular) Lasso Tool (L)

Set the Tool options on the Options Bar. Click and drag your mouse around your selection, release your mouse and your selection is drawn. If you're not happy with your selection, hit the Esc Key and start over. To toggle back and forth to the Polygonal Lasso Tool (L) to make straight line segments, hold the Alt key and release the mouse and click your mouse where you want your straight line to end (watch the cursor change, the option bar will not change).

How to Use the Magnetic Lasso Tool (L)

You will either love or hate the Magnetic Lasso Tool (L). The Magnetic Lasso clings/snaps to high contrast edges you drag over on your photo/image. The perfect image to use the Magnetic Lasso on would be a white golf ball on green grass. The Magnetic Lasso (L) clings to the edge of the ball because of the dramatic color changes. Dragging slowly usually works better than dragging quickly.

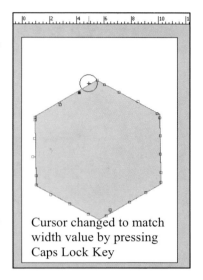

Cursor changed to match width value by pressing Caps Lock Key

Set the Tool options in the options bar. Click once to set your anchor point and drag your mouse without clicking. The Magnetic Lasso (L) should start to set anchor points automatically depending on your Frequency setting by snapping to the edge of what you're selecting. Click if you want to set an anchor point. Backspace or Delete if you want to remove an anchor point. Hold the Alt key if you want to toggle on/off the Polygonal Lasso Tool (L) to make straight line segments (watch your cursor because the Option Bar will not change). When you get back to your starting point, click on the starting point. Double click or Ctrl click if you are not over the starting point and want to close your selection.

Use the Esc Key to cancel at any time to start over if you're not happy with your selection.

How to Use the Polygonal Lasso Tool (L)

Set the Tool options on the Options Bar. Click to set your anchor point and click again where you want your first straight line segment to end, setting another anchor point. Keep clicking to add straight line segments. To remove an anchor point, click the Delete or Backspace Key. Toggle back and forth to the Lasso Tool by holding the Alt key and dragging your mouse (watch the cursor change, the Option Bar will not change). To close your selection, click on the starting point (a closed circle will appear when you hover over it) or Ctrl Click or double click if you're not over the starting point.

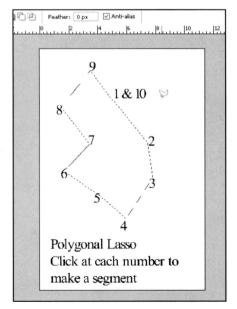

Polygonal Lasso
Click at each number to make a segment

Use the Esc Key to cancel at any time to start over if you're not happy with your selection.

Once you have your selection made, you can do different things with it: Move it to a scrapbook page. Activate the Move Tool (V) and move the selection onto your scrapbook page by dragging it up or down to the page in your Photo Bin.

To save your selection for later use, go to Select>Save Selection and name it. As long as you save the file as a PSD file, you will be able to use the selection again.

To save your selected image by itself on a transparent background you will need to delete the unselected areas. Make sure your layer is not a Background layer. If it is, make a new layer by Ctrl J and delete the original Background layer. Inverse your selection Shift>Ctrl>I or Select>Inverse and then hit the Delete Key. Save your file as a PSD or PNG file to keep the transparent background.

The Magic Wand Tool (W)

The Magic Wand (W) cursor looks just like the magic wand I wave daily over my thighs, the trouble is nothing ever happens. I think Photoshop Elements bought their wand from a better manufacturer than I did, because their wand actually works!

The Magic Wand (W) makes selections based on similar colors. It works perfectly with one click of the mouse when selecting one solid color from an image. If you throw in a few more shades of the color and click several times it may not work as well, depending on the settings you've chosen.

What you can do with the Magic Wand Tool (W):
Make selections of similar colors depending on the amount of color variation you select.
The Magic Wand Tool (W) will select similar colors that are touching or not, or on the same layer or not, depending on the options you select.

 New Selection

Every time you click the wand you create a new selection. If you have already made a selection, it is deleted as soon as you start a new one.

 Add to Selection

Use Add to selection when you have already made a selection and you want to add to it. You must be outside the first selection to add to it but they do not have to touch. After you have made a selection, hold the Shift to Add to Selection or click on the Add to Selection button on the Options Bar. The Magic Wand Tool (W) cursor will have a (+) sign next to it.

 Subtract From Selection

Use Subtract from Selection when you want to remove from the current selection. You must be inside the selection to click and remove some of it. After you have drawn a selection, hold the Alt to Subtract from Selection or click on the Subtract from Selection button on the Options Bar. The Magic Wand Tool (W) cursor will have a (-) sign next to it.

 Intersect with Selection

Use Intersect with Selection when you want to select an area that intersects between two selections as shown on the button above. In the example of the menu button, the selection you would be left with after you click your mouse would be the shaded square where the two squares intersect. After you have drawn a selection, hold the Shift>Alt keys when you drag to Intersect with Selection or click on the Intersect with Selection button on the Options Bar. The Magic Wand Tool (W) cursor will have a (x) sign next to it.

Tolerance

The default Tolerance setting is 32. The range of settings is from 0-255. If you choose 0 the Magic Wand Tool (W) will choose only the color you have clicked on. If you choose 255, the Magic Wand Tool (W) will select every color in the image. If you are having trouble making a selection with the Magic Wand Tool (W), try a different Tolerance setting and you will probably have better luck.

Anti-Alias

Anti-Alias is used to smooth the edges of curved selections so they aren't jagged. I keep Anti-Alias turned on.

Contiguous

Contiguous means that the colors are touching. With the Contiguous box checked the Magic Wand Tool (W) will select all of the color you click on that's touching. If you're trying to select all of a certain colored stripe on a digital paper, you would need to uncheck the Contiguous button.

This picture shows an example of a non-contiguous selection. All of the particular shade of white in the sheet that I clicked on with the Magic Wand Tool (W) cursor is selected even though it's not all touching.

Sample All Layers

When Sample All Layers is checked the Magic Wand Tool (W) selects the matching color pixels from all the layers in your image. This might be helpful if you decided you wanted to change the color of several elements on your scrapbook page.

How to Use the Magic Wand Tool (W)

Activate the Magic Wand Tool (W) and click on an image with the cursor. The Magic Wand Tool (W) searches for other pixels in the image that match the color of the pixel you clicked on, depending on the Tolerance setting you entered and if you wanted to search for Contiguous colored pixels and pixels of the same colors on all layers. The selection you make will be surrounded by a selection border (marching ants). Usually with the Magic Wand Tool (W) you will need to click your mouse more than once if it is a photograph. If you want to Add to, Subtract from, or Intersect the original selection choose one of the buttons on the Option Bar, or press one of the shortcut keys.

Once you have your selection made, you can do different things with it:

Move it to a scrapbook page. Activate the Move Tool (V) and move the selection onto your scrapbook page by dragging it up or down to the page in your Photo Bin.

To save your selection for later use, go to Select>Save Selection and name it. As long as you save the file as a PSD file, you will be able to use the selection again.

To save your selected image by itself on a transparent background, you will need to delete the unselected areas. Make sure your layer is not a Background layer. If it is make a new layer by Ctrl J and delete the original Background layer. Inverse your selection Shift>Ctrl>I or Select>Inverse and then hit the Delete Key. Save your file as a PSD or PNG file to keep the transparent background.

The Magic Selection Brush Tool (F)

The Magic Selection Brush Tool (F) draws a selection for you like Magic! When this Tool is activated your cursor looks like a magic marker.

This Tool is available for use in Full Edit Mode and is the only Selection Tool in Quick Fix Mode.

When you activate the Magic Selection Brush Tool (F) you get this dialog box giving you brief instructions on how to use the Tool. Click on "Don't show again" and you won't be bothered by it again.

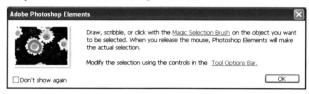

What you can do with the Magic Selection Brush Tool (F):

Make a selection of similar color and texture by quickly scribbling on the image.

New Selection

This is the default setting that lets you draw a New Selection. Draw or scribble over everything that you want to select and don't release your mouse until you have everything marked that you want in the selection. As soon as you finish drawing a New Selection and release your mouse, Photoshop Elements starts making your selection. By default the color is red but you can change it if you want to.

Indicate Foreground

After your selection is automatically drawn by Photoshop Elements, Indicate Foreground becomes the default. If you need to add more to the selection that has been drawn, click and drag again with your mouse. By default the color is red but you can change it if you want to.

Indicate Background

Indicate Background lets you subtract from the current selection and is only available after a selection has been drawn by Photoshop Elements. Click and drag over anything you want removed from the selection. By default the color of the brush is blue but you can change it if you want to.

Color

You can change the color of the brushes if you want to. The default for New and Add to Selection (Indicate Foreground) is red and the default for Subtract from Selection (Indicate Background) is blue. Click in the box to activate Adobe Color Picker, and you can pick a custom color or click the drop down arrow to pick a color from the color swatch. The default colors work well unless your image contains a lot of red and blue and it's hard to see the brush strokes. I leave mine at the default colors.

Size

Choose the size of brush you want to use.

How to Use the Magic Selection Brush

By default when you first activate the Magic Selection Brush Tool (F) the New Selection brush is active. Click and drag over the part of the image that you want to select. Try to drag over all shades of color. Your scribbling doesn't need to be precise for Photoshop Elements to make a selection. Don't release your mouse until you've dragged over everything you want to select because as soon as you release the mouse, Photoshop Elements starts processing your selection. In the example on the left I drew over everything I wanted to be in the selection. By default Photoshop Elements uses a red brush for making a selection.

Depending on how good of a selection is made, you may need to draw on some areas that you want subtracted from the selection. In my example on the right I used the Indicate Background brush to remove some of the background from my selection.

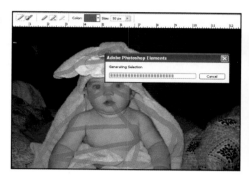 

By default the brush is blue for subtracting from the selection.

This Tool did a good job on this selection. I used the Selection Brush Tool (A) to fix a couple of little spots and I was done. This worked faster than using the Magnetic Lasso Tool (L) and the Selection Brush Tool (A).

Sometimes this Tool bogs down and struggles to work. If this happens you can add some more marks to either subtract or add to the selection to help the program. If this doesn't work, switch to another Tool momentarily and go back to the Magic Selection Brush Tool (F) and see if it works better.

The Selection Brush Tool (A)

With the Selection Brush Tool (A), paint the selection you want to keep or paint a mask of what you don't want.

What you can do with the Selection Brush Tool (A):

Make a selection by painting it either in selection or mask mode.
Clean-up a selection made with another selection Tool.

Add to Selection

Unlike some of the other selection Tools the Selection Brush Tool (A) does not have a New Selection setting. To start a new sew selection or add to an existing selection choose Add to Selection.

Subtract From Selection

Use Subtract from Selection when you want to remove from the current selection. You must be inside the selection to click and remove some of it. After you have drawn a selection, hold the Alt key to Subtract from a Selection or click on the Subtract from Selection button on the Options Bar.

Brush Presets

Click the drop down arrow and choose a brush to make your selection. There are many sets of brushes that come installed with Photoshop Elements and some you can install yourself. Usually to make a selection I use a round brush (hard or soft). A soft (fuzzy) brush will give you more of a feathered selection as seen by the examples of the two brushes on the right. Depending on the selection I'm making, it might be helpful to use a square brush which also comes automatically installed.

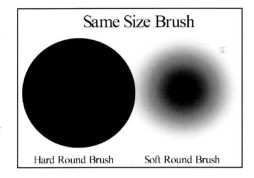

Double click on the brush that you want to select.

Size

Brush size ranges from .01 to 2500 pixels. .01 pixels is smaller than you'll ever use and 2500 pixels is 8.33 inches if you're using it on a scrapbook page, which is a pretty big brush!

To choose a brush size type the amount in the option box, use the brush size slider, or best yet use the bracket keys ([&]) to size your brushes (in any Tool). [makes your brush smaller and] makes your brush bigger. Holding the bracket key changes the size of the brush quickly.

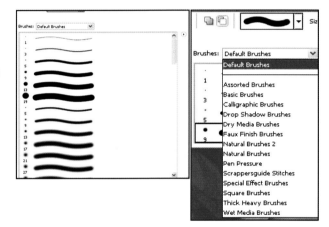

Mode

Selection-Your selection is surrounded by a selection border (marching ants). You paint over the area you want in your selection.

Mask-The area you don't want (non-selection) is covered by a red mask while the area you do want remains unchanged like masking tape. Sometimes it's easier to use the mask to make a good selection because the red overlay makes it easier to see spots you've missed. When Mask is selected two more options appear on the Options Bar: Overlay Opacity and Overlay Color.

Overlay Opacity

Choose the Opacity Level for your Mask or Overlay from 1-100%. The default is 50%, which works well. Type another amount in the box, or slide the slider to change the Opacity.

Overlay Color

This box gives you the option to choose another color for the Overlay which is another term for Mask. Red is the default color which works well, but if you want to change it click in the color box which brings up the Adobe Color Picker or click on the drop down to choose another color. If you are working on an image with a lot of red it might be useful to change the color of the overlay but normally I leave mine set at the red default color.

You can switch between Selection and Mask to make your selection.

The selections below were first made with the Magnetic Lasso Tool (L) and then cleaned up with the Selection Brush (A). The example on the left is in Selection Mode and the example on the right is in Mask Mode.

 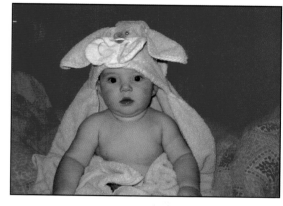

Hardness

Hardness is similar to Feathering. Hardness sets the opacity and the edge sharpness. This example explains it better. I used the same brush to make both selections and I made the selection on the same exact spot on both images. In the example on the left Hardness was 100%, in the example on the right Hardness was 8%. Changing the setting for Hardness can make a big difference in the end result of your selection.

To make the brush softer by 25% Shift>[, to make the brush harder by 25% Shift>].

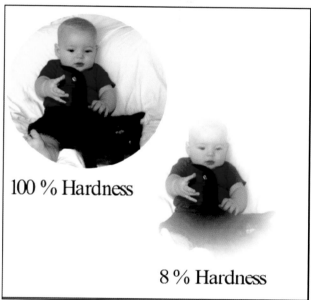

100 % Hardness

8 % Hardness

How to Use the Selection Brush Tool (A)

I use the Selection Brush Tool (A) to make small selections or to clean up selections made with another selection Tool. To make a new selection, paint over an area that you want to select and you will see the selection border (marching ants). If you paint too big of an area, you can hold the Alt key to subtract from the Selection or use the Subtract from Selection button on the Option Bar.

To clean up a selection made with another Tool like the Magic Wand Tool (W), paint out the stray pixels that remain and I smooth out the edges. If the selection is too large, hold the Alt key to paint back in the area that was removed in error.

Using the Selection Brush in Mask Mode makes it easier to see the selection you're making sometimes. The key to using the Mask Mode is to remember that it's opposite from Selection Mode, you paint what you don't want.

To draw a selection in a straight line, hold the Shift key as you drag your mouse or Click and then Shift click at the end of your selection.

To remove a selection in a straight line like shown in this example, Alt click on one side of the selection and then Alt>Shift Click at the end.

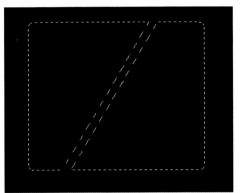

Once you have your selection made you can do different things with it:

Move it to a scrapbook page by activating the Move Tool (V) and move the selection onto your scrapbook page by dragging it up or down to the page in your Photo Bin.

To save your selection for later use, go to Select>Save Selection and name it. As long as you save the file as a PSD file you will be able to use the selection again.

To save your selected image by itself on a transparent background you will need to delete the unselected areas. Make sure your layer is not a Background layer. If it is, make a new layer by Ctrl J and delete the original Background layer. Inverse your selection Shift>Ctrl>I or Select>Inverse and then hit the Delete Key. Save your file as a PSD or PNG file to keep the transparent background.

The Magic Extractor

The Magic Extractor isn't officially classified as a selection Tool because it's not listed on the Toolbar but I'm going to cover it in this section because it makes selections by using the information you give it. The instructions for using the Magic Extractor are written right across the top of the dialog box.

Open the photo you want to use to speed up the process and crop your photo to remove areas that won't be in your selection. This saves the Magic Extractor from having to remove them.

To find the Magic Extractor go to Image>Magic Extractor.

When you open the Magic Extractor, the Foreground Brush will be active by default. Click or draw on the areas that you want to keep in your selection.

Activate the Background Brush and click or draw on the areas you want to be removed. Click Preview and you will see your image with the background removed.

Be sure to mark all colors and textures with the appropriate brush so that the Magic Extractor knows to remove or keep them.

Foreground Brush (B)

Click to indicate areas to be used for selection. Default color is red but can be changed by clicking in red color box and picking new color.

Background Brush (P)

Click to indicate areas to be excluded from selection. Default color is blue but can be changed by clicking in blue color box and picking new color.

Point Eraser Tool (E)

Use to erase the Foreground or Background Brush if you make a mistake.

Add to Selection Tool (A)

Use to add to current selection

Remove from Selection Tool (D)

Use to remove from current selection

Smoothing Brush (J)

Use to smooth edges of your selection after you preview it. Zoom in to use it.

Zoom Tool (Z)

Use to zoom into image

Hand Tool (H)

Use to move around your image

Magic Extractor

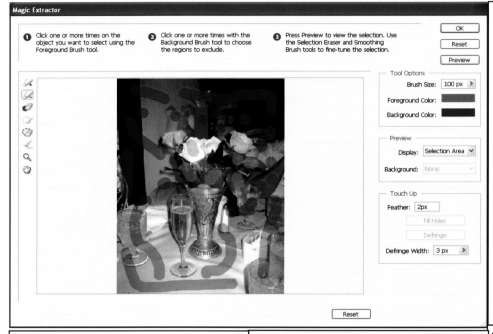

Brush Size can be increased to a maximum of 100 pixels and can be adjusted by using the Bracket keys or entering it in the Brush Size box.

Background default is None which is the checkerboard transparency. Other Backgrounds can be picked which can be helpful to show how good of a selection the Magic Extractor Made.

Click Preview and see how the Magic Extractor removes the unwanted background areas. If you need to fine tune it, use the other tools.

Use Fill Holes to fill holes that were removed in error.

Defringe will smooth jagged edges as will the Smoothing Brush. Set this between 1 and 50 pixels.

Reset will remove all blue and red marks. Click OK to accept your selection, or add more blue & red marks and preview again until you're happy with the results.

A Tool To Type and Journal

Type/Text Tool (T)

This Tool is will make your journaling look beautiful every time. Make your own professional looking titles, monograms, patterns, journaling entries. No more ink smudges, Liquid Paper, or starting over when you've made a mistake. With Photoshop Elements you can just Undo (Ctrl>Z) and start over!

The best part of using the Type Tool (T) is that you'll never run out of letters like you do in a sticker pack. The second best part is that you'll never have any letters left over from the sticker pack that you save for years trying to find the perfect use for them!

This Tool may be called The Type Tool (T) or The Text Tool (T) in various tutorials you read.

What you can do with the Type Tool (T):
Make your own titles, monograms, journaling, patterns, and stickers.
Cut words out of your photos or digital scrapbook paper.
Use letters for decoration.
Type in any color imaginable that matches your scrapbooking supplies and photos.
Use any font installed in your computer in any size.

What you can't do with the Type Tool (T):
This took me a while to figure out, and when I'm tired, I still do it. It's one of those ID 10 T errors I've told you about! You can't type a shortcut that's a letter when you have the Type Tool (T) activated. If you've got the Type Tool (T) activated and you want to go to the Move Tool (V) and you type the shortcut "V" all you'll get is a V on your page!

You can't use spell check in Photoshop Elements. Maybe when Adobe releases Photoshop Elements 10 they'll have it but until then you can copy and paste your journaling into a word processing program like Microsoft Word and run spell check there. Remember spell check finds words spelled incorrectly. If you write about your son Matt, the computer won't know that his name is misspelled when you type "Mat" the word!

If you get stuck while using the Type Tool and can't get the program to move on, you probably haven't checked your checkmark to commit your text.

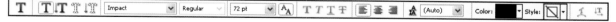

Horizontal Type, Vertical Type, Horizontal Type Mask, and Vertical Type Mask Tools are all shown on the option bar when you first select the Type Tool. In my example Horizontal Type is selected and when I start to type, the other three options will disappear and the menu bar will look like the one below.

Horizontal Type Tool (T)
This is the normal Type Tool you'll use most of the time.
This Tool types from left to right.

Vertical Type Tool (T)

Vertical Type is sometimes used but it's hard to read up and down as you can see in the example. The Vertical Type Tool is designed for Chinese and Japanese Characters.

Horizontal Type Mask Tool (T)

Instead of typing text, this Tool types a horizontal type selection. If this Tool is activated, as soon as you click on your page to type, the page turns pink. Your type appears as part of your image until you check OK and then it turns into a selection (marching ants). This selection can be used to cut letters out of pictures and scrapbook paper, much like the Group with Previous method.

Vertical Type Mask Tool (T)

Instead of typing text, this Tool types a vertical type selection. If this Tool is activated, as soon as you click on your page to type, the page turns pink. Your type appears as part of your image until you check OK and then it turns into a selection (marching ants). This selection can be used to cut letters out of pictures and scrapbook paper, much like the Group with Previous method.

Font Family

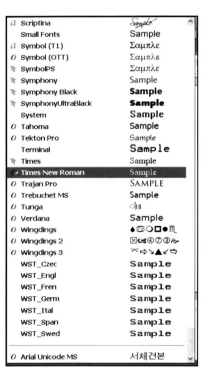

This drop down list shows all of the fonts that are installed on your computer. Fonts come automatically installed on your operating system. If you've installed digital scrapbooking programs like Creating Keepsakes, you will have CK fonts installed in your computer just by installing their software. Hallmark card making programs automatically install Hallmark fonts. Thousands of fonts, free and for purchase, are available in stores and on the internet.

A shortcut to find the font you are looking for is to type the first letter of the font name in the Font Family name box and then click on the drop down area. If you entered the letter "T" you will be automatically taken to the first font that starts with the letter "T". Once the font name is highlighted you can use your arrow keys to move up or down in the font list. Press enter when you find the font you want.

My font list will look different than yours because we will both have different fonts installed.

Times New Roman is the default font. Scriptina, a free font available at many sites is my favorite font.

Using different fonts is a lot of fun! Most digital scrapbook magazines and digital scrapbook store galleries list the fonts that are used on their pages. To find a particular font, do an internet search by going to a site like Google.com and typing in the font name. Usually you can find them this way. Collecting free fonts on the internet can be just as addicting as collecting free digital scrapbooking elements. Don't spend so much time collecting fonts that you never get to scrap.

See the section on Downloading a Free Font in the Shopping and Downloading and Installing Section.

Beware that installing a lot of fonts on your computer can slow it down. A corrupt font can crash your computer.

Photoshop Elements gives you a preview of how your font will look in the word "Sample". The default preview size is medium and it's really too small. To change your font preview size to large go to Edit>Preferences>Type and change it to Large. You'll be happy you did and this change will be permanent until you manually change it again.

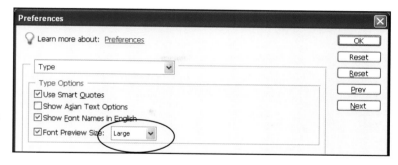

If you are following a tutorial that tells you to select a fat, thick, or wide font, what the author means is a font that is wider than most, like **Impact.** If you were going to write words cut out of a photo a fat font would display parts of the photo.

Font Style

Not all fonts have different styles particularly, free fonts downloaded from the internet. These are the styles for Times New Roman. If the drop down arrow is gray there are no other styles available and you may be able to use the faux styles.

Font Size

Choose the size you want for your font. Sizes from 6 to 72 points are listed on the drop down list but any number between .01 and 1296 can be entered manually.

An easy way to change your Type size is to select your type and select the font size option box at the same time. With both of them selected, roll your mouse wheel to increase or decrease the font size, as you do this the type changes size on your page.

The shortcut to decrease/increase the size of your text by 2 pts (if pts is your selected unit of measurement) is Ctrl>Shift (< for decrease and > for increase).

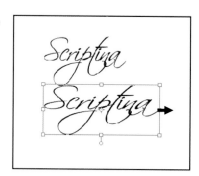

Another way to size text is to grab a side sizing box and stretch it sideways to fill in an area for titles or journaling. Some fonts respond better to this technique than others, so try it out. The example shows the same size text with the bottom copy made wider by dragging to the right; the type is no taller just wider. Dragging by a top or bottom sizing handle will make type taller and works well with some fonts but usually not Scriptina

Remember that 72 points is an inch.

If you would prefer to see your type size displayed in millimeters or pixels, go to Edit>Preferences>Units & Rulers and change it there.

Anti-Aliased

I recommend keeping this on at all times to smooth out the edges of your type. The "S" on the right has Anti-Aliased turned off and you can see the jagged edges as compared to the one on the left. Turning this on or off applies to the entire layer. In this example I had to make two separate layers to have one with and one without Anti-Aliased.

To turn it on or off, click on the AA button on the Option Bar, right click on your text, or go to Layer>Type>Anti-Alias On or Anti-Alias Off.

Faux Bold

If your font does not have a bold font style, you can have Photoshop Elements make a fake one for you. Even if your font does have a bold font style, you may be able to get a faux one too. This is not available for all fonts and doesn't always work the best.

Times	Bold
Times	Faux Bold
Times	Regular
Times	*Italic*
Times	*Faux Italic*
Times	***Bold Italic***
Times	***Faux Bold Italic***
Times	Regular Underline
~~Times~~	~~Regular Strikethrough~~

Using Faux Bold can change the proportions of your font and not always for the better, so be careful when you use this setting.

Click on the Bold T or right click when adding text to add Faux Bold.

Faux Bold text cannot be warped; if you try to warp text with Faux Bold you will be asked if you want to remove Faux Bold.

The short cut to toggle Faux Bold on/off is Ctrl>Shift>B.

Faux Italic

If your font does not have an italic font style, you can have Photoshop Elements make a fake one for you. Even if your font does have an italic font style you may be able to get a faux one too. This is not available for all fonts. Using Faux Italic can change the proportions of your font and not always for the better, so be careful when you use this setting.

Click on the Italicized T or right click when adding text to add Italic Bold.

The short cut to toggle Faux Italic on/off is Ctrl>Shift>I.

Underline

If you want to underline your text select this option. This option can be used with faux italic, faux font, and strikethrough. Just remember, if you don't want the spaces between your words underlined, you need to turn it off on the spaces.

The shortcut to toggle Underline on/off is Ctrl>Shift>U.

Strikethrough

I'm not really sure when you'd want to strikethrough your type, but if you do, this Tool is for you. This option can be used with faux bold, faux italic, and underline. Just remember, if you don't want the spaces between your words with the strikethrough you need to turn it off on the spaces.

The shortcut to toggle Strikethrough on/off is Ctrl>Shift>/.

Text Alignment

Horizontal Type Tool
Text Alignment Options

Vertical Type Tool
Text Alignment Options

Just as in a word processing program, you have the normal Text Alignment boxes with the exception of Justify, but I can show you a little trick on how to Justify your text.

Left Align Text

With Point Type when using the Horizontal Text Tool (T) your text starts at the insertion point and goes to the right. When you press enter for a second line, it aligns with the left edge of type. With Paragraph Type, your type lines up on the left edge of the bounding box.

Using the Vertical Text Tool the text lines up on the top.

The shortcut for Left/Top Align Text is Ctrl>Shift>L.

Center Align Text

With Point Type using the Horizontal Text Tool (T) the type centers from your first insertion point. If you hit the return key for a second line of text it will center below the first line of text. Sometimes this is a little bit confusing so try it out. With Paragraph Type your type is centered in the bounding box.

Using the Vertical Text Tool the text lines up Center Vertical.

The shortcut for Center Align Text is Ctrl>Shift>C.

Right Align Text

With Point Type, when using the Horizontal Text Tool (T) your text starts at the insertion point and goes to the left. When you press enter for a second line, it aligns with the right edge of type. With Paragraph Type, your type lines up on the right edge of the bounding box.

Using the Vertical Text Tool the text lines up on the bottom.

The shortcut for Right/Bottom Align Text is Ctrl>Shift>R.

Justify

If you really want to have justified type, (like a newspaper article) on your scrapbook page, there is a way to do it that usually works. With Microsoft Word select Justify Text and type out your text. Make sure your text is perfect, because with this method you cannot edit your text in Photoshop Elements. Ctrl A to Select All and then Ctrl C to copy your text in Microsoft Word. Go to your scrapbook page and Ctrl V to paste it and your justified text is pasted as a regular image layer on your page. Size it, but be careful that it won't be pixilated. Remember, you can't fix any errors or make any changes once it's pasted onto your scrapbook page.

To try and get Justify to work in Photoshop Elements, drag out a text box with the Type Tool (T) and then type Ctrl>Shift>F. Now when you type your text it will be justified, however, it doesn't always work on the last line of text.

Leading

Leading is the distance between the lines on which the type line sits.

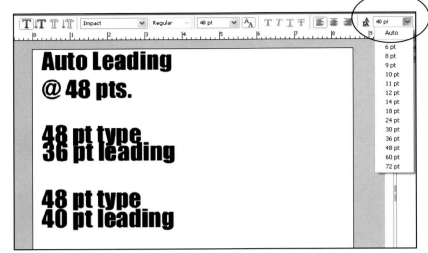

To keep the bottom descending type from colliding with the tops of the letters on the next layer, Photoshop Elements automatically adds 20 percent of space between the two layers.

If you want to move your type lines closer, especially if you are using a large font size, you can change this amount by manually entering a number or choosing one from the drop down list.

Leading can also be increased if you want to space your lines further apart like when making cards.

Color

The Type color is automatically the Foreground color. To change the color of the text, select the text by double clicking on the Text Layer thumbnail, then select a new color and check the checkmark.

Clicking in the color box will bring up the Adobe Color Picker where you can pick your own color or you can click on the drop down arrow and pick a color from the default color swatch. You have an option to load other color swatches.

Style/Layer Style

The Style box on the Type Tool (T) Options Bar is a mini version of the one found in the Layers palette Special Effects Layers Styles menu.

You must commit your text by clicking on the check mark before you have the option to add a layer style.

To find a Layer Style, click on the drop down arrow and a thumbnail or list view will be shown of the layer style selected. To choose another Layer Style, click on the small blue triangle in a circle to the right of the thumbnails and select another one from the list. I find it easier to use the Layer Styles in the Layers palette.

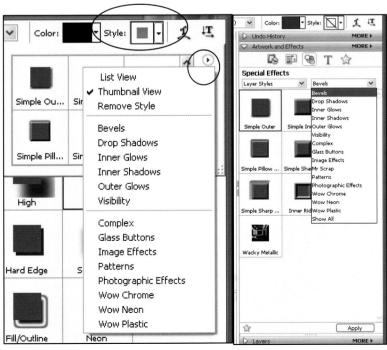

To add a Layer Style:
Double click the layer style thumbnail
Select the thumbnail and click Apply
Drag the thumbnail to your photo or scrapbook page

There are a lot of ways you can change your text by adding a Layer Style. More than one Layer Style can be added to your text at a time.

You do not have to simplify your text to add a layer style.

When you add a Layer Style to your Text Layer you will get a small sun icon on the far right end of the layer in the Layers palette.

To Remove a Layer Style right click on the layer and choose Clear Layer Style or click the More button on the Layers palette and choose Clear Layer Style.

 Create Warp Text

Faux Bold text cannot be warped.

Using Warp Text is a fun way to make scrapbook page titles and other interesting text.

To Warp Text, activate the Type Tool (T). Select the Horizontal Type Tool (T), choose a Font Family, Font Style, Font Size, Text Alignment and Text Color. Click where your want your type to start and a little square is added to your page, this is your insertion point.

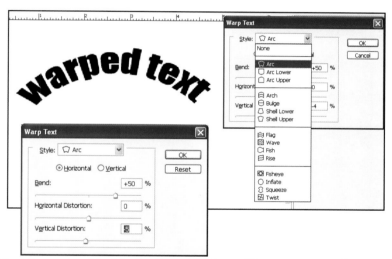

As soon as you click on your page, a new Text Layer is added in the Layers palette. You must commit your text by clicking on the checkmark before you have the option to warp your text. Choose a Warp Style from the drop down box and your text is warped. Slide the Bend, Horizontal Distortion, and Vertical Distortion to change the warp. There are many other styles you can try out. Holding the Alt key changes the Cancel button to Reset. Click OK when you're happy with the result.

Changing the bend percentage from +50% to -100% produces a big change in my text. This is one way that you can make Text in a circle, but not the best way. Using a Text Path created in Photoshop is the best way to write in a circle.

Clicking on the Warp Text button, right clicking and choosing Warp Text or Layer>Type>Warp Text

will also bring up the Warp Text dialog box.

To Unwarp Text, select the Type Layer that is warped. Click on the Warp Text button. On the drop down list choose None and your text is no longer warped. Click OK.

Once your Text is warped, the layer thumbnail will change to show the warp symbol.

Change the Text Orientation

Clicking on this button will change your horizontal text to vertical text and vice versa. This is a fast way to see if maybe you want to change the direction of your text. Right clicking after you commit your text and choosing Horizontal or Vertical, or going to Layer>Type>Horizontal and Layer>Type>Vertical will do the same thing.

Simplify Your Type Layer

If you want to add filters, paint, gradients, patterns, or use the Eraser Tool (E), Healing Brush Tool (J), Clone Stamp Tool (S), or Paint Bucket Tool (K) you have to simplify your text. Because simplified text cannot be edited, my recommendation is to make a copy of your text and simplify the copy. Before you simplify your text make sure it is the final size you'll be using because simplified text does not size well. Hide your original layer by clicking off the eyeball in the Layers palette. This way, if you don't like how your filter or other effect came out, you can simply delete that layer and don't have to retype your text. Simplified type (pixel based) does not print as crisp as your original type (vector based).

To Simplify your Type Layer:

Layer>Simplify Layer
Right click on the layer and select Simplify Layer
Click on the More button on the Layers palette. Choose Simplify Layer.

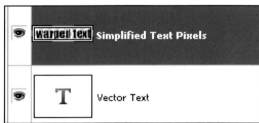

How to use the Point Type Tool

To type a line or two this method works well, but if you're typing more than that, use the paragraph method below.

Open a scrapbook page or a photo and activate the Type Tool (T).

Select the Horizontal Type Tool, Font Family, Font Style, Font Size, Text Alignment and Text Color. Click where your want your type to start and a little square is added to your page; this is your insertion point. As soon as you click on your page, a new Text Layer is added in the Layers palette. Your type will run right off the page, so when you want to make another line, hit the Enter Key and you are returned to the line directly under your insertion point.

Click the checkmark or select another Tool when you're done typing to commit your type. As soon as you commit your type you will see that the name of your layer is approximately the first 30 characters of what you typed.

To move your text, select it and press the Ctrl key to temporarily activate the Move Tool (V), or activate the Move Tool (V) and move it that way.

How to use the Paragraph Type Tool

When I'm journaling or typing a large amount of text, it's easier to create a Bounding Box to put my text in because I spend less time trying to line everything up. Open a scrapbook page or a photo and activate the Type Tool (T).

Select the Horizontal Type Tool, Font Family, Font Style, Font Size, Text Alignment and Text Color. Click and drag a Bounding Box to where you want your text. Use any of the sizing handles to change the size of your Bounding Box. Depending on the text alignment box you have selected, your cursor may be on the right, left, or center of the bounding box. The example shows Center Text Alignment. You do not get the little square insertion box when using this method. As soon as you drag out the bounding box, a new Text Layer is added in the Layers palette. Your type will be contained in the Bounding Box and will automatically go to the next line so you don't need to hit the Enter Key. If you type more text than will fit in the Bounding Box, you can resize the box or change your font size so that what you've typed will fit in the Bounding Box. If you can't see the text in the Bounding Box, it won't print on your scrapbook page.

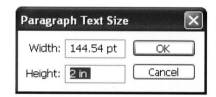

To move your text, select it and press the Ctrl key to temporarily activate the Move Tool (V), or activate the Move Tool (V) and move it that way.

How to use the Paragraph Type Tool to Make a Text Box in an Exact Size

If you know the exact size of the text box you want to make, with the Type Tool (T) active, Alt Click on the scrapbook page and a Paragraph Text Size box appears. Enter the size you want in inches, and it automatically converts it to points. Your Bounding Box appears on your page. If you need to size it you can drag one of the sizing handles.

Adding Stylized Text from the Artwork & Effects Palette

Click the "T" in the Artworks and Effects Palette and choose one of the styles by double clicking the thumbnail, selecting the thumbnail and clicking Apply to Document, or drag the thumbnail to your photo or scrapbook page.

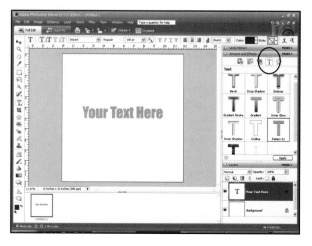

A new Text Layer is added to your Layers palette and centered on your image are the words "Your Text Here". Type in your text. To change the text, drag over the text with your cursor to select it all or double click on the Text Layer thumbnail. If you drag with your cursor a little too far to the beginning or end of the text you may get a selection (marching ants). Hit the Esc key and start over, moving in a

little bit so you are dragging right over the text.
Commit your text if you are happy with it or cancel it.
Use the Move Tool (V) to move your text.

How to Edit your Text Layer

To edit your text, activate the Type Tool (T) and select your text. There are several ways to select your text:

Double Click on the Text Layer thumbnail and all of your text is selected.
Double click on a word and the word is selected.
Triple click on a word and the whole line is selected.
Quadruple click (this is not easy!) on a word and the whole paragraph is selected.
Click in your text and then right click and choose Select All to select all text on your text layer. If you don't click in the text first when you right click it will say Edit Text.

You can also click and drag over the text, but sometimes if you don't do it exactly right, you get a selection of marching ants and you need to start over. As soon as you click to start typing, the old text will disappear and you can type your new text.

Clicking once in your text gives you the ability to start typing immediately without wiping out the original text, in the event you needed to add one letter or a space. To select one character to the left or right after you've clicked in the text, use Shift and the left or right Arrow Keys. You will add another character every time you press the keys. To select one line up or down, use Shift and the up or down Arrow Key. This adds another line each time you press the keys. To select one word to the left or right, use Ctrl>Shift and the left or right Arrow Key. This adds another word each time you press the keys.

To move the cursor one character left or right use the left or right Arrow Key. To move one line up or down use the up and down Arrow Keys. To move one word left or right use Ctrl and the left or right Arrow Key.

With the Type Tool (T) active, and with your text layer selected, click inside your text and tap the "Home" Key on your keyboard to move your cursor to the start of the line. To move the cursor to the start of the text on this layer, type Ctrl and the "Home" key. To move the cursor to the end of the line, click the "End" Key on your keyboard. To move the cursor to the end of the text on this layer, type Ctrl and the "End" Key.

Don't forget to commit your text.

Update Text Layer

If you open a scrapbook page that was constructed on another computer or with a different version of Photoshop Elements, you might get the following warning: "Some text layers might need to be updated before they can be used for vector based output. Do you want to update these layers now?"

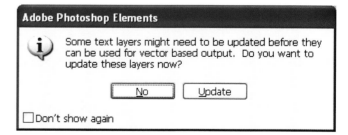

Every time I've gotten this warning I've checked "No" because I've never been able to find any information on Adobe Help or in any books regarding it. One person on the Photoshop Elements User Forum said to try it and then if you didn't like the update to close the file without saving it, which seems like good advice.

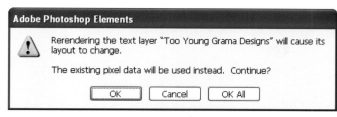

Missing Fonts

If you open a PSD file that was constructed on another computer, you may get a message that says you are missing fonts. This may be a problem if you attend a hands-on computer class and bring your scrapbook page home to complete it. You have two options. Install the font that was used to construct the file if you know what it is and where to find it, or you can go to Layer>Type>Replace Missing Fonts and choose another font to find a suitable replacement.

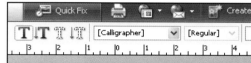

Kerning

The dictionary defines kerning as: "The setting of two letters closer together than is usual by removing space between them."

In Photoshop Elements you can't change the kerning in a normal way, but you can kind of cheat. Notice that in the bottom row the letters are actually touching. I did this using Asian Text Options.

Go to Edit>Preferences>Type and click in the box that says Show Asian Text Options.

On the bottom row of type in my example I used the highest percentage on the Mojikumi setting of 100% which is the only option available for horizontal text.

Tate-Chuu-Yoko does the same thing on vertical text.

Cutting And Straightening Tools

The Crop Tool (C)

Think of this Tool as your paper cutter that cuts your photos into rectangular shapes with perfect edges and corners every time. What ever you can do with your straight edge paper cutter you can do with the crop Tool only better, and you don't have any trash to clean up.

You'll be using this Tool a lot if you didn't take my advice in the Camera section to fill your frame with people.

What you can do with the Crop Tool (C):

Crop out unwanted backgrounds, people, etc. from your photos to help you focus on the focal point of the photo.
Crop your photos to a specified size for printing on standard sized photo paper at home or at a photo lab.

What you <u>can't</u> do with the Crop Tool (C):

Crop a photo on a multi-layer scrapbook page. If you try it, you'll end up cropping all layers of your page the size of your photo which isn't a good thing normally!

Beware of Cropping too much.

It's great to crop your photos, but don't crop out everything to fill your photo with people. I've been in several classes where cropping is discussed and the teacher has said when cropping heritage photos not to crop out the background because it's interesting to see the cars, buildings, etc. of that era. In my mind I'm thinking, "In the year 2525 if our scrapbooks do survive, won't future generations be interested in our cars and such"? For some reason, I'm the only one that ever asks these types of questions in a class, and my questions usually result in strange looks from the teacher and other students!

Aspect Ratio

Aspect ratio allows you to crop your photos in direct proportion to standard photo sizes if you want to. When you click on the drop down arrow, you are given eight options to choose.

No Restriction

You can click and drag your mouse out any size you want and crop it. If you're working on a scrapbook page, card, or a photo for the web and want just a certain part of the photo, you can crop it this way. When you crop your photo with No Restriction, the resolution of your photo does not change.

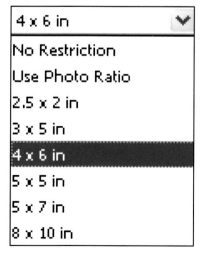

4 x 6 in

No Restriction
Use Photo Ratio
2.5 x 2 in
3 x 5 in
4 x 6 in
5 x 5 in
5 x 7 in
8 x 10 in

Use Photo Ratio

In my example shown, the photo is 17.067 inches wide and 11.378 inches high. Instead of just eyeballing the photo by using my rulers, I checked the lower left corner of my photo (if your screen doesn't display document dimensions click the black drop down menu triangle and choose document dimensions)or you can go to Image>Resize>Image size for the exact dimensions. This is the same proportion as a 6 inch wide by 4 inch wide photo. How did I figure this out? First I cheated and I tried to crop the photo with a 6 x 4 aspect ratio and it worked out fine with no left over space. Then I tried the math: $17.067 \div 11.378 = 1.5$ the same as $6 \div 4 = 1.5$. To think that I had trouble with college algebra! For this photo you wouldn't want to use photo ratio because it would be easier to just use 6 x 4, but other photos you may want to use photo ratio. When you crop your photos with Use Photo Ratio, your resolution does not change.

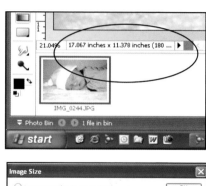

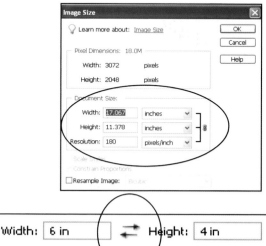

Using Pre-Set Aspect Ratios

The pre-set size you'll probably use most often is 4 x 6. When you choose 4 x 6 to crop your photo, you'll discover that you're cropping 4 inches wide and 6 inches high. If you want it 6 inches wide and 4 inches high, you can type it in yourself or you can just click on the two opposite facing arrows and it will automatically swap the dimensions. When you crop your photos with Pre-Set Aspect Ratios, your resolution changes automatically.

If I wanted to print this photo as an 8 x 10 at home or at a photo lab, part of it would be cropped as shown. If I cropped it before it was printed, I would have the option of choosing what portion is cropped off. The selection (light area inside marching ants) is what would be printed for the photo, and the dark portion would be cropped off. If I sent this photo to a photo lab and did not crop it myself first, the photo lab would decide which part to crop off.

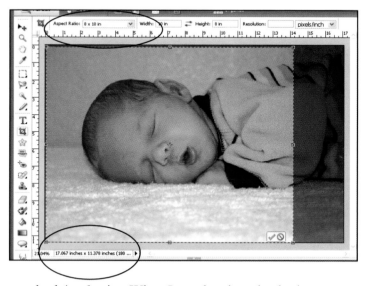

Several years ago I had a beautiful photo that my son's football team photographer took and cropped to 5 inches by 5 inches. I didn't pay attention to what size it was, I just liked it and wanted a copy of it.

I took this to my neighborhood Costco and ordered a standard 4 x 6 print. When I got the photo back, the heads were chopped off and on one side there was a one inch strip of white. I thought they'd made a mistake so I uploaded the photo again and printed it two more times with the same end result. The last time I picked up the photo I asked the technician, "Why did Costco print my photo wrong?" He told me that the size of the digital photo was a different aspect ratio than the photo paper. At the time I had no idea what he was talking about. Now after learning how to use Photoshop Elements, I understand it completely and I chalk it up to one of those ID 10 Terrors!

Isn't it a little bit scary to think you've purchased a book about digital scrapbooking written by someone who did something like that at Costco? However, if you stand back and watch at photo lab counters everywhere, there are a lot of confused people!

In retrospect now that I've learned a thing or two, if I would have ordered the photo as a 5 x 7 their heads would have stayed intact and I would have had a 2 inch strip of white on one side that I could have cut off with a paper trimmer.

How to Crop

Never crop your original photo! Never use the Crop Tool (C) on a multi-layer scrapbook page, see the instructions at the end of this section to do this. You can either duplicate it when working on it by File>Duplicate and the program automatically gives it a new name of the original name followed by the word copy, or you have the option of typing in your own new name. If your photo is IMG123 you can name the cropped one IMG123-cropped or IMG123-1. However you save your files, just make sure you will remember your system.

Cropping is one of the easiest things to do in Photoshop Elements. With the Crop Tool (C) activated, your cursor turns into the Crop Tool (C) icon. Click and drag your mouse across the area that you want to keep. The light area inside the marching ants is

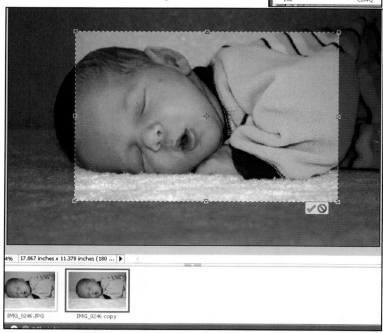

what will remain after you click the checkmark or press enter. The dark area, called the shield will be discarded. If you want to move your selection, just click inside the selection and drag it.

To accept the crop, click the checkmark, press enter, double click inside the selection, or right click and select crop.

If you don't want to crop the image, press the Esc Key or ⊘ button.

If you've selected no restriction, you can enlarge your crop area by dragging out or pushing in any of the sizing arrows. If you've chosen one of the preset aspect ratios, you can only enlarge or reduce your selection by dragging or pushing on one of the corner sizing arrows.

To rotate your selection in the event your photo is crooked, click outside the sizing arrow and you get a two headed curved arrow and you can rotate that way. You can also use the Straighten Tool (P).

If you decide not to crop it or to just start over, click on the ⊘ or right click with your mouse and select cancel.

Crop Tool Preferences

The default setting for the Crop Tool is to use a shield. The shield is the dark area that will be cropped off. If you turn off the shield you will only have marching ants to show the area to be cropped. The shield default color is black and can be changed to any color you choose. You can set the opacity of the shield from 1% to 100%. This example shows the shield set to 100%.

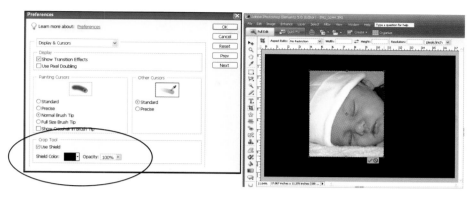

To change the Crop Tool Preferences to Edit>Preferences>Display & Cursors.

To toggle the crop shield on and off use the "/" key.

Custom Size Cropping

If you want to crop photos or digital scrapbook paper a certain size, it's easy. In the width box type the size you want. For my example I'm going to use a 1.25 inch square. I type 1.25 in both boxes and it automatically enters inches. If you're working in cm you can change it.

As soon as you type anything in the width box the Aspect Ratio drop down changes to Custom. Since I am going to drag this photo onto a scrapbook page with 300 resolution and want it to be a 1.25 inch square I enter 300 for the resolution. (Photoshop Elements will automatically resample this photo but since I'm making it smaller I'm not concerned about it.)

The true beauty of cropping with Photoshop Elements is that by cropping a 1.25 inch square I can end up with these different photos. Try to do this with a regular paper cutter!

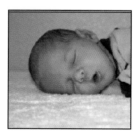   

This scrapbook page was made by cropping all nine photos in 2.5 inch squares at 300 resolution. I dragged them on a 300 resolution new page. I filled the background with black using the Paint Bucket Tool (K). Next I used the Move Tool (V) to position them on the page the way I wanted them. You can also use the Align and Distribute features of the Move Tool (V) to place them perfectly. I used white to write the name with the Type Tool (T) and to add a Stroke Outline (Edit>Stroke Outline Selection inside Location 10 px) around each photo. This page can be done in five minutes!

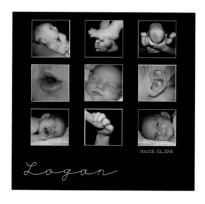

Don't Crop on a Scrapbook Page With The Crop Tool!

If you drag your photo onto a scrapbook page and decide that you should have cropped off a little bit don't use the Crop Tool (C) to do it! If you try it, as soon as you check your checkmark all you'll be left with is your cropped photo and all the other layers will be cropped to the same size as your photo. If and when you do this just Ctrl>Z to Undo because every new scrapper does it at least once!

If you need to crop a photo on a multi-layer scrapbook page follow these directions exactly:

Click on the layer you want to crop.
Activate the Marquee Tool (M) and make a selection of the area you want to keep.
Make sure you are still on the layer you want to crop.
Inverse your selection (Shift>Ctrl>I) and you will now have marching ants around the outside of your page and around the area you want to crop.
Hit the Delete Key.
Hit the Esc Key to get rid of the marching ants.

If you know the exact part of your layer that you want to crop off, you can select it and delete it by clicking the Delete Key but make sure you're on the right layer.

Snap to Grid and the Crop Tool (C)

If you have Snap to Grid turned on, your Crop Tool (C) may behave erratically and not want to crop where you want it to crop. To turn this off go to View>Snap To>Grid and click to remove the check mark.

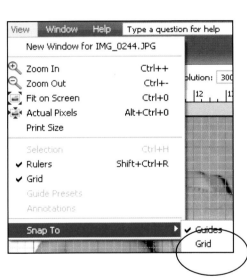

If your Crop Tool (T) still doesn't behave click on the Crop Tool icon in the options bar and click "Reset Tool".

Other Ways to Crop a Photo-Image>Crop

Make a selection on your photo with the Marquee Tool (M), Lasso Tool (L), Magic Wand Tool (W), or Selection Brush (A) and choose Image>Crop. Your photo will be cropped close to your selection border, but in a rectangular shape.

The Cookie Cutter Tool (Q)

The Cookie Cutter Tool (Q) cuts your images into shapes just like cookie cutter cuts cookie dough. If you are a paper scrapper think of it as your own personal die cut machine, corner rounder, or punch. The difference with using the Cookie Cutter Tool (Q) is that you can crop your images in many different shapes in any size and you don't have clean up all those little tiny pieces of paper on your floor!

At first glance the Cookie Cutter Tool (Q) appears to be the same Tool as the Shape Tool (U). While they use the same shape libraries, the Cookie Cutter Tool (Q) cuts or crops images and the Shape Tool (U) makes shapes in the color of the Foreground color. One of the questions I've answered on the message boards a few times is from a scrapper that's trying to make a talk bubble and as soon as she draws it out her photo is cropped because she's using the Cookie Cutter Tool (Q) instead of the Shape Tool (U). If you want to add a talk bubble to a photo you need to be using the Shape Tool (U).

What you can do with the Cookie Cutter Tool (Q):
Cut out paper or photos in fancy shapes to use on scrapbook pages or cards.

Shape

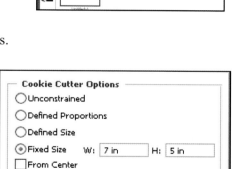

Click on the drop down triangle to the right of Shape.
This is the library of shapes that were last used. If you don't see the library you want, click on the small circle with a triangle in it at the top of the current library. It will display all of the libraries that are available. Any shapes that you loaded in from another source will also show up here. Notice the line that says All Elements Shapes. It means only the ones that came preloaded. Sports_Shapes was installed by me and does not show up in the All Elements Shapes Library.

Hover over each individual shape square and a description will pop up.
Double click a shape to accept it and the library box will close

Shape Options

Just like the Shape Tool (U) gives you options to draw your shape, the Cookie Cutter Tool (Q) gives you the option on how to crop your shapes.

Unconstrained means however you drag out the shape the Cookie Cutter Tool (Q) will cut it. If you drag a heart out that is tall and skinny the Cookie Cutter (Q) will cut a tall and skinny heart. If you want to drag from the center, use the setting From Center.

Defined Proportions will keep the shape in the proportions of the example. When you drag out a heart it will have the same proportions as the heart in the example. From Center can also be selected with Defined Proportions

Defined Size will crop the photo in the size that the designer created it. You won't know what size that is until you release your mouse. If you don't like the size, you can use the sizing handles. From Center can be selected with Defined Size.

Fixed Size crops to the exact dimensions you enter. If you enter 2 inches wide by 2 inches high and you pick a rectangle, the Cookie Cutter Tool (Q) will crop a 2 inch square. Size can be entered as inches, centimeters, or pixels. From Center can also be selected with Fixed Size.

From Center will draw the shape outward from the center. If you want to crop a daisy into a shape start at the daisy center and draw outward to get it perfectly centered in the shape. From Center can be selected with all the other options too.

Feather

Enter a number here from .2-250 pixels to soften the edge of your image that's cropped. When you feather an edge, it blends into the next layer. Once you get used to the photos from your camera, you'll decide on a feather amount that you like. If you want a sharp edge enter .2 here.

Crop

With this option it is a little bit hard to notice the difference, but there is a big difference. First of all, don't check this if you're working on a multi-layer scrapbook page or you'll end up with a mess than you can easily Undo by Ctrl>Z.

With Crop not checked, if you are working with a 4 x 6 photo and you crop a 2 x 2 heart your transparent (checkerboard) background will still be 4 x 6 and your heart photo will be 2 x 2 _after_ you check the checkmark.

With Crop checked, using a 4 x 6 photo and cropping a 2 x 2 heart after you check the checkmark your heart photo will be 2 x 2 and your background will be just slightly larger than 2 x 2.
It's my recommendation to keep this off!

How to Use the Cookie Cutter Tool (Q)

Select the shape you want to use from the shape library, the shape option (Unconstrained etc.), and the feather amount if you want a soft edge.

Click and drag across the photo if you are using unconstrained or Defined Proportions.

For Defined Size and Fixed Size, you click where you want to crop and don't drag.

As soon as you let go of the mouse, a transparency grid appears around the photo. The transparency is the area that will be deleted as soon as you check the checkmark. Notice the options bar on the top of the photo is now the Free Transform Tool and the thumbnail in the Layers palette shows a dark grey background. You can now size the heart, rotate, or skew it here by using the sizing handles explained in the Move Tool (V) Section. While it appears that the photo is actually already cut, it's not until you check the checkmark. When you're happy with your crop, check the checkmark.

As soon as you check the checkmark, you'll see the Cookie Cutter option bar again and the thumbnail in the Layers palette now has a transparent (checker board) background.

When working on a multi-layer scrapbook page it's OK to use the Cookie Cutter Tool (Q) to crop a photo or digital paper. Be sure that you are on the right layer before you use the Cookie Cutter Tool (Q) and make sure that "Crop" is not checked in the options bar.

The Cookie Cutter has a rounded square that makes a great rounded rectangle mat or rounded corner photo.

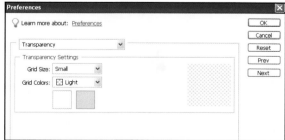

If viewing the edges of your photo is difficult because of the checkerboard pattern, you can temporarily make another layer and fill it with white. This helps check your feathered edge before you drag it onto a scrapbook page or card. You can also change your transparency by going to Edit>Preferences>Transparency. Here you have the option to change the grid size to None, Small, Medium, or Large. Other colors are available instead of the standard gray and white and, if you don't like their other options, you can make a custom checkerboard in your spare time!

You can add sets of custom shapes to be used with the Cookie Cutter Tool (U) from places like http://www.adobe.com/exchange. Go to the Photoshop section and then Custom Shapes section. Make sure the files you download say they are compatible with Adobe Photoshop Elements 5. Shapes are a CSH File and look like the one shown here.

Talk Bubbles
CSH File
9 KB

With Photoshop Elements turned off, copy your new custom shapes folders to C:\Program Files\Adobe\Photoshop Elements 5.0\Presets\Custom Shapes.

Make sure that you are displaying all hidden folders. To make sure you're displaying hidden folders, go to My Computer > Tools > Folder Options>View>click the button for Show Hidden Files and Folders.

Adding lots of custom shapes will slow down your computer, so add them selectively.

The Straighten Tool (P)

How often do you pull your tripod out and take a photo? For me the answer is never! Many of the photography books on the market will tell you that one sign of an amateur photographer is that the photos they take aren't straight. Using the Straighten Tool (P) quickly and easily straightens out any photo whether it was taken with your camera or scanned.

What you can do with the Straighten Tool (P):
Straighten photos that were taken with a digital camera.
Straighten photos that were scanned crooked as a slide, negative, or print

This is the original photo I'll be using to demonstrate the Canvas Options available. This picture is one of the doorways where my daughter's wedding reception was held. I'm hoping that if I use enough photos from her wedding in this book, the IRS will agree the entire cost of the wedding was a business expense! So far all they do is laugh! This photo is obviously not taken by a professional photographer but I'd need another whole book to tell that story! Adding to the problem of it being crooked is the painted curb and stripe down the middle of the street which makes it even more obvious that it's out of whack!

Grow or Shrink Canvas to Fit

The photo is straightened but because some of the corners were moved outside of the canvas area when it was straightened, the canvas has grown. The white areas are blank background. The original size of this photo was 7 inches wide & 5.25 inches high. After straightening it the photo grew to 7.357 inches wide by 5.737 inches high.

To do the same thing without the Straighten Tool (P), go to Image>Rotate>Straighten Image. By comparison to using the Straighten Tool, my original 7 inch wide photo x 5.25 inch high photo only grew to 7.01 inch wide by 5.26 inch high. Using the Straighten Tool (P) worked much better for me.

Using either method no pixels are clipped so you would then have to crop this photo yourself to make it into a rectangle shape suitable for printing.

Crop to Remove Background

The photo is straightened and the blank background edges are cropped off. Notice there is less of the street at the bottom and also less of the trees at the top. The original photo was 7 inches wide by 5.25 inches high. After Straightening with the Straighten Tool (P) with Crop to Remove Background selected, it's now 6.617 inches wide by 4.753 inches wide.

To do the same thing without the Straighten Tool (P) go to Image>Rotate>Straighten and Crop Image. Using this method didn't straighten the photo as well as using the Straighten Tool. The same photo is now 6.99 inches wide and 5.259 inches high The Straighten Tool (P) worked much better for me on this one too.

Using either method, pixels will be clipped but you won't have to crop the image yourself to get back to a rectangle shape. This is the fastest way to straighten and crop a photo. The downside is that you may not like the way the program crops your particular photo.

Crop to Original Size

The image is straightened and some of the corners go off of the canvas. The program does not enlarge the canvas to show the corners and keeps the original size of 7 inches wide by 5.25 inches high. The white areas are blank background. You would have to crop this photo yourself into a rectangle shape suitable for printing.

Rotate All Layers

When working on a multi-layer scrapbook page, you might want to straighten something however, I don't recommend having this checked as it rotates ALL layers just as the name implies.

If you're editing a photo that has multiple layers (like adjustment & filter layers) and you don't want to merge all of the layers before straightening you would check the box to Rotate All Layers and all of the layers would move together.

How to use the Straighten Tool (P)

If you want to straighten your image horizontally, click and drag a straight line horizontally on the image. The line does not have to go across the entire photo. In my example I drew the line along the curb because I knew it was straight.

If you want to straighten vertically, hold the Ctrl key and click and drag a straight line vertically.

On my example photo, dragging horizontally or vertically produced the same result.

Touch Up Tools

The Red Eye Removal Tool (Y)

Nothing is more annoying than taking a perfect photo only to find when you check the photo you've got two red demon eyes gleaming back at you. Red eyes are caused by your camera's flash bouncing off your subject's retina. Red Eye is usually worse with blue eyes when the photo is taken in a darkened room. Turning on your camera's Red Eye setting helps limit this problem, but it can be aggravating to your subjects because it flashes several times when you take the picture. They feel like they've been blinded by all of the extra flashes, but this is necessary to constrict their retina before the photo is actually taken. Other ways to minimize red eye problems is to turn on a light in the area or move to a better lighted area and have your subjects look away from the camera. With the Red Eye Tool (Y), usually with one click you can remove red eyes, and with Photoshop Elements 5, you can set up automatic red eye removal if you choose to.

What you can do with the Red Eye Removal Tool (Y):

Remove red eyes manually or automatically.

Pupil Size

Normally, using the pupil size default of 50% works great. If it doesn't, try adjusting the percentage up or down. If the pupil size is too small, then you'll still have red around the edges. If the pupil size is too large, then the whole eye will be darkened which isn't good if the eye is light blue.

Darken Amount

Once again, normally using the X default of 50% works great. If it doesn't, try adjusting it too. Adjusting this too low will turn the pupil a light grey, and if you adjust it too high, the pupil will be completely black.

Auto

When you hover over this button it says "Automatically find and fix red eye", however, when I click on this button nothing happens with my red eyes in the photo below. Another photo that I used this on did have the red eyes fixed, but they were very dark. Try using this button and doing it yourself.

How to Use the Red Eye Tool (Y)

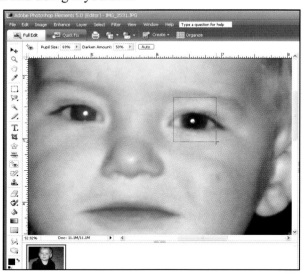

Click on the red area of the eye and usually the Red Eye Tool (Y) will fix it immediately. Zooming in very close also helps when using the Red Eye Tool (Y). The photo at the right didn't fix completely with one click because only about half of the red was removed. Next I tried clicking and dragging a box around the eye and it still didn't work 100%. Because his pupils are so big in this photo I increased the Pupil Size to 69% and the red eye was removed on that eye in one click. Be careful using the darken amount at a high setting because it makes the eye look like it has a solid black mark in the middle instead of a pupil.

If you change your settings and want to get back to the default settings, you can reset the Tool by clicking on the Red Eye Tool (Y) icon on the options bar and picking reset Tool. All Tools have this setting.

The shortcut to remove red eye is Ctrl>R.

Removing Red Eye in the Organizer

To remove red eyes from your photo while viewing them in the Organizer click to select the photo or photos and go to Edit>Auto Red Eye Fix. You can also select the photo and use the shortcut Ctrl>R. If you have more than one photo selected in the Organizer, it will say Auto Red Eye Fix Selected Photos.

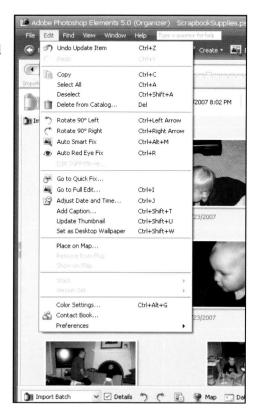

When you fix red eye in the Organizer it automatically saves the original and the fixed photo in a version set.

Turning Off Automatic Red Eye Removal

You can have Photoshop Elements automatically remove red eye on your photos when you import them through the Get Photos feature of the Organizer from your camera or card reader. This takes longer to import your photos and I prefer to fix my red eyes myself, so I turn it off.

Go to the Organizer and click on File>Get Photos>From Camera or Card Reader.
Then click on Advanced Dialog.
Remove the checkmark from Automatically Fix Red Eyes and import some photos. The next time you import photos it won't automatically fix the red eyes.

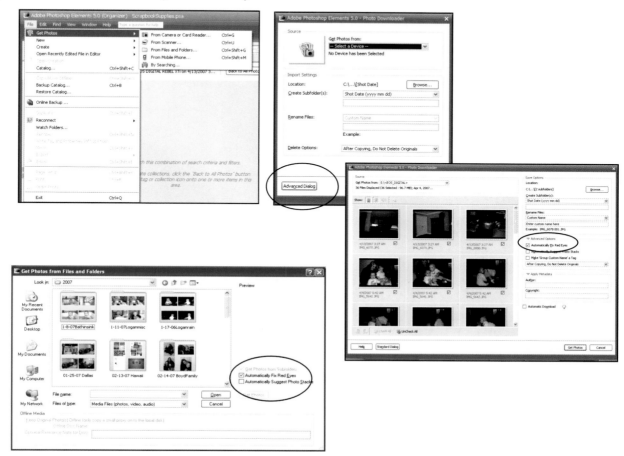

Turn Off Automatic Red Eye Removal When Downloading Your Pictures & Digital Scrapbooking Elements

You will want to turn off Automatic Red Eye Removal from Files & Folders where you'll be storing your Digital Scrapbook Elements because it takes a lot longer to bring your elements into the Organizer.

In the Organizer Go to: File>Get Photos>From Files and Folders Remove the checkmark from Automatically Fix Red Eyes

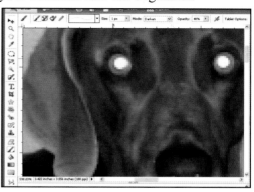

Pet Eye

The Red Eye Tool (Y) doesn't normally fix pet eye because it searches for red pixels and usually in pets the eyes don't turn red, but try it first to see if it helps. If not, here are two methods that work with varying results:

Method #1
Zoom way in until you can see the individual pixels in the eye. Activate the Eyedropper Tool (I) and pick a color of the eye that is the correct color. If the eye is completely blown out, you can pick the color from another photo. Activate the Brush Tool (B) and use a 1 pixel size brush or use the Pencil Tool (N) and fill in the areas that are colored incorrectly. You may have to use more than one color and don't forget to add some white for a highlight effect.

Method #2
Select the yellow green area with the Magic Wand Tool (W). Do not select the highlight in the eye. Feather the selection by going to Select>Feather (Alt Ctrl D) and enter 1-2 pixels, this will soften the selection.

Duplicate the Layer by Layer/Duplicate Layer or Ctrl>J. Make sure you are on your new layer and go to Enhance/Adjust Color/Hue and Saturation (Ctrl>U) . Select the color you want to remove in the drop down box and reduce the saturation to 0. You want a gray eye.

Go to Enhance/Adjust Lighting/Brightness and Contrast or Enhance/Adjust Lighting/Levels and adjust the markers until the eye looks right. If you adjust it too far either way, it will look fake.

The Spot Healing Brush (J)

The Spot Healing Brush Tool (J) is nested with the Healing Brush Tool (J) on the Toolbar, the one you used last will show on the Toolbar. Both of these Tools work great for retouching problem areas in photos. For smaller areas use the Spot Healing Brush Tool (J).

What you can do with the Spot Healing Brush (J)
Quickly and easily fix pimples, moles, wrinkles, a stain on clothing, dirt, scratches, or any other imperfection on a photo with one click of your mouse.
The Spot Healing Brush Tool (J) does not require you to sample an area first to fix the problem area with like the Healing Brush Tool (J) does.
The Spot Healing Brush Tool (J) works better on small areas.

Show Selected Brush Presets & Size
Choose a brush from the drop down menu, my suggestion is to keep the default brush. Manually type in the pixel size brush you want or slide the slider when you click on the side arrow. You can also adjust brush sizes by using your bracket keys. The left bracket [decreases the brush size and the right bracket] increases the brush size. Pick a brush size a tiny bit bigger than the area you're trying to fix and you'll have better luck.

Type-Proximity Match

The Spot Healing Brush Tool (J) blends the area around the problem area to fix the spot. If you are removing a mole in the center of someone's cheek Proximity Match will work well because there isn't too much contrast on a cheek. However if you're fixing something on the edge of their lip, you may run into difficulty because there is contrast on the lip line like this photo shows.

Type-Create Texture

The Spot Healing Brush Tool (J) blends the area you want to fix to create a texture. When I've tried to use this feature I haven't had much luck. If Proximity Match doesn't work well then try the Healing Brush Tool (J).

Sample All Layers

With this not selected, Photoshop Elements will use only the active layer to heal. Select this box and Photoshop Elements will use all Layers which may or may not work OK. If you make a blank layer on top of your image and check Sample all Layers, every thing that the Spot Healing Brush Tool (J) does will be placed on the new layer (make sure top layer is active layer). You can then adjust opacity and make other adjustments on this layer.

How to Use the Spot Healing Brush Tool (J)

Select the Spot Healing Brush Tool (J) and any options you want to use including Sample All Layers. Make a new blank layer above your image. Pick a brush size that is just a little bit larger than the area you want to fix. For a small fix like a mole or pimple, click and release your mouse. The change is not completed until you release the mouse. For larger areas you can click and drag the mouse. If you want to make further changes, click on the top layer and adjust opacity, etc.

The Healing Brush Tool (J)

The Healing Brush Tool (J) is nested with the Spot Healing Brush Tool (J) on the Toolbar. The Tool you used last will show on the Toolbar. Both of these Tools work great for retouching problem areas in photos. For larger areas use the Healing Brush Tool (J). The Healing Brush Tool (J) is very similar to the Clone Stamp Tool (S) except that the Healing Brush Tool (J) blends when it copies.

What you can do with the Healing Brush Tool (J):

Quickly and easily fix pimples, moles, wrinkles, a stain on clothing, dirt, scratches, or any other imperfection on a photo with one click of your mouse.
You can remove things from a uniform background like removing a piece of trash from a sandy beach.
The Healing Brush Tool (J) requires you to sample an area first to fix the problem area unlike the Spot Healing Brush Tool (J).
The Healing Brush Tool (J) works better on large areas.

Brush

It's best to choose a brush that is just slightly larger than the area you want to fix. Click on the black triangle or the black brush to open a brush menu. Adjust the brush size by sliding the slider bar or typing in the size you want. You can also adjust brush sizes by using your Bracket keys. The left Bracket key[decreases the brush size and the right Bracket key] increases the brush size. To make your brush fuzzy with soft edges, decrease the hardness. Spacing sets the space between the brush marks in a stroke. You can slide the slider or enter a percentage in the box. Roundness-100% is completely round, 0% is a line and you can adjust between 100% and 0%. At 100% roundness you won't notice the difference in Angle but if you change the roundness to a lower percentage you can change the Angle. I usually only adjust the brush size with the brackets and don't touch any of this.
Pen Pressure-Requires the use of a pressure sensitive tablet.
Stylus Wheel-Requires the use of a tablet Tool with a thumbwheel.

Mode

Mode determines how your patch is going to blend with existing area. Start with Normal. Replace preserves film grain and textures. For more information see the section on Blending Modes.

Source

Sampled-Uses pixels from your image to fix your problem area. Use this option to fix your photos.

Pattern-Click the Pattern Picker drop down to choose a pattern. While I don't think you'd ever want to replace a freckle with bubbles you can make your own custom pattern (like a fabric texture) from another photo to use when fixing a photo.

Aligned

Align Selected-When you Alt Click to set a sample (copy) point, a crosshair also appears and moves along with the cursor to sample as it moves. By watching the crosshair you can see where the Healing Brush Tool (J) is sampling.

Align Not Selected-When you Alt Click once to set a sample point, Photoshop Elements will use this same sample for all of the areas you fix however many times you click and drag.

Sample All Layers

With this not checked, Photoshop Elements will use only the active layer to heal. Select this box and Photoshop Elements will use all Layers which may or may not work OK. If you make a blank layer on top of your image and check Sample All Layers, everything that the Healing Brush Tool (J) does will be placed on the new layer (make sure top layer is active layer). You can then adjust opacity and make other adjustments on this layer.

How to Use the Healing Brush Tool (J)

Select the Healing Brush Tool (J), Check Sample All Layers. Make a new blank layer above your photo. Alt Click on an area that you want to use as a source point to fix the problem area. If you don't Alt Click first you'll get a warning that tells you to Alt Click.

Click and release the mouse for the change to show up. You can also click and drag for larger areas. The larger the area you fix the longer it takes Photoshop Elements to complete the task. If you want to make further changes, click on the top layer and adjust opacity, etc.

Healing With Two Different Photos

You can use the Healing Brush Tool (J) to sample from another photo. To do this you will need to be able to see them both so select Cascade or Tile View. Alt Click on the photo you want to sample from and then click on the problem area in the photo that needs to be corrected. Color modes must match to do this unless one is grayscale.

The Clone Stamp Tool (S)

The Clone Stamp Tool (S) is nested with the Pattern Stamp Tool (S) on the Toolbar, the tool you used last will show on the Toolbar. Both Tools share the same (S) shortcut. The Clone Stamp Tool (S) copies from one area and pastes it onto another. The Clone Stamp Tool (S) is similar to the Healing Brush Tool (J) except it does not blend when it copies like the Healing Brush Tool (J) does.

What you can do with the Clone Stamp Tool (S):

Use the Clone Stamp Tool (S) to copy from an area on the same photo or from another photo. This can be used to fix problem areas or to copy and paste an area quickly.

Brush

It's best to choose a brush that is just slightly larger than the area you want to fix. Click on the black triangle or the black brush to open the brush menu. Choose the brush you want to use from the drop down menu. It's usually best to use a soft brush so that the cloned area blends in wherever you stamp it.

Brush Size

Adjust the brush size by sliding the slider bar or typing in the size you want. You can also adjust brush sizes by using your Bracket keys. The left bracket [decreases the brush size and the right bracket] increases the brush size.

Mode

Mode determines how your cloned area is going to blend with existing area. Start with Normal. For more information see the Filters and Blending Modes Section.

Opacity

Drag the Opacity slider up and down or type in a percentage setting. A lower setting allows layers below to show through.

Aligned

Aligned Selected - When you Alt Click to set a sample (copy) point, a crosshair also appears and moves along with the cursor to sample as it moves. By watching the crosshair you can see where the Clone Stamp Tool (S) is sampling from. In this example the white circle is the brush and the + is the crosshair. The Clone Stamp Tool (S) will copy from the crosshair area in the size of the brush and stamp it on the area within the brush area.

Aligned Not Selected - When you Alt Click once to set a sample point, Elements will use this same sample for all of the areas you fix however many times you click and drag.

Sample All Layers

When not checked, Elements will use only the active layer to clone. Select this box and Photoshop Elements will use all layers which may or may not work OK. If you make a blank layer on top of your image and check Sample All Layers everything that the Clone Stamp Tool (S) stamps will be placed on the new layer (make sure top layer is active layer). You can then adjust opacity and make other adjustments on this layer.

How to Use the Clone Stamp (S)

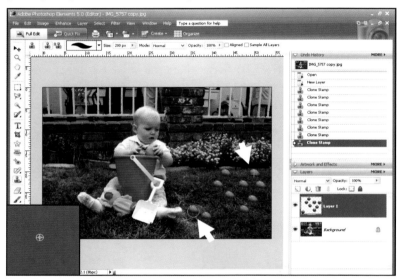

Open the image you want to clone (Ctrl>O). In this photo I am adding more Easter eggs to the grass area. When I used this photo for my scrapbook page I cloned live grass over the dead grass areas. Since I am going to add eggs, I want the Clone Stamp Tool (S) to clone the same egg over and over again. Therefore I am going to make sure the checkmark is removed from the Aligned box. I've chosen a soft round brush that is slightly larger than the egg which is 200 px. Alt click on the egg and you will see your round brush turn into a bulls-eye symbol as shown in the example.

Make a new layer with the New Layer icon in the Layers palette and then click on the grass area and you will have pasted another egg on the grass on the new layer. Making a new layer on which to stamp your cloned egg gives you more options for changes in the future. Every time you click, you will paste another egg. The example shows the + on the top right egg is the area that is being copied. The white circle is the brush that is stamping the copied egg where the brush is. Alt clicking on an area of healthy grass would paste good grass on top of the dead grass. To get a more realistic look for cloning the grass, add the checkmark to the Aligned box and click or click and drag to fill in areas from wherever the cross hair is on the photo. Watch the crosshair because if it goes over the baby or another part of your photo that is what you'll be stamping.

The Pattern Stamp Tool (S)

The Pattern Stamp Tool (S) is nested with the Clone Stamp Tool (S) on the Toolbar. The tool you used last will show on the Toolbar. Both Tools share the (S) shortcut.

What You Can Do With The Pattern Stamp Tool (S):

Stamp patterns that you have created or purchased yourself. Making, saving, and loading patterns is covered in the Cool Stuff to Do Section. Patterns also come installed in Photoshop Elements. Other ways you can fill layers or selections with patterns include using the Paint Bucket Tool (K), Layer>New Fill Layer>Pattern, or an Adjustment Fill layer.

    Size: 21 px Mode: Normal Opacity: 100%  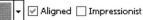 Aligned □ Impressionist

Brush

It's best to choose a brush that is just slightly larger than the area you want to stamp. Click on the black triangle or the black brush to open a brush menu. Choose the brush you want to use from the drop down menu.

Brush Size

Adjust the brush size by sliding the slider bar or typing in the size you want. You can also adjust brush sizes by using your Bracket keys. The left Bracket [decreases the brush size and the right bracket] increases the brush size.

Mode

Mode determines how your stamped area is going to blend with existing area. Start with Normal. For more information see the Filters and Blending Modes Section.

Opacity

Drag the Opacity slider up and down or type in a percentage setting. A lower setting allows layers below to show through.

Aligned

Aligned Selected-(Right Example)
Your pattern is stamped in alignment.
Aligned Not Selected-(Left Example)
Pattern is stamped over an over again wherever you click or click and drag. Un-checking Align allows you to stamp some areas more than others as shown in the examples.

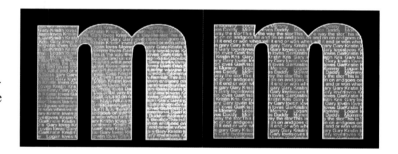

Impressionist

With Impressionist selected the pattern is stamped as if it was painted with paint dabs. When using this setting not much of your original pattern usually remains.

How to Use the Pattern Stamp Tool (S):

Choose the pattern you want to stamp and set the other options on the options bar. Click or click and drag to stamp the pattern. In my example I typed the letter "M". I selected the letter by Ctrl Clicking on the layer thumbnail to produce the selection outline (marching ants). I made a new layer and then stamped on the new layer. Because I had the selection made, my pattern was only stamped inside the marching ants on the new layer. By deselecting the Alignment box I can overlap my pattern if I want a messier look. Next I made a new layer, made a Stroke Outline and finally I deselected by pressing the Esc key.

Tools That Erase

The Eraser Tool (E) consists of three different Tools:
Eraser Tool (E)
Background Eraser Tool (E)
Magic Eraser Tool (E)

When you think of a regular eraser you think of fixing a mistake. The Photoshop Elements Eraser is sometimes used to fix a mistake but most commonly it's used to remove unwanted areas. The last Eraser Tool (E) used will show on the Toolbar.

All three Eraser Tools (E) can be used together or independent of each other.

Hold the Shift key and type the letter E to toggle through all three Tools if you've selected "Use Shift key for Tool switch" as a Preference option (Ctrl K or Edit>Preferences).

I don't use the Eraser Tool (E) very much because normally I make a selection with one of the selection Tools and delete the selection. Typical of Photoshop Elements, there are many ways to accomplish a task.

What you can do with the Eraser Tools:

Normal people use the Eraser Tool (E) to erase unwanted areas of their images.

Digi-scrappers (not to say we aren't normal) erase with different brushes for decorative effects.

Eraser Tool (E)

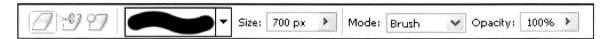

This is what I call the "Regular" Eraser. It doesn't do anything fancy for you, it just erases where you click and drag it.

Show Selected Brush Presets

Choose a brush from the drop down list by clicking on the downward facing black triangle. Choose one of the Default Brushes or any other brush from the drop down list. I normally use a soft or round hard brush depending on what I'm erasing. The soft brush erases a fuzzy area almost like it was feathered. The hard brush at 100% Opacity is like cutting out an area with scissors.

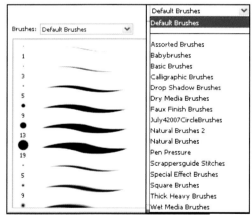

Size

Brushes can be sized from 1-2500 pixels. Use the Bracket keys. [to decrease your brush size or] to increase your brush size. Holding the Bracket key changes the brush size quickly. Clicking on the arrow in the box will allow you to use a slider to adjust your brush size, or you can manually enter a size in the box. Brush sizes are entered in pixels only.

Mode

Brush Mode erases with any of the brushes that come included with Photoshop Elements or you have installed into your Brushes Folder. For scrappers this is a great Tool. Choose a fancy brush and erase to show the layer below as an embellishment. The Brush Mode allows you to erase with a soft edge. There are many brushes available in the Brush Mode, which is why I never use the Pencil or Block Mode.

Pencil Mode erases with a hard edge, if you want a very precise area erased, use this setting.

Block Mode erases with a cursor that is a 16 pixel square brush. When you choose this mode, you are unable to change the brush size or opacity which is pretty limiting. There are square brushes in the brushes menu that you may want to use instead because you can adjust their sizes.

Opacity

The Opacity default is 100% which means you are erasing 100% of everything. Your Background color shows through the erased areas if you're erasing a Background layer. If you're erasing a regular/image layer, the erased area is completely transparent. Lowering the Opacity by typing in the amount in the box or using the slider will allow part of the erased image to remain. You cannot adjust Opacity when using the Block Mode. If you want to adjust the Opacity when erasing with a square shape, choose one of the square brushes.

How to use the Eraser Tool (E)

Open an image and activate the Eraser Tool (E). Choose a Brush, the Brush Size, Mode (I keep this set at Brush), and Opacity from the Eraser Tool (E) Option Bar.

The Eraser Tool (E) only erases the active layer you have selected in the Layers palette.

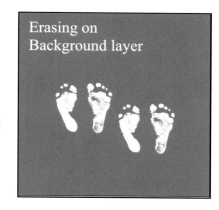

Erasing on Background layer

If you are erasing on a Background layer and want a transparency (checkerboard) to show through, double click on the layer in the Layer Palette and click on the OK button to turn it into a regular layer.

Erasing on a Background layer where the Background color is white gives the effect of stamping on your image with a white brush. This example shows a light blue background that I used my baby feet brush to erase on. The feet look like I stamped them with a white brush, but in reality I just used the Eraser Tool (E) to erase the blue Background layer so my Background color of white is showing through.

Make a duplicate of the layer you're going to erase for a back-up by Ctrl>J and hide it by clicking on the eyeball icon. Zoom into the area that you want to erase. Click and drag on the area that you want to erase. Release your mouse often to erase small parts at a time. Many times you're very involved in erasing and you erase a little too much. When this happens you have to undo. When you Undo (Ctrl>Z) you undo all of your erasing since the last time you released your mouse.

This example shows a regular layer that has been erased with the Eraser Tool (E). I know this is not a Background layer because transparency (checkerboard) is showing through. Making a selection will protect the selected area from being erased, which is helpful if you're erasing for a decorative look. In this example I made a rectangular selection and inverted it so that the area outside of the rectangle is selected. When I erase, only the areas in the selected area will be erased.

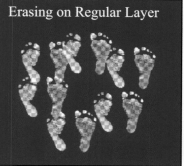

Erasing on Regular Layer

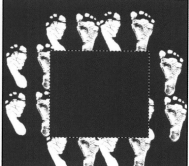

In this example white is my Background color which is why it's showing through. I could do the same thing using the Brush Tool (B) by stamping white which would give me more options, but you can do it this way as well.

Background Eraser Tool (E)

The Background Eraser Tool (E) works best when there is a high contrast between the areas you want to erase and the area of your image you want to keep.

If you are working on a Background layer it is automatically converted to a regular layer when you activate this Tool and your erased areas are transparent (checkerboard).

Using the Background Eraser Tool (E) instead of the Magic Eraser Tool (E) gives a softer less jagged edge to your image.

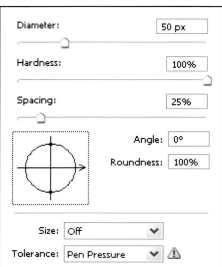

Brush

Diameter
To size your brush the [Left Bracket key makes it smaller or the] Right Bracket key makes it larger, or click on the downward facing black triangle. This opens the brush options pull down menu where you can slide the diameter slider to make it bigger or smaller.

Hardness
To make a softer edged brush, lower the Hardness setting.

Spacing
Spacing sets how far apart your brush strokes are when you click and drag. The default is 25% and I leave mine at 25%.

Roundness
Roundness allows you to change your round circle shaped brush to more of an oval shape.

Angle
Angle allows you to adjust the angle of your brush. Adjusting the angle of a round brush does nothing. Use this if you want to adjust the angle of a brush where you also changed the roundness.

Size
The Size setting allows you to change the size of your brush by using pressure on a pressure sensitive tablet or by using a stylus wheel on a pressure sensitive tablet. If you aren't using a tablet like a Wacom tablet turn this off.

Tolerance
The Tolerance setting (there are two) allows you to change the tolerance by using pressure on a pressure sensitive tablet or by using a stylus wheel on a pressure sensitive tablet. If you aren't using a tablet like a Wacom tablet turn this off.

Limits

Contiguous
Erases all colored areas that match the hotspot color and are touching; only the area inside the circle is erased.
Discontiguous
Erases all colored areas that are similar to hotspot color; only the area inside the circle is erased.

Tolerance

The default Tolerance setting is 50%. The range of settings is from 0-100%. This decides how much the color has to match the color in the hotspot. If you are having trouble erasing with the Background Eraser Tool (E), try different Tolerance settings and you will probably have better luck. The higher the Tolerance setting the more areas will be erased.

How to use the Background Eraser Tool

Make a duplicate of the layer you're going to erase for a back-up by Ctrl>J and hide it by clicking on the eyeball icon. Change any option on the options bar that you need to. Zoom into the area you want to erase.

With your Background Eraser activated, your cursor turns into a circle with a crosshair inside of it. The crosshair is called the hotspot. Do not let the hotspot touch any of your image that you want to keep.

Click and drag on the area that you want to erase, don't let the hotspot touch any area you want to keep. Release your mouse often to erase small parts at a time. Many times you become very involved in erasing and you erase a little too much. When this happens you have to Undo. When you Undo (Ctrl>Z) you undo all of your erasing since the last time you released your mouse.

Magic Eraser Tool (E)

The Magic Eraser Tool (E) is like the Magic Wand Tool (W) and the Eraser Tool (E) combined into one Tool. Using the Magic Wand (W) to make a selection and pressing the delete key is what the Magic Eraser Tool (E) does, but all at one time instead of in 2 steps.

If you are working on a Background layer it is automatically converted to a regular layer when you activate this Tool and your erased areas are transparent (checkerboard).

When working with a regular layer, if your transparency is locked (checkerboard icon in the Layers palette), the area that is erased is filled with the Background color.

Use the Magic Eraser (E) to erase areas where the colors are similar depending on the Tolerance setting you use. The Magic Eraser Tool (E) is the only eraser that can be used to erase the same color from all layers of your image by checking the Sample All Layers box.

Tolerance

The default Tolerance setting is 32. The range of settings is from 0-255. If you choose 0, the Magic Eraser Tool (E) will choose only the color you have clicked on. If you choose 255, the Magic Eraser Tool (E) will select every color in the image. If you are having trouble erasing with the Magic Eraser Tool (E), try different Tolerance settings and you will probably have better luck.

Anti-Alias

Anti-Alias is used to smooth the edges of curved selections so they aren't jagged. I keep Anti-Alias turned on.

Contiguous

Contiguous means that the colors are touching. With the Contiguous box checked, the Magic Eraser Tool (E) will erase all of the color you click on that's touching. If you're trying to erase all of a certain colored stripe on a digital paper you would need to uncheck the Contiguous button.

Sample All Layers

When Sample All Layers is checked the Magic Eraser Tool (E) erases the matching color pixels from all the layers in your image.

How to Use the Magic Eraser

There is no brush setting size for the Magic Eraser Tool (E) so if you want to erase a tiny area, press the Caps Lock Key to turn on the crosshair cursor.

Activate the Magic Eraser Tool (E) and click on an area in the image that you want to erase with the cursor. The Magic Eraser Tool (E) searches for other pixels in the image that match the color of the pixel you clicked on. The areas it erases will depend on the Tolerance setting you entered, if you want contiguous colored pixels, and if you want pixels of the same colors on all layers. Once you click on your image, the Magic Eraser Tool (E) erases the matching pixels. If it's a photograph and depending on the image, you usually need to click your mouse more than once and in several different places to erase what you want.

You will probably have to use the regular Eraser Tool (E) to clean up your images because this Tool usually leaves jagged edges. Using the Defringe feature Enhance>Adjust Color>Defringe Layer is sometimes helpful in cleaning up the edges or halos as they are sometimes called. Try different pixel settings to see what works best for your particular image.

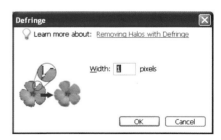

Tools That Paint, Stamp, And Draw

The Brush Tool consists of four different tools:
Brush Tool (B)
Impressionist Brush Tool (B)
Color Replacement Tool (B)
Pencil (N)

The last tool used will be the one that shows on the Toolbar and on the far left of the Option Bar which can be confusing. Once you select the Brush Tool (B), the far left icon on the Options Bar will change to the Brush Tool (B). Hold the Shift key and type the letter B to toggle through all four tools if you've selected "Use Shift Key for Tool Switch" as a Preference option (Ctrl>K or Edit>Preferences). All of these tools can be used together or independent of each other.

The Brush Tool (B) paints soft edges while the Pencil Tool (N) draws hard edges. Anti -Alias which is used to smooth edges is automatically applied to the Brush Tool (B) and cannot be added to the Pencil Tool (N).

Tips for any tools that use brushes:

Tap the bracket keys to adjust the size of your brushes. The left bracket key [makes your brush smaller and the right bracket key] makes your brush larger. Press and hold the bracket keys to adjust the size of your brush quickly.

Shift>[makes your brush softer by 25% every time you click. Shift>] makes your brush 25% harder every time you click.

To paint/draw a straight line hold the Shift key as you drag your mouse.

To paint/draw a straight line between two points click your mouse and then move the cursor and Shift Click.

The Brush Tool (B)

This tool is sometimes called the "Regular" Brush Tool. This brush paints your Foreground color. It does not make selections like the Selection Brush Tool (A) does. Digi-scrappers use brushes like traditional scrappers use rubber stamps. Using a brush as a stamp gives you the option of changing the size of your stamp and the color with the click of your mouse. If you have rubber stamps or doodles that you frequently use, scan them and make them into brushes. Use these brushes all the time without worrying if you have the right color stamp pad or if it's dried up. There are stitching brushes you can use that look just like you stitched your page with your sewing machine. Step by step instructions on how to make your own brushes are in the Cool Things to Do with Patterns and Brushes Section.

Decorative brushes are available as freebies or for purchase at all of the digital scrapbooking websites. Stamping decorative brushes on your scrapbook pages and cards adds a professional look to them. Directions on downloading and installing brushes can be found in the Shopping, Downloading and Installing Section.

Always stamp your brushes on a new blank layer so you can make changes to them later on.

What you can do with the Brush Tool (B):

Paint/Stamp areas of color in the shape of your selected brush with the Foreground color on your image.

Show Selected Brush Presets

Choose a brush from the drop down list by clicking on the downward facing black triangle. Choose one of the Default Brushes or any other brush from the drop down list.

Size

Brushes can be sized from 1-2500 pixels. 2500 px is approximately 8.33 inches on a 300 resolution scrapbook page. Use the bracket keys (left bracket key) [to decrease your brush size or] (right bracket key) to increase your brush size. Clicking on the arrow in the box will allow you to use a slider to adjust your brush size or you can manually enter a size in the box. Brush sizes are entered in pixels only. If your cursor shows as a crosshair you either have the Caps Lock key activated or you have a very small brush.

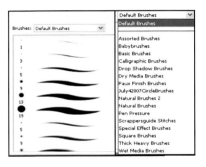

Mode

Choose a Blending Mode here. Normal is the default setting and all Blending Modes are available for use. Blending Modes change how your painted area blends with the other areas of the image. Blending Modes are explained in detail in the Filters and Blending Modes Chapter.

Opacity

The Opacity default is 100% which means you are painting a solid color. Lowering the Opacity by typing in the amount in the box or using the slider will adjust how opaque your painted area is.

Airbrush

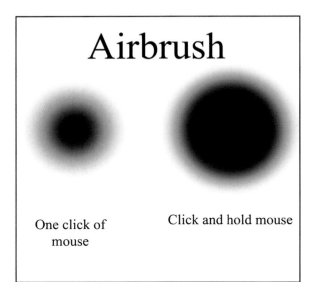

Airbrush

One click of mouse

Click and hold mouse

Click on the airbrush icon and a small thin rectangular outline indicates that it's activated. The Adobe airbrush works just like a regular airbrush or aerosol paint can. Click once and a light layer of paint is "sprayed", hold down your mouse button and the paint gets thicker. In this example the brush size was the same for both painted areas. The airbrush is not available for all brushes.

Tablet Options

To set the brush options you want to control with pen pressure on your Wacom Tablet, check the boxes on this drop down list.

More Options

Fade

Fade options are 0-9999. When set at 0, your brush strokes don't fade. In this example the Fade option was set at 4. I clicked and dragged with my mouse and 4 brush strokes were painted and then stopped until I clicked and dragged again. The first brush stroke is the Foreground color and the next three brush strokes fade out.

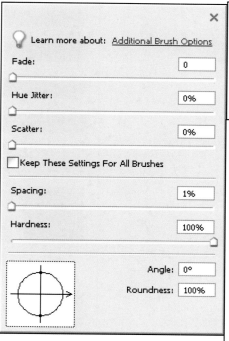

Fade = 4 Spacing = 150%

Foreground Color-Red
Background Color-Blue

Fade 6, Hue Jitter 50%, Spacing 150%

Fade 6, Hue Jitter 100%, Spacing 150%

Hue Jitter

Hue Jitter options are 0-100% and specify how the brush stroke switches from the Foreground and Background Colors.

Scatter

In the example, I clicked and dragged from the left of my scrapbook page to the right side and released exactly the same. The only difference was the scatter setting. Setting scatter at 100% added more brush strokes and scattered them farther from my cursor.

Scatter 100%

Scatter 0%

Spacing

In this example I used the same size brush and clicked and dragged approximately the same distance. The spacing percentage sets the distance between the brush strokes. The Option Bar will show a preview thumbnail of how the stroke will look. The thumbnail examples shown are for 1% and 200% spacing.

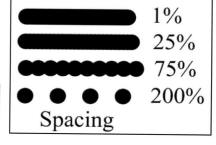

1%
25%
75%
200%
Spacing

Keep These Settings for All Brushes

Normally I leave this box unchecked because I am only making changes for one brush at a time. If you find that you are having trouble setting your brush options check to see if you selected this in error.

Hardness

Hardness softens the edges of the brush. The Option Bar preview changes with the hardness of the brush selected, but the change is not as obvious as when the spacing is changed.

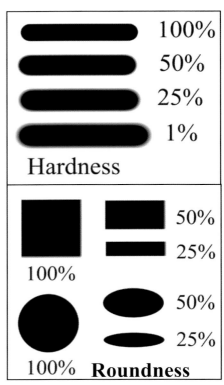

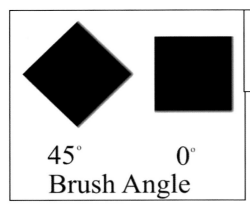

Angle

Rotating the angle of some brushes (not a circle) will change the look of the brush. Enter the angle percentage or drag the arrowhead to the angle you want.

The Option Bar brush thumbnail also changes when you change the brush angle.

Roundness

Roundness changes the ratio between the length and width of the brush. The roundness can be changed by dragging the dot on the angle icon. The Option Bar brush thumbnail changes to reflect the change in the brush roundness.

How to save a brush you modified

If you like a brush that you modified by changing one of the brush options, save it so you don't have to try to remember the settings later on. Go to the brush drop down menu and click on the right facing blue triangle and choose Save Brush. The brush is automatically named but you can choose a different name and then click OK. If you want to rename the brush later, right click on the brush in the drop down menu and choose Rename and type the new name over the old name. Your new brush will show up at the bottom of the list of brushes you are currently working with.

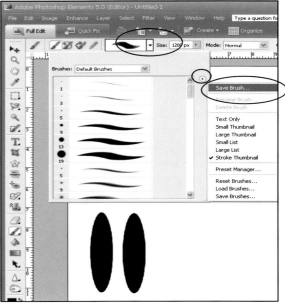

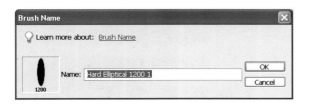

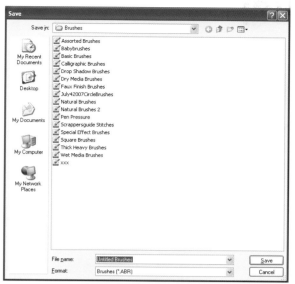

How to delete a brush

Right click on the brush in the drop down menu and choose delete.

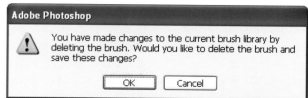

How to Use the Brush Tool (B)

Make a new blank layer before you add any brushwork to an image so that you have the option of changing it if you decide you don't like it as you complete your project.

Click once and release   Click, drag, and release

Since the Brush Tool (B) paints with the Foreground color, check to see if this is set to the color you want to paint with. Choose the brush, brush size, and any options. By placing your brushwork on its own layer, you can change the Opacity and Blending Modes at any time. Click and release to add one brush mark (stamp). Click, drag, and release to add a brush stroke (draw or paint).

The Impressionist Brush Tool (B)

The Impressionist Brush Tool (B) paints on your image to give it a hand painted look. The Impressionist Brush tool (B) is like the Blur Tool (R) after too much coffee. Other ways to achieve the same effect are using the Brush Strokes Filter and The Smudge Tool (R).

What you can do with the Impressionist Brush Tool (B):

Paint an image to look like it was painted by a painter in the Impressionist era.
Use the brush stokes alone or with the original image to make background papers or patterns.

Show Selected Brush Presets

Choose a brush from the drop down list by clicking on the downward facing black triangle. Choose one of the Default Brushes or any other brush from the drop down list.

Size

Brushes can be sized from 1-2500 pixels. If you are going to paint on a photo to turn it into a painting, it's usually better to paint with a small brush. Use the bracket keys [(left bracket key) to decrease your brush size or] (right bracket key) to increase your brush size. Clicking on the arrow in the box will allow you to use a slider to adjust your brush size or you can manually enter a size in the box. Brush sizes are entered in pixels only. If your cursor shows as a crosshair, you either have the Caps Lock key activated or you have a very small brush.

Mode

Choose a Blending Mode here. Normal is the default setting, and not all Blending Modes are available for use with this tool. Blending Modes change how your painted area blends with the other areas of the image. Blending Modes are explained in detail in the Filters and Blending Modes Chapter.

Opacity

The Opacity default is 100% which means you are painting a solid color. Lowering the Opacity by typing in the amount in the box or using the slider will adjust how opaque your painted area is. Duplicating your photo layer and lowering the Opacity on the painted layer lets the detail from the original photo show through the painted layer which can be a nice effect.

More Options

Click on the brush icon next to More Options to display the dialog box.

Style

Style controls the shape of the brush stroke as shown in the example.

Area

Area sets the size of the brush stroke and how many times it strokes every time you click your mouse.

Tolerance

Tolerance is similar to the Tolerance setting on the Magic Wand Tool (W). Tolerance determines how similar the colors have to be to be changed by the tool.

How to use the Impressionist Brush Tool (B)

Always duplicate your image first before using this tool for a few reasons. If you don't like the end result you can delete it, and by varying the Opacity, you can create different results.

In the butterfly example, I duplicated the layer and used the default style setting of tight short and painted on the butterfly only. The effect of the brushwork was more than I wanted, so I lowered the Opacity on the painted layer to 17% so that the original butterfly showed through from the layer below.

In the example of the brush strokes you can see how this tool could be used to make background paper for your scrapbook pages. In this example my Background layer was black as was my Background color. My Foreground color was white. I made a new layer and painted on the new layer. Because I made a new layer, I can adjust the Opacity and Blending Modes in the future.

The Color Replacement Tool (B)

The Color Replacement Tool (B) is used to replace a color in your image with the Foreground color. It does not paint a solid color like the Brush Tool (B) does but a color that has all of the highlights and shadows like the original color did.

What you can do with the Color Replacement Tool (B):
Change the color in your image to the Foreground color like the color of someone's blouse.
Add color to a black and white photo

Brush

It's best to choose a brush that is just slightly larger than the area you want to edit. Click on the black triangle or the black brush to open a brush menu. Adjust the brush size by sliding the slider bar or typing in the size you want. You can also adjust brush sizes by using your Bracket keys.

The left Bracket key [decreases the brush size and the right Bracket key] increases the brush size. To make your brush fuzzy with soft edges, decrease the hardness. Spacing sets the space between the brush marks in a stroke. You can slide the slider or enter a percentage in the box. Roundness-100% is completely round, 0% is a line, you can adjust between 100% and 0%. At 100% roundness you won't notice the

difference in Angle, but if you change the roundness to a lower percentage you can change the Angle. I usually only adjust the brush size with the brackets and don't touch any of this.
Pen Pressure-Requires the use of a pressure sensitive tablet.
Stylus Wheel-Requires the use of a tablet Tool with a thumbwheel.

Mode

Mode choices are Hue, Saturation, Color, and Luminosity. I usually only use the Color mode.

Sampling Options

Sampling: Continuous samples the colors as you drag your mouse
Sampling: Once will replace only the color you clicked on when you began
Sampling: Background Swatch

Limits

Contiguous
Changes all colored areas that match the hotspot color and are touching.
Discontiguous
Changes all colored areas that are similar to hotspot color, only the area inside the circle is changed.

Tolerance

The default Tolerance setting is 30%. The range of settings is from 0-100%. This decides how much the color has to match the color in the hotspot. If you are having trouble, try different Tolerance settings and you will probably have better luck. A higher percentage will replace more colors than a lower setting.

Anti-Alias

Anti-Alias is used to smooth the edges of curved areas so they aren't jagged. I keep Anti-Alias turned on.

How to use the Color Replacement Brush Tool (B)

Duplicate your image by Ctrl>J. Choose a Foreground color that you want to use for your new color. In my example, the flowers were pink and I changed my Foreground color to blue. Click on the color to be replaced and then drag over the areas where you want the color changed. In this example I chose Sample Once, Discontiguous and Tolerance 31%. Because my Tolerance setting was low, I will have to go back over the areas on the edges and replace the color again to fine tune my image. For an additional effect, lower the Opacity on the top layer to have the original color layer show through.

The Pencil Tool (N)

The Pencil Tool (N) is just another brush that paints or draws with hard edges as compared to the Brush Tool (B) that paints with soft edges. The pencil tip is referred to as a brush. Any round brush you use with the Pencil Tool (N) will have jagged edges. Anti –Alias which is used to smooth edges is automatically applied to the Brush Tool (B) and cannot be added to the Pencil Tool (N).

What you can do with the Pencil Tool (N):

Paint/Stamp areas of color in the shape of your selected brush with the Foreground color on your image. Sketch using your mouse or preferably a Wacom Tablet.

Show Selected Brush Presets

Choose a brush from the drop down list by clicking on the downward facing black triangle. Choose one of the Default Brushes or any other brush from the drop down list.

Size

Brushes can be sized from 1-2500 pixels. The default brush size is 1 px. Use the bracket keys. [(left bracket key) to decrease your brush size or] (right bracket key) to increase your brush size. Clicking on the arrow in the box will allow you to use a slider to adjust your brush size or you can manually enter a size in the box. Brush sizes are entered in pixels only. If your cursor shows as a crosshair, you either have the Caps Lock key activated or you have a very small brush.

Mode

Choose a Blending Mode here. Normal is the default setting, and all Blending Modes are available for use. Blending Modes change how your painted area blends with the other areas of the image. Blending Modes are explained in detail in the Filters and Blending Modes Chapter.

Opacity

The Opacity default is 100%, which means you are painting a solid color. Lowering the Opacity by typing in the amount in the box or using the slider will adjust how opaque your painted area is.

Auto Erase

Auto Erase doesn't really mean Auto Erase! This feature paints with the Background color over the Foreground color that's been drawn with the Pencil Tool (N).

With your Background/Foreground colors set at the defaults of black and white, try this out yourself. In this example the background is white with a blue rectangle. A black (foreground color) line has been drawn with the Pencil Tool (N) on the layer above the rectangle. Switching to Auto Erase and dragging over the black line, causes the black line to turn white (background color). If the blue rectangle wasn't on the white background it would work fine. I don't use this feature.

How to Use the Pencil Tool (N)

Make a new blank layer before you add any brushwork to an image so that you have the option of changing it if you decide you don't like it as you complete your project.

The Pencil Tool (N) paints with the Foreground color, verify you have the correct color. Choose the brush, brush size, and any options. By placing your brushwork on its own layer, you can change the Opacity and

Blending Modes at any time. Click and release to add one brush mark (stamp). Click, drag, and release to add a brush stroke (draw or paint).

Tools To Fill Layers Or Selections With Color

The Paint Bucket Tool (K)

The Paint Bucket Tool (K) should probably be called the Magic Fill Tool. This tool fills a layer or selection with the foreground color or pattern by searching for matching color wherever you click, depending on the options you've chosen. The cursor for the Paint Bucket Tool (K) is an overflowing paint bucket can. Using the Paint Bucket Tool (K) is a quick way to fill layers or selections on your scrapbook pages.

What you can do with the Paint Bucket Tool (K):
Fill a layer or selection with your Foreground color or a pattern that you've chosen.

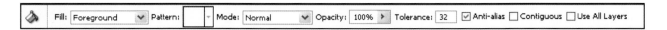

Fill
Foreground fills with your Foreground color located in the foreground color box at the bottom of the Toolbar. Pattern fills with a pattern that you choose from the pattern drop down list.

Pattern
Click on the dropdown list and your default patterns are probably displayed. You must have Pattern selected as a "Fill" to enable you to click on the drop down arrow. Click on the side arrow to change the size of the pattern thumbnails, reset, load, save or replace patterns, and display other pattern sets available to use.

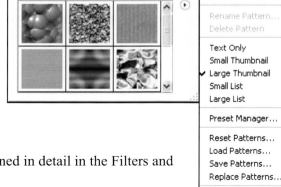

Mode
Choose a Blending Mode here. Blending modes are explained in detail in the Filters and Blending Modes Chapter.

Opacity
The Opacity default is 100%, which means you are filling with a solid color or pattern. Lower the Opacity by typing in the amount in the box or using the slider to make your fill more transparent.

Tolerance
The default Tolerance setting is 32. The range of settings is from 0-255. If you choose 0, the Paint Bucket Tool (K) will choose only the color you have clicked on to fill. If you choose 255, the Paint Bucket Tool (K) will select every color in the image to fill. If you are having trouble filling an area with color or a pattern with the Paint Bucket Tool (K), try different Tolerance settings and you will probably have better luck.

Anti-Alias

Anti-Alias is used to smooth the edges of curved areas that you fill so they aren't jagged. I keep Anti-Alias turned on.

Contiguous

Contiguous means that the colors are touching. With the Contiguous box checked, the Paint Bucket Tool (K) will select all of the colors you click on that are touching and fill them. If you're trying to fill all of a certain colored stripe on a digital paper you would need to uncheck the Contiguous button because they're not touching.

Use All Layers

When Use All Layers is checked, the Paint Bucket Tool (K) fills the matching color pixels from all the layers in your image. This might be helpful if you decided you wanted to change the color of several elements on your scrapbook page.

How to Use the Paint Bucket Tool (K)

Click inside a selection or layer on a color that you want to fill with your Foreground color or pattern.
If you are not happy with how the Paint Bucket Tool (K) filled the areas, adjust the setting on the Option Bar.

The Gradient Tool (G)

The Gradient Tool (G) fills a selection or layer with a color that fades into another color or into a transparency. Gradients can be used to make your own papers or elements. A Gradient setting of Foreground to Transparency with an Adjustment Layer can be used to make montages.

The default setting for the Gradient Tool (G) is Foreground to Background. When you click and drag your mouse with the default selected, you'll be filling with the Foreground color first and fading into the Background color. The point in which the foreground ends and the background begins is at the halfway point. Changing these options is easy.

Applying a filter to a Gradient can soften its look or change the look entirely.

What you can do with the Gradient Tool (G):

Fill a layer, selection, or pattern with a gradient to make a digital paper.
Fill a doodle, shape, or element with a gradient to blend the colors.
Fade images into each other when making a montage – See Montage Section
Fill the sky in a photo with a Gradient to simulate a blue sky or a beautiful sunset.

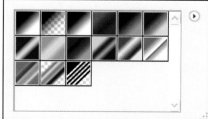

Choose Gradient

Click on the drop down list and you have a choice of the 15 default gradients. Hover your mouse over the thumbnail and you can see the Gradient name. The checkerboard indicates that the Gradient fades to a transparency. Click on the side arrow to change the size of the gradient thumbnails, reset, load, save or replace gradients, and display other gradient sets available to use.

Edit Gradient

This box looks way too complicated at first but it's really not. In this box you can choose a gradient and completely customize it for your own needs. Once you've made your changes here, click OK and then drag your gradient. The Alt key toggles the Cancel/Reset key. Load and Save are also available from the Gradient drop down list. When you make a new Gradient, click the New button and your Gradient is added to the thumbnails. If you want to remove it, right click on the thumbnail and choose Delete.

Save-To Save a Gradient that you made, which would be helpful if you are using it for a logo or plan on using it several times, name the Gradient and click on the Save button. You will be saving it in the Gradient Folder located in the Presets Folder, which is in the Adobe Photoshop Elements Program File. I also save mine in a file called PSE Gradients because if I have to reload my program they will probably be lost. Restart the program and you can load the Gradient you saved. Name-The Gradient shown is the Spectrum Gradient and its thumbnail is circled. Because I moved the blue color stop slightly my Gradient Name is now changed to Custom. To rename it, double click in the field and type a new name.

Stops-To change where the opacity changes and where each color starts and stops, drag one of the stops that looks like a tiny ink bottle or type in the Location percentage. To enter a location percentage, drag the Opacity stop or type the percentage in the box. To adjust the Opacity in my example, click on one of the Opacity stops and the Opacity area is no longer grayed out; type the percentage number in the box. If you are planning on saving an image with a transparency remember to save it in the right file format (PNG or PSD) because a JPEG will fill your transparency with white.

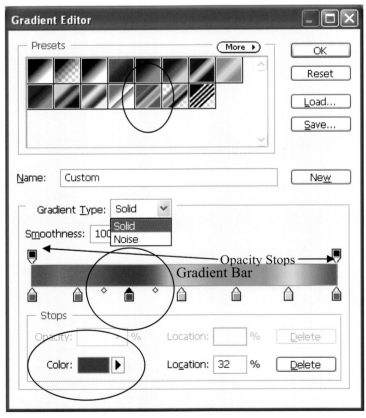

The Opacity stops are located on the top of the Gradient Bar and the Color Stops are located under the Gradient Bar. Once you move one of the stops, the small black diamonds appear to mark the exact spot the color/opacity starts and stops. These can be dragged to make changes. In my example I moved the blue color stop so the diamonds mark the start and stop of the blue in the gradient. To delete the blue color from the Gradient, click on the Delete button or drag the color stop down from the Gradient Bar and it's all gone. To change a color, double click inside the color on the color stop or in the color box and the Adobe Color Picker is activated, choose a color and click OK. To use a color from your image in the Gradient, hover over the Gradient Bar and your cursor becomes the Eyedropper Tool. Click on the color stop you want to change, and then go to your image and click and the color stop is changed to the color from your image.

To add an additional Opacity, stop click just above the Gradient Bar. To add an additional Color stop, click just below the Gradient Bar and a new stop will be added which is your foreground color, double click in the stop to change it.

The Gradient Type can be changed to Solid or Noise and when you choose noise, different options are displayed. At the end of this section I have some examples of Solid and Noise Gradients. Smoothness sets the transition smoothness between the colors.

Mode

Choose a Blending Mode here. Blending modes are explained in detail in the Filters and Blending Modes Chapter.

Opacity

The Opacity default is 100% which means you are filling with a solid color gradient. Lower the Opacity by typing in the amount in the box or using the slider to make your fill more transparent.

Reverse

This reverses the colors in your gradient. By checking this box your starting color will become your ending color and your ending color will become your starting color.

Dither

I keep this box checked to make the colors blend together better.

Transparency

This box must be checked if you have any transparency in your Gradient or it won't work correctly. I keep it checked all the time.

Types of Gradients

With Photoshop Elements you can draw 5 different types of gradients:

Linear
Radial
Angle
Reflected
Diamond

Once you choose one of these Gradients, it will remain your default Gradient until you switch to another one.

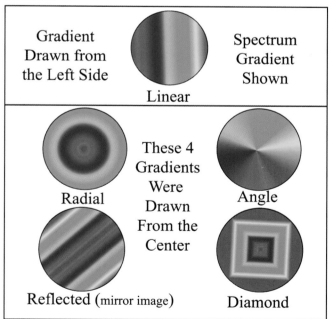

Gradients will look different depending on the settings you use and the direction from which you draw the gradient.

The Gradients in this example were drawn in a selection made by the Elliptical Marquee Tool (M).

How to use the Gradient Tool (G):

Open a new image and make a new layer or selection. It's a good idea to put your Gradient on its own layer so you can edit it in the future. Choose your gradient and settings. Click and drag your mouse and when you release your mouse the Gradient is drawn. The whole layer or selection will be filled with the Gradient. Depending on how far you click and drag at a time will make a difference on how the Gradient looks. The farther you drag your mouse (even off the edge of your page), the smoother your gradient will be drawn.

Using the Foreground to Background Gradient with red as my Foreground color and blue as my Background color, the image on the left was drawn by clicking in the bottom left corner and dragging all the way across to the upper right corner. The image in the center was drawn with everything exactly the same, except that my first click was a couple of inches from the bottom left corner and released about 2 inches later. Dragging from the center produces the Gradient on the right.

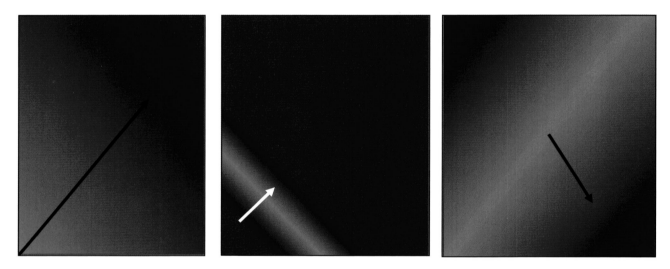

Adding a Gradient to a shape drawn with the Custom Shape Tool (U) dresses it up rather than just filling the shape in a solid color. To do this, draw your shape and choose your Gradient. In all of these examples I used Foreground to Background Gradient. Pick your Foreground and Background color at the box located at the bottom of the Tool Bar. Ctrl Click on the Shape Layer thumbnail so that you have a selection around the shape. Make a new Layer with the New Layer icon in the Layers Palette. Click and drag your Gradient. Undo if you don't like it, and try it again. If you make a mistake and don't want to wait for the computer to finish the Gradient, press the Esc key.

Solid vs Noise Gradients

This is the Spectrum Gradient in all examples drawn from the center outward to the lower right corner with the Radial Gradient setting selected. No other changes have been made, except what's noted below.

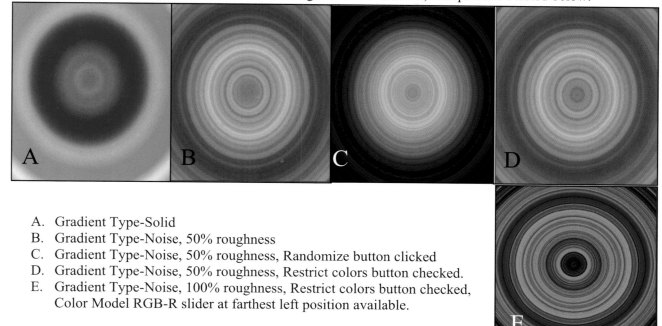

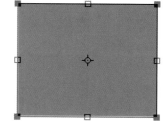

A. Gradient Type-Solid
B. Gradient Type-Noise, 50% roughness
C. Gradient Type-Noise, 50% roughness, Randomize button clicked
D. Gradient Type-Noise, 50% roughness, Restrict colors button checked.
E. Gradient Type-Noise, 100% roughness, Restrict colors button checked, Color Model RGB-R slider at farthest left position available.

Tools That Make Shapes

The Shape Tool (U) is located third from the bottom on the Toolbar. The last tool used will be the one that shows on the Toolbar and on the far left of the Option Bar, which can be confusing. Once you select the Shape Tool (U), the far left icon on the Options Bar will change to the Shape Tool (U). Hold the Shift key and type the letter U to toggle through all seven tools if you've selected "Use Shift Key for Tool Switch" as a Preference option (Ctrl>K or Edit>Preferences). All of these tools can be used together or independent of each other.

All Shape Tools share the same U shortcut, which can be activated by typing the letter U unless you are using the Type Tool (T).

Shape Selection Tool (U)

The Shape Selection Tool (U) is used to select and move shapes without having to switch to the Move Tool (V), which saves time. If the Shape has been Simplified (rasterized), the Shape Selection Tool (U) will no longer work and you'll have to use the Move Tool (V) instead.

Show Bounding Box

The Bounding Box marks the edges of the shape and the center as soon as you click on the shape. When this box is not checked, there will still be a slight outline around the shape.

Combine

To combine two or more shapes on <u>one</u> layer, click on the Combine button. This is similar to linking the shapes, except that you can't unlink them unless you Undo (Ctrl>Z)

How to Use the Shape Selection Tool

Activate the Shape Selection Tool (U) and click and drag the shape to move it to a different location. Dragging one of the sizing handles on the sides or corners will transform the shape and the Transform Option Bar will be displayed.
Shape Selection Tool (U)
When there is more than one shape on a layer, the Shape Selection Tool (U) must be used to move <u>one</u> of the shapes. The Move Tool (V) will move all of the Shapes on the layer together as if they are linked.

Shape Tools (U)

The six Shape Tools (U) are the Rectangle Tool (U), the Rounded Rectangle Tool (U), the Ellipse Tool (U), the Polygon Tool (U), the Line Tool (U), and the Custom Shape Tool (U).

What can you do with the Shape Tools (U):

Add shapes to your scrapbook pages and cards like you would add die cuts to a traditional scrapbook page.
Use shapes to make templates for your photos (Group with Previous) and scrapbook papers.
Create logos and other shapes by combining shapes.
Create web buttons for web pages.
Use shapes to make custom patterns.

Shared Shape Tool Options:

All of the options for these tools are essentially the same, except for a few that are specific to their tool like Radius for the Rounded Rectangle Tool. Any tool specific option will be listed under the section pertaining to that tool.

Unconstrained

Unconstrained means however you drag out the shape, the Shape Tool (U) will draw it. If you drag a heart out that is tall and skinny, the Shape Tool (U) will draw a tall and skinny heart. If you want to drag from the center also use the setting From Center.

```
┌─ Custom Shape Options ──────────────┐
│ ○ Unconstrained                      │
│ ◉ Defined Proportions                │
│ ○ Defined Size                       │
│ ○ Fixed Size    W: [      ]  H: [      ] │
│ □ From Center                        │
└──────────────────────────────────────┘
```

Square/Circle

This option draws a square or circle instead of a rectangle or oval depending on the tool selected. It's usually faster to just draw with your mouse while holding the Shift key.

Defined Proportions

Defined Proportions will keep the shape in the proportions of the example. When you drag out a heart, it will have the same proportions as the heart in the example. From Center can also be selected with Defined Proportions

Defined Size

Defined Size will crop the photo in the size that the designer created it. You won't know what size that is until you release your mouse. If you don't like the size, you can use the sizing handles. From Center can be selected with Defined Size.

Fixed Size

Fixed Size crops to the exact dimensions you enter. If you enter 2 inches wide by 2 inches high and you pick a rectangle, the Shape Tool (U) will draw a 2 inch square. Size can be entered as inches, centimeters, or pixels. From Center can also be selected with Fixed Size.

From Center

From Center will draw the shape outward from the center. If you want to draw a daisy into a shape, start at the daisy center and draw outward to get it perfectly centered in the shape. From center can be selected with all the other options too.

Create a New Shape Layer

Creates a new shape on its own layer. This option will usually be selected. By default your first shape layer is named Shape 1.

Add to a Shape Area

Adds more shapes to an existing shape layer. All shapes will be on the same layer; the layer thumbnail will reflect this also. Holding the Shift key will also do the same thing.

Subtract from a Shape Area

To subtract from a shape, click on this box and drag over the shape you want to subtract from. This is a little bit confusing because the old shape boundary shows on your screen and layer thumbnail as does the boundary of the shape you used to subtract with. These lines do not print.

Intersect Shape Areas

The area that overlaps between two shapes is left over. Both of the layer boundaries show on your screen and layer thumbnail but will not print.

Exclude Overlapping Shape Areas

This is the opposite of intersect shape areas. The areas that do not intersect are filled with color. The layer boundaries show on your screen and layer thumbnail, but will not print.

Color

The Foreground color is the default color for a new shape. With your shape layer active, changing the Color box also changes the color of the shape. Click inside on the drop down list to choose a color or click inside the color to activate the Adobe Color Picker.

If you've Simplified the shape, you can no longer change the color by changing the Color box. Ctrl Click to make a selection border (marching ants) around the shape and then fill the selection by Alt>Backspace the shortcut for fill with Foreground color.

Style

Automatically add a Layer Style without having to go to the
Artwork and Effects palette. The default is No Layer Style. The
option to remove a Layer Style is also here.

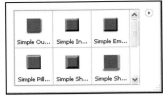

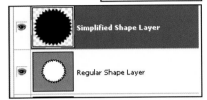

Simplify

Shapes are raster images. In simple terms, a raster image has sharp edges no matter how
you size them. If you Simplify (rasterize), your shape layer is turned into a pixel based
shape. When you size a pixel based shape, your edges will no longer be sharp. Simplify a
shape layer only when you have to and when you won't need to change the size.

If you can't remember if you Simplified your shape layer, look at the layer
in the Layers palette. A Simplified shape layer will have a transparent
background on the layer thumbnail, which is indicated by a checkerboard as
shown in the example. The layer name does not change when the shape is
simplified. The layers were renamed only for illustration purposes.

To move a Simplified shape, you will have to activate the Move Tool (V) as the Shape Selection Tool (U)
only works on shapes that have not been Simplified.

Once you've Simplified a shape, you can no longer change the color by activating the layer and changing the
Foreground color.

Rectangle Tool (U)

The Rectangle Tool (U) is used to draw rectangular shapes.

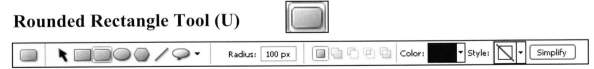

Snap to Pixels

Snap to Pixels moves your rectangle to the edge of a pixel so that you get a sharper shape. Keep this on when
using this tool.

All other options for this tool are explained under Shared Shape Tool Options.

Rounded Rectangle Tool (U)

Snap to Pixels

Snap to Pixels moves your rectangle to the edge of a pixel so that you get a sharper shape. Keep this on when
using this tool.

Radius

The default setting is 10 px, and the options available are from 0-1000 px. A 0 px radius is a straight edged
rectangle. Holding the Shift key to draw a square and setting the radius at 1000 will draw a circle.

All other options for this tool are explained under Shared Shape Tool Options.

Ellipse Tool (U)

To draw a circle, hold the Shift key when dragging out your shape with the mouse.

All other options for this tool are explained under Shared Shape Tool Options.

Polygon Tool (U)

The Polygon Tool (U) draws from the center outward by default.

Sides

Choose between 3 and 100 sides to make your polygon.

Radius

Specifies the distance from the center of the polygon to the furthest points.

Smooth Corners

To round your corners, choose this option. On some polygons smoothing the corners will turn it into a circle.

Star

To change a polygon into a star by inverting the angles, choose this option.

Indent Sides By:

This option is available only if you are drawing a star. The default setting is 50%. Using a larger percentage will make the star thinner.

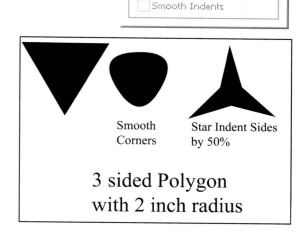

Smooth Corners   Star Indent Sides by 50%

3 sided Polygon with 2 inch radius

Smooth Indents

This option is available only if you are drawing a star. To curve the inside edges of your star, choose this option.

All other options for this tool are explained under Shared Shape Tool Options.

Line Tool (U)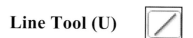

To draw lines with or without arrowheads use the Line Tool (U)

Weight

Set a pixel width for your line. The default is 1 px, but any amount between 1 px and 1000 px can be entered.

Arrowheads

Start & End-An arrowhead is added at the beginning or end of the line or both.

Width & Length-The default setting for Width is 500% and the default setting for length is 1000%. Any amount between 10% and 1000% can be entered to set the Arrowheads size, which is a percentage of the line width.

Concavity-The default setting is 0% but a percentage between -50% and +50% can be entered to add a curve to the Arrowhead.

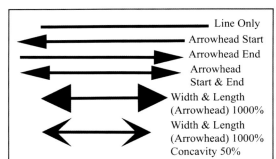

All other options for this tool are explained under Shared Shape Tool Options.

Custom Shape Tool (U)

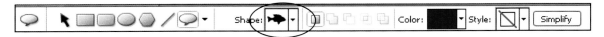

Shape

Click on the drop down triangle to the right of Shape. This is the library of shapes that were last used. If you don't see the library you want, click on the small circle with a triangle in it at the top of the current library. It will display all of the libraries that are available. Any shapes that you loaded in from another source will also show up here. Notice the line that says All Elements Shapes. It means only the shapes that came preloaded. Sports_Shapes was installed by me, and does not show up in the All Elements Shapes Library.

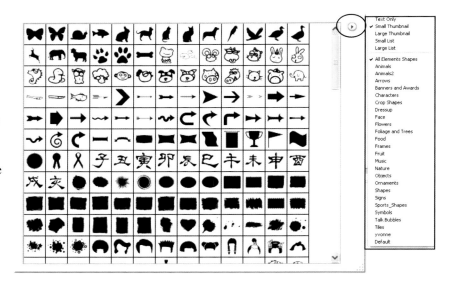

Hover over each individual shape square and a description will pop up. Double click a shape to accept it and the library box will close

All other options for this tool are explained under Shared Shape Tool Options.

How to use the Shape Tools (U):

Activate the Shape Tool (U) by typing the letter U, or clicking on it on the Toolbar. Choose the shape, size option, color, and layer style preference. Click and drag the shape and then release your mouse. Your shape will be drawn on its own layer.

To draw several shapes exactly the same, switch to the Shape Selection Tool (U) or the Move Tool (V) and hold the Alt key. Click, drag, and release your mouse to add each additional shape. To constrain the shapes to a straight line, you will have to use the Move Tool (V) and hold the Shift key at the same time you're holding the Alt key. Use the Align and Distribute options on the Move Tool (V) to space them evenly to make a border.

How to make a shape look like it was punched:

Make 2 layers filled with different colors so the effect is obvious. Draw your shape with one of the Shape Tools (U) so that it is the top layer (3rd layer). Ctrl Click on the shape layer thumbnail so that the shape is surrounded by marching ants. Go to the middle layer and press the Delete key so that the shape selection is deleted from that layer. Delete the shape layer. Add a drop shadow to the top layer with the shape layer cut out of it.

More Touch Up Tools

The Blur Tool (R)

The Blur Tool (R) is nested along with the Sharpen and Smudge Tool. Located second from the bottom on the Toolbar, all three tools share the same (R) shortcut. The last tool you used will be the one that shows on the Toolbar and on the far left of the Option Bar, which can be confusing. Once you select the Blur Tool (R), the far left icon on the Options Bar will change to the Blur Tool (R). Hold the Shift key and type the letter R to toggle through all three tools if you've selected "Use Shift Key for Tool Switch" as a Preference option (Ctrl K or Edit>Preferences).

The Blur Tool (R) blurs images out of focus, and is the opposite of the Sharpen Tool (R), which brings images into focus. Depending on how big of an area you want to blur, using one of the Blur Filters may work better for you.

What you can do with the Blur Tool (R):

Blur a distracting or unattractive background to bring attention to the focal point of your photo.
Soften small flaws like wrinkles.
Soften rough edges of a selection that you cut and pasted onto another image.

Brush Preset Menu

Click the drop down arrow and choose a brush. There are many sets of brushes that come installed with Photoshop Elements and some you can install yourself. A soft (fuzzy) brush will give you a softer blurred effect. Double click on the brush that you want to use.

Size

Brush size ranges from .01 to 2500 pixels. .01 pixels is smaller than you'll ever use and 2500 pixels is 8.33 inches on your scrapbook page. To choose a brush size, type the amount in the option box, use the brush size slider, or best yet, use the Bracket keys to size your brushes (in any tool). [(left bracket key) makes your brush smaller, and] (right bracket key) makes your brush bigger. Holding down the Bracket key changes the size of the brush quickly.

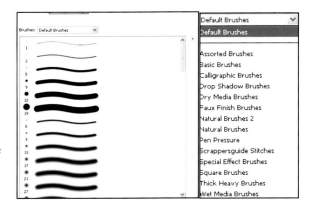

Mode

Choose a Blending Mode here. Normal is the default setting; Darken, Lighten, Hue, Saturation, Color, and Luminosity are your choices. Blending Modes change how your blurred area blends with the other areas of the image. Blending modes are explained in detail in the Filters and Blending Modes Chapter.

Strength

Set the amount of blur you want with each stroke. A higher setting blurs more than a lower setting. The default Strength setting is 50%.

Sample All Layers

When Sample All Layers is checked, the Blur Tool (R) uses all of the colors to blur the image not just the active layer. The active layer is the only layer that will be blurred if this is selected.

How to Use the Blur Tool (R)

Duplicate (Ctrl>J) the layer that you are going to blur. In my example, the left image is the original. Click and drag your mouse over the area that you want to blur. In my example on the right, I dragged across the flowers. It may take a little while for the blur effect to show on your screen.

To contain the blur to a specific area like the flowers in my example, make a selection first with one of the selection tools. If you are not happy with how the Blur Tool works try a Blur Filter from the Filter drop down menu.

The Sharpen Tool (R)

The Sharpen Tool (R) is nested along with the Blur and Smudge Tools. Located second from the bottom on the Toolbar, all three tools share the same (R) shortcut. The last tool you used will be the one that shows on the Toolbar and on the far left of the Option Bar, which can be confusing. Hold the Shift key and type the letter R to toggle through all three tools if you've selected "Use Shift Key for Tool Switch" as a Preference option (Ctrl K or Edit>Preferences).

Once you select the Sharpen Tool (R), the far left icon on the Options Bar will change to the Sharpen Tool (R). The Sharpen Tool (R) is the opposite of the Blur Tool (R). Instead of blurring images out of focus, it brings them into focus much like a camera lens.

To sharpen a selection or all of an image in Standard Edit mode, go to Enhance and choose Auto Sharpen, Adjust Sharpness, or Unsharp Mask. In Quick Fix, you can choose Auto sharpen or use a slider to adjust the amount of sharpening you want to apply.

Sharpening an image too much will make your photo appear grainy.

What you can do with the Sharpen Tool (R):

Increase the focus of your image by sharpening areas of the image that you click and/or drag over.

Brush Preset Menu

Click the drop down arrow and choose a brush. There are many sets of brushes that come installed with Photoshop Elements and some you can install yourself. To sharpen I use a round brush (hard or soft). A soft (fuzzy) brush will give you a softer sharpened effect. Double click on the brush that you want to select.

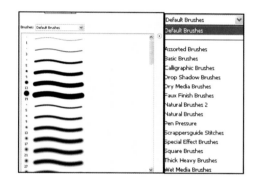

Size

Brush size ranges from .01 to 2500 pixels. .01 pixels is smaller than you'll ever use and 2500 pixels is 8.33 inches on your scrapbook page. To choose a brush size, type the amount in the option box, use the brush size slider, or best yet use the Bracket keys to size your brushes (in any tool). [makes your brush smaller, and] makes your brush bigger. Holding down the Bracket key changes the size of the brush quickly.

Mode

Choose a Blending Mode here. Normal is the default setting; Darken, Lighten, Hue, Saturation, Color, and Luminosity are your choices. Blending Modes change how your blurred area blends with the other areas of the image. Blending modes are explained in detail in the Filters and Blending Modes Chapter.

Strength

Set the amount of sharpening you want with each stroke. A higher setting sharpens more than a lower setting. The default Strength setting is 50%. Start at a lower strength of 25% or less, and if you don't achieve the results you want gradually adjust the setting higher so you don't over sharpen and get a grainy look.

Sample All Layers

When Sample All Layers is checked the Sharpen Tool (R) uses all of the colors to sharpen the image not just the active layer. The active layer is the only layer that will be sharpened if this is selected.

How to Use the Sharpen Tool (R)

Duplicate (Ctrl>J) the layer that you are going to sharpen. Click and drag your mouse over the area that you want to sharpen. If you want to sharpen an area like an eye, make the size of your brush the same size as the eye and click without dragging. It may take a little while for the sharpen effect to show on your screen but be careful you don't over sharpen, like the example of the butterfly on the right.

To contain the sharpening to a specific area, make a selection first with one of the selection tools. If you are not happy with how the Sharpen Tool (R) works, try one of the Sharpening commands in the Enhance Menu.

The Smudge Tool (R)

The Smudge Tool (R) is nested along with the Blur and Sharpen Tools. Located in the second from the bottom spot on the Toolbar, all three tools share the same (R) shortcut. The last tool you used will be the one that shows on the Toolbar and on the far left of the Option Bar, which can be confusing. Hold the Shift key and type the letter R to toggle through all three tools if you've selected "Use Shift Key for Tool Switch" as a Preference option (Ctrl K or Edit>Preferences).

Once you select the Smudge Tool (R), the far left icon on the Options Bar will change to the Smudge Tool (R). The Smudge Tool (R) mixes colors as you drag your cursor across the image. It's almost as if the image was still wet from being printed and you dragged your finger across it. Using the Smudge Tool (R) is similar to using the Liquify Filter.

What you can do with the Smudge Tool (R):

Make subtle changes in an image, like adding a smile.
Make a finger painting out of an image to use for a background.

Brush Preset Menu

Click the drop down arrow and choose a brush. There are many sets of brushes that come installed with Photoshop Elements, and some you can install yourself. To smudge I use a round brush (hard or soft). A soft (fuzzy) brush will give you a softer effect. Double click on the brush that you want to select.

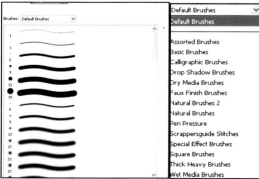

Size

Brush size ranges from .01 to 2500 pixels. .01 pixels is smaller than you'll ever use, and 2500 pixels is 8.33 inches on your scrapbook page. To choose a brush size, type the amount in the option box, use the brush size slider, or best yet use the Bracket keys to size your brushes (in any tool). [makes your brush smaller, and] makes your brush bigger. Holding down the Bracket key changes the size of the brush quickly.

Mode

Choose a Blending Mode here. Normal is the default setting; Darken, Lighten, Hue, Saturation, Color, and Luminosity are your choices. Blending Modes change how your blurred area blends with the other areas of the image. Blending Modes are explained in detail in the Filters and Blending Modes Chapter.

Strength

Set the amount of smudging you want with each stroke. A higher strength setting blends more than a lower setting will. The default Strength setting is 50%.

Sample All Layers

When checked, color from all visible layers will be used to smudge. If not checked, only colors from the active layer will be used to smudge. The active layer is the only layer that will be smudged if this is selected.

Finger Painting

When checked, your Foreground color is smeared at the very beginning of the stroke. If it's not checked, only colors from the active layer are used. To see how this works, set your Foreground color to a completely different color than the image that you want to smear, and try it.

To toggle to the Finger Painting Option press the Alt key.

How to Use the Smudge Tool (R)

Duplicate (Ctrl>J) the layer that you are going to smudge. Click and drag your mouse over the area that you want to smudge. Depending on your computer, it may take a little while for the smudging to show on your screen.

To contain the smudging to a specific area, make a selection first with one of the selection tools. If you are not happy with how the Smudge Tool (R) works, try the Liquify Filter.

The Smudge Tool (R) only works on areas with different colors, so nothing will happen if you are trying to smudge an area of just one color until you drag over another color.

The Sponge Tool (O)

The Sponge Tool (O) is nested along with the Dodge and Burn Tools. Located in the bottom spot on the Toolbar, all three tools share the same (O) shortcut. The last tool you used will be the one that shows on the Toolbar and on the far left of the Option Bar, which can be confusing. Once you select the Sponge Tool (O), the far left icon on the Options Bar will change to the Sponge Tool (O). Hold the Shift key and type the letter O to toggle through all three tools if you've selected "Use Shift Key for Tool Switch" as a Preference option (Ctrl K or Edit>Preferences).

The Sponge Tool (O) adds or removes color from a color image, and increases or decreases the contrast for grayscale images. It's best to use this tool for small areas. If you want to change large areas, it would be easier to use Enhance>Adjust Hue/Saturation (Ctrl U) for color images and Enhance>Adjust Lighting> Brightness/Contrast for grayscale images.

What you can do with the Sponge Tool (O):

Draw attention to an area on an image by removing or adding color.

Brush Preset Menu

Click the drop down arrow and choose a brush. There are many sets of brushes that come installed with Photoshop Elements and some you can install yourself. To smudge, I use a round brush (hard or soft). A soft (fuzzy) brush will give you a softer effect. Double click on the brush that you want to select.

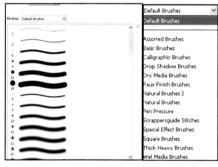

Size

Brush size ranges from .01 to 2500 pixels. .01 pixels is smaller than you'll ever use and 2500 pixels is 8.33 inches on your scrapbook page. To choose a brush size, type the amount in the option box, use the brush size slider, or best yet use the Bracket keys to size your brushes (in any tool). [(left bracket key) makes your brush smaller, and] (right bracket key) makes your brush bigger. Holding down the Bracket key changes the size of the brush quickly.

Mode

Desaturate is the default setting and removes color in a color image like a sponge soaking up water. The Sponge Tool (O) decreases the contrast in a grayscale image.

Saturate adds color to a color image and increases the contrast in a grayscale image.

Flow

The default setting for Flow is 50%. Adjust this slider higher to increase the rate of saturation/desaturation (depending on mode selected). Enter a percentage amount in the text box or use the slider to adjust the flow.

How to Use the Sponge Tool (O)

Duplicate (Ctrl>J) your layer so you have a copy for safe keeping in case you're not happy with your results. Click and drag over an area that you want to adjust the color.

In this example, the original image is on the left. I decreased the saturation in the background and increased the saturation on the butterfly.

To contain the Sponge Tool (O) to the butterfly, I made a selection with the Magnetic Lasso Tool (L) first.

The Dodge Tool (O)

The Dodge Tool (O) is nested along with the Sponge and Burn Tools. Located in the bottom spot on the Toolbar, all three tools share the same (O) shortcut. The last tool you used will be the one that shows on the Toolbar and on the far left of the Option Bar, which can be confusing. Once you select the Dodge Tool (O), the far left icon on the Options Bar will change to the Dodge Tool (O). Hold the Shift key and type the letter O to toggle through all three tools if you've selected "Use Shift Key for Tool Switch" as a Preference option (Ctrl K or Edit>Preferences).

The Dodge Tool (O) lightens areas of an image and is the opposite of the Burn Tool (O). It's best to use this tool for small areas. If you want to lighten large areas, it would be easier to use Enhance>Adjust Lighting> Shadows/Highlights.

What you can do with the Dodge Tool (O):

Lighten up small dark areas of an image, like shadows.
Bleach your teeth in a photo without a trip to the dentist, or whiten the eyes of a jaundiced new born baby for a birth announcement.

Brush Preset Menu

Click the drop down arrow and choose a brush. There are many sets of brushes that come installed with Photoshop Elements and some you can install yourself. To use the dodge tool, I use a round soft brush. Double click on the brush that you want to select.

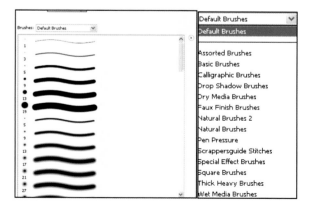

Size

Brush size ranges from .01 to 2500 pixels. .01 pixels is smaller than you'll ever use, and 2500 pixels is 8.33 inches on your scrapbook page. To choose a brush size, type the amount in the option box, use the brush size slider, or best yet use the Bracket keys to size your brushes (in any tool). [(left bracket key) makes your brush smaller, and] (right bracket key) makes your brush bigger. Holding down the Bracket key changes the size of the brush quickly.

Range

Choose one of the following settings to adjust different areas of your image:

Shadows to adjust the dark colors in the image.
Midtones is the default setting, and is used to adjust the middle tones of color

Highlights to adjust the light colors in an image

Exposure

The default setting for exposure is 50%. It's better to start with a lower exposure setting and paint over an area several times.

How to Use the Dodge Tool (O)

Duplicate your layer (Ctrl>J) so you have a copy for safe keeping in case you're not happy with your results. Click and drag over an area that you want to lighten. In this example, the original image is on the left. I lightened the background around the butterfly.

Reduce the opacity of the layer you are using the Dodge Tool on, so the duplicate layer shows through and see if you like the effect.

To contain the Dodge Tool (O) to the butterfly, I made a selection with the Magnetic Lasso Tool (L) first.

The Burn Tool (O)

The Burn Tool (O) is nested along with the Sponge and Dodge Tools. Located in the bottom spot on the Toolbar, all three tools share the same (O) shortcut. The last tool you used will be the one that shows on the Toolbar and on the far left of the Option Bar, which can be confusing. Once you select the Burn Tool (O) the far left icon on the Options Bar will change to the Burn Tool (O). Hold the Shift key and type the letter O to toggle through all three tools if you've selected "Use Shift Key for Tool Switch" as a Preference option (Ctrl K or Edit>Preferences).

What you can do with the Burn Tool (O):

Lighten up areas of an image that are too dark.
Burn the edge of elements to give an aged look.

The Burn Tool (O) darkens areas of an image to bring out detail, as long as it's there to begin with. The Burn Tool (O) is the opposite of the Dodge Tool (O). It's best to use this tool for small areas. If you want to darken large areas, it would be easier to use Enhance>Adjust Lighting> Shadows/Highlights.

Brush Preset Menu

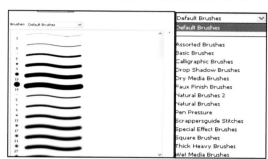

Click the drop down arrow and choose a brush. There are many sets of brushes that come installed with Photoshop Elements, and some you can install yourself. To use the Burn Tool (O), I use a round soft brush. Double click on the brush that you want to select.

Size

Brush size ranges from .01 to 2500 pixels. .01 pixels is smaller than you'll ever use and 2500 pixels is 8.33 inches on your scrapbook page. To choose a brush size, type the amount in the option box, use the brush size slider, or best yet use the Bracket keys to size your brushes (in any tool). [(left bracket key) makes your brush smaller, and] (right bracket key) makes your brush bigger. Holding down the Bracket key changes the size of the brush quickly.

Range

Choose one of the following settings to adjust different areas of your image:

Shadows to adjust the dark colors in the image
Midtones is the default setting, and is used to adjust the middle tones of color
Highlights to adjust the light colors in an image

Exposure

The default setting for exposure is 50%. It's better to start with a lower exposure setting and paint over an area several times.

How to Use the Burn Tool (O)

Duplicate your layer (Ctrl>J) so you have a copy for safe keeping in case you're not happy with your results. Click and drag over an area that you want to darken. In this example, the original image is on the left. I darkened the background around the butterfly.

Try reducing the Opacity of the layer you're using the Burn Tool on so the duplicate layer shows through and see if you like the effect.

To contain the Burn Tool (O) to the butterfly, I made a selection with the Magnetic Lasso Tool (L) first.

Measuring Tools

Rulers

View>Rulers or the shortcut Shift>Ctrl>R turns the Rulers on and off. Rulers are not available when you're in Quick Fix Mode. When activated, Rulers are only visible on the left and top sides of the Image Window if you have an active image as indicated below by the two arrows. Rulers help you find the center or other location on your active image. I keep my rulers on all the time.

Double click on one of the rulers or go to Edit>Preferences>Units & Rulers to change the method of measurement. Available units of measurement are: pixels, inches, cm, points, picas, or percent. If you change the unit of measure in the Info Palette (Window>Info>More button), it will also change the rulers units of measure.

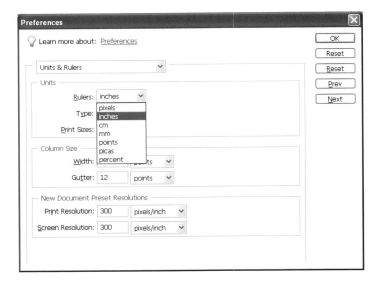

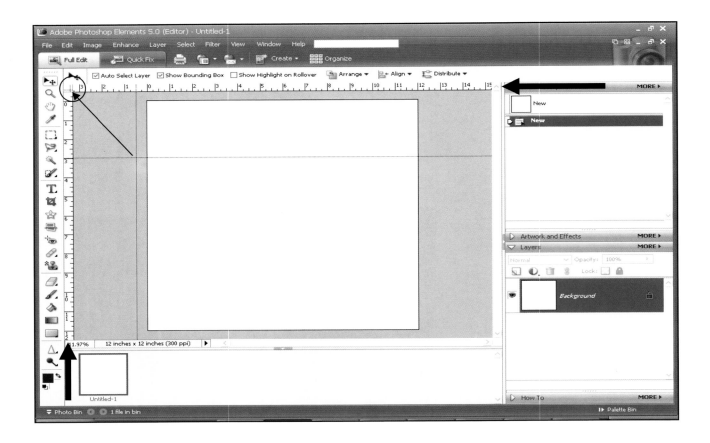

To change the zero origin of the ruler, click where the two dotted lines intersect in the area circled, and drag down towards the bottom left side of your screen. As you drag, you'll see the two intersecting lines move as shown in the example. You might want to change the zero origin if you want to have 0 in the middle of your scrapbook page to help you center items. I have a plastic ruler I bought to do the same thing on my traditional scrapbook pages. To return the 0 point to the default setting, double click on the crosshairs.

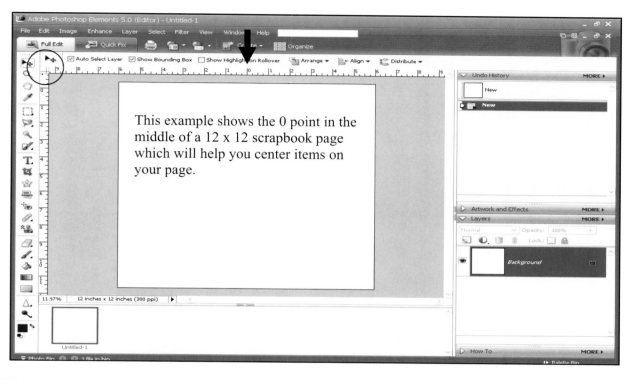

Grids

View>Grid turns on your Grid lines. Grid lines are shown in both Standard Edit and Quick Fix modes. I used my grid lines a lot more to help me line up items before the Alignment and Distribute Commands were added to the Move Tool (V) in version 5. Grid lines are not printed when you print your project.

Edit>Preferences>Grid has settings to allow you to change the color, spacing, and style of the gridlines. Lines, dashed lines or dots can be used for the lines. Choose a color from the drop down list or choose custom, and the Adobe Color Picker lets you choose a custom color for your style of grid. You may want to change the color of the lines if the Grid lines are too close to the color on your page you're working on and you can't see them.

In the example shown, my image will have a gridline every one inch and it will be divided four times.

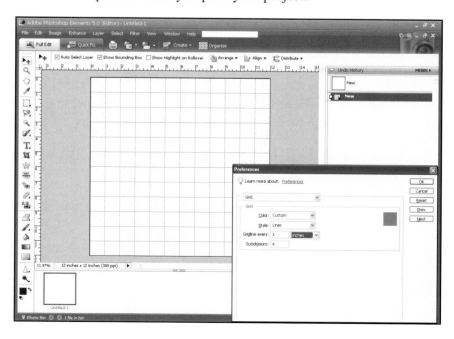

Using these settings the grid will be marked every ¼ inch.

Some tutorials will advise you to change your Grid lines to indicate the center of your scrapbook page or card. In this example, on a 12 inch square scrapbook page the gridlines are set every 6 inches with 1 subdivision, which breaks the page into 4 even squares. Another way to do this would be to change the inches to percent and type in 50% and the page would automatically be divided in half.

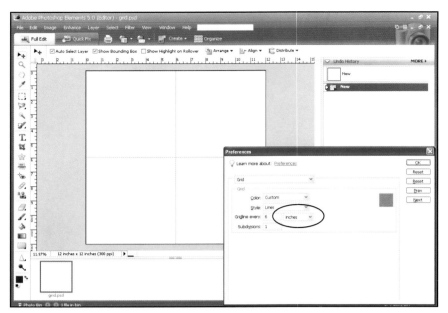

When I want to do something like this, I usually make a separate layer and draw a brush stroke with the Brush Tool (B). I center it on the page with a color that does not match the page so I remember it's there. I need to remember to discard the brush line layer before I print or I'll get a line down the middle of my page. Either way works, but changing the gridline is probably a safer way to go!

Snap To Grid

View>Snap to Grid will cause your images to snap to the gridlines if Grid is turned on. Sometimes snap to grid makes your tools behave erratically. If your Move Tool (V) or Crop Tool (C) especially are acting strange, check to see if this is turned on.

Before the Align and Distribute Commands in the Move Tool (V) were introduced, Snap to Grid was helpful to line up images on a straight line. I haven't used Snap to Grid since I installed Adobe Photoshop Elements 5.

Cursor Options

If you're not happy with how your cursor is displayed, you have the option of changing it in your preferences. Go to Edit>Preferences>Display & Cursors and choose a different setting. Click on the radio button to display a preview of how your cursor will look. I usually use the Normal Brush Tip setting.

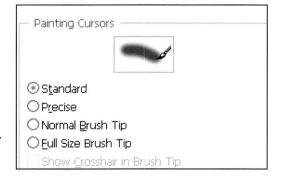

You probably never think about how hard your cursor works for you. To see a good demonstration of how hard your cursor really works go to: http://www.1-click.jp. Be sure to move your mouse around and also to click so you get a good understanding of everything involved in making your cursor work hard for you.

Layers

Understanding Layers is the key to using Photoshop Elements. Traditional scrapbookers usually have an easy time understanding Layers because they already work with real layers of paper, photos, and embellishments.

If you are a traditional scrapper, imagine your completed but not glued down scrapbook page in front of you. Your page consists of a background paper, photos, photo mats cut out of cardstock or printed papers, journaling, brads or other fasteners, and other embellishments. If you were to put the photo mat on top of the photo you wouldn't be able to see the photo. If you put the background paper on the very top of the other items you'll only see the background paper. Putting your paper layers in the right order is the same as putting your digital layers in the right order.

If you have never scrapped before think of a pizza, hopefully you've made a pizza, or at least eaten one before! On the bottom is your crust followed by pizza sauce, mozzarella cheese, different toppings like pepperoni, and then maybe some parmesan cheese or spices. If you put your crust on the very top, you will have a big mess! Just as if you would put the sauce on top of all of the toppings. However if you mix up the pepperoni and mushrooms layer order it will probably be OK.

Layers in Photoshop Elements are just like traditional scrapbooking or making pizza! Get your layers in the right order, and it looks great. If your layers aren't in the right order, it's simple to move them around. Without layers you can't add your head to the body of a beauty queen! The biggest problem beginning digital scrappers have is layers. Master layers, and digital scrapping is easy!

All About Layers

A layer is like a clear piece of plastic that you place over the top of your photo or other image. Making changes on the layer doesn't affect the original image layer below it. JPEG , TIFF, PNG, and BMP files have only one layer. By using layers you can edit all or part of your original image.

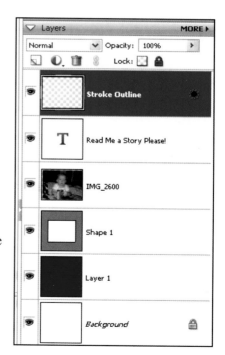

When you make and save changes on different layers, you have the ability to delete or edit these changes later. Saving a file as a PSD file saves all of the layers intact. A photo straight from your camera is one layer. A scrapbook page can be many layers depending on how many photos, papers, embellishments, etc. you have. Photoshop Elements is capable of supporting more layers than your computer can probably handle without running out of memory. According to Adobe Help, Photoshop Elements allows 8,000 layers in an image with their own Blending Mode and Opacity. Thank goodness I've never gotten anywhere near that amount of layers!

The more layers your scrapbook page is, the larger your file size will be and the slower your computer will run. Working on a 24 inch wide by 12 inch high double page layout slows your computer more than if you were working on a single 12 by 12 page. It's easier for me to do the double page layout even though the computer runs a little bit slower.

Layers Palette Options

The Layers palette is usually in the Palette Bin. If it's been removed for some reason, go to Windows>Layers or F11.

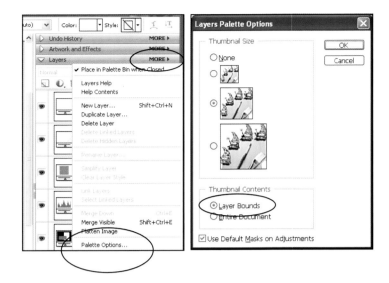

To set your Layers palette Options, click on the More button on the top right corner of the Layers palette. Click on Palette Options and you have four choices for your layer thumbnail size. The third size is the default size and the size I show in my examples.

You have two choices for Thumbnail Contents: Layer Bounds or Entire Document.

As a digital scrapper choose Layer Bounds.

Using the example of several pieces of the Candy Fairway kit from Miss Mint, you can see a big difference between the two choices. Using Layer Bounds you can actually see what the content of your layer is. Entire Document Example shows the whole 12 x 12 page on the Layer Thumbnail and the brad and bow are tiny. The paper looks the same on both examples because it's 12 x 12 and fills the entire layer.

Layer Bounds Example   Entire Document Example

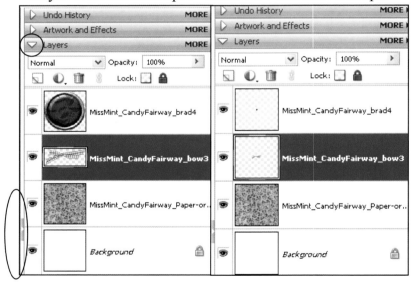

My layers in the above example are named with the file name because I used the Move Tool (V) to drag my elements up from the Photo Bin to my scrapbook page. Had my elements been the active image and I dragged them down in the Photo Bin to my scrapbook page, they would have been labeled Layer 1, Layer 2, etc.

If you are working on a double page spread, you might want more room on your image window to temporarily view the whole page close up. To close/open your Palette Bin, you can click on the word Palette Bin on the bottom right corner of your screen. If you want to make your Palette Bin not so wide, you can grab the triangle on the side (circled in the preceding example) and drag it inward. Dragging all the way to the right will hide the Palette Bin completely. I use a wide screen monitor so I like to have the Palette Bin as wide as possible in order to read all of the layer names. Clicking on the triangle to the left of the word Layers on the Layers palette tab will collapse the Layers palette.

The Layers Palette

Selected/Active/Targeted Layer

Selected/Active/Targeted Layer all means the same thing. To make changes to a layer, you must select it first in the Layers palette. To select a layer, click on the layer thumbnail or on the layer name. In the example to the right, the top layer is my selected layer. Your selected layer will be blue or in some cases dark gray. This example shows the Layers palette removed from the Palette Bin, so yours will look a little bit different.

To select the layer above your active layer Alt] (Bracket key), to select the layer below your active layer Alt [.

If Auto Select Layer is checked on the Move Tool (V), you can also click on the image on your scrapbook page and the appropriate layer will be highlighted on your Layers palette.

Sometimes you need to select more than one layer at a time to merge, link, etc. There are two different ways to do this.

On your Layers palette:
To select several layers in a row, click on the top layer and then Shift click on the bottom layer and those two layers and all in between will be selected.

To select several layers not in a row, click on the top layer and then Ctrl click on all of the other layers. All of the layers you clicked on will be selected.

On your scrapbook page with Auto Select Layer on the Move Tool (V) turned on:
Click on your first element and then Shift click on the next element and you will see them highlighted on the Layers palette.

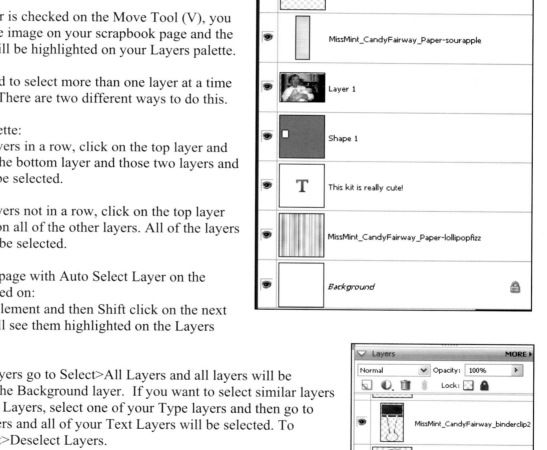

To select all your layers go to Select>All Layers and all layers will be selected except for the Background layer. If you want to select similar layers like all of your Text Layers, select one of your Type layers and then go to Select>Similar Layers and all of your Text Layers will be selected. To deselect go to Select>Deselect Layers.

 ## Eyeball Icon/Visibility Toggle/Layer Visibility Indicator

Click on the eyeball to turn your layer on and off. If the eyeball is turned off, the layer is "hidden" and there is an empty box where the eyeball was. In this example the brad is hidden.

Hidden Layers

You might want to hide a layer because you're working on its duplicate, or you're not sure that you will use it on your page but don't want to delete it quite yet.

Make a Text Layer with notes to yourself on things that you want to remember regarding the construction of your page. Turn the layer on and off so you don't see it.

The Digital Scrapbook Teacher puts an instruction layer on all of our layered templates that can be easily turned on when you want to read them.

When you save your scrapbook page as a PSD file, your hidden files are saved intact. If you save as a JPEG file your hidden layers are discarded.

Hidden layers don't print if you're printing at home from a PSD file.

Alt click on the eyeball on one layer, and all of the visible layers in your file are turned off except for the layer you clicked on originally (hidden layers remain turned off). Alt click again on the eyeball, and the layers are all turned back on.

Delete Hidden Layers

To delete a hidden layer, drag it to the trash can icon or go to the More Button on the Layers palette and click on Delete Hidden Layers.

Layer Thumbnail

The Layer Thumbnail is the tiny little square that shows what's on the layer as shown circled in the example. All layer types have their own thumbnail. This is an image/regular layer thumbnail. I changed the layer boundary by clicking the More button on the Layers palette and changing it in Palette Options. If your thumbnail shows a speck for a brad, it's helpful to change this. The directions were shown in detail in the preceding Layers Palette Options in this chapter.

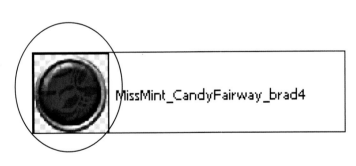

To make a selection (marching ants) of the layer contents, Ctrl click on the thumbnail. This is a trick you will use over and over again, so try to remember it.

Layer Name

The Layer Name is to the right of the Layer Thumbnail, by default your Background layer is named by the program. As you add regular layers, they are named Layer 1, Layer 2, etc. Shape Layers are named Shape 1, Shape 2, etc. Text Layers are named by the text that your write. Adjustment and Fill Layers are named with what kind of adjustment or fill they are.

If you build your scrapbook page by dragging the elements from the Photo Bin up to your page as shown in the Move Tool (V) instructions, your layer name will automatically be the file name of the scrapbook element. This is very helpful when you need to identify your supplies. In the example shown above, the layer is named MissMint_CandyFairway_brad4 because that is the name assigned to the file by the designer.

Rename A Layer

Naming your layers is helpful because many times you can't tell by looking at the layer thumbnail exactly what you're looking at. Changing the Thumbnail Contents to Layer Bounds helps a lot with this too. If you're adding a filter to a photo, you can rename the layer with the name of the filter so you can remember what you did to the photo. There are lots of reasons to rename a layer and it's very simple to do.

To rename a layer, select the layer and do one of the following:
Double click on the layer name.
Right click on the layer.
Layer>Rename
Click the More Button on the Layers palette and select Rename. Type in the new layer name in the highlighted area..

Layer Stacking Order

Layers are created in numerical order (unless you've dragged up from the Photo Bin when creating a scrapbook page where they're named by their file name). Layers do not have to stay in numerical order and can be moved to change their order.

Your Background layer will always be your bottom layer unless you convert it to a regular layer.

One of the biggest mistakes new digital scrappers make is putting their elements in the wrong order. The top layer of the Layers palette is what will be the top element on your scrapbook page. If you stack a 12 x 12 piece of paper on top of anything, you're not going to be able to see what's below it. If you have your photo mat on top of your photo, you won't be able to see the photo. If you can't see something on your page that you know is there, look at your Layers palette and figure out which element is in the wrong order.

How To Move Layers In The Layers Palette

The easiest way for me to move one or more layers in the Layers palette is to select them by clicking on them, or Ctrl click to select several and drag them up or down in the palette. As soon as you start to drag the layer up or down you will see your cursor arrow has turned into a white fist. As you move up and down the Layers palette you will see the lines between the layers change a little bit. Drop your layer in between those lines.

You can also use one of the other two methods below:
Go to Layer>Arrange or on the Move Tool (V) Option Bar and choose one of the following commands or use the shortcut listed:

Shift Ctrl] (Bracket key)   Bring to Front (Top)
Ctrl] (Bracket key)   Bring Forward (Up)
Ctrl [(Bracket key)   Send Backward (Down)
Shift Ctrl [(Bracket key)   Send to Back (Bottom)

Use the Move Tool (V) Arrange feature to move layers up and down in the Layers palette.

Create New Layer

There are several ways to make a new blank image/regular layer. New Layers are automatically entered in numerical order starting with Layer 1. You have the option of moving the layer's stacking order and do not have to keep them in numerical order.

When you create a new layer in one of the following ways, you are given the option of changing Blend Modes, Opacity, and Grouping with a previous layer:

Alt>New Layer Button
Layer>New>Layer
Shift>Ctrl>N
Click on the More button in the Layers palette and choose New Layer
If you just want a blank layer click OK.

Clicking on the New Layer Icon makes a new blank Image/Regular layer.

When making a New Layer by any method, the new layer automatically becomes the active layer.

A new layer is added on top of the layer you previously selected. This is why when making a digital scrapbook page it's important to have your top layer active when you add other elements to the page. If you have a lower layer active and make a new layer, your new layer may be hidden by the layer stacked on top of it.

When you drag an element onto your scrapbook page with the Move Tool (V), it automatically becomes a new layer so you don't have to make a new layer for it.

Text, Shapes, Fill and Adjustment layers also become their own layer automatically.

Putting things like Stroke Outlines and brush work on their own layers is a good habit to get into. This will save you a lot of time and headaches in the end because you have the ability to go back and edit or delete the contents of the layer.

To add a new layer under your selected layer, Ctrl click on the New Layer icon.

Copy/Duplicate A Layer Or Selection

If you want to add a filter, or simplify a Text layer, it's a good idea to duplicate your layer and keep the original layer untouched in case you need it later. This is a very good habit to get in to.

To Duplicate a Layer make sure the layer you want to duplicate is active and:

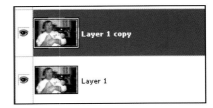

Ctrl>J
Layer>New>Layer Via Copy
Drag the layer thumbnail to the New Layer icon

With the Move Tool (V) activated, you can Alt Click and drag to duplicate the element that you are dragging. This works really well with elements like brads. Add Shift to Alt Click and the elements you copy will be in a straight line. This tip alone is worth the price of this book! You will get an exact copy of your layer placed in the layer on top of your original layer, and the new layer name will now be followed by the word "Copy".

To have the option of naming your duplicated layer and sending it to another file use:

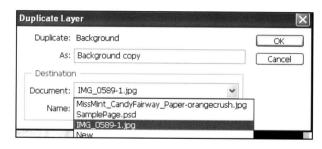

Layer>Duplicate Layer
Right click on the layer and select Duplicate Layer
Click the Layers palette More Button and select
Duplicate Layer

This is one way that you can work on a duplicate image because it's important not to work on your original photos. By selecting the destination of SamplePagePSD, my photo is pasted right in the middle of the scrapbook page just as if I used the Move Tool (V) to move it there.

To copy a selection onto its own layer, make a selection and then Ctrl>J (or Layer>New>Layer Via Copy). Your selection only is pasted on the layer above your original layer with a new layer number without the word "copy".

Copying a selection using Layer>New>Layer>Via Cut (Shift>Ctrl>J) will put your selection on its own layer with a new layer number. It will also leave a hole in the original layer where the selection was cut.

Duplicate an Image

Duplicating an image in your Photo Bin is a little bit different than duplicating a layer, but I will cover it here to avoid confusion.

To Duplicate an Image:

Right Click on the image in your Photo Bin and select Duplicate Image

File>Duplicate

You can pick a new name for your duplicated image or keep the name that's given to it automatically, which is the original name followed by copy.

 ## Create New Adjustment or Fill Layers
See the Adjustment layer Section under Layer Types

 ## Delete Layers

There are several ways to delete a layer. With the layer selected that you want to delete, do one of the following. You will be asked to confirm that you want to delete the layer:

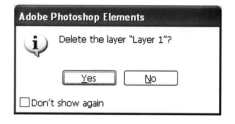

Click on the More Button at the top of the Layers palette and then select Delete Layer.
Click on the Trashcan icon.
Go to Layer>Delete Layer.

Right click on the layer you want to delete and select Delete Layer.

Click in the "Don't show again" box if you don't want to see this box again.
To delete a layer without having to confirm your change drag the selected layer to the Trashcan icon or Alt click on the Trashcan icon.

If you delete your Background layer you will have a transparent (checkerboard) background.
If you are not 100% positive you want to delete your layer you can turn the eyeball icon off and hide the layer. Hiding the layer makes it invisible on your scrapbook page but the layer will still remain in your Layers palette.

Link Layers

Linking Layers together is helpful when working with a multi-layered scrapbook page. Once you get your elements on a page where you want them link them together so that you don't inadvertently move them. Link a photo layer to a mat layer, link brads to scrapbook paper, etc. By linking your elements together you can move, copy, paste, and size them all together.

The Digital Scrapbook Teacher links all of our template shapes so that you don't inadvertently move one of them out of alignment. If you want to move around the template shapes to make your own special creation just unlink them.

Linked Layers do not have to be stacked directly on top of each other; they can be spread out through your Layers palette.

To Link a Layer:

Select all of the layers you want to link on the Layers palette by Ctrl clicking on each one and then:
Click on the link symbol.
Right click and choose Link Layers.
Go to the More Button on the Layers palette and select Link Layers.

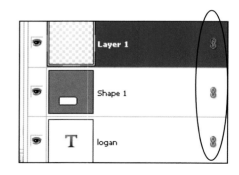

Once you link the layers, a link symbol will show to the right side of the layer name. The only time the link symbol will show up is when one or all of the linked layers are selected.

You can also select your layers to link by Shift clicking on several layers on your scrapbook page when the Auto Select Layer option of the Move Tool (V) is activated, and then linking them by one of the three methods above.

To Unlink

To unlink a linked layer select one linked layer in the Layers palette and click on the Link icon on the top of the Layers palette and only that layer is now unlinked.

To unlink all layers linked together select all of the linked layers and:
Click on the Link icon.
Right Click on one of the layers and choose Unlink Layers.
Click on the More button on the Layers palette and choose Unlink Layers.

Delete Linked Layers

With one of the linked layers, selected click on the More Button on the Layers palette and select Delete Linked Layers and all of your linked layers are deleted that are linked to the selected layer. If you have another set of linked layers that was not linked with the selected layer they will not be deleted.

Select Linked Layers

With one of the linked layers selected, do one of the following:
Click on the More Button on the Layers palette and choose Select Linked Layers
Right click on one of the linked layers and choose Select Linked Layers

Merge Linked Layers

To Merge one set of Linked layers, select one of the linked layers and do one of the following:
Ctrl E (Shortcut)
Layer>Merge Linked
Click on the More Button on the Layers palette and choose Merge Linked Layers
Right click on one of the linked layers and choose Merge Linked Layers

Any of the layers that were linked to the selected layer will now be merged together.

Merging And Flattening Layers

When you are working on a multi-layer scrapbook page sometimes it's helpful to merge some of your layers. Before merging your layers be sure that you do not plan on making any changes to those layers. If I'm working with a lot of small photos or elements like brads and rivets, I'll merge them all together in one layer. By merging these layers I reduce my file size, which sometimes will make my computer work faster. I also reduce the number of layers stacked in my Layers palette, which makes it easier to work with.

To upload your scrapbook pages to a photo lab or printing service, you must save your page as a JPEG file. When saving as a JPEG all of your layers are going to be merged into one layer. If you have any transparent areas they will be filled with white. I recommend saving a layered PSD file that saves all of your layers so you can make changes in the future to your scrapbook pages.

There are several options when it comes to merging your layers. Usually I just select the layers I want to merge in the Layers palette and then Ctrl>E, but here are the other options available:

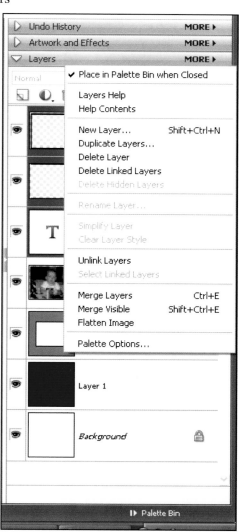

Merge Layers

To merge layers, first select the layers that you are going to merge by clicking on the first layer and Ctrl clicking on the other layers and do one of the following:
Ctrl>E (shortcut)
Layer>Merge
Click on the More Button on the Layers palette and Choose Merge Layers
Right Click on one of the selected layers and choose Merge Layers

All of the layers will be combined into one layer and the new layer is now named whatever your top merged layer was originally named.

Merge Down

The active layer is merged with the layer directly below it. Click on one layer and then:
Ctrl>E (shortcut)
Layer>Merge Down
Click on the More Button on the Layers palette and Choose Merge Down
Right Click on one of the selected layers and choose Merge Down

You must have a layer below your selected layer for this to work. When you Merge Down, the new layer name is the name that the lower merged layer was originally named.

This option is not available if the lower layer is a Shape, Type, or Fill Layer that has not been simplified. If the bottom layer is an Adjustment layer, this option is not available.

Merge Visible

To merge all layers that are visible (Eyeball icon is turned on), select any layer that is visible then:
Shift>Ctrl E (shortcut)
Layer>Merge Visible
Click on the More Button on the Layers palette and Choose Merge Visible
Right Click on one of the visible layers and choose Merge Visible

All visible layers will be merged into one and the hidden layers will remain on the Layers palette. The new file name will be the name of the layer that was selected before you merged them.

Merge Linked

To Merge one set of Linked layers, select one of the linked layers and do one of the following:
Ctrl E>(Shortcut)
Layer>Merge Linked
Click on the More Button on the Layers palette and choose Merge Linked Layers
Right click on one of the linked layers and choose Merge Linked Layers

Any of the layers that the selected layer was linked to will also be merged together.

Merging Adjustment and Fill Layers

If you are going to merge layers to conserve on file space, don't bother merging Adjustment or Fill Layers consisting of only white filled masks because they don't increase file size very much.

Adjustment and Fill Layers can't be used as the bottom or target layer in a group of layers that you merge.

To permanently apply an adjustment or fill layer below, merge them with the layer below them. Once you merge an Adjustment layer with the layer below it, the lower layers are no longer affected by the Adjustment layer.

Merge All Visible Layers into a Target Layer

To merge all of your layers into one layer and still keep all of your separate layers:

Ctrl>Shift>Alt>E (your left hand will be very busy on this one!)

Your new combined layer will be placed above the layer that was last selected and will be named Layer and the next number available.

Merge Clipping Mask/Merge Grouped Layers

You will only get this option if your selected layer is the bottom layer of a grouped layer:

Ctrl>E (shortcut)
Layer>Merge Clipping Mask
Click on the More Button on the Layers palette and Choose Merge Clipping Mask
Right Click on one of the selected layers and choose Merge Clipping Mask

All of the layers will be combined into one layer and the new layer is now named what ever your bottom merged layer was originally named.

If your bottom layer in the clipping group is a Shape or Text Layer you must Simplify it first to get this option, otherwise you can highlight both layers and merge them.

Flatten Image

Flattening your image merges all visible layers into the Background layer, any hidden layers are deleted. Transparent (checkerboard) areas are changed to white. Flattening an image reduces the file size.

To Flatten your Image:
Layer>Flatten Image
Click on the More Button on the Layers palette and choose Flatten Image
Right Click on one of the selected layers and choose Flatten Image

It is a good idea to save your file as a PSD file before you Flatten your image because once you save it after you flatten it, all of your layers are gone.

Lock Transparent Pixels

Locking transparent pixels only locks the transparent (checkerboard) part of your layer. The actual item on the layer is able to be painted or filled with color. If you were to use a brush on a decorative doodle, you would paint on the doodle and the transparent part of the layer. By locking the transparency you only paint on the doodle.

To Lock Transparent Pixels, select the layer and then click on the Transparent (checkerboard) icon next to Lock. To unlock, click on the icon again or type the "/" key.

If you duplicate a layer that you've locked the transparency, the duplicated layer will also have the transparency locked.

Shape and Type layers have their transparency locked automatically until their layer is simplified.

To fill a layer with transparency with your Background color without locking the transparency, use the shortcut Ctrl>Shift>Backspace. To fill an image with your Foreground Color and preserve the transparency, use the shortcut Alt>Shift>Backspace.

 ## Lock All/Locked Layers

To lock a layer, click on the Lock All icon on the Layers palette, to unlock, click on it again or type the "/" key. The lock will appear on any layer that is locked. The Background layer is locked all the time and cannot be unlocked unless you convert it to a regular layer. You can move locked layers up and down in the stacking order except for the Background layer. You can crop locked layers with the Crop Tool (C).

You cannot do the following on a locked layer unless it's the Background layer:

Paint with the Brush Tool (B)   Delete the Locked Layer
Apply a filter   Fill with a Gradient (G)
Fill will the Paint Bucket (K)   Erase with the Eraser Tool (E)
Use the Clone Stamp Tool (S)   Use the Healing Brush (J)
Use the Straighten Tool (P)   Use the Cookie Cutter Tool (Q)
Use the Sponge Tool (O)   Use the Blur Tool (R)
Add Layer Styles   Add Photo Effects

Opacity Slider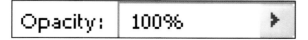

To adjust the Opacity of a layer, you can type in the percentage you want in the box or slide the slider that pops up once you click on the right facing arrow. For a solid layer use 100% opacity. As you lower the opacity of a layer it becomes transparent. An easy way to make a vellum type paper is to lower the opacity on the layer.

A Background layer is the only type of layer where you can't adjust the opacity. The shortcut to adjust the Opacity for an active layer is to activate the Move Tool (V) and type 9 for 90%, 8 for 80% etc. To set the opacity to 35 %, type 35 quickly, type 0 for 100%.

Blending Modes

Blending modes combine pixels from the layer that you apply the
blending mode to with all of the layers below it. The layers are not combined. See the Filters and Blending Mode Section.

Types of Layers

Background Layer

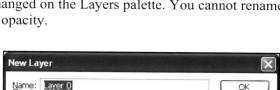

When you open a photo in Photoshop Elements from your digital camera or a scanned image it is automatically called Background. A Background layer is always locked which is why it has the small padlock symbol to the right of the layer name. While the Background layer is locked, it has different properties than regular Locked Layers. Be sure to read about Locked Layers in this section. The Background layer must always be the bottom layer and its stacking order cannot be changed on the Layers palette. You cannot rename a Background layer nor can you change the blending mode or opacity.

There are two ways to change a Background layer to a regular layer. With both methods you get the option to rename the layer and change the mode and opacity.

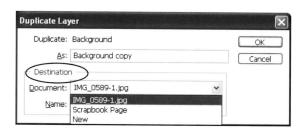

Double click on the layer name where it says Background then click OK if you don't want to change the Mode or Opacity. Your layer will now be named Layer 0.

Layer>New>Layer from Background.
Clicking OK will rename the Background layer Layer 0 and it will no longer be locked.

Another way to change the Background layer to a regular layer is to duplicate it by clicking on the More button on the Layers palette and choosing Duplicate. When you click OK you will have a duplicate copy of your Background layer named Background Copy. Using this method you can send the photo to another file (Destination) that you have open in your Photo Bin such as a scrapbook page in progress by choosing another destination. By choosing scrapbook page in this example, this photo was pasted right on the Scrapbook page. Choosing New duplicates the photo in your Photo Bin.

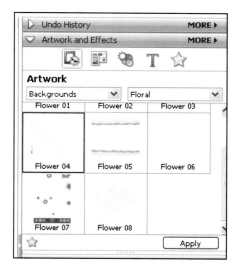

I usually copy the Background layer with the shortcut Ctrl>J. The copy is named Layer 1. Then I delete the original Background layer or hide it so it's not distracting.

If you use the Background Eraser Tool (E) on your Background layer, it will be automatically converted to a regular layer.

If you are working with the Backgrounds in the Artwork & Effects Palette, by double clicking the thumbnail it will automatically become your Background layer.

If you have already opened an image that is your Background layer and want to add one of the Artwork Backgrounds for decoration, be careful.

The new Artwork Background will replace your image Background layer by deleting it. If you're going to use the Artwork Backgrounds, make sure you change your photo to a regular layer first or start with the Artwork Background to begin with.

To change an image/regular layer into a Background layer select the layer and go to Layer>New>Background From Layer. If there are any transparent areas in the layer, they will be filled with the background color.

Image Layer

An Image Layer is also called a Regular Layer. An Image Layer is made up of pixels and can be blank. As you add more image layers to a scrapbook page their Layer # will increase.

Raster and Vector Layer

You'll probably never need to understand what Raster or Vector images are but, just in case you run across the term, you'll have a little bit of an understanding what they are.

Raster images are made up of pixels. When you zoom into a raster image, you can see all of the pixels that make up the image. Bitmap image is another name for Raster images. Raster images are best used for photographs.

Vector graphics are made up of paths which have a mathematical relationship with points, and beyond that I'm pretty well lost! Vector graphics are best used for type or illustrations because they keep their sharp edges.

Type/Text Layer

Type layers are made automatically when you type with the Type Tool (T). Type layers can be adjusted to any size and still keep their detail. It's a good idea to use the Anti Alias setting. Type layers are vector based.

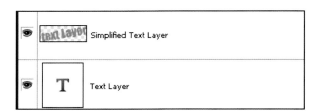

You must Simplify a Type layer to use the Paint Bucket (K), Red Eye Removal (Y), Cookie Cutter (Q), Eraser (E), Brush (B), Healing Brush (J), Clone Stamp (S), Gradient (G), Blur (R), Sponge (O) Tools, or add filters. A Simplified Text Layer Thumbnail will show a transparent (checkerboard) background. The Type layer name will be the first 29 characters or spaces that you type. When a Type layer is simplified it will keep it's original name.

Shape Layer

Shape layers are made automatically when you make a shape with the Shape Tool (U). Shape layers can be adjusted to any size and still keep their detail and smooth edges.

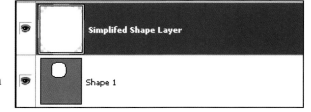

You must Simplify a Shape layer to use the Red Eye Removal (Y), Cookie Cutter (Q), Eraser (E), Brush (B), Healing Brush (J), Clone Stamp (S), Gradient (G), Blur (R), Sponge (O) Tools, or add filters. A Simplified Shape Layer Thumbnail will show a transparent (checkerboard) background. When the Shape layer is simplified, it will keep its original name. Shape layers are vector based.

Layer Mask

Photoshop Elements gives you the option for adding a Layer Mask when you add an Adjustment or Fill layer.

If you never plan on using a Layer Mask and find another square on your Layers palette distracting, you can uncheck the box and you'll no longer get a Layer Mask on your Adjustment layers. I would suggest you keep it on so that a Layer Mask will be added automatically every time you add an Adjustment layer.

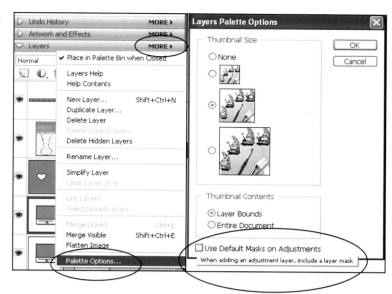

This example shows a Brightness/Contrast Adjustment layer and a Color Fill layer with and without the Layer Mask. The Layer Mask is the solid white square to the left of the layer name shown circled.

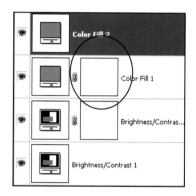

Using a Layer Mask allows you to make changes to only part of your image. Think about when you take a picture. Many times part of the picture is fine and doesn't need to be corrected. With a Layer Mask you can choose the area in the image you want your Adjustment layer to be applied to.

An all white Layer Mask is automatically applied when you add an Adjustment layer. With an all white Layer Mask the Adjustment layer is completely applied to the layers below (or just one layer below if it's grouped). Applying black with the Brush Tool (B) to the Layer Mask causes the areas on the layer(s) below to have the Adjustment layer Masked or not applied.

Think of masking tape not allowing paint to spatter on a window. Using varying shades of gray will apply different degrees of the adjustment to the layer(s) below. A light gray will allow a lot of the adjustment to show, and dark gray will only allow a little bit of the adjustment to show. Using a Mask works well when you take a photo and part of the photo is fine. For example, the people in the foreground look good, but the beautiful mountains in the background are washed out. Applying an Adjustment layer and masking the people allows you to relatively easily, make the mountains beautiful again.

You can also use the Eraser Tool (E) to paint on the Layer Mask but the painting is reversed. Use white to mask and black to reveal.

If you make a selection on your layer that you are applying your Adjustment layer to, the changes will only be applied to the selection. For example, if you want to change the color of a stripe on some digital paper, select the stripe and then apply a Hue/Saturation Adjustment layer and adjust only that stripe. The Layer Mask Thumbnail will show the selected stripes in white and the unselected areas of the paper in black.

To apply black or gray to the Layer Mask, use your Brush Tool (B) and click on the Adjustment layer and paint on your picture. In my example I wrote the word "Hi" with my Brush Tool (B) on my image. You can see it on my Layer Mask Thumbnail. You can also use the Gradient Tool (G) to add a gradient to the Layer Mask. Click on your photo and drag the gradient across it. The Color Fill Layer Mask shows a gradient on it.

To see only what you've added to the mask layer by painting or with the gradient, Alt Click on the mask thumbnail. All other layers are turned off and your Layer Mask is displayed in black and white. Alt Click again on the mask thumbnail to return to normal.

To see your Layer Mask in red, Shift>Alt Click on the mask thumbnail. All of your other layers are still turned on but you can see your mask layer in red. If parts of your image are red, it's pretty hard to see.

To turn your Layer Mask off, Shift Click on the Layer Mask thumbnail. A large red X is placed over the Layer Mask Thumbnail and it's turned off on your image.

It's a good idea to link your Adjustment layer and your image layer together so that if you move or size one, they are both sized or moved together.

One technique used to blend two layers together in a montage is to create a blank Levels, Brightness/Contrast or Hue and Saturation Adjustment layer. Don't make any changes, just click OK so you have a blank Adjustment layer. Group (Ctrl G) this blank Adjustment layer with your top photo. With a soft fuzzy brush, paint black (with the Adjustment layer selected) on the areas that you want to disappear. Your photos now blend together beautifully. If you make a mistake and paint over too much, you can paint over it with white to fix it. This method is more forgiving than the method of using the Eraser Tool (E) without an Adjustment layer, because you can easily fix your mistakes at any time. With an Eraser you would have to Undo everything, and if you've closed your file, you can't do that.

See Montages for more detailed instructions.

Deleting a Layer Mask

To delete a Layer Mask, click and drag the Layer Mask box to the trash can icon. You will be asked to confirm that you want to delete it.

Fill Layers

Fill Layers allow you to fill a layer with color, gradient, or pattern.

To add a Fill Layer, go to Layer>New Fill Layer>and choose Solid Color, Gradient, or Pattern. You can also add a Fill Layer by Clicking on the Create Adjustment layer Button which is the half black/half white button located next to the New Layer Icon at the top of the Layers palette.

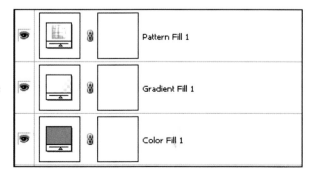

Fill Layers do not affect the layers below them like Adjustment layers do. You can change the blend mode, opacity, and stacking order of a fill layer.

Fill Layers include a Layer Mask unless you have changed your setting in your Palette Options. To paint on a Fill Layer with the Brush Tool (B) or Pant Bucket Tool (K), you must Simplify it first or you will be painting on the Layer Mask.

You must Simplify a Fill Layer to use the Red Eye Removal (Y), Cookie Cutter (Q), Eraser (E), Healing Brush (J), Clone Stamp (S), Gradient (G), Blur (R), Sponge (O), or add filters. When the Fill Layer is simplified, it will keep its original name.

When you add a Color Fill Layer you are given the opportunity to pick a color for the layer with the color picker. With a Gradient Fill Layer you can choose your gradient, shape, angle, scale %, reverse, dither and, if you want to, align it with the layer. The Pattern Fill Layer allows you to choose the pattern you want and, if you want to, link it with the layer, the scale %, and snap to origin.

Other ways to fill a layer or selection with a color or a pattern is to use the Paint Bucket Tool (K), or Edit>Fill Layer/Selection (Shift>Backspace). To fill a layer or selection with the Foreground color, use the shortcut Alt>Backspace. To fill a layer or selection with the Background color, use the shortcut Ctrl>Backspace.

If your layer has transparency in it, filling the layer/selection with any of the methods above will fill the layer entirely with color/pattern. To fill with Foreground color and preserve transparency, Alt>Shift>Backspace. To fill with Background color and preserve transparency, Ctrl>Shift>Backspace. If you are using the Edit>Fill Layer/Selection (Shift>Backspace) command, be sure to put a checkmark in the box that says Preserve Transparency.

Adjustment Layers

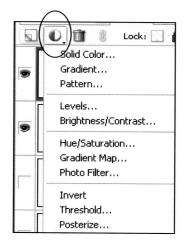

There are many advantages to using Adjustment layers. The biggest advantage to using an Adjustment layer is that the change isn't permanent. You can also use multiple Adjustment layers on one image, on the whole image, or on a selected area of the image.

To add an Adjustment layer to a layer (or a selection on the layer), select the layer and then click on the Create Adjustment layer Button. The first three choices listed after you click on the Create Adjustment layer Button are Fill Layers, which do not affect the layers below them.

An Adjustment layer will affect all the layers under it. If you want the Adjustment layer to affect only the first layer underneath it, Group it together by Ctrl>G.

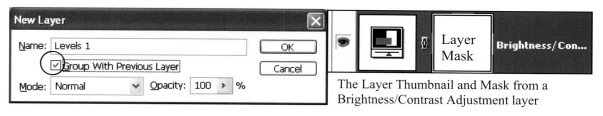

The Layer Thumbnail and Mask from a Brightness/Contrast Adjustment layer

If you want to restrict which layers the Adjustment layer affects, go to Layer>New Adjustment layer>Choose the Adjustment layer you want. When you get the New Layer dialog box, be sure to check Group with Previous and then it will only affect the layer (s) that are grouped with it.

Adjustment layers enable you to make changes without changing the original image and can be easily changed or deleted. When you make a change on an image such as brightness and contrast by using the Enhance Menu, you make the change right on the image layer. If you decide you are unhappy with this change, you can start over by using Undo to delete all of the changes you made after that change. If you have closed your file, your Undo History is cleared and you will be unable to Undo your change. If you used an Adjustment layer to make the same change, all you would need to do is double click the Adjustment layer thumbnail to display the dialog box and change the settings. Adjustment layers are saved when you save your file as a PSD file, enabling you to make changes to them anytime. If the effect of the Adjustment layer is too strong, you can lower the Opacity on the Adjustment layer. If you only want to make an adjustment on part of your image you can use the Adjustment layer's Mask to do this. You can make several Adjustment layers on one image without harming your original image.

Adjustment layers include a Layer Mask unless you have changed your setting in your Palette Options.

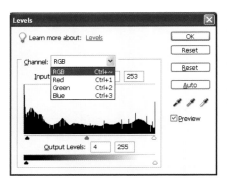

Levels Layer>New Adjustment layer>Levels, or use the Adjustment layer button on the Layers palette. This allows you to adjust shadows, highlights, and mid tones independent of each other by sliding the three sliders at the bottom of the Histogram. You can also change a color cast using RGB, Red, Green or Blue Channels. You can always try the Auto button first, if you don't like the results, try moving the sliders. The Output Levels Sliders on the very bottom make your darkest pixels darker and your lighter pixels lighter.

Brightness/Contrast

Layer>New Adjustment layer>Brightness/Contrast or use the Adjustment layer Button on the Layers palette. To adjust brightness/contrast to all or a selected portion of your image, adjust the sliders. Sliding either slider to the right increases, sliding to the left decreases. Be sure that the Preview box is checked or you won't be able to see your results until after you check OK.

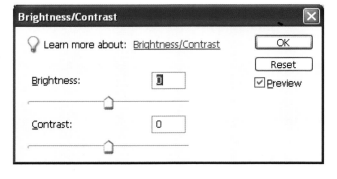

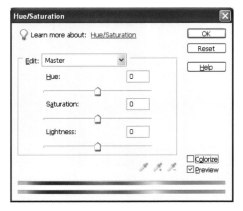

Hue/Saturation Layer>New Adjustment layer>Hue/Saturation or use the Adjustment layer button on the Layers palette. Use the Hue slider to adjust the color of your photos or scrapbook supplies. Adjusting the Saturation slider makes the colors brighter or muted. I usually increase the saturation on photos I take in Hawaii because my camera doesn't capture how blue the sky and water is. Lightness should be used on just a portion of the photo. Check the Preview box to see your changes before you click OK. Check the Colorize box if you are working with a black and white photo.

Gradient Map Layer>New Adjustment layer>Gradient Map, Filter>Adjustments>Gradient Map (no Adjustment layer), or use the Adjustment layer button on the Layers palette. Choose the gradient you want to use from the drop down menu. Shadows are mapped to the starting color of the gradient (shown at the left of the gradient box), midtones are mapped to the midpoint (shown at middle) of the gradient, and highlights are mapped to the ending color of the gradient (shown at right). Choosing Reverse will do the opposite. To smooth the transition between the gradient bands, choose Dither. Check the Preview box or you won't see changes until you click OK.

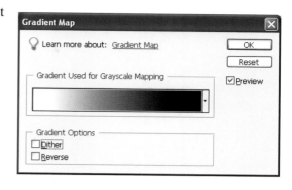

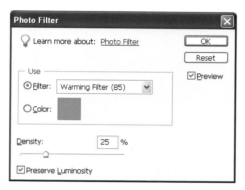

Photo Filter Layer>New Adjustment layer>Photo Filter, Filter>Adjustments>Photo Filter (no Adjustment layer), or use the Adjustment layer Button on the Layers palette. Choose one of the preset filters by clicking on the drop down arrow or click on the Color button and choose your own color with the color picker. Set the Density by sliding the slider or entering a percentage. The higher the Density, the more color is applied. The image will be darkened with the color unless you keep Luminosity checked. Keep Preview checked or you won't see your change until you click OK.

Invert (Ctrl>I), Layer>New Adjustment layer>Invert, Filter>Adjustments>Invert (no Adjustment layer), or click on the Adjustment layer

button on the Layers palette. This filter inverts the colors in your image. If you have used a true black and white negative, you can make a black and white positive which is a black and white photo. You photo looks like a negative when you use this filter.

The Invert filter will not work with color negatives because of the orange mask that is on them. Use a scanner that is capable of scanning color negatives.

Threshold Layer>New Adjustment layer>Threshold, Filter>Adjustments> Threshold (no Adjustment layer), or click on the Adjustment layer Button in the Layers palette. Reset/Cancel by holding the Alt Key. This turns the image to Black and White only. Sliding all the way to the right turns almost all black and all the way to the right turns almost all white.

Posterize Layer>New Adjustment layer>Posterize, Filter>Adjustments> Posterize (no Adjustment layer) or click on the Adjustment layer button in the Layers palette. Reset/Cancel by holding the Alt key. Posterize makes your image look like a cartoon image because it reduces the number of continuous tones. Level 4 is the default. Make sure Preview is checked or you have to wait to see the effect until after you click OK.

Grouping Layers, Layer Clipping Groups, Clipping Masks

Different terms are used for grouping layers by different people.

This is a great **EASY** way to do cool things on your scrapbook pages!

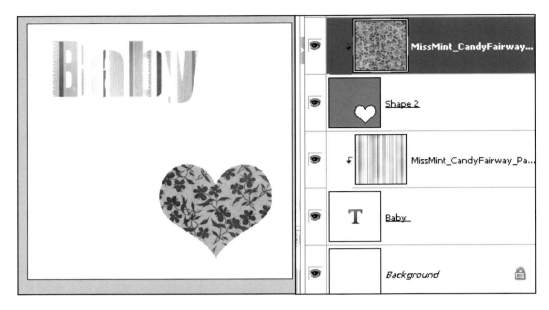

Grouping layers has an end result similar to using the Cookie Cutter Tool (Q), but with much more versatility. When you cut a shape with the Cookie Cutter Tool (Q) your image is cropped. If you didn't get a certain area of your image inside the shape you cropped you have to Undo and do it again. By grouping your layers you can move the image around inside the shape you grouped it. Just activate the Move Tool (V) on the image layer and move it around. If you want to cut a shape or text out of a photo or digital paper, it's easy with grouping layers.

You do not have to cover all of your shape. If you only want to cover half of a shape or text with a digital scrapbook paper, drag it over only half of the shape and then Ctrl>G.

In a clipping group it is the bottom layer that will be the shape of the group. All layers grouped with the bottom layer take on the opacity and blending mode of the bottom layer of the group. Layers that are grouped must be stacked directly on top of each other in the Layers palette. The bottom layer of the group's name is underlined and the upper layers are indented and identified by a bent downward facing arrow, as shown in the example.

If you want to move the clipping layer up or down in the Layers palette, you will need to select them all and move them or link them together and move them, or they will become ungrouped.

Group

To Group two or more layers make sure your selected layer is directly above the layer you want to group it with and:
Ctrl>G (shortcut)
Layer>Group with Previous

 Alt Click on the line dividing the two layers you want to group will give you a symbol with a black and white circle and a left facing arrow. Click and they are grouped.

Make a new layer by:
Alt New Layer Button
Layer>New>Layer
Shift Ctrl N
Select the More button in the Layers palette and choose New Layer. Specify that you want to group this layer with previous by checking the box shown circled.

Once you group your two layers, the top layer in the group takes on the shape of the layer below it. The example above shows the word Baby grouped with a striped paper and a heart shape grouped with a floral paper. As soon as they are grouped, all of the excess paper disappears and it's as if you used a die cut machine to cut them out. The cool thing about this die cut machine is you can make changes to what you've cut out. The other cool thing is that the store can't say you broke their die cut machine and ask you to pay for it! If I don't like how my stripes show up on my Baby word, I use the Move Tool (V) on the paper layer to move the stripes. If I want to move my "Baby" word to another place on the page, I select both layers and use the Move Tool (V) to move them. I can also link my grouped layers by selecting them both and clicking on the Link icon, or I can merge my grouped layers.

Ungroup

To Ungroup select one of the grouped layers and:
Shift>Ctrl>G (shortcut)
Layer>Ungroup
Drag the grouped bottom layer above the other grouped layers on the Layers palette
Drag the top grouped layer up between two ungrouped layers on the Layers palette

 Alt Click on the line dividing the two layers you want to group will give you a symbol with a black and white circle and a left facing arrow. Click and they are ungrouped.

Layer Groups

The circled layers in the example above are actually a Layer Group that was created in Photoshop. To use a layer group in Photoshop Elements you must simplify it first.

Layer Styles

To dress up your scrapbook pages and cards, use one of the many layer styles available in the Special Effects area of the Artwork and Effects palette. If your Artwork and Effects palette is not installed in your Palette Bin, go to Window>Artwork and Effects. Using one of the many layer styles available will enable you to add a drop shadow to an element, or make it appear to be a piece of cactus. While I've never used the Cactus layer style, I use the drop shadow all the time!

To add a layer style to a layer, locate the layer style from the drop down list and double click the layer style thumbnail. Dragging the layer style thumbnail to your image or clicking on the Apply button will also apply the layer style.

At least one style from each layer style category can be applied to a layer, which means that each layer can have several layer styles applied to it. When you apply a layer style to a layer, a small sun is added to the far right side of the layer in the layers palette, as

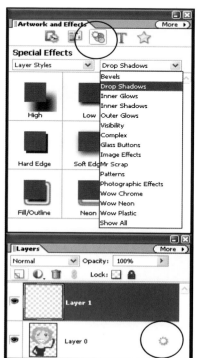
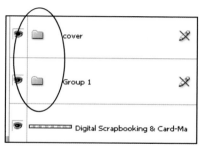

shown in the example. Layer styles cannot be applied to a Background layer. If you add a layer style like a drop shadow or outer glow to a photo, you will not be able to see the effect because it is applied to the outside edge of the photo. If the photo is moved to a scrapbook page or card, you'll see it.

Favorite Layer Styles

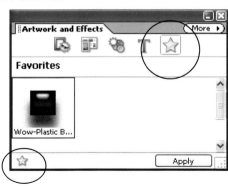

To add a layer style as one of your favorites, click on the layer style thumbnail and drag it down to the Favorites star located at the bottom of the Artwork and Effects palette shown circled. To use the layer styles you've marked as your Favorites, select the Favorites star icon at the top of the Artwork and Effects palette shown circled. To remove the layer style from your Favorites, right click on the layer style thumbnail and choose Remove from Favorites.

To Remove a Layer Style

Do one of the following to remove a layer style:
Right click on the sun icon on the layer in the Layers palette and choose Clear Layer Style
Drag the sun icon to the trashcan
Click on the More button on the Layers Palette and choose Clear Layer Style
Go to Layer>Layer Style>Clear Layer Style

Copy and Paste a Layer Style to Other Layers

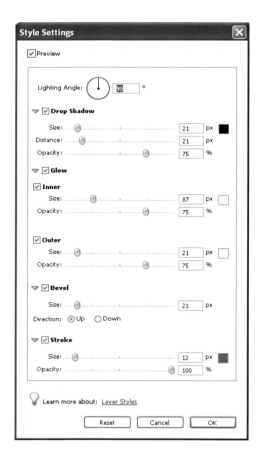

To save time it's easier for me to apply all of my drop shadows at the same time when I'm done with my project. To do this, apply a drop shadow (or any other layer style) to one layer. Click on that layer so that it's the active layer and go to Layer>Layer Style>Copy Layer Style. Select the other layers that you want to apply the layer style to and go to Layer>Layer Style>Paste Layer Style, and the same layer style is pasted to all of the other layers. Using this method is helpful if you've modified a layer style and don't want to modify it for each layer. Holding the Alt key and dragging the sun icon to another layer will also copy and paste all layer styles to another layer.

Show/Hide All Effects

To hide all of the layer styles you have applied to your project, go to Layer>Layer Styles>Hide All Effects. To turn them back on go to Layer>Layer Styles>Show All Effects.

Adjusting Layer Styles

To adjust a layer style, double click on the sun icon on the layer in the Layers palette or go to Layer>Layer Styles>Style Settings.

Make adjustments by sliding the sliders or entering amounts for pixels or percentages in the appropriate boxes.

Adjusting the lighting angle can be done by typing it into the box or rotating the angle in the circle. Dragging the layer style, such as a drop shadow, on the scrapbook page while the Style Settings dialog box is open will also produce the same effect. Changing the lighting angle on one layer will change it on all layers.

Stroke is similar to a Stroke Selection Outline except that you cannot choose to put the stroke on the center or inside of the selection. There is no option to add this stroke to its own layer but because it's a layer style, you can remove it in the future without Undo-ing all of your prior steps. You cannot adjust the Blending Mode of this stroke like you can with a Stroke Selection Outline.

Scale Layer Style Effects

To adjust the size of the layer style go to Layer>Layer Styles>Scale Effects.

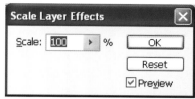

Types of Layer Styles

Adding different layer styles to the same image will produce completely different results. In this example, the original red diamond is shown with different layer styles. Looking at the bottom row you would never guess that the original image was red.

Adjusting the Layer Style Settings on these examples would also change their appearance.

The following layer styles are included when you purchase Photoshop Elements 5. Many websites offer layer styles for purchase or as a freebie. To install a layer style, see the Shopping, Downloading, & Installing section

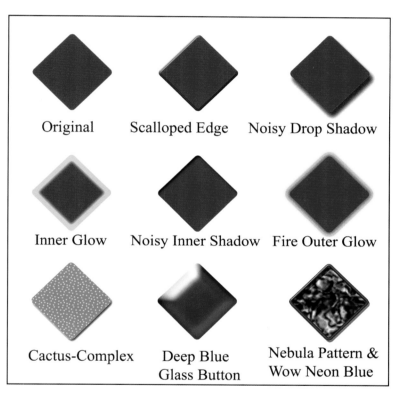

Bevels

To change a flat image into a three dimensional image, use one of the bevel layer styles. An easy way to make a brad is to make a circle shape and add a bevel to it. Layer>Layer Styles>Style Settings gives you options to change your bevels, including the size and direction.

Drop & Inner Shadows

To make your elements appear to be popping off the page rather than part of the page, apply a layer style. The drop shadows included with Photoshop Elements are not as realistic as they could be and usually need a little bit of adjusting. For this reason I use the Mr. Scrap Pop Actions available at PolkaDotPotato.com. If you use the standard drop shadows, be sure to adjust them so they aren't so obvious. New in Photoshop Elements 5 is the ability to adjust the color of the drop shadow. Layer>Layer Styles>Style Settings gives you options to change your shadows, including the size, distance, opacity and color.

Inner & Outer Glows

A lighting effect is placed inside or outside your image. Layer>Layer Styles>Style Settings gives you options to change the size, opacity, and color of the glow.

Visibility

To ghost an image choose Ghosted and it appears that the Opacity of your image has been reduced. Hide displays only the layer style and not the original image. Show brings you back to your original image.

Complex

This is where the layer styles begin to get very interesting! Add a cactus or sunset sky effect to your layer. Most of these images have a bevel and shadow included with them. As of yet, I've never actually used one of these layer styles myself but they're fun to play with.

Glass Buttons

Turn an image into a glass or plastic looking button for a decorative element or webpage. It doesn't matter what the color of your image is to start with because when you choose one of the thumbnails, it's changed to the glass button color you choose.

Image Effects

To add weather, fade, puzzle, water reflection, mosaic tile, circular vignette effects and others, choose this category of layer styles.

Patterns

I'm not sure how many times you'll want to use a Satin Sheet layer style but if you do, you'll find it in this layer style category. Dry Mud, Denim, Brick Wall and others can also be found here. Some of the colored effects like Tie Died Silk appear to be from the 60's.

Photographic Effects

Photographic Effects are very similar to colored filters.

Wow Chrome

If you're looking for realistic chrome effects, you'll find five of them here.

Wow Neon

To add a bright neon outline around your image in 14 different colors, choose this category.

Wow Plastic

Wow Plastic has 11 different colors that you can choose to change your image into brightly colored plastic.

Filters & Blending Modes

Filters and Blending Modes add an artistic touch to your images, whether they are photos or scrapbook elements. How you apply a filter will produce subtle or extreme changes on your images. Remember to always make a duplicate copy of your image before editing it in any manner.

Filters & Textures

Filters and Textures can be applied by choosing a filter from the Filter Menu listing or from the Artwork and Special Effects Palette. To add a filter from the Special Effects Palette, double click on the thumbnail or drag the thumbnail to your image. The filter is the same, regardless of where you activate it. The thumbnail of the green apple shows how the apple will look with the filter applied. Textures are found in the Filters Texture Category but for some reason people can't remember this, so I've chosen to mention them separately.

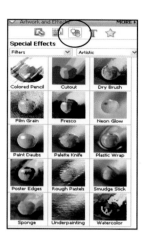

The Filter Gallery shows in the Preview Window you what your image will look like with the filter applied to it. Most of the filters available can be previewed in the Filter Gallery shown below. The Filter Gallery can be accessed by going to the Filter Menu and choosing Filter Gallery.

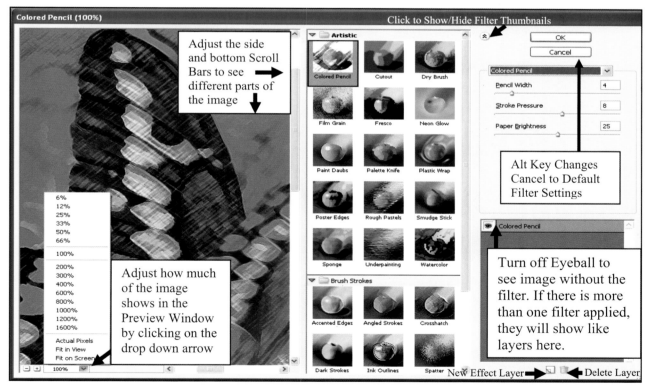

Filters are listed by category, in alphabetical order, and inside each category they are also listed in alphabetical order.

When choosing a filter from the Filter Menu, any filter without the ... behind it, will automatically add the filter without any options. If you choose your filter from the Special Effects palette or from the Filter Gallery, you won't know if the filter is applied automatically.

After you've already applied a filter, the short cut to apply a filter again during the current session with the same exact settings, is Ctrl>F. The filter will also appear at the top of the filter list. To apply the same filter again, but with different options, press Ctrl>Alt>F.

Filters can be applied to a layer or to a selected area of a layer. Sometimes filters take a long time to apply. To speed up the time you spend trying out filters, apply a filter to just a small selection of your image and it won't take the computer as long to do the work. Because filters cause your computer to work extra hard, it's sometimes helpful to clear your Undo History and Clipboard before you apply them. To do this, go to Edit>Clear>Undo History & Clipboard Contents. Closing other computer programs you may have open will also help speed up your computer.

Correct Camera Distortion Filter

This filter is primarily used to straighten out photos that the Straighten Tool (P) didn't entirely fix. This filter can also be used to distort the shape of images, and to add vignettes for photos. When using this filter to straighten images, try a little bit of adjustment at a time.

Remove Distortion – if your image bulges outward, move the slider to the right. If your image pulls in, slide the slider to the left. Vignette – Lightens dark areas in corners caused by a camera lens. If you have this problem, slide the slider to the right. Perspective Control – If your building is tilted, as the one in the example is, slide the slider to correct it. The photo next to the slider helps with figuring out which one you want to use. Angle – Rotates the whole photo, if you get motion sickness beware! Edge Extension – scales your photo bigger or smaller.

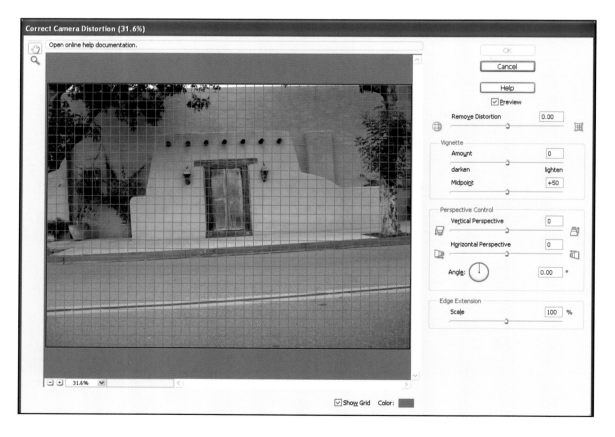

Adjustment Filters

Adjustment Filters are usually used to edit images.

Equalize

The brightest areas of the image are remapped to represent white, and the darkest areas are remapped to represent black. The brightness is equalized. I haven't had great luck with this filter.

Gradient Map

The grayscale range of the image is mapped to the colors of a gradient, specified by the drop down box. The default Gradient is the Foreground to Background Color. Click inside the Gradient box to adjust the Gradient.

Invert (Ctrl>I)

Used to invert the colors in an image. This can be used to make a positive image from a scanned black and white negative. Because color negatives have a orange mask, this won't work with color negatives. This filter was used to make a realistic Rubber Stamp in the Cool Things to Do Section.

Posterize Levels:3

Posterize

To give a Warhol type effect, this filter lets you choose the number of colors for each channel (Red, Green, Blue) in an image. The pixels are mapped to the closest matching level. This reduces the colors in an image and creates more flat areas. Lower levels produces more flat areas. The default setting is 4 levels and can range from 2-255. The image to the right was done with a level 3 setting.

Threshold

Color and Grayscale images are converted to a black and white high contrast image. This is used to find the darkest and lightest areas of an image. By changing the Threshold Level (default is 128), anything lighter than 128 will be converted to white, and any thing darker than 128 will be converted to black.

Photo Filter

Similar to putting a clear colored piece of plastic over an image or taking a photo with a filter on your lens. Choose a preset filter or click on the color button and choose a custom color. Adjust the Density of the filter, and if you want to, Preserve the Luminosity. The same Photo Filters can also be added as an Adjustment Layer, which would allow you to make changes to it. The most popular filter is the Sepia filter.

Artistic Filters

To turn your photos and scrapbook elements into works of art, apply an artistic filter. Most of the names of the filters describe them perfectly, but I've included an example of each one along with the settings I used. The original photo before any filters were applied is shown to the right

Colored Pencil

Turns your image into a colored pencil drawing and changes the background to a solid color, which can be adjusted. Adjust the Pencil Width, Stroke Pressure, and Paper Brightness to change the look of the image. The settings for the example are: Pencil Width 2, Stroke Pressure 15, Paper Brightness 50.

Cutout

This filter gives your image the appearance that it was cut out of little pieces of paper. Adjust the Number of Levels, Edge Simplicity, and Edge Fidelity. The settings for the example are: Number of Levels 2, Edge Simplicity 6, and Edge Fidelity 2.

Dry Brush

This filter looks as if the dry brush technique was used on the image. Adjust the Brush Size, Brush Detail, and Texture. The settings used for this example are; Brush Size 10, Brush Detail 10, and Texture 3. The same exact filter was applied twice because only applying it once didn't make much of a change.

Film Grain

To make your image look like old film, use this filter. This filter eliminates banding in blends Adjust Grain, Highlight Area and Intensity. In this example, the settings are: Grain 11, Highlight Area 20, Intensity 5.

Fresco

This filter uses short, round, quickly applied brush dabs to paint a layer on your image. Adjust the Brush Size, Detail and the Texture. This example used: Brush Size 2, Brush Detail 8, and Texture 1, and was applied to the photo exactly the same two times.

Neon Glow

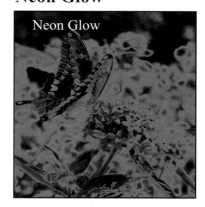

Neon Glow uses the Foreground, Background, and a Glow color to soften and colorize an image. Adjust the Glow Size, Glow Brightness, and Glow color with the Adobe Color Picker. In this example, the Glow Size was 2, the Glow Brightness was 18, and the Glow Color was Royal Blue.

Paint Daubs

To make your photo appear to be painted, use the Paint Daubs Filter. Brush Size, Sharpness, and different brushes can be specified. The choices for the brush are: Simple, Light Rough, Dark Rough, Wide Sharp, Wide Blurry, and Sparkle. The example shown used: Brush Size 39, Sharpness 10, and the Sparkle Brush.

Palette Knife

Imagine a painting painted with a thin coat of paint applied by a palette knife that allows the canvas to show through. Options available to adjust are: Stroke Size, Detail, and Softness. The example settings are: Stroke Size 25, Detail 0, and Softness 0.

Plastic Wrap

The Plastic Wrap Filter makes your image look like it was covered in plastic wrap. Adjust Highlight Strength, Detail, & Smoothness. The example settings are: Highlight Strength 15, Detail 9, & Smoothness 7.

Poster Edges

This filter is similar to Posterize except that it draws black lines on the edges. Adjust Edge Thickness, Edge Intensity, and Posterization. The example settings are: Edge Thickness 10, Edge Intensity 10, and Posterization 6.

Rough Pastels

This filter makes your image look like it was roughly sketched with pastel chalk on a textured background. Set the Stroke Length, Stroke Detail, and Texture. Choose a Texture of brick, burlap, canvas, sandstone or load a texture; set the Scaling, Relief, and Light Source. You can also invert the Texture. The example shown used the maximum settings on all options with a brick texture.

Smudge Stick

The darker areas of your photo are smudged using this filter, while the lighter areas lose their detail and become brighter depending on the settings chosen. Adjustable settings are: Stroke Length, Highlight Area, and Intensity. The example shown used: Stroke Length 10, Highlight Area 9, and Intensity 5.

Sponge

When using this filter, your image looks like a contrasting color was sponged on it. Adjustable settings are: Brush Size, Image Definition, and Edge Smoothness. The example shown used: Brush Size 7, Image Definition 25, and Smoothness 2.

Underpainting

This filter makes your image look like it was roughly painted on a textured background. This filter is similar to Rough Pastels. Set the Brush Size, Texture Coverage and Texture. Choose a Texture of brick, burlap, canvas, sandstone or load a texture; set the Scaling, Relief, and Light Source. You can also invert the Texture. The example shown used the maximum settings on all options with a brick texture.

Watercolor

Your image is painted like a watercolor painting. The detail is simplified in the image. Set the Brush Detail, Shadow Intensity, and Texture. The example shown used the following settings: Brush Detail 14, Shadow Intensity 0, and Texture 3. I applied the same filter five times. Even though I had Shadow Intensity at 0, my image was very dark after applying the filter five times. I lightened the image using the Shadows/Highlights and Brightness/Contrast settings in the Enhance Menu under Adjust Lighting.

Blur Filters

Blur Filters blur your selection or layer. By blurring a distracting background, you emphasize the focal point of your photo. In the examples that follow, I made a selection of the dog and blurred the beach background. Using a filter from the Blur Menu is much faster than using the Blur Tool (R). Always make a duplicate of your image before you apply any filter. Lock transparent pixels must not be selected on any layer that you are applying a Blur Filter to.

Average

This filter averages all of the colors in the selection or layer, and turns them into a solid color.

Blur

The Blur Filter blurs the selection or layer, but not very much. The Blur Filter was applied three times in this example.

Blur More

The Blur More Filter blurs more than the Blur Filter but the effect is not that dramatic. In the example, the Blur More Filter was applied six times.

Gaussian Blur

The Gaussian Blur Filter is probably the most used Blur Filter. This filter is used to soften wrinkles and to give a dreamy look to photos. Choose a radius amount and check your results in the preview window. This example used a 6 pixel radius.

Motion Blur

To make your layer or selection appear to be in motion, choose the Motion Blur Filter. Choose the Blur Angle, and Distance. In this example the Blur Angle is 0 and the Distance is 50 px.

Radial Blur

The Radial Blur Filter gives a sense of motion to the layer or selection that it's applied to. In the top example, I chose the maximum amount of Spin Blur at the best setting to show the maximum amount of radial blur available. The Blur Center was at the default setting of centered on the image as indicated by the bulls-eye type image. This can easily be moved by clicking and dragging the center around inside the Blur Center box. The bottom example shows the maximum amount of Zoom blur at the Best setting. I moved the Blur Center to the upper right area of the photo, as indicated by the line drawing. To move the Blur Center, just click and drag it with your mouse. Using Draft Quality quickly gives you a grainy result.

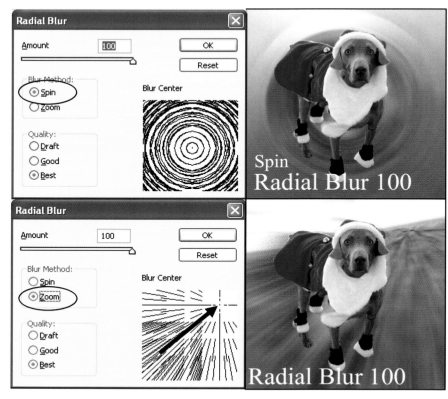

Smart Blur

Choose a Radius, Threshold, Quality, and Mode to precisely blur your layer or selection. The Normal Mode blurs only the edges where the color changes. Edge Only adds black and white edges, while Overlay Edge applies white to the areas of color changes.

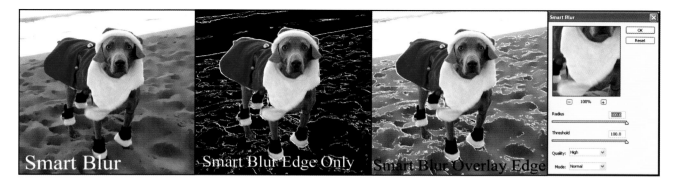

Brush Stroke Filters

Brush Stroke Filters give a painted or inked look to your images. Using these filters is a great way to make beautiful digital scrapbook backgrounds. My example is a photo of some plants I took in Hawaii.

Accented Edges

Used to emphasize the edges in your image, this filter adds a white chalky accent when the edge brightness is set to a high number, and a black ink look when it's set to a low number. The settings for this example are: Edge Width 3, Brightness 31, and Smoothness 13.

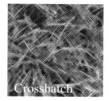

Angled Strokes

Dark and light areas are painted in opposite facing diagonal strokes. The settings for this example are: Direction Balance 50, Stroke Length 13, and Sharpness 3.

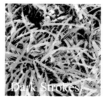

Crosshatch

Rough texture is added to your image to look like it was crisscrossed with a pencil. The settings for this example are: Stroke Length 27, Sharpness 20 and Strength 1(amount of crisscross passes).

Dark Strokes

Light areas of your image are painted with long white strokes and dark areas are painted with short tight strokes. The settings for this example are: Balance 4, Black Intensity 2, White Intensity 9.

Ink Outlines

To get a pen and ink type image, use the Ink Outlines Filter. The settings for this example are: Stroke Length 32, Dark Intensity 28, Light Intensity 25.

Spatter

To achieve an airbrush look, use the Spatter Filter. The settings for this example are: Spray Radius 9, Smoothness 2.

Sprayed Strokes

To paint the dominant colors of your image with angled strokes, use the Sprayed Strokes Filter. The settings in this example are: Stroke Length 12, Spray Radius 19, Stroke Direction Horizontal.

Sumi-e

To replicate the Japanese style of painting black ink on rice paper, use the Sumi-e Filter. The settings for the example are: Stroke Width 3, Stroke Pressure 1, Contrast 0.

Distort Filters

To create a three dimension effect or reshape in other ways, try one of the Distort filters.

Diffuse Glow

To make your image look as if a diffusion filter was used when the photo was taken, use the Diffuse Glow filter. The settings for this example are Graininess 10, Glow Amount 9, Clear Amount 15.

Displace

Displacement Maps are beyond the scope of this book. If you are interested in Displacement Maps, EclecticAcademy.com offers some great Photoshop Elements classes taught by Sarah Froehlich. If you are a subscriber, PhotoshopElementsUser.com also has some great tutorials available online. The American Flag example is from one of the lessons in the Photoshop Pizzaz class at EclecticAcademy.com.

Glass

To make your image appear as if you are viewing it through obscure glass such as frosted or block glass, choose this filter. The settings for this example are: Distortion 20, Smoothness 7, Glass Block, Scaling 200%

Liquify

This is not a good filter to put into the hands of someone like me who loves to play jokes on their friends. With this filter, I can give someone a Pinocchio nose, Dr. Spock ears, or make them look like a Conehead. I can also use it to perform miracle plastic surgery fixes; the sad part is that the fixes are only in the photos. For tips on how to use this filter to perform free plastic surgery, see the Perform Plastic Surgery Without A Medical License Section. Using the Warp feature of this filter, I was able to transform my grandson into an alien in seconds flat. Imagine what I could do with this filter if I had a lot of time on my hands.

The best way to learn to use the Liquify filter is to sit and play with it; it's also a lot of fun. In my example, once I got one portion of the photo complete, like the ear, I clicked the OK button. Then I went onto the eyebrows because otherwise, if you press Cancel or Revert, you have to start completely over. Try using the Reconstruct Tool that looks like a brush on the left side if you want to just remove part of the change you've made.

Ocean Ripple

To make your images appear as if they are underwater, use the Ocean Ripple Filter. The settings for this example are: Ripple Size 11, Ripple Magnitude 9.

Pinch

Imagine you picked up and pinched a paper photo right in the middle. This is what the Pinch filter does. In this example I applied the filter twice to show the effect at the maximum setting of 100%. Moving the slider to the opposite side at -100% pinches the image outward for a completely different effect.

Polar Coordinates

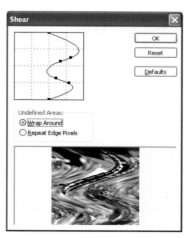

The Polar Coordinates filter is used in an example in this book to make a circle brush and to put text into a circle. It can also be used to modify an image to make it look as if you're viewing it through a cylinder. This example was used with the Rectangular to Polar setting. Using the Polar to Rectangular Setting produces a completely different effect.

Ripple

As the name implies, applying the Ripple filter to an image also gives the effect of being under water. The end result of applying the filter to a straight line is shown in the example. This filter can be used to apply a deckled edge to a frame, or to make an edge template.

Shear

The Shear filter distorts your image along a curve that you set. Watch the preview box to see if you like the change before you click the OK button.

Spherize

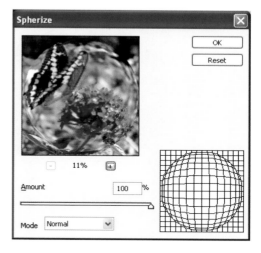

To make your image appear as if it has been wrapped around a sphere, apply the Spherize filter with a positive percentage in the amount box. This filter applies a bubble type glass ball effect. To make your image appear as if it's inside the sphere choose a negative percentage amount.

Twirl

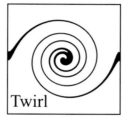

Depending on the settings used, the Twirl filter twirls your image into a circle. This example shows a straight line made with the Brush Tool (B) drawn horizontally across a scrapbook page. The maximum angle value of 999° was used to achieve this effect. Use this filter on photos or on other images to make your own digital paper and other elements.

Wave

The Wave filter is used to make an Edge Template in the Template section of this book. This filter can be used to change your image into a wavy pattern or to make digital paper and accents for your pages. This example shows a straight line made with the Brush Tool (B) drawn horizontally across a scrapbook page. It almost looks as if you're reading an EKG printout.

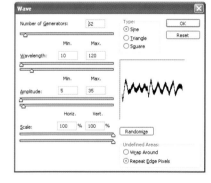

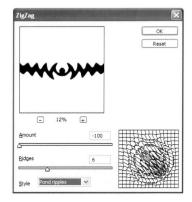

Zig Zag

Applying a Zig Zag filter to your photos creates pretty wild effects. You may want to use this filter if you are making your own digital paper. This example shows a straight line made with the Brush Tool (B) drawn horizontally across a scrapbook page. Maybe this is how the Batman logo was made.

Noise Filters

Noise is what causes your images to appear grainy. These filters blend areas in your images to disguise noise, dust, scratches and other problems, with the exception of the Add Noise filter.

Add Noise

The Add Noise filter adds pixels to an image to make an edited photo look more realistic. It can also give the appearance that the photo was shot with high speed film. Just to show the effect, this example shows a higher setting than you would want to use.

Despeckle

There are no options to choose for the Despeckle filter. Photoshop Elements automatically finds the edges in the selected layer and blurs the entire layer except for the edges. The Despeckle filter blurs the noise but still keeps the detail of the edges. Use this when you have scanned magazines or other items that have noise or banding that you cannot remove.

Dust & Scratches

If you have old photos that have been scanned with various imperfections on them, try the Dust & Scratches filter first and see if it removes most of your problem areas.

Median

The Median filter also reduces noise with blending techniques. Try this filter also when you have scanned images or other items that have noise or banding that you can't remove. It also can be used to remove the look of motion if the photo appears blurred.

Reduce Noise

The Reduce Noise filter helps remove various kinds of noise caused by poor lighting and caused by photos taken with a low camera setting, such as a mobile phone.

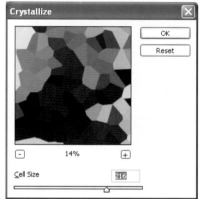

Pixelate Filters

These filters are used to define images or selections.

Color Halftone

A halftone is an image made up of dots. To simulate this effect, use this filter for something like an Andy Warhol type effect. This example shows high values entered in the radius (12) and channel (200) fields just to show the effect.

Crystallize

The Crystallize filter changes your image into crystals of a size that you specify. The larger the cell size, the more abstract the appearance of the image.

Facet

The Facet filter is applied automatically and does not give you an option to change the intensity of the filter. To increase the effects of this filter, apply it more than once. This filter can make an image look like it's hand painted or an abstract painting. The effect of the filter was so subtle that I did not include an example of it.

Fragment

The Fragment filter is also automatically applied without options to adjust the intensity of the filter. This filter blurs the image slightly. To increase the effects of this filter, apply it more than once. The effect of this filter was so subtle that I did not include an example of it.

Mezzotint

This filter seeks to replicate an old print making process where the printing plate was roughed up by a tool that made dots or lines. Choose dots, lines, or strokes of varying degrees to apply to your image. The example used the Coarse Dots option.

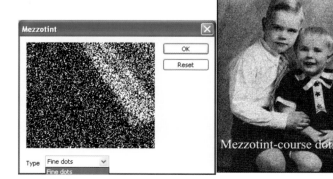

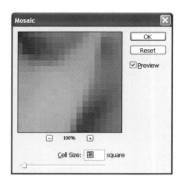

Mosaic

To make your image appear as if were drawn with blocks of color, choose this filter. The Mosaic filter allows you to choose the cell size. Depending on your image, choosing the largest cell size leaves your altered image unrecognizable.

Pointillize

The Pointillize filter changes your original image into dots and uses your background color to fill in the background of the image. Adjust the cell size for varying results.

Render Filters

The Render Filters category has seven filters that can best be classified as special effects filters.

3D Transform

I have used this filter to make a photo cube and a book that appeared to be placed on a flat table. Both of these exercises were a little bit difficult.

Clouds

To make a blackboard background paper or a clouds background paper, use the Clouds filter. This filter uses the Background and Foreground colors to make a cloud type pattern. This filter is applied automatically, but if you want to intensify the effect, just apply it again. Set your Background color as white and your Foreground color as blue for a nice sky, or green for a chalk board background for a scrapbook page.

Difference Clouds

This filter is similar to the Clouds filter except that instead of generating soft fluffy clouds, more distinctive lines are formed. This filter also uses your Foreground and Background Colors. I have used this filter in a class to replicate the look of marble

Fibers

The Fibers filter adds the look of fiber to your image using your Foreground and Background colors. To add this effect to an image, apply the filter to a duplicate layer and then lower the Opacity on the filter layer.

Lens Flare

The Lens Flare filter adds a lighting effect to your image. To move the source of light to another location, drag the light with your cursor. Change the brightness and type of the light source easily with the slider or Lens Type buttons

Lighting Effects

The Lighting Effects filter has a multitude of lighting effects you can add to your image, as shown in the drop down list in the Lighting Effects dialog box. You can easily change the area that is affected by the lighting by dragging the light to another location in the image.

The type of light can be a spotlight, omni light, or directional light. The Intensity and Focus can be adjusted along with Gloss, Material, Exposure, Ambience, and Texture Channel. This is a fun filter to try out.

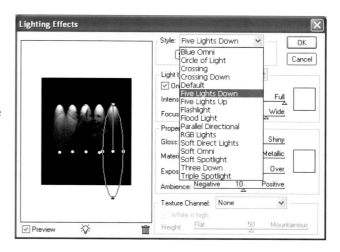

Texture Fill

To use the Texture Fill filter you will need to have an image that has been saved as a Grayscale PSD image. To change an image to Grayscale, go to Image>Mode and select Grayscale. Save this image as a PSD file. When you select this filter; to apply it you will be directed to a dialog box that will require you to locate the image you want to use for the Texture Fill. Your only choices are PSD files that will show in the dialog box. If you choose an image that is not Grayscale, you'll get a notice that says sorry, it won't work. The Texture Fill shown in the example uses the Rocky Beach Photo which is included on the CD that came with this book.

Sketch Filters

To make your image look as if you drew it yourself, use one of the sketch filters. Duplicating your layer and applying the sketch filter to the top layer and then reducing the Opacity on that layer will give you a great effect too. The colors you choose for your Foreground and Background colors will play a role in how your filter applies. If you apply the filter and your screen appears to be blank, check to see if your Foreground color is white and change it.

Bas Relief

The Bas Relief filter uses the Foreground color and Background colors to carve an image. This image is accented by light and you can choose the source of from various locations. The example used the following settings: Detail 15, Smoothness 3, Light, Top. The Background color is black and the Foreground color is white.

Chalk & Charcoal

The Chalk & Charcoal filter uses the foreground color to draw diagonal charcoal lines in the dark areas of your image. The background color is used to draw the lighter areas in chalk. The example used the following settings: Charcoal Area 6, Chalk Area 6, Stroke Pressure 1. These were the default settings. The Foreground color is black and the Background color is white.

Charcoal

The Charcoal filter uses your Foreground to draw the edges of your image and the Background color to color the paper. The example used the following settings: Charcoal Thickness 3, Detail 5, Light/Dark Balance 99. The Foreground color is black and the Background color is white.

Chrome

The Chrome filter makes it appear that your image has been covered in chrome. The example used the following settings: Detail 4, Smoothness 7 (Default Settings).

Conte´ Crayon

The Conté Crayon filter uses the Foreground color to fill in the dark areas of your image and the Background color to fill in the lighter areas of your image. Different textures can be used to make it appear that your image was sketched on bricks, canvas etc., or you can load your own textures. The example used the following settings: Foreground Level 11, Background Level 7, Texture Canvas, Scaling 100%, Relief 4, Light Top.

Graphic Pen

The Graphic Pen filter uses ink strokes in Foreground color to replace all color in the image and uses the Background color to color the paper. The example used the following settings: Stroke Length, Light/Dark Balance, Stroke Direction Right Diagonal (Default Settings). The Foreground color is black and the Background color is white.

Halftone Pattern

The Halftone Pattern filter uses your Foreground and Background colors to give your image a halftone effect. You are given a choice of circles, dots or lines to choose from. The example used the following settings: Size 5, Contrast 20, Circle Pattern Type. The Foreground color is black and the Background color is white.
This filter can be used to add this effect to digital scrapbook paper, text, mats, etc.

Note Paper

The Note Paper filter uses the Foreground and Background colors to make your image appear to be handmade paper. This filter is great to use when making digital scrapbook paper. The example used the following settings: Image Balance 25, Graininess 14, Relief 11. The Foreground color is black and the Background color is white.

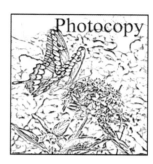

Photocopy

The Photocopy filter uses the Foreground and Background colors to make your image appear as if you copied it with a copy machine. The example used the following settings: Detail 10, Darkness 19. The Foreground color is black and the Background color is white.

Plaster

The Plaster filter uses the Foreground and Background color to make your image appear as if it's been cast in plaster. The example used the following settings: Image Balance 20, Smoothness 2, Light: Top. The Foreground color is black and the Background color is white.

Reticulation

The Reticulation filter adds a grainy effect to your image using the Foreground and Background colors. The settings used for this example are: Density 18, Foreground Level 33, Background Level 11. The Foreground color is black and the Background color is white.

Stamp

The Stamp filter uses the Foreground and Background colors to make your image appear to have been stamped by a rubber stamp. The example used the following settings: Light/Dark Balance 26, Smoothness 1. The Foreground color is black and the Background color is white.

Torn Edges

The Torn Edges filter uses the Foreground and Background color to make your image appear as if it's been torn into pieces. The example used the following settings: Image Balance 25, Smoothness 11, Contrast 17 (Default Settings). The Foreground color is black and the Background color is white.

Water Paper

The Water Paper filter makes your image appear to be painted onto a textured wet paper. The example used the following settings: Fiber Length 50, Brightness 60, Contrast 80.

Stylize Filters

The Stylize Filters produce amazing results that you can use to make your own digital scrapbook papers or to add a special touch to a photograph.

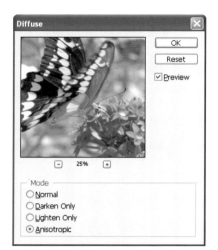

Diffuse

The Diffuse filter moves pixels around to soften the focus of the selected area depending on which Mode you choose.

Emboss

The Emboss filter makes your image appear as if it's been embossed in a gray color. The edges of the image are still the original color and show through the gray filled area.

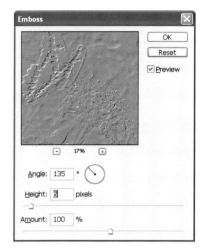

Extrude

The Extrude filter makes your image appears as if it has been split into tiny blocks or pyramids that are protruding out of the image. Using the option Solid Front Faces will remove most of the detail of the image and leave only colored blocks. The example used the following settings: Type-Block, Size-50 Pixel, 50 Depth, Random.

Find Edges

The Find Edges filter changes your background of your image to white and emphasizes the edges by outlining them with a darker color. This filter is automatically applied and does not give you the opportunity to adjust any settings.

Glowing Edges

The Glowing Edges filter changes your background to black and makes it appear that the edges of the image have been turned into neon lights. The example used the following settings: Edge Width 6, Edge Brightness 6, Smoothness 5.

Solarize

For an interesting effect, the Solarize filter combines a photo along with a negative. This is one filter you need to try yourself because this small image does not do it justice. This filter is automatically applied.

Tiles

The Tiles filter makes your image look as if it's small tiles pieced together. Select your Foreground or Background color to be placed underneath the tiles. The example used the following settings: Number of Tiles 10, Maximum Offset 15%, Fill Empty Area With: Background Color. The Background color is black.

Trace Contour

The Trace Contour filter outlines the areas where the brightness fades into lighter areas like a contour map. The settings used in the example are: Level 82, Edge Upper.

Wind

The Wind filter makes your image look as though the wind is blowing through it. You can choose how strong of a wind you'd like and also the direction the wind is blowing from.

Texture Filters

Texture filters make your image look as if it is really textured. I have had several people run their finger across projects I've made because it appears to be so real they think they should be able to feel the texture. Using one of these filters allows you to give a plain colored filled layer the look of an expensive textured cardstock.

Craquelure

The Craquelure filter paints your image so realistically that you can see the cracks in the paint. I apply this filter to photos and background paper and love it. The settings used for the example are Crack Spacing 65, Crack Depth 10, Crack Brightness 0.

Grain

The Grain filter uses different types of grain to add a texture to an image. The Regular and Soft Grain Types look like the Noise Filter to me. If you don't like the effect of the filter, try changing your background color because some of the filters use it. The settings used for the example shown are: Intensity 100, Contrast 100, Grain Type Clumped.

Mosaic Tiles

The Mosaic Tiles filter makes your image look as if it's mosaic tile that you buy at the tile store that's hooked together on mesh. This tile even has the grout already applied. The settings for this example were set at the maximum to enable you to see them in the small example: Tile Size 100, Grout Width 15, Lighten Grout 10,

Patchwork

The Patchwork filter turns your image into tiny little squares that to me looks more like needlepoint than a patchwork. The settings for this example were set at the maximum strengths available to enable you to see the effect in the small example: Square Size 10, Relief 15.

Stained Glass

The Stained Glass filter makes your image look just like stained glass with the lead in between the glass pieces in the Foreground color. Tell your friends you spent hours on a photo that you've applied this filter to, and they'll believe you. The settings used for this example are: Cell Size 11, Border Thickness 2, Light Intensity 1.

Texturizer

The Texturizer filter makes your image look like it was painted on burlap, bricks, canvas or sandstone. This is also a great way to make your background appear to be expensive cardstock instead just a plain colored filled layer. The settings used for this example are: Texture-Burlap, Scaling 200%, Relief 21, Light: Top.

Not only can you use the four default textures with the Texturizer filter, you can add other filters from the Adobe Photoshop Elements Texture file. Some of the textures available to use include: Puzzle, Stucco, Snake Skin, Footprints, and Feathers. Be sure to read about making a photo into a puzzle and how to make your own texture in the Cool Stuff To Do Section. To load another texture, click on the arrow (circled), click on Load Texture and navigate to the Textures here: C:\Program Files\Adobe\Photoshop Elements 5.0\Presets\Textures.

Video Filters

The DeInterlace & NTSC Colors filters are used for television reproduction and are beyond the scope of this book .

Other Filters

Photoshop Elements lets you create your own custom filters. The only problem is you have to enter codes in all of these tiny little boxes. To be completely honest, I have no idea how to do it but when I put some random numbers in the boxes, I got some pretty interesting results. With all of the great filters already included, I don't really feel the need to make any custom filters at this time.

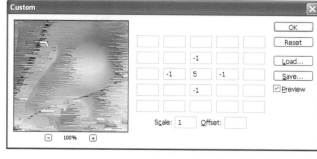

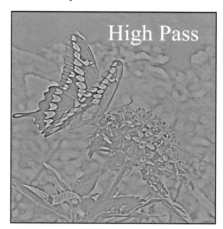

High Pass

The High Pass filter is the opposite of the Gaussian Blur filter because it keeps edge details where there is a big difference in color.

Maximum

The Maximum filter applies a choke, a printing term which means it replaces areas of color with the lightest of colors from the surrounding areas.

Minimum

The Minimum filter does the opposite of the Maximum filter. In printing terms it's called a spread, which means it replaces areas of light color with the darkest of colors from the surrounding areas.

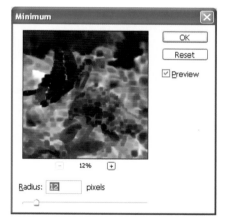

Offset

The Offset filter moves a selection by using the amounts entered by you. In this example, I entered amounts which were close to half of the width and height so it divided the image in four almost equal parts, as shown by the Image Size dialog box. If you want to duplicate this effect, go to Image>Resize>Image size. In the Offset filter dialog box Horizontal box, enter half of the image's Width measurement, and in the Vertical box enter in half of the height measurement.

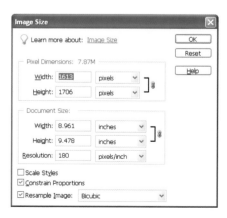

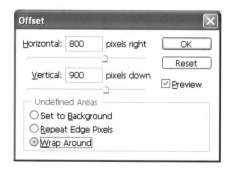

Plug-In Filters

Plug In filters are sold or given away by various websites and are not covered in this book. You can only use filters that are for Windows. A Mac filter will not work in the Photoshop Elements Windows version.

Digimarc Filter

If there is a Digimarc watermark on an image you will be able to read it by using this filter. I have never been able to find a Digimarc so far, with the images I've checked, but if it does find a watermark it will direct you to the Digimarc website where you can get more information about the owner of the copyright

Blending Modes

Blending Modes can be used with layers and brush tools and control how one layer affects the layers below it. For this reason you cannot apply a Blending Mode to a Background layer. When you have an image that is just a Background layer, the Blending Mode drop down list is not available as seen in the top example. To apply a Blending Mode to a Background layer Ctrl>J (Layer>New via Copy) and copy the Background layer. Apply the Blending Mode to the Background copy layer. With two or more layers, you are able to click on the drop down arrow to display the list of Blending Modes. When using a tool that utilizes brushes, the Blending Modes are listed on the specific tool option bar. All of the Blending Modes may not be available for use.

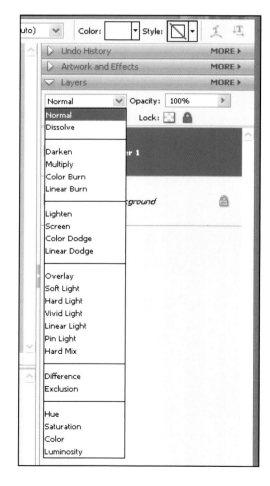

When you have a few minutes, the best way to start using Blending Modes is to just play around with them. Try blending a photo with a digital paper or vice versa. Blending Modes can be applied to brush work on their own separate layer to create great effects.

There are several ways to select a Blending Mode. Clicking on the drop down arrow and selecting one works just fine. Highlighting the Blending Mode name and rolling your mouse wheel or tapping the up and down Arrow keys will scroll through the list and display the changes to your image at the same time. Holding the Shift and the + and – key will also do the same thing.

Adjusting the layer's Opacity will also change the effect of the Blending Mode. To adjust the Opacity, use the slider. Enter an amount in the Opacity box, hover over the word Opacity until the two headed arrow appears, or use the keyboard shortcut of typing 1 for 10% when several tools are active.

Duplicating a layer with a Blending Mode (Ctrl>J) intensifies the effect of the Blending Mode.

The following examples use two layers to demonstrate exactly what Blending Modes do. The top layer shown on the top left is strips of solid color along with a black and white patterned area. The bottom layer is different paper from the Pistacchio kit designed by Denise Liemert at Polkadotpotato.com that's included on the DVD that came with your book. I used a different Blending Mode and Opacity for each selection that is identified by the Blending Mode name and the Opacity.

Blending Modes are kind of like filters, you need to have a general idea of what kind of effect you want to create, and then just try it. I can use the technical jargon regarding pixels being darkened and lightened or I can show you an example. Below is my non-techie description of blending modes and an example. Try them out with your photos and digital papers for an impressive look.

The Blending M odes are broken up in groups in the drop down list according to what they do.

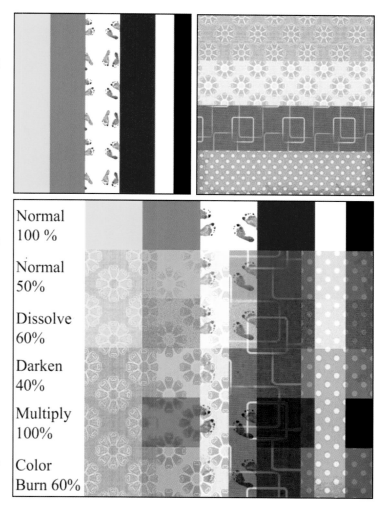

Normal (Shift >Alt>N)

Normal is just plain normal, the only way the top layer will affect the layer below it is if you lower the Opacity.

Dissolve (Shift >Alt >I)

Dissolve almost looks like you've added Noise with a Noise filter when you reduce the Opacity of the layer, at 100% Opacity you won't notice much difference.

Darken (Shift >Alt>K)

Darken makes the darker areas of the different layers displayed leaving the lighter areas to virtually disappear. Darken works exactly opposite of the Lighten Blending Mode.

Multiply (Shift >Alt>M)

Multiply darkens the entire image. I use this when I have a photo where the faces are blown out with the flash and are stark white. Multiply also works well with photos that are faded.

Color Burn (Shift>Alt>B)

Color Burn also darkens an image almost as if you used the Burn Tool (O) on it.

Linear Burn (Shift >Alt >A)

This is another Blending Mode that darkens and decreases the bright areas of the layer below.

Lighten (Shift>Alt >G)

Lighten chooses the lighter colors and replaces the darker colors.

Screen (Shift>Alt >S)

Screen lightens an image. I use screen on photos that are too dark. Make several layers and apply the Screen Blending Mode to lighten the photo gradually.

Color Dodge (Shift >Alt>D)

Color Dodge also brightens, unless you blend it with black and then nothing happens.

Linear Dodge (Shift >Alt >W)

Linear Dodge brightens similar to Color Dodge. There is also no change when you blend it with black.

Overlay (Shift >Alt >O)

Overlay will brighten or darken the colors depending on the original color in the image. Patterns preserve the highlights and shadows of the original image.

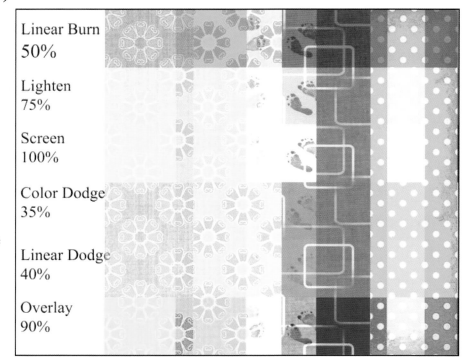

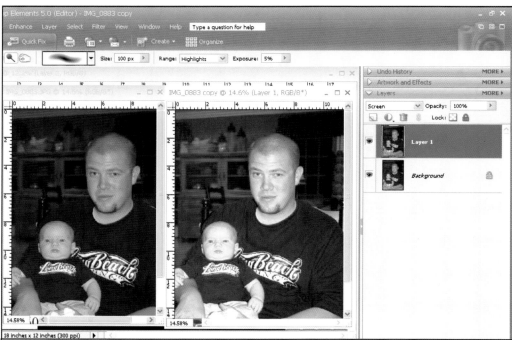

The photo on the left is the original. I duplicated the Background layer (Ctrl>J) and applied the Screen Blending Mode to lighten the photo. If the photo is very dark you can duplicate the layer several times.

Soft Light

(Shift >Alt >F)

Like the name implies, Soft Light looks as if you're shining a soft spotlight on your image. Depending on what you've applied with a painting or editing tool, Soft Light will darken or lighten the colors. If you've painted with a color 50% or more gray, the image is darkened. Less than 50% gray and it's lightened. If you paint with solid black or white, the image will be darker or lighter but will not be pure black or white.

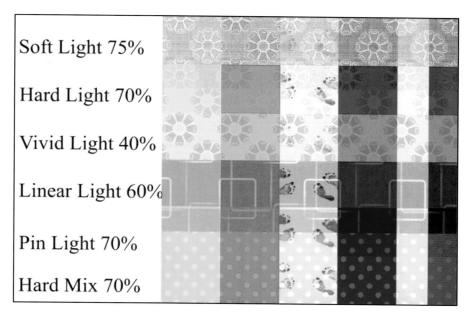

Hard Light (Shift>Alt>H)

Hard Light looks as if you're shining a powerful spotlight on your image. If you've painted with a color 50% or more gray, the image is darkened. Less than 50% gray and it's lightened. If you paint with solid black or white, the image will be darker or lighter but will not be pure black or white.

Vivid Light (Shift>Alt>V)

Vivid Light is like using the Burn or Dodge Tools (O) on the colors in your image to increase or decrease the contrast.

Linear Light (Shift >Alt >J)

Linear Light is similar to using the Burn or Dodge Tools (O) on the colors in your image to decrease or increase the brightness.

Pin Light (Shift>Alt>Z)

Pin Light changes colors depending on the blend color. If the blend color is dark, then the darker colors are replaced while the lighter colors don't change. If the blend color is light, the lighter colors are replaced and the darker colors don't change.

Hard Mix (Shift>Alt >L)

Hard Mix reduces colors to the RGB (Red, Green, Blue) & CMYK (Cyan, Magenta, Yellow, Black) colors and white.

Difference (Shift>Alt >E)

Difference uses the brightest between the two layers. Blending with black makes no change as you can see in the example, but blending with white inverts the colors.

Exclusion (Shift>Alt> X)

Exclusion is very similar to Difference, except that the contrast is lower.

Hue (Shift>Alt>U)

Hue uses the saturation and lightness of the base image along with the hue from the blend layer to create a new color.

Saturation (Shift>Alt>T)

Similar to the Hue Blending Mode, but Saturation uses the lightness and hue of the base image with the saturation of the blend layer to create a new color.

Color (Shift>Alt >C)

Similar to Hue and Saturation Blending Modes, Color uses the lightness of the base image with the hue and saturation of the blend layer to create a new color. This is sometimes used to tint photos.

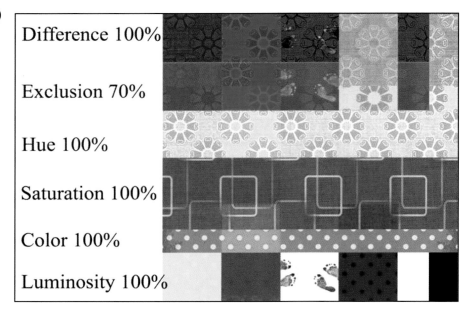

Difference 100%

Exclusion 70%

Hue 100%

Saturation 100%

Color 100%

Luminosity 100%

70% Hard Light

Color Burn 100%

Overlay 100%

A scanned wedding invitation layer with various Blending Modes applied is placed over a photograph layer. These Blending Modes almost make it appear that the wedding invitation background has been removed and only the text remains.

Luminosity (Shift >Alt>Y)

The Inverse of the Color Blending Mode is Luminosity. It uses the hue and saturation of the base image with the lightness of the blend layer to create a new color

Fixing Your Photos Quickly

There are many Photoshop Elements books on the market today that deal primarily with editing your photos. People spend hours editing one photo at a time. I am not one of those people, although I have to admit I did spend a lot of time editing a photo, taken at night, of a large painting job my son worked on. In this section are some quick tips to edit your problem photos. Other fixes are sprinkled through the Tools and Layers Sections.

Always duplicate (File>Duplicate) your image before you edit it in any way. Photos can be edited in the Editor, which is sometimes called the Standard Edit or Full Edit Mode or in the Quick Fix Mode. The example below shows the Quick Fix Mode. The Zoom Tool (Z), Hand Tool (H), Magic Selection Brush (F), Crop Tool (C), and the Red Eye Tool (Y) are the only tools available for use in Quick Fix Mode. All of these tools work just like they do in Full Edit Mode, and are explained in the Tools Section of this book. Photos can be rotated using the Rotate arrows, which rotates the image 90° every time you click on the arrow.

One of the nice things about Quick Fix is that the image can be viewed both before and after changes were done.

The first thing to try in Quick Fix, is the top button on the right which is Smart Fix. Click on the button and see if you like the change. A lot of times this one change is all that a photo needs. Auto Smart Fix can also be applied in the Organizer. From the Edit Menu, choose Auto Smart Fix Selected Photos (Ctrl>Alt>M). From the Editor, choose Enhance>Auto Smart Fix (Alt>Ctrl>M). The After photo in this example has Smart Fix applied.

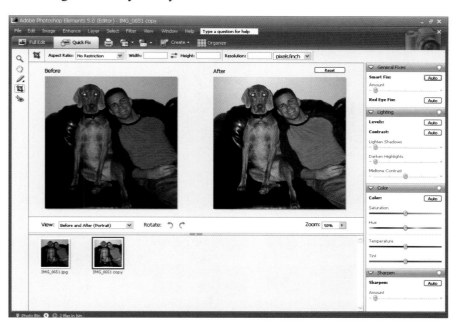

Click on the Reset button on the top right to undo the change or Ctrl>Z for Undo. If you go to the Editor and then return to Quick Fix, the reset button will no longer be available and your before and after photo will no longer show your beginning image. To adjust Lighting, Color, and to Sharpen the image, choose one of the Auto buttons below Smart Fix or slide the sliders. These changes can also be done automatically or manually in the Editor by choosing the Enhance Menu. In addition, Adjustment layers can be added to photos to change Levels, Brightness/Contrast, and Hue/Saturation. The advantage of Adjustment layers is that the changes you make can easily be edited in the future, as long as you save your file as a PSD file, with all of the layers intact. Adjustment layers are explained in detail in the Layers section.

Too much Quick Fix or any other type of editing is not a good thing. When I first began using Photoshop Elements, I thought all I needed to do was use Quick Fix on all of my photos and Save my only copy of the photo that way. What I found after I had them printed was that some of them looked awful in print, and I no longer had my originals to edit again. So…if you wonder why I'm always telling you to duplicate your photos, you now know I have a good reason for it.

Sometimes you only need to edit part of your photo, because editing all of it will ruin the parts of the photo that have no problems. Or, maybe you want to make a change to just a portion of the photo. The easiest way to do this is to make a selection with one of the selection tools and apply the changes only to the selected area. As shown in this example, I made a selection of the pumpkin and adjusted the Hue and Saturation by sliding the sliders in the Hue/Saturation dialog box.

Other ways to edit the color in your photos is to choose Enhance>Adjust Color>Color Variations. Click on each color to achieve the results shown in the preview boxes. Increasing red two times and green one time will usually give you a Sepia effect as shown in the After photo.

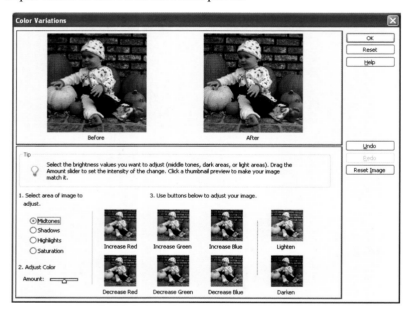

Enhance>Adjust Color>Adjust Color For Skin Tones is supposed to fix the rest of your image based on the skin tone area you select. I have never had great luck with this command.

Enhance>Adjust Color>Adjust Color Curves is new to Adobe Photoshop Elements 5. This gives you another opportunity to adjust the color of your image. To display the Advanced Options as shown, click on the drop down arrow (circled). The sliders change the curve on the graph. Adobe Help in my version says that there is a tutorial at Adobe.com that explains how to use this feature.

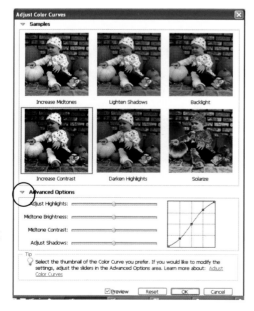

When you're done fooling around with your photo (duplicate of your original), and want to return to the image when last saved, choose Edit>Revert. Opening your Undo History (Window>Undo History) allows you to return to the point when you opened your photo, as long as you didn't make more than 50 changes, (unless you changed your Undo preferences). To change how many steps your Undo History will hold, choose Edit>Preferences>General (Ctrl>K) and change the amount of History States. Be aware that saving a lot of steps (History States) slows your computer.

Design, Color, & Journaling

Design

I am not a designer by any means. I prefer simple classic lines for everything in my life including my scrapbook pages and cards. My theory is "less is more". I've met many scrappers who aren't happy until their traditional page is covered in embellishments six inches deep. I'm sure these scrappers look at my pages and thing they're missing something or I'm too cheap to cover them with lots of expensive embellishments. Unfortunately these are the same scrappers who usually have no journaling what so ever on their page. I'm scrapping to save my memories, not win an art contest. Design is a very personal thing.

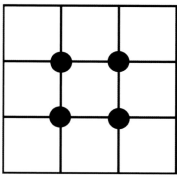

For design ideas, I usually turn to the magazines I subscribe to or buy on a newsstand, if they've caught my eye. I also save digital and paper copies of pages I like so I can refer to them when I finally have some time to scrap. I use simple templates for page designs sold by **The Digital Scrapbook Teacher** to construct most of my pages. By changing the template just a little, I can make a page look completely different from another one constructed with the same template. Using a template saves me a lot of time because the design is already done and perfectly lined up. All I have to do is add my photos, some digital paper, embellishments and text, and I'm done.

If you don't have an artistic bone in your body like me, scraplifting is a great way to go. I regularly begin a with another page I've seen before in mind. The funny thing is, my page ends up looking completely different than the one I originally liked. Sometimes my page looks better and sometimes…OK we won't go there!

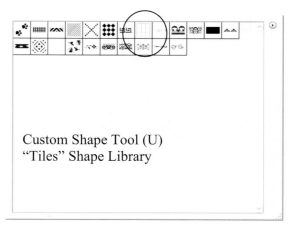

Custom Shape Tool (U)
"Tiles" Shape Library

Besides my "Less is More" rule, I also follow the Rule of Thirds that I explained in the photography section. Essentially, if you divide your scrapbook page or card into thirds vertically and horizontally with lines; the areas where those lines intersect should be your focal point. The really cool thing is that Photoshop Elements has a tool built right in to help you mark you page. Activate the Custom Shape Tool (U) and choose the Grid from the shape library. Choose Fixed size from the Custom Shapes Tool (U) Option Bar and enter the size of the project you're working on. Click once, and your Grid is positioned on your page. Use the Shape Selection Tool (U) to move it into position and use it to plan your page. When you're done with it, delete it or hide it by clicking on the eyeball icon.

Color

I have struggled with color since the days when I was determined to be a great quilter. The actual sewing of the quilt was no problem, but the colors of my fabrics never matched quite the way I'd hoped they would. I had the same trouble picking out the perfect card stock to match my scrapbook layouts. I'd love to be like a friend of mine who flipped through a stack of more than a hundred paint swatches and chose the perfect paint color for my house in less than a minute, but it's just not going to happen. The Eyedropper Tool (I) in Photoshop Elements makes color issues a thing of the past for me. It's simple to pick a color from one of my photos or scrapbook elements. I can match other elements of my scrapbook page or card to my photos and scrapbook supplies with the click of my mouse.

Many websites are now available with free color wheels and color swatches with great color combinations that I could never come up with on my own. Many of the websites give the hexadecimal or RGB numbers to match your color to exactly. If they don't give you the numbers, simply use the Eyedropper Tool (I) to sample the color. I have to admit, I use these websites now instead of trying to figure out matching colors on my own. Some great sites I've found are:

www.steeldolphin.com/color_scheme.html
www.njit.edu/~walsh/rgb.html
www.htmlhelp.com/cgi-bin/color.cgi
www.colorschemer.com/online.html
www.wellstyled.com/Tools/colorscheme2/index-en.html
www.behr.com/behr/workbook/indes.jsp (you must create a free account to use this, but it's worth it!)

Bazzill Basics Paper is now selling a book called Chemistry (of) Color 2007 that gives you the RGB formulas to match their cardstock along with more than 50 layout ideas.

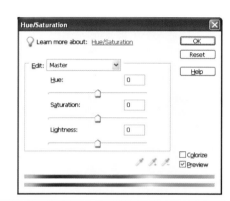

If you really want to pick colors for color schemes I'll show you the trick I used before I got lazy and started using the websites.

Sample a color that you want to match to other colors with the Eyedropper Tool (I) so that it's your Foreground color. Activate your Marquee Tool (M) and draw out a selection. The size or shape of the selection doesn't matter because you're just going to discard it. Make a new layer with the New Layer icon on the top of the Layers palette. Alt>Backspace to fill the selection on the new layer with your Foreground color. Tap the Esc key to remove the selection border (marching ants), Ctrl>U (Enhance>Adjust Color>Adjust Hue/Saturation) and the Hue Saturation dialog box will be activated. By adjusting the different boxes, you can choose a pleasing color scheme. The new color you make will be your new Foreground color.

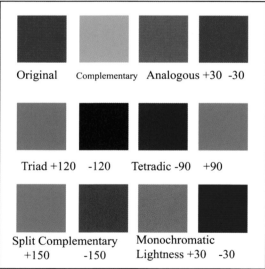

Original   Complementary   Analogous +30 -30

Triad +120   -120   Tetradic -90   +90

Split Complementary   Monochromatic
+150   -150   Lightness +30   -30

Monochromatic color (variations of the same color in lightness) Slide the Lightness slider, do not adjust Hue and Saturation.

Analogous color (colors adjacent on the color wheel) To get two analogous colors, put a number in the Hue box to make the first color, such as 20. Go back to your starting color and put a -20 in the Hue box.

Complementary color (opposites on the color wheel): put -180 or +180 in the Hue box. For a complementary color only you can Ctrl>I to apply the Invert filter.

Triadic color (three colors equally spaced on the color wheel): In the Hue box put +120 and -120.

Tetradic color (Four colors in two complementary color pairs): In the Hue box put +90, -90, +180.

Split Complementary color (2 colors an equal distance away on the color wheel from the complementary color): In the Hue box put +150 and -150.

Scrapbook Journaling & Card Wording Tools

As a traditional scrapper I found I waited to do my journaling until I was sure I knew what I wanted to write, and tried to write in my best penmanship. As a result, I have many pages with pictures but no journaling. As I got better with the computer I used it to do my page titles and some journaling. Now I've found with digital scrapbooking, I journal much more than I ever did before. Writing in cards is similar to journaling because you have to find the right words to say.

Journaling doesn't have to be perfect. Write something, anything about your page. You've seen the pretty pages in the scrapbook magazines. The journaling is wonderful beautiful thoughts that were probably written by an English major. Start with the basics-Who, What, When, Where, and go from there. Your journaling can be serious, funny, or even sad so that when someone looks at the page, they understand what it's all about.

Years ago I attended a scrapbook class about journaling. The instructor showed us several nice scrapbook pages with and without journaling, then she made a point that I'll never forget. She said that if you don't journal, the page is saying that all that matters is how the person in the photo looks. She also told us that if we don't write things we'll forget them. I've always had a great memory and I was in my late 30's at the time and didn't really believe that I'd forget. Well…fast forward a few years and I'm now what Oprah considers the new 30! What Oprah didn't mention, probably because she forgot, is that you do forget things more as you age. The whole idea behind scrapbooking is to tell a story. When you journal on your scrapbook page, people will know the story of what was going on because they'll read it themselves. The teacher had us tell some stories of our lives; some were sad, and some were hilarious. I told a funny story about my son when he was three years old. After leaving the class, I decided I'd make a scrapbook page about the story even though my son was now a 6'4" strapping football player. Here's the story on my son's scrapbook page:

I wanted this Christmas to be special. The past year had been a tough year for all three of us and I wanted to get the perfect gift for you and your sister. You were always easy to buy for, anything that was all boy fit you perfectly! I'd found you a big yellow Tonka truck that I knew you'd love. Your sister is girly at times, but not all the time. This Christmas season I looked all over for the perfect gift to get her but I didn't have much luck. Finally I found it, a small white jewelry box with a pink ballerina that twirled around to music when the lid was opened. I had one when I was a little girl and loved it. I was sure she would love it too. Christmas morning was a blur as both of you tore through your presents. Then we were off to Grama & Poppa Kelley's. You both loved your presents but I could tell Kristin was less than thrilled about the jewelry box. We got home late that night and you both fell asleep in the car. I carried you in first and put you on your bed and then carried Kristin in. After I got you both in your pajamas and in bed, I went into the living room to clean up the path of the Christmas cyclone.   As I was cleaning up I heard the music from the jewelry box playing down the hallway. Aha! Kristin really did like her jewelry box after all. I crept down the hallway and peeked into her room expecting to see a heartwarming scene, instead I saw Kristin fast asleep. I thought maybe in my post Christmas exhaustion I was hearing things until I heard the jewelry box again. As I looked into your room, there you were with your back to me huddled under your bunk bed. Kristin's little pink ballerina jewelry box was also under the bed. You sat and watched the ballerina twirl around. Suddenly you slammed the lid shut and shouted: "OK lady now you're trapped in there!" I've never looked at a pink ballerina jewelry box quite the same!

The scrapbook page is a simple one with just the story and a pink ballerina, but if I'd just had a photo of him with the jewelry box I'd never remember the story. As a matter of fact I don't even have a photo on the page, nor did I take one that night.

You'll find that digital scrapbooking makes it much easier to journal on your pages. You've got choices of more fonts than you could ever install in your lifetime, available for free. You can even buy a font of your own handwriting for a very reasonable price to make it look like your journaled yourself when in fact, the computer did it.

While spell check still isn't available in Photoshop Elements, you can copy and paste your text from your scrapbook page into a Word document and spell check it that way. Just be warned that everything is not caught on spell check. If you write: "I'm knot inn thyme four tee". The computer doesn't know that you really meant to write: "I'm not in time for tea".

The easiest way to get familiar with the Text Tool (T) is to practice, and the best way to practice is to journal! I'm sure you've got a Pink Ballerina type story, scrap it and journal it before you forget!

Websites to Help With Journaling & Card-Making

There are several free sites available to help you come up with creative titles, phrases, sayings, poems and journaling ideas. Some of my favorite sites are:

www.PeppermintCreative.com/phrases.php
www.dennydavis.net
www.worldofquotes.com
www.goodquotes.com
www.brainyquote.com
www.famous-quotations.com/asp/categories.asp
www.thinkexist.com
www.quotegarden.com
www.thenaspoems.com
www.rubberstampinglinks.com/poems-quotes.html

There are probably thousands more sites on the internet that offer free journaling ideas. To find more go to Google.com and type in poems, phrases, etc.

Journaling & Card-Making Tips

Try not to use more than three fonts on a page. Using the right font can make your page or card, but using too many fonts will drive the reader crazy.

Use only one space after a sentence.

Use the right font for the page or card. A font with footballs on it isn't appropriate for a New Baby Girl card (I know this example is a little bit extreme!)

Set the Leading on the Text Tool (T) to space your lines of text for you instead of trying to use the enter key.

Try using different text alignment. If you always use left align, try right align or center align for a different look. Drag out a text box with the Text Tool (T) to constrain your writing to a confined space instead of trying to use the enter key to control it.

DON'T USE ALL CAPS BECAUSE IT MAKES IT TOO HARD TO READ.

Copy and paste your text into a word processing program and check the spelling. Zoom in very close and look at all of the text before you print it because spell check doesn't catch all errors.

If you don't want to write on the page and you're not printing your page on 2 sides, journal on a piece of cardstock or even a mailing label and secure it to the back of the page where you can see it.

How To Do The Basics

Photoshop Elements Basics

Maximize View And How To Get There

All of my examples are shown in Maximize View because I prefer to work this way. Working in Maximize View is like a traditional scrapbooker working with one page in front of her with her other supplies neatly lined up very close by. For me, and many of the students I've taught, Cascade or Tile View is like working with all of your stuff in a big pile and continually sorting through it. Try the different views and see which way you like better. To switch to Maximize Mode if you're not already there, go to the upper right corner of your screen and hover over the box that says Maximize Mode and click on it. You should now only see one image in your image window.

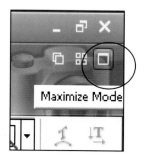

How To Get A Photo/Scrapbook Element Into The Editor

Photoshop Elements does not differentiate between photos and scrapbook elements; to it, they are all images even if the term "photos" is used. The procedure for getting photos into the Editor is the same as getting scrapbook elements. Before proceeding, if you have not read the Organizing Chapter, I highly encourage you to read it first.

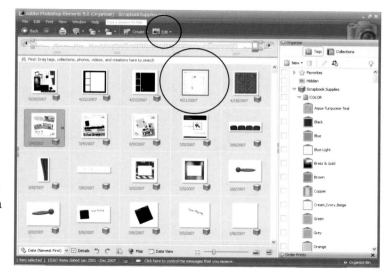

If you have imported your images into the Organizer, go to the Organizer and click on the thumbnail of the image(s) you want. You will know they are selected when they have a blue outline around them. Once selected, Ctrl>I or click on the Edit button at the top of the screen and choose Full (Standard) Edit. The images will open in the Editor.

Click and then Shift Click on the last image in a group to select several images in between both images. Click and Ctrl click on each image to select images not in a row.

If your images are not stored in the Organizer but in folders, go to the Editor and Ctrl>O or File>Open and find the folder where your images are stored. Double click on the folder or click once on the folder and click the Open button and the

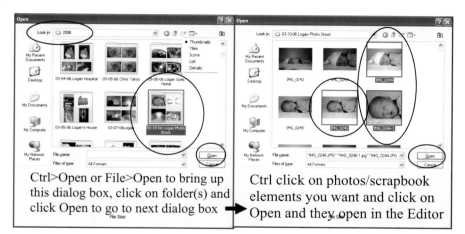

Ctrl>Open or File>Open to bring up this dialog box, click on folder(s) and click Open to go to next dialog box

Ctrl click on photos/scrapbook elements you want and click on Open and they open in the Editor

folder will open for you. Select the images you want to use by clicking on the first image and Ctrl clicking on the other images. If you have several images in a row you can click and then Shift click on the last image to select all images in between. You will know they are selected when they have a blue outline around them. Click on the Open button and they will open in the Editor. One image will show in the image window and the other images will show in the Photo Bin, as shown in the example.

How To Make A New Blank File/Document (Scrapbook Page, Card, Etc.)

Making a new file is the same no matter what kind of project you're working on. The only difference is that you enter different width and height dimensions. To make a new file, go to File>New or Ctrl>N. To open a file with the same specifications as the last one you opened, type Alt>Ctrl>N, this is a big timesaver. Always name your File because you'll have to name it when you Save it anyway, so you might as well do it now and it will help you identify it in the Photo Bin.

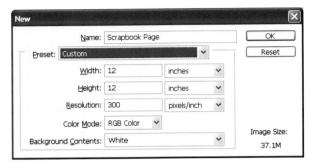

There are a few Preset sizes, but I rarely make anything in those sizes, so I always type in my own dimensions. When you type in your own dimensions, the Preset line changes to Custom. Enter the dimensions for the project you're creating. If you're a 8.5 x 11 scrapper enter that here. If you're making a card that's 10 x 7, enter that here.

Be sure that you click the drop down box to enter inches because just typing the letter "I" won't do it. If you get a strange sized file after you click OK, it probably reverted back to pixels, so close it and start over.

Resolution will always be 300 pixels/inch.

Color Mode will always be RGB.

Background Content is usually white unless otherwise stated. A Transparent background will appear as a checkerboard pattern, but is actually blank. The checkerboard pattern does not print on your project nor do grid lines if you use them.

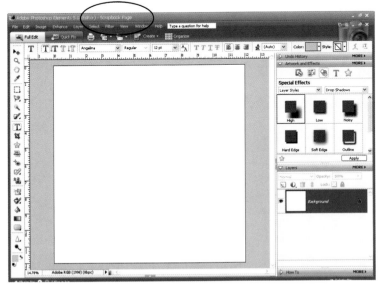

Click OK and your new file becomes the active image. At the top of the Editor screen is the name of your new file. Your new blank file is the Background layer.

Setting Your Grid Lines To Show The Center Of Your File/Document

Grid lines are not printed on your project, but are helpful in locating the center of your document. Go to View>Grid. Go to Edit>Preferences>Grid

Using these settings will divide your project into quarters.

An easy way to center your photos and other elements on your card or scrapbook page is to activate the Move Tool (V) and move the bounding box center sizing handles directly on top of your grid line.

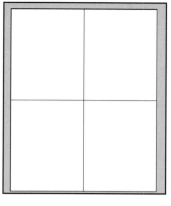

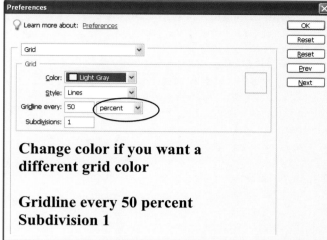

Change color if you want a different grid color

Gridline every 50 percent
Subdivision 1

Watch The Edges!

Depending on how you print your projects, you may have a problem with the edges. For this reason I make it a rule not to put any text or elements closer than ¼ inch to the edge of my page. Check out your printer/photo lab and you can probably adjust this one way or the other, but be careful if you change printers.

Scrapbooks

Plopper/Quick Page/Ready Made Page

Many sites offer scrapbook pages that are already completed by the designer, all you need to do is add the photos. Different sites call their products by different names, but the term I tend to hear the most is plopper. This is a very fast way to make a nice page and who says you have to admit that you didn't make the whole thing?

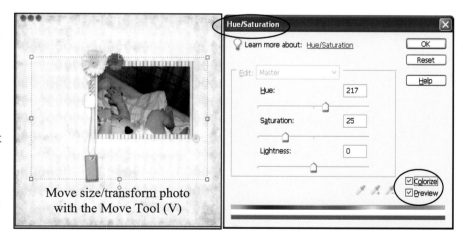

Move size/transform photo with the Move Tool (V)

Make a new blank document 12 x 12 inches (instructions are at the beginning of this chapter). Open the quick page file and a photo (instructions are at the beginning of this chapter). The page I'm using is in the Crazy Universe Folder on the CD that came with this book. Drag the quick page onto your new blank document. Select the Background Layer and drag your photo onto your scrapbook page. Because you were on the Background Layer, it should be sandwiched in between the quick page and the Background Layer. Your photo is probably centered on the page, so activate the Move Tool (V) and drag it to the hole in the page and size/transform it by dragging or pulling on the corner sizing handles. Once the photo is centered, you're done unless you want to add text with Type Tool (T).

Because this baby is a boy, I didn't want to put him on a purple page (his dad has issues with things like that). I sampled a blue color from the image with the Eyedropper Tool (I) by activating the tool and clicking in the blue area that I wanted to use. This changed my foreground color. Next I selected the quick page layer and went to (Ctrl>U) Enhance>Adjust Color>Adjust Hue & Saturation. I clicked the colorize box and as soon as I did, my page turned blue. I added some text with the Type Tool (T) Scriptina font and I'm done. Ctrl>S or File>Save and choose a place to save your page. I save all of my scrapbook pages in my Scrapbook Pages folder in a sub-folder for each scrapbook I'm making. I always know where to find my pages this way. Changing the color of this quick page allows it to be used for many different occasions.

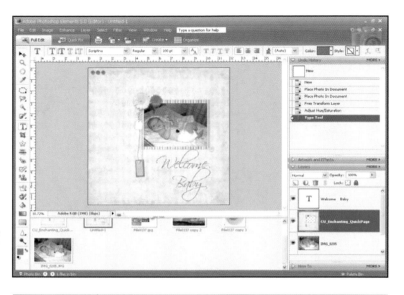

How To Mat A Photo

Adding a mat to a photo simply outlines it to bring more emphasis to the photo. Photos can be matted several different ways. Adding a drop shadow to the photo and the mat makes the photo pop off the page. Link your mat and photo together by selecting both layers and clicking on the Link icon on the top of the layers palette. By linking your layers, when you move or size your photo, the mat will also move or size along with it.

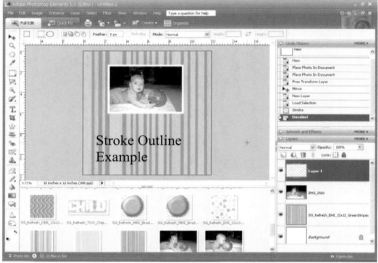

The fastest way to add a mat is to use the Stroke Outline (Selection). Make a new blank layer for each Stroke Outline. Select the image by Ctrl clicking the layer thumbnail and then go to Edit>Stroke Outline (Selection). Choose a color, size, and location of your outline and press OK. Stroke Outlines are explained in detail in the Selection Tools section.

To cut photos and mats into shapes, use the Custom Shape Tool (U) and drag out a shape. Position the shape under the photo/paper. Select the photo layer and Ctrl>G (Layer>Group with Previous) and your photo/paper will now appear to be cut into the shape. If you want to change this, you can Undo or select the top layer and Shift>Ctrl>G to Ungroup.

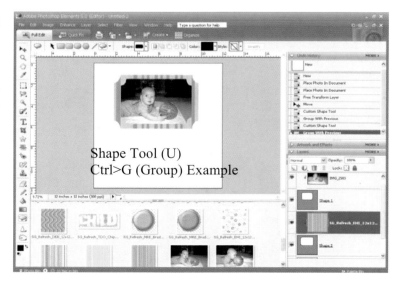

To add a solid mat under your photo, drag out a Shape using one of the Shape Tools (U). Begin on the layer below your photo on a scrapbook page, and it will automatically be placed under the photo. If you forget and your shape is on top of your photo, drag the layer down in the Layers palette.

Frames from the Artwork section of the Artwork and Effects palette can be used to mat your photos by selecting the photo and double clicking on the frame. Right click on the frame to make any adjustments.

To use a scrapbook paper to mat a photo, position your photo on top of the scrapbook paper on your page. Select the scrapbook paper layer in the Layers palette. Do not use the Crop Tool (C) or you will crop off your whole scrapbook page. Use the Marquee Tool (M) to draw an outline around your photo the size you want your mat to be. Shift>Ctrl>I to inverse your selection so that the part of the scrapbook paper you want to cut off is selected. The example shows the steps to this point. Tap the Delete key and then the Esc key to remove the marching ants. If it didn't work right, you probably didn't have the scrapbook paper layer selected, so try it again.

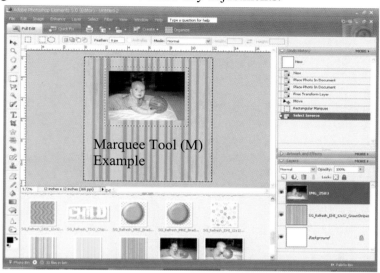

Single Simple Scrapbook Page-Photos Only

Make a new blank document the size you want your scrapbook page (instructions are at the beginning of this chapter). Turn on your gridlines and use the setting to divide the scrapbook page into quarters (instructions are at the beginning of this chapter). My example will show a 12 x 12 inch scrapbook page. Open the photos you want to use on your page (instructions are at the beginning of this chapter). Duplicate and edit your photos for lighting, color, etc. issues and crop out any obvious areas you don't want, (see the Editing your Photos chapter). Never edit your original photos, edit the duplicate.

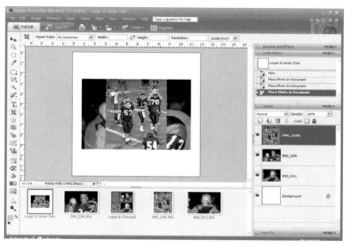

Shift>Ctrl S (File>Save As) and specify the location you want to save your scrapbook page. I save all of my scrapbook pages in my Scrapbook Pages folder in a subfolder for each scrapbook I'm making. This way, I always know where to find my pages.
With your blank scrapbook page as your active image, drag your photos onto your blank scrapbook page by dragging up from the photo bin. Your photos will all land in the middle of the page and will be stacked on top of each other, so don't panic if you only see one. Check your Layers palette and you'll see all of the photos on the different layers. My example has three photos and the Background layer, even though only one photo shows on the scrapbook page.

Activate the Move Tool (V) and move and size/transform your photos by clicking on the photo and moving it. Remember to check the checkmark to accept the change when you size/transform the photo. Place your photos where you want them on the page.

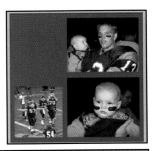

Right click on your photos in the Photo Bin and choose close so you clean up your work area a little bit.

Choose a Background color for your page. To choose a color from an image, activate the Eyedropper Tool (I) and click in a color to select it. I chose the dark blue from the football uniform. To pick a color from the Color Picker, double click in the Foreground color square and choose a color. Ctrl>S (File>Save).

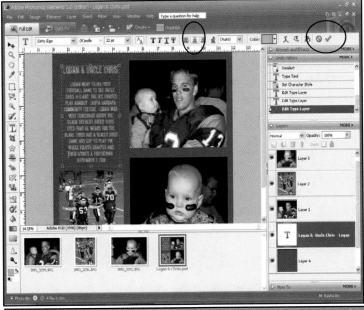

Click on the Background layer and make a new layer with the New Layer icon on the Layers palette. The new layer should be right above the Background layer. Type Alt>Backspace to fill the new layer with the Foreground color.

Choose a color for your text and a stroke outline with the Eyedropper Tool (I). I chose the orange from the football uniform.

Activate the Type Tool (T), click and drag out a paragraph box, type your text in the box. Change the alignment of the text by using the appropriate alignment setting located on the Type Tool options bar. Don't forget to click the checkmark or you won't be able to go on to the next step. The font in the example is Dirty Ego, downloaded for free from www.Dafont.com.

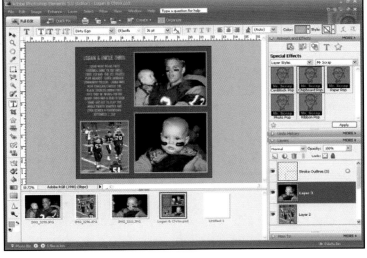

Add mats to the photos (instructions are at the beginning of this chapter). I used a 30 px Stroke Outline and chose Inside Location on each of the photos in the same orange color that I used for the text. I put all 3 Stroke Outlines on their own layer.

Add drop shadows to the Stroke Outline Layer.

From the Artwork & Effects Palette, choose Special Effects and Layer Styles. Pick a low drop shadow so that it looks real. I use the Mr. Scrap drop shadow from PolkaDotPotato.com and I like it a lot better than the drop shadows included with Photoshop Elements.

Ctrl S or File>Save. This is a simple page that's actually finished in a few minutes (after you practice a little bit!).

Single Scrapbook Page Or Flat Card Using A Digi-Kit

Using a digi-kit seems a little bit scarier than just using your photos to digi-scrap. If you think about your digital scrapbook elements as just another image, you'll see that it's exactly the same.

The kit I'm using for this example is the Refresh kit that has been contributed by Scrapgirls.com. It's on the DVD that came with your book. Scrapgirls.com sends out a newsletter six days a week filled with great tips, inspiration, and a freebie, not to mention great products for sale.

Follow the steps in the beginning of the section to open your photos and scrapbook elements into the Editor. Make a new file and be sure to name your new file. Turn your grid lines on to divide your page in half so you can position images correctly. Open your photos and scrapbook supplies from the Organizer or from your folders following the instructions in the beginning of this section.

With your blank file as the active image showing in the image window, choose a paper to use for your background in the Photo Bin. Click, hold and drag it up onto the blank page. This may take a little while. If you clicked and released your mouse on the paper in your Photo Bin, the paper became your active image. Find the blank file in your Photo Bin and try it again. You will now have your paper on top of your Background layer.

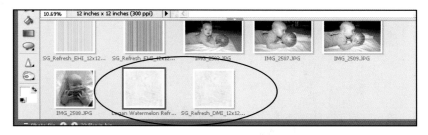

In the Photo Bin, right click on the paper (not your new page) and choose Close. This is one spot where people get very confused, and if you don't close the paper now, you will get confused and make a mistake. As shown in the example, the last two images in the Photo Bin look exactly the same. There are two ways you can tell which page you're working on: Check the name of the file. The highlighted one is named Logan Watermelon Refresh so I know that is what I named my scrapbook page. The other one has the file name given to it by Scrapgirls.com. If you didn't name your page, or you're still not sure, check each image in the image window by selecting it. When you select the Logan page, you will see it has the paper and a Background layer. The other file will just be the paper. You do not want to scrap directly on your paper for a couple of reasons. By making a new file, you are assured that the resolution is 300 and acceptable for printing without checking on the supplies. If you drag lower resolution elements onto your page, you'll know it immediately because they'll be very small. The other reason is that if you scrap directly on the paper, and you Save it, you've just saved over your scrapbook paper and can't reuse it. While it might take an extra second to start with a New File Ctrl>N (File>New) it's worth it.

Edit and crop your photos before you put them on your scrapbook page. Sometimes you aren't sure exactly how much of a photo you want to crop. In that case, you can crop it on the scrapbook page using the Marquee Tool (M). Do not use the Crop Tool (C) on a scrapbook page or it will crop the whole page. Select the photo layer in the Layers palette, activate the Marquee Tool (M), make a selection of the area you want to delete, and tap the Delete key. Tap the Esc key to remove the selection border (marching ants).

If you have a sheet of several embellishments or Alphas and you want to use only one, as shown in this example, activate the Marquee Tool (M) and draw a selection around the element you want to use. Activate the

Move Tool (V) and click in an area that is not transparent (checkerboard), and drag the element down to your page in the Photo Bin. You will only move the element that you selected. If you try to move a letter without the selection, you will drag the whole sheet of letters onto your page.

With your scrapbook page file as your active image, click, hold, and drag photos and elements from the Photo Bin up to your page. Dragging up from the Photo Bin names your layers with the file name which is very helpful. All of your images will be placed in the center of your blank page. If you don't see them, look in the Layers palette to see if they are underneath the other items. Moving all items to get to your page from the Photo Bin is the fastest way to digi-scrap. In the beginning, you may want to move them one at a time and then position them on your page so you don't get confused. In my example below you can see how all the elements are all stacked on top of each other (circled). Looking at the scrapbook page, you don't realize that there is another photo and paper that you don't see. When you look at the Layers palette (I removed it from the bin so you can see it better) you can see the yellow paper and the other photo.

Move your photos/elements with the Move Tool (V) on your page. Mat your photos following the instructions in this section. Link your photos and mats together so that when you move or size them they move or size. This save you lots of unnecessary work. If you move the linked layers up and down in the Layers palette they do not move together. You will have to select both layers at the same time and move them. If you are having difficulty moving small objects like brads or rivets, zoom in to see them better or turn off Auto Select Layer on the Move Tool (V) Option Bar. To toggle the Auto Select Layer on/off, hold the Ctrl key when the Move Tool (V) is active. Add titles or journaling using the Text Tool (T) Alphas.

Finally, add drop shadows to your layers to make the items pop off the page. I think I've mentioned several times I use the Mr. Scrap Pop Action available at Polkadotpotato.com. With a little bit of practice, you can make a simple page shown above in just a couple of minutes.

Double Scrapbook Page

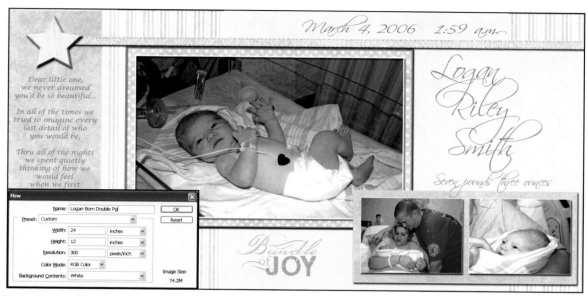

Scrapping a double page layout at one time is easier for me because it takes less time and it's easier for me to line up both sides of my page at one time. Sometimes making a double page will slow down your computer because it's such a big file. For this reason I do not store my scrapbook pages in my Organizer.

Make a new file twice as wide as a regular page; if you scrap 12 x 12, your double page will be 24 wide by 12 high. If you are an 8 ½ x 11 scrapper, your page will be 17 wide by 11. Choose 300 resolution and a white background, name your page with the word double in it. Turn on your Grid Lines. You will need to know where the center of your page is because you'll eventually be cropping it right down the middle. In my example, that's made with the Our Little Prince kit from ShabbyPrincess.com and the Scriptina font, my large center photo will end up being cropped through the center. While this may seem strange to you at first, think about how many times you've seen this in a magazine and it looks fine.

Construct your double page just as you would a single page. Use two copies of the background paper if you want the same paper across the whole page. Use the Grid Lines as a guide to help you always know where the center of the page is.

The difference in using a double page comes when it's time to print it because, unless you have access to a huge printer, you have to cut it in half. Activate the Crop Tool (C) and set the size of your crop on the Option Bar as 12 inches wide, 12 inches high, 300 resolution. Start at the upper left corner, and drag down. Make sure your crop covers the whole right side of the page and click the checkmark. The right side of your page has been cropped off.

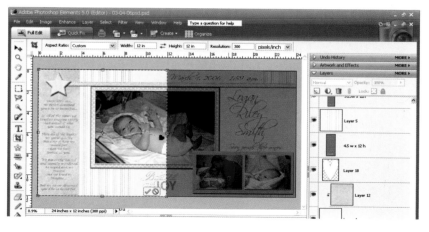

Even though you cropped some layers off, they will still show in the Layers palette, which is correct.

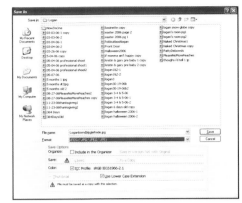

If you are printing on a home computer, you can go ahead and print the left side of your page right now from the PSD file and it works great. If you are going to send it to a photo lab, you must save this half of your page as a JPEG. Shift>Ctrl>S (File Save As) to save. Name your page something so that you know it's the left page. Choose JPEG as the file type. Go back to your file, Undo the crop and repeat these steps for the other side of the page. If you make changes to the double wide PSD file, remember that you will have to repeat the steps to save it again as a JPEG.

Cards

Cards are essentially just like a scrapbook page. Some cards are flat, and some you fold. The big difference in making a folded card is that ½ of the card is placed upside down so that when you fold it they both face the right way.

Cards can be mailed with or without an envelope. Check with the US Post Office website at www.USPS.gov to use the right amount of postage. If you are using an envelope that is larger, smaller than normal, or square be aware that there is an extra charge for this. If you want to mail a flat card without an envelope, you can do that. All you need is the address and postage on the back. Some people think that you need printing like what you see on a postcard that you purchase. I mail photos as postcards all the time. If you don't want to pay for a postcard stamp, read about how to ship your friends and relatives photos without any postage fees in the Printing and Saving Your Pages Section.

Paper of any kind can be used to print your cards, however I've had better luck with precut and scored cards. When I cut regular card stock and score it myself, the edges never quite look finished but you can try your luck at it yourself. Use a regular piece of copy paper cut the size of your card to make a folding template. Fold the copy paper so that the corners line up correctly and then lay it over your card as a pattern. Nothing works better to create a crisp fold than a plastic Chinese spoon purchased at a 99¢ store. Put your finger in the spoon part and slide it across your fold. The flat bottom flattens out your fold like you can't believe.

Postcards, Flat Cards, & Posters

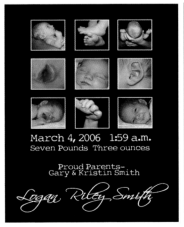

Post cards, posters, and flat cards used for invitations and birth announcements are nothing more than a different sized scrapbook page. In this postcard example, I opened my image (Ctrl>O), duplicated my layer (Ctrl>J), and then I used Quick Fix to adjust the lighting. In this 6 x 4 example I cropped my image in a standard size that a photo lab will develop. With my Foreground color set to white, I used the Custom Shape Tool (U) to draw a talk bubble. Since the talk bubble faced the wrong way, I went to Image>Rotate>Layer Flip Horizontal. I activated the Text Tool (T) and dragged out a text box with my mouse by clicking and dragging. I set my alignment to center and typed my text. I Ctrl clicked on the talk bubble layer and then made a new blank layer with the New Layer icon on the top of the Layers palette. To add a Stroke (Selection) Outline, go to Edit>Stroke (Selection) Outline. I chose an outside location in black that was 10 px wide. I added a bevel and the Mr. Scrap drop shadow available at PolkaDotPotato.com to the talk bubble. I added the type to the fence rail and used the skew function to line it up correctly. Finally, I Ctrl clicked on the layer thumbnail for the Background layer copy and added a white Stroke Outline with an inside (must choose inside) location 40 px wide. Once printed; add a note, a postcard stamp and address to the back of this photo, and drop it in the mail. This card could also be emailed just like a photo.

An inexpensive way to make a party invitation or birth announcement is to make a new 5 x 7 file and create your card just as you would a scrapbook page. You can even leave a spot for a ribbon or other embellishment. The birth announcement shown on the previous page was printed very inexpensively as a 5 x 7 photo. For ideas on birth announcements, do an internet search entering "birth announcements" in the search field. There are many beautiful but expensive cards available for purchase on the web and also shown in magazines. Pick up a few ideas, and use your digital scrapbook supplies to make your own custom announcement.

For Christmas, I normally bake cookies, but last year instead of baking I made my neighbors cookie dough and rolled it in wax paper. I tied the ends with ribbon and added a custom printed label. The label was nothing more than a Costco 4 x 6 inch photo that I made using the Santas Lil' Elfer clip art sets by Carolee Jones at PcCrafter.com. My neighbors loved the custom Christmas invitation, but I think they liked the cookie dough better!

Many photo labs now print posters inexpensively. A poster is constructed the same way as a postcard is, but in a larger size. To increase the size of your photo, be sure to read the instructions in the Resolution section.

Single Fold Card

Make a new blank document the size you want your card (instructions are at the beginning of this chapter). Turn on your gridlines and use the setting to divide the card into quarters (instructions are at the beginning of this chapter). My example will show the dimensions for a 8.5 x 11 inch card. One good thing about making a card in this dimension is that envelopes are very affordable to purchase at the large office supply stores.

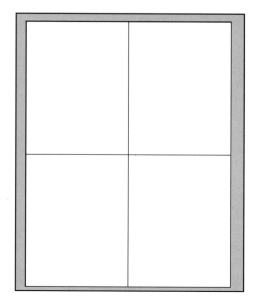

Drag a digital paper onto the card so that your card is no longer white. Drag your logo (logos are covered at the end of the Cards section) to the top center of the card. Because the logo will be on the back, we need to flip it upside down. Go to Image>Rotate>Layer 180° and your logo will be flipped upside down. Move the logo with the Move Tool (V) and size it by dragging on the sizing handles on the bounding box if necessary.

Make a selection with the Marquee Tool (M) on the bottom of the card to place a photo or digital scrapbook paper in it. I made my selection in the example little bit smaller than the bottom half of the card so I could add a border around it. I could have made it the entire bottom half so that the image covered the front of the card, this is my personal preference.

Choose a photo or scrapbook paper that you want to paste into the selection. Select>All (Ctrl>A), and then Edit>Copy (Ctrl>C). Go back to your card document and make a new layer by clicking on the New Layer icon in the Layers palette and Edit>Paste>Into Selection (Shift>Ctrl>V). Your image will be pasted into the selection. Activate the Move Tool (V) if you want to move it around or size it slightly.

Drag any other elements that you want to use onto the card with the Move Tool (V). In my example, I used the Miss Mint Candy Fairway kit. I made another selection with the Rectangular Marquee (M) tool for the strip of striped paper, and pasted it in by repeating the steps above. I dragged on the rick rack and stitching with the Move Tool (V). I added drop shadows to the rick rack, strip of striped paper, and the rectangular piece of paper. Lastly I typed "Thank You" using the Angelina Font. Not bad for a two minute card! To turn the grid lines off go, to View>Grid. Print the card and fold it down the middle. Real buttons, a bow, or real rick rack can be easily added to this card.

In this example, I followed the same directions and pasted a photo inside the selection instead of digital scrapbook paper. I added text on the photo, and two stroke outlines around the photo. I used colors from the photo for the stroke outline and the text by using the Eyedropper Tool (I) to first set my foreground color. To make the stroke outline, I Ctrl clicked on the photo layer, made a new layer, and then went to Edit>Stroke outline and chose an inside location outline 8 px. wide. For the outer stroke outline, I made a rectangular selection using the Rectangular Marquee Tool (M), made a new layer, and then went to Edit>Stroke Outline and made an outline 25 px wide outline from the same color. For the logo, I used the 2 Peas Price Check font (available at TwoPeasInABucket.com) and just wrote "I Love You" and centered it on the back of the card after I rotated its layer 180°. For "Thinking of You", I used Papyrus and centered it on the front of the card. Add a drop shadow on either Stroke Outline if you want to.

If you regularly like to add photographs to cards, you could make a template to print on cardstock and then paste the real photo on top of it. Add type to the photo before you print it. Make a new blank document the size you want your card (instructions are at the beginning of this chapter). To do this, make a shape slightly

larger than the photo you will be using and then make a stroke outline around that. If you want to, add a logo and then simply glue a photo onto it. In this example, I made a shape with the Shape Tool (U) ¼ inch larger than a 4 x 6 photo. My shape is 4.25 x 6.25 I used the Fixed Size setting on the Shape Tool to make my shape exactly the right size. I centered my black shape by using the grid lines as a guide; notice the center sizing handle is centered right on the grid line. To make the Stroke Outline, I used the Marquee Tool (M) in Fixed Size Mode and made an outline 6.75 w x 4.75 h. Make a new layer, and then go to Edit>Stroke Outline. This Stroke Outline is 25 px wide with an inside location. If you want one add a logo. Keep some of these on hand and when you need a note card, paste a photo onto the shape and it will have two nice outlines around it. They sell these in photo stores for people to show off their photos, and they're expensive.

Using the Marquee Tool (M) to make a selection to paste into works great for making cards. In this example I made an oval selection that I feathered after I made a new document (instructions are at the beginning of this chapter). I made a new layer and pasted my photo into the selection Shift>Ctrl>V and it was automatically feathered. I added the text "Hawaii" with the font MP Peony. Finish it off with a logo, and you've got a nice card. I centered my photo on the card by using the sizing handles on the bounding box that become visible when you activate the Move Tool (V). The Undo History lists all my steps, and the settings for the Eliptical Marquee Tool (M) are shown on the options bar.

If you make cards like this on a regular basis, you can make a template and save the selection for the feathered oval by going to Select>Save Selection and naming the selection. Save the file and open it when you want to make another card. Load the selection, select another photo and paste it into the selection, and your card is done in minutes. As soon as you open the card, File>Save As (Shift>Ctrl>S), so you don't save over your template.

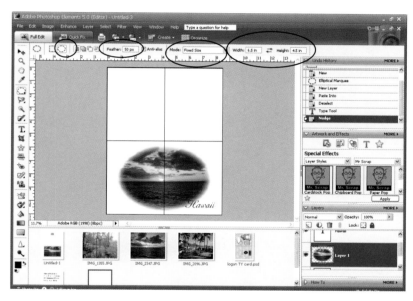

This card can be used leaving the inside blank, or you can add printing inside. When adding type to a card, changing the Leading on the Type Tool (T) Option Bar is helpful for spacing your text lines closer or farther apart. Leading is explained in the Tools section of this book.

If you want to add printing to the inside of your card, you can do it two different ways. The long way is to make another new file, and use the Grid lines to locate the center fold in your card to type your text. Save this as a separate file, print out the card, and then print the center printing on the back of the card.

The fast tricky way is to turn the Eyeballs off on all of the layers, other than the Background layer, and type your text. Print your inside text, then turn off the inside text layer, and turn back on the other layers. Print the card part now but make sure the Eyeball on the inside text layer is turned off. Essentially, you have the inside and outside of your card all in one file, which can be good and bad. It's good if you remember what you did later on, if you want to reuse it, and bad if you forget and can't figure out what you did.

Double Fold Card

To make a double fold card with an 8 ½ x 11 inch piece of card stock that fits in a standard envelope, make a new file, Ctrl>N, 8.5 inches wide by 11 inches high. Change your Grid Lines (Edit>Preferences>Grid) to Gridline every 25% with 1 Subdivision. To turn on your Grid Lines, choose View>Grid. In my example, my grid lines are black for illustration purposes. I have also added shapes in different colors to illustrate the layout of the card. If you make double fold cards like this a lot, you may want to create a template like this. Turn off the colored layers as you complete your card, and it's easy. The top two sections of the card will need to have the text or image rotated. To do this, choose Image>Rotate>Layer 180°. If your whole card rotates, you didn't choose Layer and your whole image was rotated.

Note Cards

Set up a note card with the above specifications. Make a template for the top and bottom note card. It is faster to make the card for Card 1 and then duplicate it and move it with the Move Tool (V) up to the Card 2 area. In my example, I added cut and fold lines for illustration purposes only. With your Grid Lines turned on, you will be able to use them for placement. To add text to the inside for a party invitation, make a new template or turn off the layers and make a new text layer for Card 1. Duplicate the text and move it up to Card 2.

Printing Cards

In most cases you'll be printing your cards at home. The hardest part of printing a two sided card is figuring out how your printer prints. My advice is to print a test card first on regular copy paper, and then print the inside text on the back of it. If it works out the first time, you're lucky. My printers print differently. When I figured it out I taped a note on the printer because I kept forgetting and constantly had to reprint my cards.

To save you a lot of headaches, be sure to read the card folding tips at the beginning of this section.

Envelopes

Printing on an envelope is essentially the same as printing a flat card with the exception that you will also be printing the address. I printed personalized envelopes for a birthday party for my father and received a lot of positive comments. No one had ever seen anything like it, but in reality it was just as easy as making the card. I had a photo of him, a mini calendar of the month, with the date circled, along with some other embellishments on the front of the envelope. People told me they couldn't forget the date because it was right on the envelope. I typed each address individually for each envelope, but you can use a mail merge program to do it too.

All you need to do is make a new document (directions at the beginning of this chapter) the same size as the envelope. Measure the envelope yourself, don't always believe the dimensions on the box. Design your envelope. If you're only doing a few, type the address each time on the file before you print it. Check your printer to see if they have a setting for the size of envelope you're using. If they don't enter a custom size. When you enter the custom size for the envelope, type something like "Card Envelope 7.25w x 5.25h" and save it. This way the next time you want to print an envelope that size, it's already set up in your printer.

Card Logo

One of my favorite parts of making my own cards is the logos that I've designed; Hallmark has their own logo, so why shouldn't you? So far I've only designed funny logos. The example is one that I've used a lot since my grandson was born. The text reads: "No babies were traumatized in the making of this card", "Too Young Grama Designs". This logo always gets a laugh, and everyone is astounded that I have a personalized barcode.

To make the bar code, download a barcode font from a free website and type what you want, the barcode and the type are both written at the same time. To make the bar code even more realistic, place it on a white rectangle shape to look like a label.

You can get much fancier than this and one day when it comes time to make a fancy card I will, but for now, I've had a great time with this one. You may want to warp your text or make a shape with the Shape Tool (U). The possibilities are endless, just have fun with it!

Open a new document as shown in the instructions in the beginning of this section. Make the document the size you want your logo. This logo is 2 inches high 1.5 inches wide. There are three different layers of type "No babies…", "Too Young.." and "Priceless Baby". Add the photo (and what a special photo it is!) I placed the photo on top of a black oval shape with a feathered edge because I had problems with the photo and didn't want to take the time to fix it, and I've just left it that way. Move your text, photo, and shape around with the Move Tool (V). Save your logo, both as a PSD file and as a JPEG file. Saving as a PSD file will allow you to make changes to it later. Saving as a JPEG will make it fast and easy to drag onto a card that you're making at the last minute.

Making An Instant Scrapbook Using the Adobe Create Menu

This is a scrapbook that maybe even my non-scrapping Editor might try. Using this feature works much easier if you have your photos in the Organizer. I didn't have these particular photos in the organizer that I'm using for the demonstration, so I made a new catalog. In the Organizer, go to File>Catalog and choose New and name the catalog. The Organizer will open in the new catalog. I then imported these photos into this catalog. When you have this done, go to the top of the Organizer and click on the Create button. Choose Photo Layout from the drop down list.

Select all of the photos in the organizer that you want to use for the photo layout pages by clicking, and then Ctrl clicking or Shift clicking (all in a row) on all of them.

Choose the size of your page, layout, and a theme. When you click on the theme, you will see a preview of how it will look. It will also tell you how many pages your project will be.

Click OK and you are taken to the Editor where it starts making all of the pages itself.

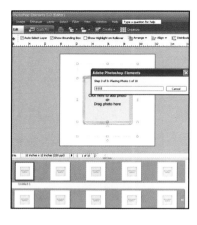

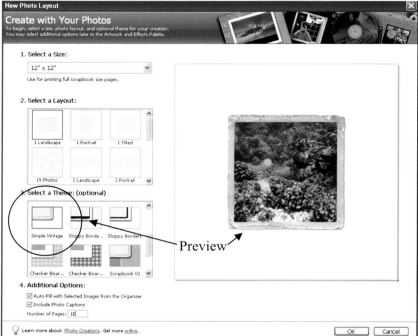

When your pages are finished, you can add paper and other embellishments to them, just like other pages you've made. If the frame does not fit right, and quite a few won't, right click on the frame and choose Fit Frame to Photo. To move the frame around, use the Move Tool (V) and move it just like any other image. If you size the frame by dragging on a corner sizing handle, you will automatically size the photo too.

When you save this, it is saved in a PSE format, along with a folder with individual PSD files. If you want to have some of these pages printed, you will need to open the folder and change the individual PSD files to JPEGs. When you open the PSE file, all of the pages are opened in the Editor.

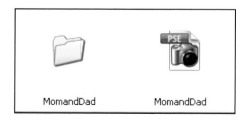

Templates

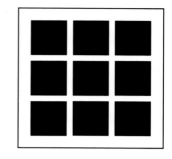 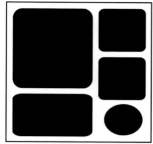

What Is A Template?

If you're a traditional scrapbooker, you've probably bought plastic templates that help you cut out shapes or lay out your scrapbook page. To use a traditional template, you trace the template shape on your photo or paper and then cut each one of them out, one by one with scissors. Position your photos and paper on your scrapbook page, glue them down, add a few embellishments, and you'd be done. Traditional templates are time savers because you don't have to spend your time working on a design that is balanced and pleasing to the eye. Using a traditional template to make a traditional page takes time, but then again everything in traditional scrapbooking takes time!

As a digital scrapbooker you can also use templates that are made digitally. There are templates available to make layouts, shapes, paper, curled edges, photo corners, tags, alphas, embellishments, and just about anything else you can think of!

Using a page layout template speeds up your work because you have the design work all done for you. No thumbing through magazines and books or surfing the web to find the perfect layout you like that will work with your photos. No spacing and measuring everything to make sure all of your photos are balanced. If you have a lot of photos to scrap, or you're short on time and patience, templates are definitely the way to go. You can make your own templates or buy them.

What Kind of Templates Are Easier To Use?

The Digital Scrapbook Teacher prefers to use layered templates. I'll explain the difference and show you how to make and use both types of templates on the next few pages.

Layered Templates (PSD)

Layered Templates are easier for beginners, which is why **The Digital Scrapbook Teacher** sells this type of template in her classes and on her website. Each template is several layers. For example, to use one with 9 squares, you would open the template and nine photos in Photoshop Elements. Next you would drag a photo over a square and group it with the square, that's it. Complete it 9 times and you're done. Each square can be grouped with a photo or a digital scrapbook paper.

Single Layer Templates (PNG)

A PNG template is a single layer template with holes cut in it that you place your photos in. Some of these templates allow you to place your photos underneath the holes so that they show through. Most single layer templates need you to paste your photos into the holes, which can be confusing sometimes. The big advantage of a PNG template is that it is a smaller file and takes up less space on your hard drive.

Single Layer Templates (JPEG)

A JPEG template is a single layer template with the areas for pictures filled with a solid color (usually black or white). The only time you will usually see a JPEG template is when the areas for photos overlap each other. The photo areas can be cut out or selected, so that you can paste your photos into them.

How To Make Eight Different Pages With One Layout Template

For a different look rotate the template 90° by going to Image>Rotate>90° Right (or Left).

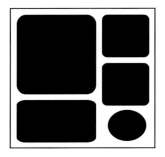 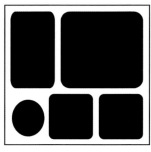 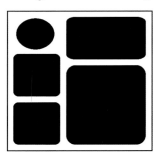 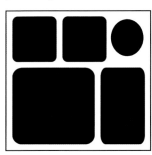

Flip your template by going to Image>Rotate>Flip Horizontal and you get four other choices.

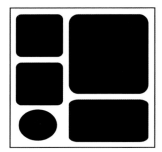 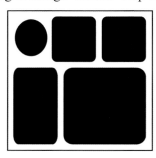 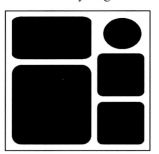 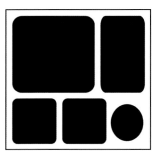

By using one 12 x 12 template, you can make eight different pages in any square scrapbook size. Flipping and rotating your template pages gives a uniform and balanced look to your 2 page scrapbook layout.

Turn off one of the shape layers to add journaling or an embellishment. Turning off a shape layer and adding a different shape layer yourself will also give the template a completely different look.

Included on the CD that came with your book are three12 x 12 templates and two 8 ½ x 11 templates for you to use. **The Digital Scrapbook Teacher** also sells CDs of templates sets. Included in each one of our templates is a layer with easy to understand instructions written right on the template. This is something that other companies don't do. When you're done reading the instructions, just turn off the layer and they disappear. When you get stuck you can turn the instruction layer back on by clicking on the eyeball instead of searching through your files trying to remember where you saved their instructional file. Each template includes a layered template (we've found they're easier to use, especially for beginners) and a single layered template either in PNG or JPEG format. In addition, all of the template shapes are numbered and match to the layer number so they're easier to work with. The shapes are also linked so that if you want to move them as a group, you can. This helps you so that you don't move one shape by mistake and mess up your design. If you want to unlink the shapes, we've also explained that in our instructions. All of our templates are created in 300 ppi resolution and in RGB color. Check TheDigitalScrapbookTeacher.com website for our latest templates set or use the order form included with this book. You'll find the templates here are priced less than half of other websites.

I Scrap 12 x 12 - How Am I Going to Use This 8 ½ x 11 Template?

While some people still scrap in 8 ½ x 11 format, most people scrap in some size of a square format whether it's 12 x 12 or smaller. If you scrap in 8 ½ x 11, you're happy to use them as they are, but you can also use them if you scrap 12 x 12 too. Remember in digital you can change pretty much everything! Some of my favorite hybrid scrapbook pages have started with an 8 ½ x 11 template.

The example below shows a 24 wide x 12 inch high layout which is two 12 x 12 pages side by side. Full directions on how to do this can be found at How to Make a Double Page Layout in Half the Time in the How to Do the Basics Chapter.

First I made a 24 wide by 12 inch high new page at 300 resolution RGB color. Next I dragged on my 8 ½ x 11 template twice. I flipped one of the templates horizontally for a mirror image effect. With this particular template, flipping it vertically would also give you the same layout. The black rectangles I fill with photos or digital scrapbook paper. I cover the white area of the template with scrapbook paper or fill with color. The gray area can also be covered with scrapbook paper or filled with color. The gray area is where I usually add my traditional supplies. The top gray area is big enough for ribbon or rickrack. If I want more space on the top, I can move the template down so that I cut off part of the bottom white portion, and it works fine. On the 2 sides of the gray area, I can add some of the cute embellishments that are available at scrapbook stores.

You have a lot of options when working with digital templates.

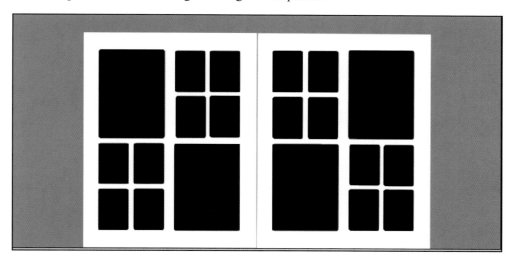

I Scrap 8 ½ x 11 - What Am I Going To Do With A 12 x 12 Template?

Resize the 12 x 12 template to 8 x 8 by going to Image>Resize>Image Size and changing the size. This example shows a 17 x 11 page which is a double 8 ½ x 11 page. I flipped one template to balance the page. In this example I flipped my template horizontally, but you can also flip them vertically for a different look. You can add digital or traditional elements around the template.

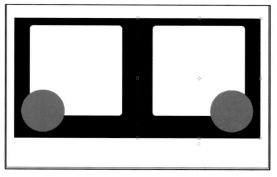

How To Make a Layered Scrapbook Layout Template (PSD)

Make a new page with the following specifications:

Pick a name for your template. If you're planning on making several you may want to set up some kind of system so you can easily find them. Since I'm going to be making a template with nine squares, I've named it 9 Squares. My example shows 12 x 12 inches but if you scrap 8 ½ x 11, you can also enter those dimensions here. If you scrap 8 x 8 inches still use the 12 x 12 setting.

Go to View and Turn on Grids, Rulers, & Snap to Grid.

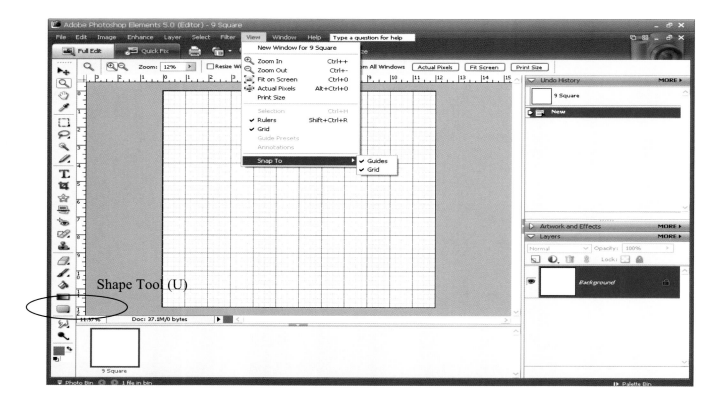

Go to File Save As (Shift>Ctrl>S) and save your template in your Scrapbook Supplies Folder. It would be a good idea to make a new folder called Scrapbook Templates if you plan on making several templates.

By default, my file will be named 9 Squares. Be sure you are saving as a PSD file.

Type D to set your Foreground and Background colors to the Default colors of black and white, although you can make your templates any color you want. If you are going to make a Template where the shapes overlap you'll need to use an additional color, such as gray.

Select the Shape Tool (U), which is the third tool from the bottom on the Toolbar. The icon on your Toolbar may look different than the one shown above, depending on the last time you used it. You may have an oval, rectangle, rounded rectangle, talk bubble, or other shape.

Decide on the design of your template. If you want to draw free form shapes you will choose Unconstrained, and you can click and drag your mouse to make your shapes any size. Every time you click and drag your mouse, you'll be making a new shape on a new layer.

I am going to make 9 squares, and I want each square to be 3 inches so I've chosen "Fixed Size" on the drop down menu. If I chose Square, I could not have set the exact size. I'm using the rounded rectangle shape, and I've set the radius at 300 px to round the corner, as shown on the next example.

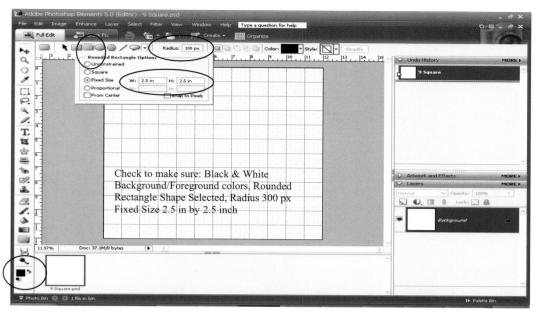

My cursor has changed to a crosshair, and when I click, the cross hair will be at the upper left edge of the shape. Since I've selected a "Fixed Size" shape, every time I click, a new black shape will be added to my page. If you are drawing an unconstrained shape, you will click and drag out each shape.

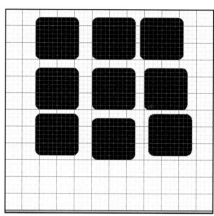

In my example I've clicked 9 times in different places to end up with my 9 squares. They're not lined up right and to fix that, I have two options. Type V to activate the Move Tool (V). If by mistake you click on your template and make another shape, drag it to the trashcan.

Option 1: I can use the Move Tool (V) and move all the squares around to where I want them. The grid helps me see where to put them and the Snap to Grid helps them stick onto the grid lines.

Option 2: Use the Align and Distribute options in the Move Tool (V), which would be faster and perfect.

To use the Align Command, select the bottom three shape layers by clicking on one layer, and then Ctrl Clicking on the other two layers in the Layers palette. Your bottom three layers should be blue.

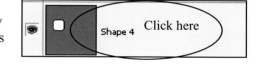

When you click on your individual layers, make sure that you are clicking in the area that says Shape 4 in the example here. If you click in the darkened square by mistake, which is the layer thumbnail, you will get a selection (marching ants) on your square. Press Esc to remove the marching ants, and click on the layer name.

With the Move Tool (V) activated, go to Align>Top Edges. Photoshop Elements will align these three shapes to the top edge of the shape that is the highest on the page. Using Align>Bottom edges would align to the lowest edge. My top row looks fairly even, but you can see the bottom row needs to be fixed. By using Align>Bottom Edges, Photoshop Elements will align the three squares even with the shape in the middle, because it's lowest on the page, so be careful which option you choose.

Using the Align Command gets a little tricky at times because you're not sure which layer it's going to line up the other layers with. If you remember this little trick, while not in proper English terms, you won't ever have a problem. The Align Command, when choosing Align Top edges, will use the most Top-most layer. Align Bottom Edges, will align everything to the most Bottom-most layer.

To center the bottom row, move the right square and the left square to where you want them. In my example, I will move them both 1 ¾ inches from the side edges of the page with the Move Tool (V). With all three layers selected, go to Distribute>Horizontal Centers. The space in between the three squares will be equal but they will remain 1 ¾ inches from the side of the page.

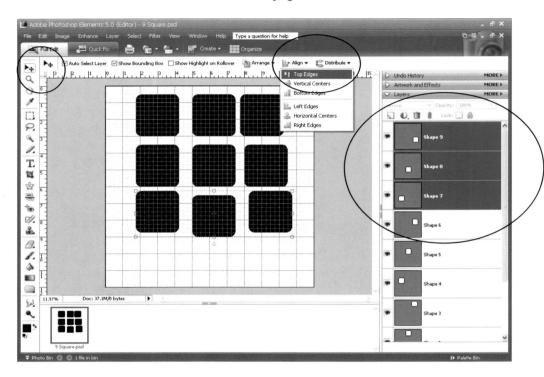

Align the top edges for each of the three rows of squares. Next, Horizontally Center each of the three rows. You can also select all of the shapes on the right side row and align Left Edges. Continue Aligning and moving the squares until you get them all lined up evenly. This may seem like a lot of work, but after you get the hang of it, it's really easy.

Turn off your Grid Lines (View>Grid Lines) so you can see your template clearly. You will also probably want to turn off Snap to Grid (View>Snap to>Grid) at the same time.

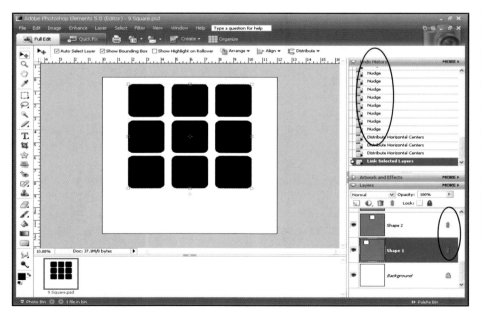

You can see by my Undo History, I've had to Nudge (Using the arrow key with the Move Tool (V) activated) a few times.

Next link the shape layers so that you don't move one by accident when you're using it. To link the shape layers, click on the top shape layer, then Shift Click on the bottom shape layer, and click on the link button.

Don't link your shapes to your Background layer. When your layers are linked, you'll see the little link on the right side of the Layers palette as shown in the previous example. If you click on the Background layer you won't see the link. To unlink them, select the layers, click on the link button, and they'll be unlinked.

With the shapes linked, I can move them around on the Background layer. I can also size them as a group by dragging one of the sizing arrows on the bounding box that surrounds all nine squares. By doing this, I get a completely different look to my template.

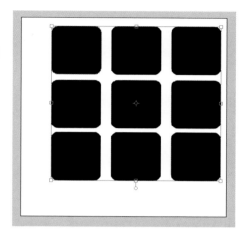

If you move your shapes around or change their size you can Undo (Ctrl>Z) your change.

Congratulations, you've made your first template!

Click File>Save or Ctrl>S and you're done unless you want to make your template a little bit easier to use by numbering your layers and adding an instruction layer.

Naming Your Template Layers

The templates you buy from **The Digital Scrapbook Teacher** have their layers numbered, starting from the top left to the lower right. If the layers overlap, this system changes a little bit but we try to start at the top left and work our way to the bottom right. This makes the template easier to use, especially when you're using a template with a lot of layers.

Because I started in the top left corner when I drew my template, my shapes are in the opposite order than I would normally use them when I scrap. Right now, my top left square is Shape 1, but it's at the bottom of my Layers palette. I am going to drag them into the order I want them in the Layers palette by dragging and dropping them. You don't have to do this; we just do it to make your life easier when you purchase our templates.

To number your layers, type T to activate the Type Tool (T). Choose a large font size. Type X to switch your Foreground and Background color so that you'll be typing in white. If you type in black on the black square, you won't see it. Make sure you are on your top layer, which should be Shape 1, and type the number 1 on top of Shape 1 and click once. After you click, you'll see that the Text layer is now named 1. Next, Ctrl Click on Shape 1 so that both layers are selected. Type Ctrl>E or Layer>Merge Layers. Because only 2 layers are selected, only the 2 layers will merge.

Your top layer will now be named 1. Continue doing this for each shape. Click on the shape you are going to name and the Text Layer is placed directly on top of the shape layer. If you make a mistake, you can drag the text layer to where you need it.

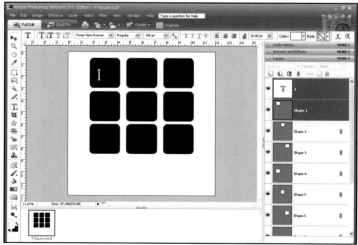

When you're finished, your template will look something like this.

Because numbering the layers unlinked them when you merged the shape layer with the type layer, you will need to link them again by selecting all of the shape layers and clicking on the link button.

Ctrl>S (File>Save) to Save.

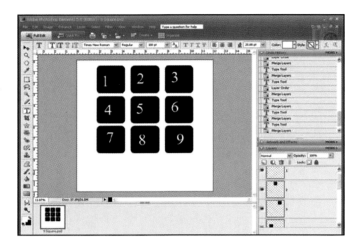

Adding An Instruction Layer

When I first learned to digi-scrap, I was frustrated by not being able to find one source of information, which is why this book and class came about. I bought templates at online stores, and they sent a different generic text document that explained how to use all of their products. This did me little good! Every template that **The Digital Scrapbook Teacher** sells includes the template instructions on its own separate layer. If you don't need them, you can turn them off or even delete them. The first line of the instructions says to File>Save As (Shift>Ctrl>S) so that you don't save over your template. The last line says, to turn off these instructions click on the eyeball on your Layers palette. It's simple, but it works. If you want to do something like this, just make a new text layer and type out your instructions.

Ctrl>S (File>Save) to Save.

Saving Your Template

Windows XP Screenshot

In the beginning, I had you save this template as a PSD file which keeps all of the layers. You may also want to save another copy as a JPEG or PNG so that you can view it easier in your Scrapbook Supplies Folder. A PSD file will only show a thumbnail of the Photoshop Elements logo, while a thumbnail of a JPEG or PNG file will be the actual image.

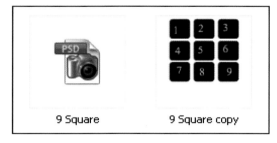

How To Use A Layered (PSD) Scrapbook Layout Template

Open your template File>Open (Ctrl>O) and find the Template Folder inside your Scrapbook Supplies folder that you hopefully made! Or, in the Organizer select the Template and go to Edit>Standard Edit or Ctrl>I.

All Templates sold by **The Digital Scrapbook Teacher** will have an instruction layer on the top layer, which can be turned off by clicking on the eyeball to turn off the layer.

The template I'm using for this demonstration is on the CD that is included with this book, and is named 9squarePSD. The first thing you need to do is File>Save As (Shift>Ctrl>S). The reason you need to do this first is because you'll get so excited about the wonderful page you're making so quickly that you'll save it, and when you save it, you've got your wonderful page, but not your wonderful reusable template! My suggestion is to save this in a Folder named Scrapbook Pages. If you're working on several scrapbooks, I would make subfolders for each one.

The original name of my template was 9squarePSD. I am saving this file in my Hawaii Folder, which is a sub-folder of my Scrapbook Page Folder. I am naming my page: Hawaii Waikiki 1. I'm saving it in Photoshop PSD format. I do not include my scrapbook pages in my Organizer because it's been my experience with <u>my</u> computer (yours may be different) that large multi-layered PSD files slow it down considerably, so I have unchecked the box "Include in the Organizer".

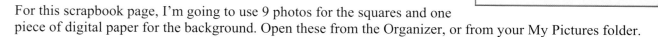

Remember to Save (Ctrl>S or File>Save) periodically when you're working on this template. This way you won't lose your work in the event you have a computer problem.

For this scrapbook page, I'm going to use 9 photos for the squares and one piece of digital paper for the background. Open these from the Organizer, or from your My Pictures folder.

In your Photo Bin will be the template, one piece of digital paper, and nine photos.

On your template, select the Background layer so it's blue in the Layers palette. Select the digital paper that you want to use to cover the Background layer and make it the active image in the window. Activate the Move Tool (V) and drag it down to your template in the Photo Bin. Because you had the Background layer selected on the template, anything you added to the template was added in a new layer right above it. If your paper came in somewhere else other than right above your Background layer, drag it into the correct position. Click Ctrl>G (Layer>Group with Previous), and your background paper is now attached to your Background layer. The digital paper I'm using is Paper Bag from the Shabby Princess Festival free kit. This kit along with other great products can be found at ShabbyPrincess.com.

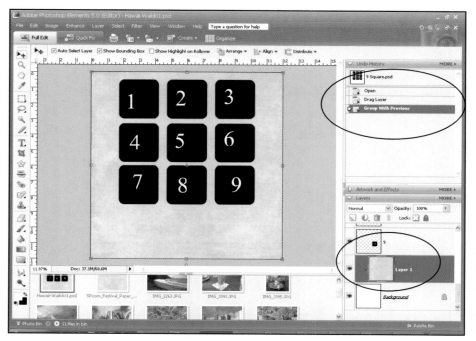

When you Group with Previous (Ctrl>G), you've created a Clipping Mask. I know I promised no technical terms but if you read somewhere else to create a clipping mask, this is what it is. Notice how the paper is now Layer 1, and it's indented with a crooked arrow pointing downward. The Undo History also lists that we Grouped with Previous.

You can now close the Paper in your Photo Bin by right clicking and choosing Close.

Rename Layer 1 Background Paper by double clicking on the layer palette and typing it in.

If you have to make any corrections to your photos (lighting, color, etc.), it is a good idea to fix them before you drag them onto your template.

We're going to start with Shape 1 and work our way down the page, so select the layer for Shape 1 on your template and then click on your photo in the Photo Bin that you want to put there.
Your photo will now be your active image. Just like the paper, drag it down to your template in the Photo Bin, and as long as you had Shape 1 selected, it will be right on top of it. Ctrl>G to Group it with Shape 1. Because you renamed the background paper, this photo will now be Layer 1 on top of your Shape 1. The first shape is named 1 if you numbered your layers as I suggested, or if you're using a template made by **The Digital Scrapbook Teacher.** You can now close the photo you just used in the Photo Bin by right clicking and choosing close.

If you are not happy with the size of the photo, you can make it larger or smaller by dragging or pushing the corner sizing arrows on the bounding box. If you're not happy with the position of the photo, you can grab the photo by the center circle move point and position it differently. If you see the black shape that means you've moved the photo too far over so the shape is showing. Reposition the photo so the shape is covered up.

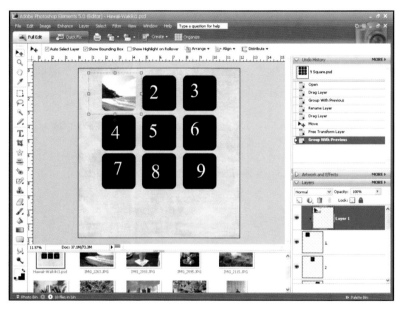

Think of the shape as a window you're looking through, and you can move the photo underneath it. The advantage of Grouping with Previous rather than using a one layered template with holes in it and the photos placed underneath the template, is that they won't overlap. In my example, the photo in Shape 1 is extending into Shape 2 if you look at the bounding box, but it's not showing in Shape 2. With a one layered template, you'd have to crop your photos or use another technique. I'll show you in the section How to Use a PNG Template. Continue this for all of the other eight squares. Select the Shape you want to add the photo to, drag the photo onto your template, and then Ctrl>G to Group with Previous.

Sometimes, especially in this example where the template shapes are small, it helps to size the photo down before you Group with Previous. Use the Move Tool (V) and push or pull the corner sizing handles to transform it to the approximate size you want. Don't forget to check the check mark to accept the sizing change.

If you Group the wrong photo with a shape, you can Undo (Ctrl Z) if you catch it right away. You can also Ungroup by Shift>Ctrl>G (Layer>Ungroup). Sometimes after you finish a template, you realize that a photo would look better in a different position and you want to swap it, so just Ungroup it and swap it.

Add a drop shadows to the shape layers not the photo layers, or they won't show up.

It is probably a good idea to link or merge your photos with their template shape. To link the photo and shape, select both layers and click on the link symbol on the Layers palette. To merge the photo and template shape, select both layers and Ctrl>E (Layer>Merge) to merge them together. Merging the photo and shape is permanent, so make sure you're finished with them before you merge them.

If you want to add mats to the individual photos, or add a large mat under all nine squares, you can add another shape(s) using the Shape Tool (U). Make sure when you add the shape that it is in the correct place on the Layers palette or you'll cover up some photos. Don't forget to save your file.

Matting Photos On A Template

Some of the templates **The Digital Scrapbook Teacher** sells have mats already included. These mats can be covered just like you've done with photos. Drag paper on top of the mat, and then Grouping with Previous (Ctrl>G). Make sure you're on the right layer before you drag the paper on, and it's easy. If you are planning on matting all of the photos with the same digital paper, you can merge all of the mat layers by selecting them all and then Layer>Merge Layer (Ctrl>E). This way, you drag the digital paper over the nine mats that are now on one layer, you Group with Previous (Ctrl>G) once, and you're done.

If your template doesn't have any mats, it's easy to add them. For example, to add a large mat to this page select the background paper layer, and draw a new shape. Draw the shape either freehand with the Unconstrained option selected on the Shape Tool (U), or by choosing another size for a fixed size like 10 x 10. Choose another color when you draw the new shapes so that all your shapes aren't the same color. When you do this, the new mat will be above the background paper, but below the square shapes on the template.

To add individual mats for each of the nine squares, it would probably be easiest to enter a fixed size of a 3.25 inch rounded rectangle square. Because the squares are 3 inches and only ½ inch apart, in this example you really can't make the mats much bigger.

Adding A Stroke Outline Instead Of A Mat On Your Template

Instead of drawing out additional shapes to make mats, you can add a Stroke (Outline) Selection to your photos or background paper for a thin mat type effect.

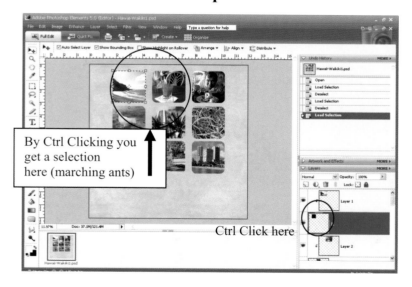

Follow these directions exactly to add the stroke outline:

1. Click on the first shape layer that you want to add the outline to. Click in the box that shows the shape (layer thumbnail), not the area that says 1. Do not select the photo layer. Ctrl Click and this will select the shape by putting marching ants around it.

2. Click on the photo layer directly above the shape layer, Layer #1.

3. Make a new layer with the new layer icon in the Layers palette. The new layer will be right above the photo that has the marching ants on it.

4. Go to Edit>Stroke (Outline) Selection. By default your Stroke Outline will be the Foreground color which, in my example above, is white. I used white but you can pick any color. I chose 30 px, Inside Location, Mode

Normal, Opacity 100%. Because you put this Stroke Outline on its own layer, we can adjust all of these settings later on if you need to.

5   Tap the Esc key or Ctrl>D to Deselect.

6   Repeat this for each shape you want to outline.

7   To put a stroke around the Background layer, you have to do it a little bit differently since you can't Ctrl Click on the Background layer and get a selection. Ctrl Click on the paper layer thumbnail and you should get a selection (marching ants) around the whole outside of the page. Make a new blank layer above the paper layer, go to Edit>Stroke (Outline) Selection, choose your color and width, and choose Inside Location. In my example, I used a white 100 px. Stroke Outline. Next I Ctrl Clicked on the Stroke Outline layer, made a new layer again, and put a thin black stroke outline as an additional accent. Because these Stroke Outlines are on their own layers, I can change their color, opacity, blending mode or remove them completely without Undo-ing other steps. I adjusted my white Stroke Outline to 60% Opacity, and my black Stroke Outline to 40% Opacity to have them blend in with the paper.

8   To add drop shadows, go to Artwork & Effects palette located above the Layers palette. Choose Layer Styles. Apply a drop shadow to the shape layers or the Stroke Outline Layers, but not the photo layers.

9   Add some writing with the Text Tool (T) and you're done. I used the font Elegant at 200 pt for Waikiki and at 46 pt for February 2007 in two different Text Layers.

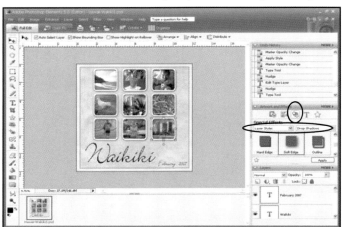

10   Ctrl>S (or File>Save) to Save. If it tells you that you already have a file with that name say OK you want to replace it because it's an earlier version of the same file.

How To Make a Single Layer Scrapbook Layout Template

Saving a Scrapbook Layout Template as a PNG and JPEG file is easy. There are several different ways to make a single layer template, depending on how complicated the template is, and if any of the shapes overlap.

Step 1

Begin by making a New File (Ctrl>N or File>New) using the settings in the example. Notice that Background Contents is Transparent. Click OK

File>Save As (Shift>Ctrl>S) and select PNG file. If it asks for Interlace, check none. When we're done, we'll also save this file as a JPEG file. You will have one transparent layer named Layer 1.

Type D to reset your default Foreground and Background colors to black and white.

Make a new layer and fill it with black (Foreground color) by typing Alt>Backspace. By default, this layer will be named Layer 2.

Method 1

Complete step 1 on the preceding page.

If you're really good with your Marquee Tool (M), you can drag out selections of rectangles, squares, ovals, and circles freehand. Tap the Delete key to make holes in the black layer (Layer 2). When you're all done, merge the black layer with the holes in it and the background transparent layer (Ctrl>E or Layer>Merge). Save, and you're done. I'm not that good with the Marquee Tool (M), so I use the other methods!

Method 2

Complete Step 1 on the preceding page.

Turn on your Grid Lines and Snap to Grid by going to View>Grid & View>Snap to>Grid.

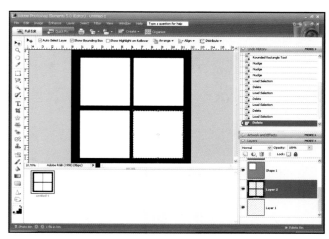

Drag out template shapes with the Shape Tool (U) just like making a layered template. In my example, I've drawn out four 5 inch rounded squares by using the Fixed Size option on the Rounded Rectangle Tool (U). I used the Move Tool (V) to line them up evenly by nudging them with the Arrow keys. Using the Align and Distribute options on the Move Tool (V) also works. Remember, the key to Align and Distribute is to select all the layers that you want to line up together.

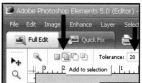

Ctrl click on the layer thumbnail for Shape 1. Select the black solid filled layer (Layer 2) and tap the Delete key. A hole has now been placed in the black layer (Layer 2) as indicated by the checkerboard pattern shown on the layer thumbnail. Repeat this for all 4 shapes so that you have 4 holes cut in your black layer (Layer 2).

Delete the four white rounded rectangle layers (Shape layers 1-4).

If you are making and saving a lot of multi-layer and single layer templates, you will want to speed up the process. You can use the Magic Wand Tool (W) to select all of the shape layers and delete them at the same time. If you are using a layered template and you numbered the shape layers, adjust the Tolerance setting to 255, which will select the entire layer. Since my shapes are not numbered, I left my Tolerance setting 20 as shown in my example. If your shapes are not numbered, you will need to Simplify each shape each time you click on it with the Magic Wand Tool (W). You will be prompted by the program each time, so just click OK. Click on the Shape 1 layer in the Layers palette and make sure that it's highlighted. Next, click on the shape on your template with the Magic Wand Tool (W) and marching ants will surround the shape. Make sure you have "Add to Selection" selected on the Magic Wand Tool (W) option bar. Next, click on the Shape 2 layer in the Layers palette so that it's highlighted and then click on the shape on your template. Both of these shapes should have marching ants surrounding the shapes. Continue doing this on each shape and then go to the black layer (Layer 2) and tap the Delete key to cut four holes.

All you want to save is the black layer with the holes. Select all of the shape layers and the transparent layer by Ctrl clicking on each layer in the Layers palette and drag them all to the trashcan together.

Save (Ctrl>S or File>Save), and you have a completed a 1 Layer Template.

When you Save, if it asks you for Interlace, choose None.

To save the template in JPEG format go to File>Save As (Shift>Ctrl>S) and choose the JPEG option and choose the options shown in this example-Matte: None, Quality 4, Baseline (Standard).

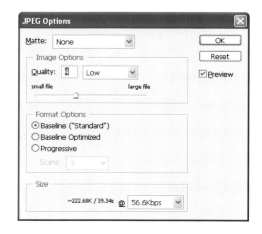

Method 3

Complete Step 1 under "How to Make a Single Layer Scrapbook Template".

Use this method if some of your shapes overlap each other.

Turn on your Grid Lines and Snap to Grid by going to View>Grid and View> Snap to>Grid.

Draw out your Shapes with the Shape Tool (U); just like making a Layered Template. If your shapes overlap, you'll need to use different colors for them. I made a rounded square with the Rounded Rectangle Tool (U) and a circle with the Ellipse Tool (U). I used the Move Tool (V) to line them up evenly by nudging them with the Arrow keys.

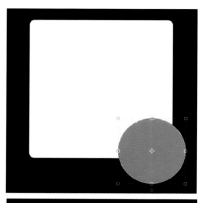

I want to have two shapes to fill with photos when my template is finished. If I delete both shape layers right now from the Background layer, I'll just have one funny shape leftover. I will need a border around the circle shape in my final template. Ctrl click on the circle shape layer thumbnail and then go to Select>Modify>Expand, (If you use this feature with a square corner your selection will be rounded. I chose to expand my selection by 80 pixels .

Next, I made a New Layer under the circle shape. Type "D" to return to your Default colors and Alt>Backspace to fill the new larger circle selection with black (Foreground color).

Ctrl Click on the white square layer thumbnail to select the large white square. Go to Layer 2 (solid black layer) and tap the Delete key. Delete the white square layer. Next, Merge the black circle layer with Layer 2 only. Click on Layer 2, Ctrl click on the black circle layer so they are both highlighted on the Layers palette, and then Ctrl>E (Layer>Merge Layers). At this point, your Layer 2 should look like the layer thumbnail below.

Ctrl click on the circle shape layer that is remaining. Select Layer 2 and tap the Delete key to make another hole in the Template.

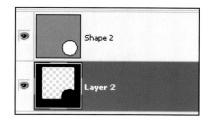

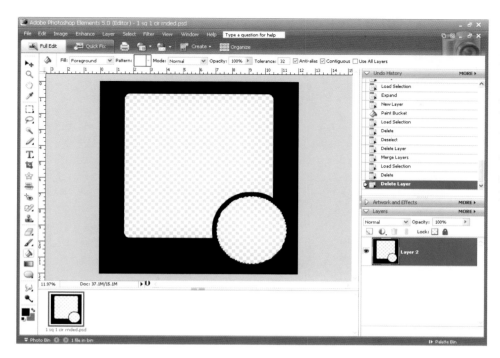

Save your Template as a PNG file to keep the transparent background. Saving your Template as a JPEG file will cause the transparent (checkerboard) areas to be filled with white.

To use this Template be sure to use Method #3 that follows.

How To Use A Single Layer Scrapbook Layout Template

There are at least 3 ways you can use a single layer template. I'll show you the easiest case scenario and then we'll go from there.

If you are using a PNG template, you will have transparent holes in your template that you can paste your photos into or slide them under.

A single layer JPEG template will have areas for photos that are filled with white or another color. If you are using a JPEG template, do the following steps so that you can use the methods listed here.

Open your JPEG template.

Always, when using a Template, save your template with a new name by going to File>Save As (Shift>Ctrl>S). This way you don't save over your blank template by mistake!

Change the Background layer into a regular layer. Double click the layer thumbnail, or go to Layer>New Layer>From Background

Activate the Magic Wand Tool (W) with Tolerance set at 32 (Default) and Contiguous not checked. Click in the color that indicates where a photo should be placed, and then tap the Delete key. If all of the photo areas are the same color, you should have all of your holes cut. If the photo areas are different colors, repeat this step until you have holes cut for all your photos.

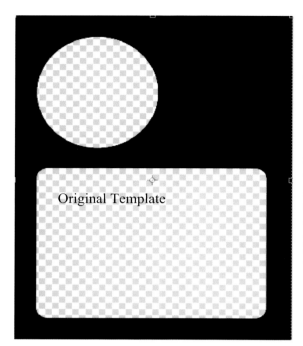

Original Template

Method #1

Always, when using a template, save your template with a new name, by going to File>Save>As (Shift>Ctrl>S). This way you don't save over your blank template by mistake!

If you have a template where there are just one or two openings for your photos, you can easily move the photos under the openings in the templates and arrange them underneath the template so they won't overlap. To cover the template, use either the Paint Bucket Tool (K) or Shift>Alt>Backspace to fill the black layer with the Foreground color. If you want to cover the template with a digital scrapbook paper, put the paper on the layer above the template and Ctrl>G (Layer>Group with Previous).

Notice in the Layers palette that the paper is on top of the template. Both photos are below the template, and the smaller round photo is under the 5x7. If you look closely, you can see the bounding box for the small round photo. All I need to do is add some embellishments, a Stroke Outline, drop shadows, journaling and I'm done!

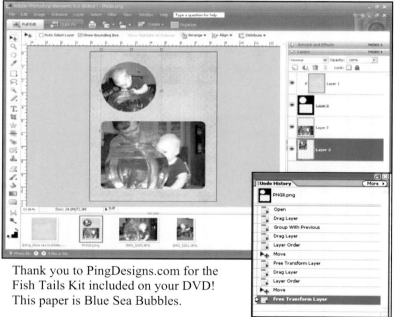

Thank you to PingDesigns.com for the Fish Tails Kit included on your DVD! This paper is Blue Sea Bubbles.

Adding A Stroke Outline Selection On A PNG Template

Make sure that you are on the template layer, and activate the Magic Wand Tool (W). Click on the template where each hole is for a photo. Make sure you have "Add to Selection" on the Magic Wand option bar selected. Un-checking the Contiguous option will select all of the photo holes at one time. Click on your top layer in the Layers palette, and make a new blank layer using the New Layer button on the top of the Layers palette. Make sure this new layer is the top layer, as seen in the example on the next page. If the new layer did not go on top and it's grouped with the scrapbook paper, Ungroup using Shift>Ctrl>G or Layer>Ungroup. When you have marching ants around all of the openings, with the top blank Layer selected, go to Edit>Stroke (Outline) Selection and choose your color, size, and location of outline. If you choose inside, the outline will be inside the opening and will cut out a little bit of your photo. If you choose center, it will center over the edge of the template. If you choose outside, it will be outside of the opening. If your selection has square corners, be aware that choosing center or outside will produce a Stroke Outline that has slightly rounded corners. A circle or rounded rectangle will do great with any of the location choices. Click OK and you'll have the Stroke Outlines on their own Layer. You can now add a drop shadow to this Layer.

Method #2

Usually when you have a single layer template, your photos overlap underneath the template so Method # 1 doesn't work. In this example, I want to use the template with the same two photos, but in addition to the photos, I want to use the Tiny Fish paper to fill two of the squares. I could drag my paper underneath the template and use the Move Tool (V) to reduce the paper in size by pushing on the sizing handles to transform it. The Tiny Fish paper would turn into microscopic fish if I did it this way! Be aware that when you use this method you do not have the capability of adjusting your photos after you've placed them in the template. If you think you might want to adjust them later, use Method #3.

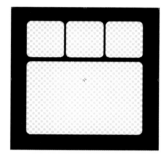

First, do File>Save As (Shift>Ctrl>S). Drag the paper you want to cover the Template with over the Template and Ctrl>G (Layer Group with Previous). Drag your photo under the template that you'll be using in the large rectangle, and size it by using the corner sizing handles. Drag the paper you want to use for decoration under the template layer and photo so that it is the bottom layer, and you will see it showing through the three squares.

Activate the Magic Wand Tool (W) with the template layer active. Make sure "Add to Selection" is activated on the Magic Wand option bar; Contiguous should be checked. Click on the two outer squares and you should have marching ants around both squares. Inverse this selection by Ctrl>Shift>I (Layer>Inverse), and you will now have marching ants around the squares and around the outer edge of the page. Go to the paper on the bottom layer and tap the Delete key. Your center square will now be transparent, and the other two squares will be filled with the paper. If you look at the paper on the bottom layer, you will see that the 12 x 12 paper has been cut into two squares on one layer. Repeat this step with final photo.

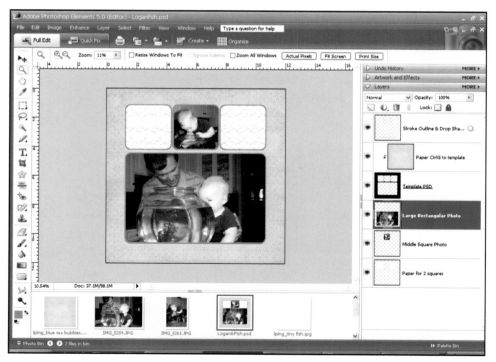

I added a Stoke Outline and drop shadows on another layer as explained under Method #1. To finish, I can add journaling and embellishments to quickly make a really cute page quickly.

If I decide that I want to move my top center square photo, I would have to Redo the steps because the photo is cut exactly to the hole.

Method #3

This is the method that works the best. It seems like a lot of steps, but it's really not. If you are using a template where the shapes overlap, this is the method you want to use!

We'll use the same template, photos, and papers that we did in Method #2.
File Save As (Shift>Ctrl>S) so you don't save over the template in error. Drag on your paper that you want to cover the Template with using the Move Tool (V) and Ctrl>G (Layer>Group with Previous).

Choose the photo you will use for the large rectangle hole, with this photo as your active image Ctrl>A (Select >All). Marching ants will be around the outside edge of the photo, then Ctrl>C (Edit>Copy). Go to the template and activate the Magic Wand (W) Tool. Select the template layer and, with the Magic Wand Tool (W), (Contiguous should be checked) click in the large rectangle hole so there are marching ants surrounding the hole. <u>Very</u> <u>important</u>-Make a new layer by clicking on the New Layer icon in the Layers palette. Shift>Ctrl>V (Edit>Paste into Selection) will put your photo right into the hole in the template on its own layer. You still have the ability to size and move the photo around with the Move Tool (V). Repeat this for every hole you want to fill.

The key to this method is to always make a new layer for each hole in the template that you fill. Make it a habit to look at the template layer after each hole you fill to make sure that there are no photos on this layer, and you'll do fine. By making a new layer for each photo you have the ability to change things around easily. If you don't make a new layer, and you want to move a photo, you will have to Undo (Ctrl>Z) all of your steps to get back to where you added the photo. The template will remain the bottom layer.

Notice in this screen shot that the middle center square is filled (it's not yet adjusted correctly), but that the bounding box for the photo actually extends much farther. The photo also doesn't show in the two other boxes. This is because you used Paste into Selection (Shift>Ctrl>V).

Add the paper to the two other squares at the same time by selecting both squares. Select the paper and paste it into the selection.
Add Stroke Outlines, drop shadows, embellishments, and journaling and you're done. Don't forget to save!

Embellishment/Custom Shape Templates

Different digital scrapbook sites sell shapes that can be used as templates. They are usually provided in a PNG format and sometimes as a Custom Shape CSH format that can be installed directly into your Custom Shapes folder. A set of these templates usually costs around $3.50, but you can make your own very easily!

How To Make An Embellishment/Custom Shape Template

By using the Custom Shape Tool, (U) you can drag out many different types of shapes. If Photoshop Elements doesn't have a shape that you want to use, you can make your own. Draw a shape with a Wacom Tablet, or draw on a piece of paper with a black Sharpie marker and scan it into your computer. In my example, I am using a leaf from the Custom Shape Tool (U) and a piece of Paper Bag paper from the Shabby Princess Festival Kit.

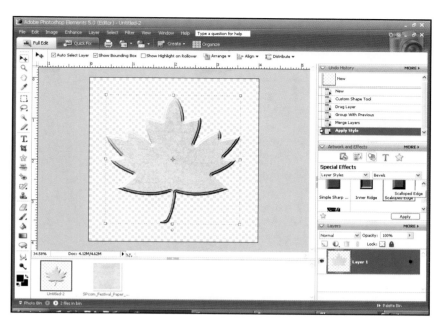

I made a new document 4 x 4 inches with a transparent background, 300 ppi and RGB color. Position the paper above the shape in the Layers palette and Ctrl>G (Layer>Group with Previous). The paper has now taken on the leaf shape. Next, select both layers and Ctrl>E (Layer>Merge). There is only one layer for your leaf shape. Now you can add a Bevel or any other kind of Layer Style you want. In my example, I used a Simple Sharp Bevel so it can be seen easier. Save this file as a PNG to keep its transparent background. You can use this as a journaling block or an embellishment at a later time. Making several leaves in different Fall colors would give a nice Autumn effect.

You do not have to make a separate document for each shape you want to make. In this example, I could have very easily put the shape on a Scrapbook Page and covered it with the paper right on the page.

Edge Templates

How to Make A Curved Edge Template

Make a new scrapbook page with the specifications shown. Pick a name for your template that you'll remember. Shift>Ctrl>S to save your file as a PSD file. Save your file to your Scrapbook Templates file so you'll know where to find it later.

Make a new layer with the New Layer icon button on the Layers palette. By default it will be called Layer 2. Activate the Pencil Tool (N) by typing the letter "N". Using the Pencil Tool (N) will give you a sharp edge compared to a softer edge you'd get using the Brush Tool (B).

Any regular type brush will work but, to make sure we're on the same page, choose a hard round brush like the one shown on the preceding page in the example by double clicking on the brush. Tap your right Bracket key ( ]) several times until your brush size is about 175 px, or enter this amount in the Size box manually.

Set your default colors by typing the letter "D". Your Foreground color should be black and your Background color should be white. Turn your Rulers on by Shift>Ctrl>R or View>Rulers.

With Layer 2 active, hold your Shift key (easy way to draw a straight line) starting at the top 6 inch mark on the ruler. Click and drag your pencil/brush from the top of the page to the bottom so you have a straight line drawn dividing your page in half.

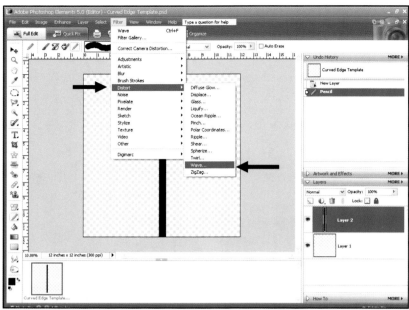

With your line drawn down the center of your page on Layer 2, go to Filter>Distort>Wave.

Use the settings that I have listed (I also used Randomize), or try out your own. If you get a warning when you try to type a number into one of the boxes, use the slider instead and then go back and try to insert the number, and it usually works. Notice how the preview box shows the changes to your line. Click OK when you're happy with the image in the preview box.

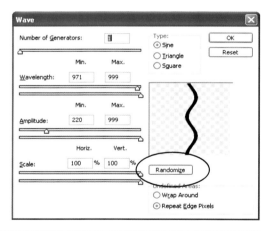

Activate the Magic Wand Tool (W) (Contiguous should be checked), and click in the area to the left of your curved line. You will have a selection area marked by marching ants. Go to Select>Modify>Expand, and expand your selection by 3 pixels. Expanding the selection will eliminate a gap between the pencil line and the fill. Fill the selection with black Alt>Backspace. Press the Esc key to remove the selection border of marching ants.

Ctrl>S (File>Save) to save your final template as a PSD layered file. To save as a single layer PNG file Shift>Ctrl>S (File>Save As), and choose PNG format (Interlace-None).

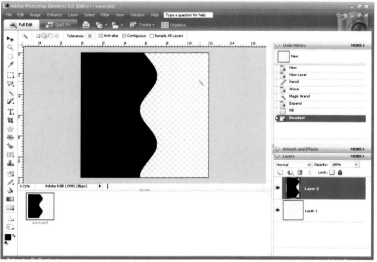

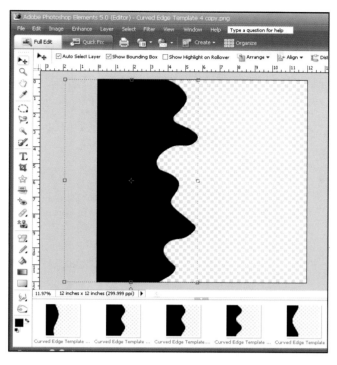

To change the look of your template, activate the Move Tool (V) and drag on different sizing handles to distort it from its original shape. The examples in the Photo Bin show how I changed my original template by using the Move Tool (V).

Applying the Wave Filter to the template again gives it a Halloween look.

Remember that Image>Rotate will rotate your template so that it goes horizontal instead of vertical, which will also give the template a different look.

The template does not have to be used this wide (6 inches at the widest point). By moving the template to the left off your scrapbook page with the Move Tool (V), you can just use part of the template's width.

Using a rectangle instead of a line will make a two sided template, as shown below. Draw a rectangle with the Shape Tool (U) (Unconstrained Size) horizontally from side to side of your paper. This is similar to the line you drew with the Pencil Tool (N) in the preceding example.

Go to Filter>Distort>Wave and click OK when you're asked to simplify your rectangle.

Use the setting shown or tryout your own settings. Keep Horizontal scale at 1% or the side edges will be distorted too.

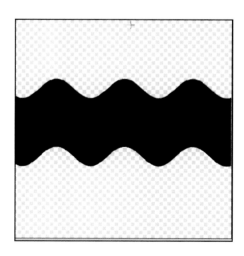
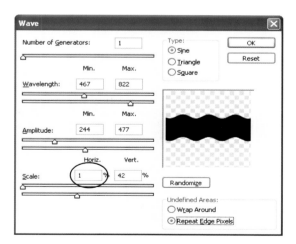

How To Use A Curved Edge Template

Method #1

Open your template and drag a piece of digital scrapbook paper over your template with the Move Tool (V) and Ctrl>G to Group with Previous. This method gives you the ability to move your paper/photo around so different areas can be shown on the template. The paper shown is from the Scrap Street Painted Summer Kit by Handmaid Designs and is on the DVD that came with this book.

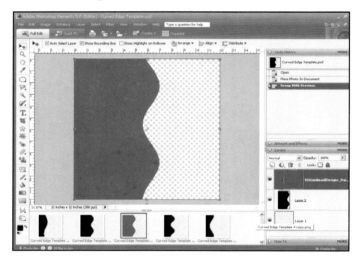

Method #2

Open your template and drag a piece of digital scrapbook paper over your template with the Move Tool (V). Ctrl Click on the template layer thumbnail so that you have a selection of marching ants. Go to your scrapbook paper layer and Ctrl>J to copy the selection. Your scrapbook paper will be cut the size of the template. Delete the full size scrapbook paper layer.

How To Make A Scalloped Or Zigzag Edge Template

Make a new scrapbook page with the specifications shown. Pick a name for your template that you'll remember.

Shift>Ctrl>S to save your file as a PSD file. Save your file to your Scrapbook Templates file so you'll know where to find it later.

Activate the Brush Tool (B) and choose the regular brush, which is the first tool on the options bar on the left.

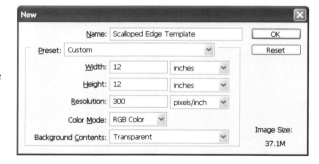

For the Scalloped Edge Template:

Set your default colors by typing the letter "D"

Choose a hard round brush from the Default brush drop down menu.

Set the brush size to 175 px.

Go to More Options on the options bar and change the Spacing to 90% and Hardness to 100%.

Make a new layer by clicking on the new layer icon in the Layers palette.

On Layer 2, go to the left side of your blank page at the 6 inch horizontal ruler line, and position your cursor (brush) so that the left edge of the cursor is almost to the left edge of your page. Your cursor is in the shape of the brush you chose. Hold the Shift key (easy way to draw a straight line) and click and drag across the page all the way to the other side and release your mouse. Your brush mark line will look like this example below. You may want to save your template at this point as another file if you think you would use this shape by itself as a template.

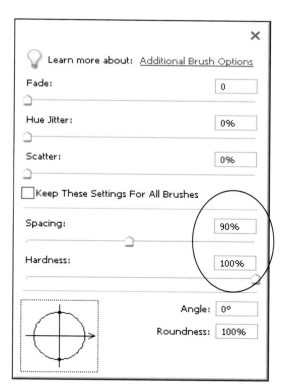

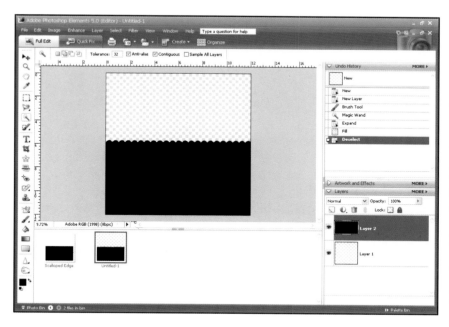

Activate the Magic Wand Tool (W) (Contiguous should be checked), and click in the white area below your brush line on the brush layer. This should only select the area under the brush line. If it selects all of it, make sure that your brush line goes from side to side and that there is no gap on the side edges. If you have a small gap on one of the sides, use the Move Tool (V) to stretch the brush line slightly. Go to Select>Modify> Expand and choose 3 pixels.

With the brush layer active, Alt>Backspace to fill with black. Tap the Esc Key to remove the selection border (marching ants).

Ctrl>S to save your final template as a PSD layered file. To save as a single layer PNG file Shift>Ctrl>S (File>Save As), and choose PNG format (Interlace-None).

To make the zigzag edge template, follow the scalloped edge template directions exactly except change your brush settings as follows:

Choose a square brush from the brush drop down menu at about 164 px.

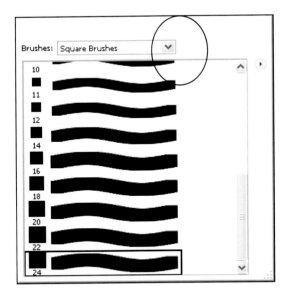 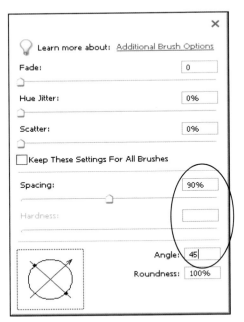

Alpha Templates

My biggest pet peeve with traditional scrapbooking is any kind of lettering. Whether it's stickers or some other type of embellishment with a letter on it, they all drive me crazy. How many times have you tried to write something only to figure out that you don't have enough of a certain letter? I can still remember making a scrapbook page for a baby shower I'd just hosted. The mother to be is a dear friend of mine and I thought it would be nice to make the pages for her. I found some darling pink letters that were in the shape of a button and bought them even though they were $3.99 a package. I was at home working feverishly to finish the project at my usual scrapbook time of two in the morning. I started to spell out Amber Catherine Miller, only to find out that there was only one "E" in the package. Amber Catherine Miller has four "E's"! I was off the next morning hoping that my local scrapbook store had another 3 packages. In the end, I paid $16 + tax for those cute letters. I don't think I've bought traditional letters since! Long before I realized I was a hybrid scrapper, I was using my computer to do titles and journaling because it was just easier for me. I still have letter stickers hanging around with just a few letters remaining, because someday I might just find the perfect use for them!

Included on your CD that comes with this book is an Alpha template designed by **The Digital Scrapbook Teacher. The Digital Scrapbook Teacher** also sells sets of Alpha templates. Our Alpha templates come with both, upper and lower case letters, numbers 0-9 and several punctuation marks. Save money overall and make your own Alpha's with our templates to match the kits you have. Visit TheDigitalScrapbookTeacher.com website, buy in a class, or order by mail with the order blank that came with this book.

How To Make Your Own Multi Layered PSD Alpha Template

Some kits don't come with Alphas so you have to use regular text or make your own titles and journaling. If you want the ability to customize your own Alphas with your own papers or don't like the Alphas that came with your set, it's easy to make your own.

Open a new document 12 x 12 inches, RGB Color, 300 ppi, with a Transparent Background.
In my example I'm going to make a simple 1 ½ inch round circle Alpha template.

Shift>Ctrl>S (File>Save>As) and pick a name and location to save this template. Save as a PSD file. I named this one Circle Alphas, and it's on the CD that was included with this book.

Type D to set your Foreground color to Black and your Background Color to White.

Activate the Ellipse Tool (U) (Oval), click on the black down facing triangle that says "Geometry Options" when you hover your mouse over it. Choose Fixed Size 1.5 inches wide by 1.5 inches high. Click your mouse, and you automatically draw a black 1 ½ inch circle without dragging the mouse; don't worry about placing them in a straight line. Click 6 times across the top of the page so you have 6 circles.

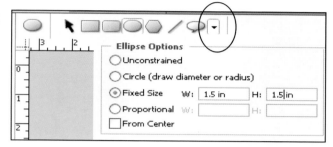

With the Move Tool (V), put one circle shape approximately ¼ inch from the top edge of the blank page. Select all of the circle layers by Ctrl Clicking on all layers in the Layers palette. Use the Align option in the Move Tool (V) and select Align>Top Edges. Next, move the far right and far left circles approximately ½ inch from each side of your blank page. Select all of the layers again and use the Distribute Command in the Move Tool (V), and select Distribute>Horizontal Centers.

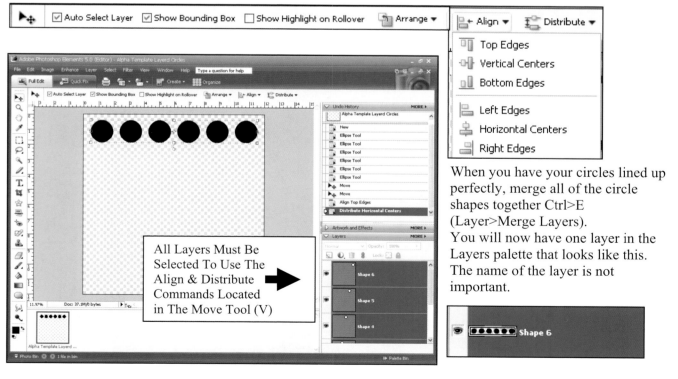

When you have your circles lined up perfectly, merge all of the circle shapes together Ctrl>E (Layer>Merge Layers).
You will now have one layer in the Layers palette that looks like this. The name of the layer is not important.

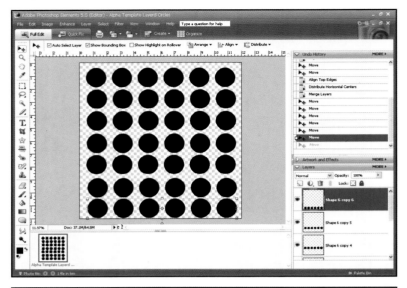

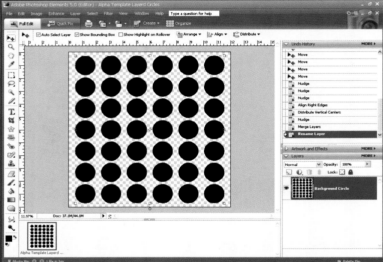

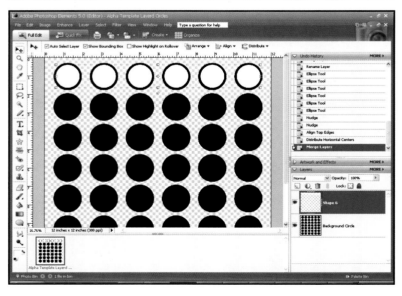

With the Move Tool (V) still activated, Alt click on one of the circle shapes, drag it down and release. You've just copied the whole row of circles. Do this six times until you have seven rows of six circles. Don't worry about the spacing.

Select all the layers by Ctrl>clicking on all of them, and Align>Right Edges, and then Distribute>Vertical Centers.

After all of your circle layers are lined up the way you want them, Ctrl>E (Layer>Merge Layers). To make the Template easier to use, I renamed the layer "Background Circle" by double clicking on the Layer. Ctrl>S (File>Save).

To make the inner circle, repeat the same steps, but change the size of your circle to 1.25 inch and the color to white.

Make 6 white circles with the Ellipse Tool (U), and place the far right and left circles directly over the black circles, which will act like a mat. Use Align>Top Edges and Distribute>Horizontal Centers, and they should all line up perfectly.

Select all six layers of the white circles and Ctrl>E (Layer>Merge Layers). As with the black circles, activate the Move Tool (V) and while holding the Alt key, click and drag one of the white circles and you will copy the Layer. Do this six times.

Use the Align and Distribute Commands to line the white circles up perfectly over the black circles by selecting all layers. When you've got them perfect, Ctrl>E (Layer>Merge Layers). You now have two layers, one of black circles and one of white circles.

Ctrl>S (File>Save).

Activate the Type Tool (T); in my example I'm using the Papyrus font at 60 pts. Use any font you want, but understand that they may not line up the same way as my example.

Click in the white circle approximately where you want to start the letter. Type "A" then move your mouse over to the next one, click and type "B", and so on. By doing it this way, each letter will be on its own layer. After you get the first row done, center the letter manually with the Move Tool (V). Sometimes it's difficult to move small letters, so you might want to Zoom (Z) in. Selecting small thin items is also hard, so you may want to turn off Auto Select Layer on the Move Tool (V) option bar. If you turn off Auto Select Layer, remember that you have to click on the layer you want to move in the Layers palette.

I duplicated this file and used all 26 letters in the alphabet, numbers 0-9, and a few punctuation marks on my template. I used the Caps Lock key to make it easier to type the capital letters. You can also type one layer with lower case and one layer with upper case letters, it's your choice!

Select all of the letter layers on one row and Align>Bottom Edges so they're all spaced out the same. The capital letter Q is a little tricky as is any letter that descends like a lower case g, y, p, q, and sometimes others depending on the font.

If you are planning on doing several Alpha templates, you may want to type all of your letters and position them correctly. Save them that way in a PSD file as 42 layers so that you can change the font and size of the letters for another Alpha template. After you save the 42 layers, you can then Ctrl>E (Layer>Merge Layers) to make one layer of letters. If you're never going to do this again you can proceed this way:

When you have the first row the way you want them with A-F layers selected, Ctrl>E (Layer>Merge Layers). Repeat this with all rows. When you have all the rows done, merge all of the letter layers so that you have just one layer of letters.

Link your three layers together by selecting all the layers in the Layers palette and clicking on the link symbol on the top of the Layers palette.

Ctrl>S (File>Save)

Your template is now finished. You can use this template over and over on different projects. Remember to immediately Shift>Ctrl>S (File>Save As) when you open it to use it and save it with another name so you don't save over the original file.

How To Use A Multi Layered PSD Alpha Template

The Digital Scrapbook Teacher also sells Alpha templates in several designs. The following directions work for our Alpha templates, and they'll probably work for Alpha templates you've purchased elsewhere. The Postage Stamp Alpha demonstrated in this example is available in a CD set of templates available on TheDigitalScrapbookTeacher.com, in our classes, or by mail with the order form that came with this book.

Open the Template and immediately Shift>Ctrl>S (File>Save As), and name it something else. Since I am going to make these Alphas to match the Fish Tails kit by PingDesigns.com I am going to name my file FishTailsPostageAlphas. This Alpha template has four layers including the letters. Open four papers from the Fish Tails kit that's on the CD included with your book.

Drag the papers over each layer with the Move Tool (V), and then Ctrl>G (Layer>Group with Previous) just like we've done with the other Templates in this section.

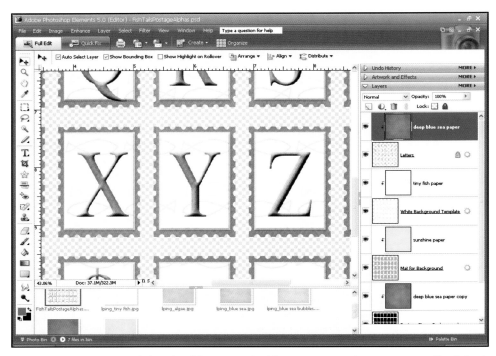

This is how your Layers palette will look. I have renamed my paper layers with the paper, so that you can see which papers I used on each layer.

I added a drop shadow to the two middle layers and a bevel to the letters. You'll add a drop shadow to the bottom layer once you place them on your page, but not now.

After you have your Alphas looking exactly like you want them, merge all of the layers together by selecting all of the layers and Ctrl>E (Layer>Merge). Merging all the layers will keep your transparent background. Do not Flatten Image or your background will be white. Save again!

To move one of the letters to your scrapbook page, draw a rectangle around the letter with the Marquee Tool (M), then activate your Move Tool (V) and drag it onto your scrapbook page. Your letter will be copied onto your scrapbook page on its own layer. Copy all of the letters that you will use the same way. Use the Move Tool (V) along with the Align and Distribute options to arrange the letters on your scrapbook page. Add a drop shadow on the Alpha after you have them placed where you want them. You can size them with the Move Tool (V). Making the Alpha very large will make them look pixilated, but making them a little bit bigger is fine.

You may want to make several sets of Alphas to match your paper kits and mix and match them. Many of the Alpha sets available at digi-scrapping sites are not identical, but generally match the other elements they're sold with. Using Alpha templates is fast and easy. If you like to mix and match your Alphas, make another set with the papers in a different order. The second set will only take you about five minutes, I promise!

How To Use A Paper Template

Some Digital Scrapbooking websites sell Paper templates that can be used to make paper to match your own color scheme. You can also combine templates with other papers to make completely different looking paper. Some templates have a distinct pattern on them, while others have textures that look like grunge, etc.

The Paper template in this illustration is in the ScrapGirls.com Refresh kit included on the CD that came with your book.

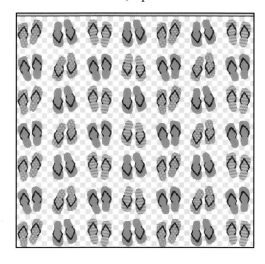

The file name of this template is: SG_Refresh_ScrapSimple_PaperTemplate, and it has cute flip flops on it for a summer themed scrapbook page.

Open the file in Photoshop Elements and immediately Shift>Ctrl>S (File>Save As). Choose a new name for your file and a place to save it. Save as a PSD file so you'll have all the layers available if you want to make a change.

Currently this template has a transparent background which is indicated by the checkerboard pattern. If you want to put a piece of digital paper underneath the flip flops, you can drag it under Layer 1 and the paper will show through on the transparent areas. Adjust the color or opacity of this background paper now, or after we get the template filled.

If you don't want to use a digital paper as the base layer, you can make a new layer with the New Layer icon. Ctrl>Click on the icon, and the new layer will appear below Layer 1 in the Layers palette, or go to Layer>New Layer. This layer will automatically be named Layer 2. Drag Layer 2 under Layer 1, and use Alt>Backspace to fill with your Foreground color. My example shows this option.

For demonstration purposes, I opened another paper in the Refresh kit called Multi-Flowers, and copied its colors to my paper template. To pick my color, I activated the Eyedropper Tool (I) and clicked on the pink of the flower on the Multi Flowers paper. I used the wheel on my mouse to zoom in very close, and picked the lightest pink I could find in the pink flowers. Depending on where you click, you may get a different Hex #. You can do this or enter the Hex # that I'm using which is fbd7e1. To enter the Hex #, double click on the Foreground color swatch at the bottom of the Toolbar, and type it in where it says "#" near the bottom (circled in example).

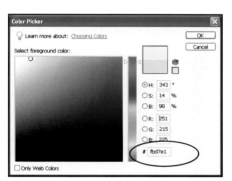

To begin filling in the template, click on Layer 1 and activate your Magic Wand Tool (W). Make sure that Contiguous on the Magic Wand Options Bar is not checked. Contiguous means it will select everything in that color that is touching; the items we are going to select are not touching! Click on the darkest gray on the strap part of a pair of flip flops, and all of the straps should be surrounded by marching ants.

Your Options Bar should look like this:

Make a new layer with the New Layer icon in the Layers palette, this will be Layer 3. Fill this layer with the Foreground color by Alt>Backspace. Your flip flop straps will now be pink. Press the Esc key to remove the selection border (marching ants).

Select another color from the Multi Flowers paper using the previous steps, this will be your new Foreground color. The purple I used is # a26fb1.

Go back to Layer 1, the template layer and activate the Magic Wand (W), click on the gray stripes or polka dots on the flip flops. All of the stripes and polka dots will be selected.

Select another color from the Multi Flowers paper using the previous steps, I chose yellow # ffe591.

Make a new layer with the New Layer icon in the Layers palette, this will be Layer 4. Fill this layer with the Foreground color by Alt Backspace. Your flip flop stripes and polka dots will now be yellow. Press the Esc key to get rid of the selection (marching ants).

Go back to Layer 1, the Template layer, and activate the Magic Wand (W). Click on the remaining gray for the solid flip flops and the other stripes. The solid flip flops and stripes will be selected.

Select another color from the Multi Flowers paper using the previous steps, I chose blue # 83d3ea. Make a new layer with the New Layer icon in the Layers palette, this will be Layer 5. Fill this layer with the Foreground color by Alt>Backspace, or with the Paint Bucket Tool (K). Your flip flops and stripes will now be blue. Tap the Esc key to remove the selection border (marching ants).

After you complete all of the steps, your template will look like the example below. If you're not happy with the colors, you can change them easily. You can add Layer Styles such as Drop Shadows or Bevels if you like them.

When you're happy with the colors, you can Shift Ctrl>E (Layer>Merge Visible). When you merge the layers, you will have one layer. Save!

Use this paper as it is, or add filters or textures to it. By placing a different paper, pattern layer, or color fill layer above and/or below it and adjusting the Opacity and Blending Modes, you can get a completely different looking paper. Have fun and experiment!

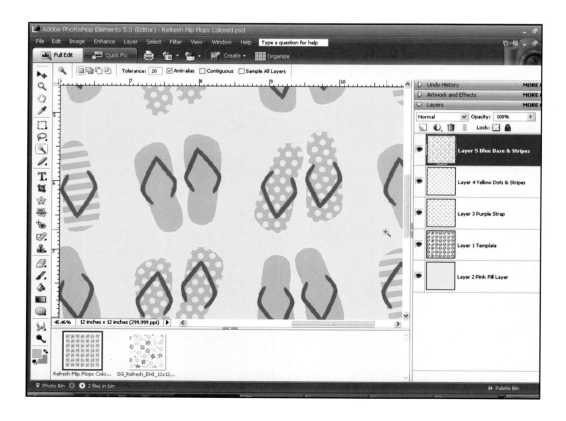

How To Use A Page Curl Template

To get a realistic looking curl on your page, you can spend a lot of time reading tutorials and trying to make one yourself. You may or may not be happy with the end result or you can just buy a Page Curl Template.

The Page Curl Template I'm using is available in PNG and PSD format from Kim Hill, owner and designer of CGEssentials.com. This example shows the PSD Format template.

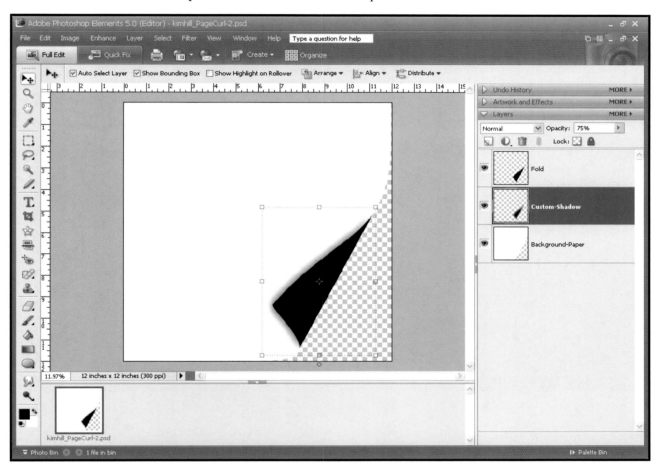

As with any template, when you start using it Shift>Ctrl>S (File>Save As). Save this file as a PSD file to keep all the layers intact. I'm going to name this FishTailPageCurl, to use with my Fish Tail Kit from Ping Designs.

This Template was created 12 x 12 RGB Color 300 Resolution, which is perfect! It consists of 3 layers.

Open two pieces of 12 x 12 digital paper for the two paper layers. The third layer is a Custom Shadow.

With the Move Tool (V), drag the paper you want to show on the top of your template on top of the layer named Background Paper. Ctrl>G (Layer>Group with Previous), and your paper is cropped to the shape of the Background Paper.

Drag your second piece of paper on top of the layer named Fold Layer. Ctrl>G (Layer>Group with Previous).

Your screen should look like this.

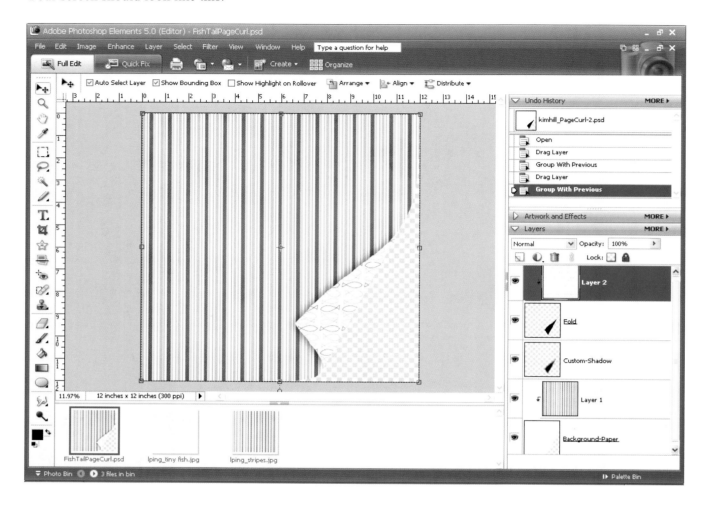

Select all 5 layers and Ctrl>E (Layer>Merge Layers).

By using a template, you made a unique looking page that looks like it really has a folded edge in less than a minute. Just think how impressed your friends will be!

If you are going to save this file now, do not flatten this image or you will lose the transparency on the bottom right corner. Ctrl>S (File>Save) to save as a PSD file, and you can also save it as a PNG file to keep its transparency.

To continue on and use this as a scrapbook page, add another paper underneath the curled page and add pictures and journaling on top of the curled paper.

Cool Stuff To Do With…

Cool Stuff To Do With Text, Shapes, & Mats

Multi-Colored Text

For multi-colored text, the easiest way to accomplish this is to type your text. Select the letters or words that you want in a different color. Choose another color from the color box on the Type Tool (T) option bar or click on the Foreground color box and choose a color from the Color Picker. Your highlighted text color will now be changed and you'll end up with something like the example. However, with this method you don't have the ability to change the color of half of a letter.

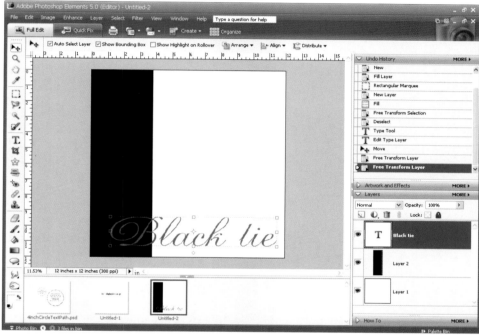

You might think that you'd never want to change the color of half of a letter, but think about when you're making a title that stretches across your scrapbook page. Many times the title crosses over several colors of digital paper. In my example shown, I've written my type in red because if I choose black or white you won't be able to see part of it.

This technique is very easy, the instructions just look a little bit long, but this can be done in just a couple of minutes.

Open a new document (Ctrl>N) that is 12 x 12 inches, 300 resolution, RGB color, with a white background. With your Marquee Tool (M) draw a rectangle on the left side of the page. Make a new layer with the new layer icon in the Layers palette. Type D to set your Default colors to black and white. Fill the selection with black by typing Alt>backspace. Activate the Type Tool (T) and type the word Black Tie. In my example I used the Devon Font in a size of 200 pts. I activated the Move Tool (V) and pulled the side sizing handles a little bit to make the font wider to fit on my page better. Make sure you have committed your text and sizing change by clicking your checkmarks. You now have 3 layers as shown in the example above.

Make 2 copies of the type layer by Ctrl>J or dragging the type layer to the New Layer icon on the Layers palette. Hide your original type layer by clicking on the Eyeball icon. By hiding this layer, you have a backup copy of your text in case you make a mistake. Change the color of the top text layer to black by double clicking on the text layer thumbnail and choosing black from the color box on the Text Tool (T) options bar.

Check the checkmark to accept the change. You won't be able to see the beginning part of your text because it's now black, this is OK. Go to the next layer and change the type to white the same way. You will not see any obvious change on your page because the white text is under the black text. Turn off the top text black layer to see if you can see the white text on the black portion of your page. You won't be able to see the rest of your text because when you write white text on a white page, it's invisible! Simplify your black and white text layers by right clicking on the layer name and choosing Simplify Layer. You will know your text is simplified because the layer thumbnail now shows a transparent (checkerboard) background. Ctrl click on the layer with the black rectangle and the marching ants will surround the black rectangle. Click on the layer with the black type which should be your top text layer and tap the Delete key. This will delete the text only in the selected area. Tap the Esc key to remove the marching ants. Link or Merge your black and white text layer so you don't accidentally move them apart by selecting both layers in the Layers palette and click on the Link icon or typing Ctrl>E to merge. You can discard the hidden text layer when you're sure you're done with the text.

Once you try this, you'll start using it all the time. Since your text is simplified you can add a filter or distress it too. If you're looking for a rainbow effect, you can make many color layers of the text and delete portions of it using the Rectangular Marquee Tool (M). Make a selection around the area you want to delete and tap the Delete key.

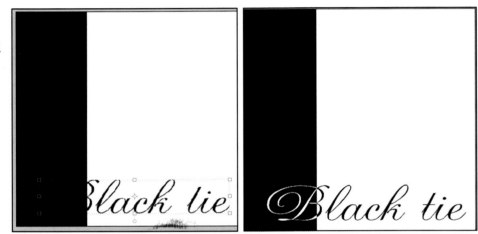

Text In A Circle

In every class that I've been in, someone always wants to know how to write their text in a circle like they show in all the magazines. I've listed three methods that will give you varying results. Text Paths are the easiest and fastest way to write your circle or other shape, but they can't be made in Photoshop Elements. Text Paths are available for purchase on some digital scrapbooking websites, but you won't find a better selection that's better priced, than at TheDigitalScrapbookTeacher.com.

Using A Text Path To Write Words In A Circle (or other shapes)

Text Paths are a fun and easy way to add words or journaling to your scrapbook pages. The great thing about them is that you can edit the type at any time and make the path larger or smaller easily.

Text Paths cannot be created in Photoshop Elements. Text paths that were created in Photoshop can be used in Photoshop Elements. TheDigitalScrapbookTeacher.com has a wide assortment of Text Paths available for purchase.

The Text Paths sold by TheDigitalScrapbookTeacher.com have the instructions included on the file.

Activate the Move Tool (V) and drag the Text Path onto your scrapbook page. To make the Text Path larger or smaller, drag one of the corner sizing handles.

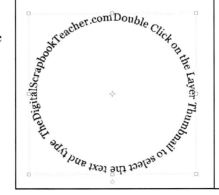

Double click on the Text Path layer thumbnail to select the text. When the text is selected, it will be highlighted like the example shown. Change the font if you want a different font because it will affect the sizing of the text.

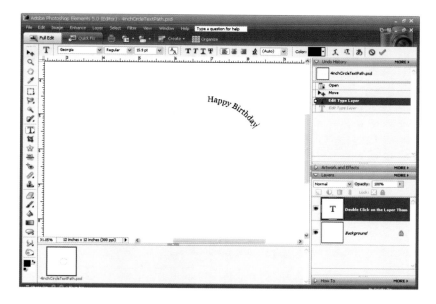

With the Text Path type selected, start typing. All of the text that was written disappears and your text is shown as you type. Continue typing your text until you get to the end of the circle or other shape.

If you're lucky, the text you type fits perfectly into your Text Path. If it doesn't (which it probably won't on your first attempt), try one of these fixes:

Add spaces in between the words.

Select the text by double clicking on the Text Path Layer thumbnail, select the font size and roll your mouse so that the font size adjusts. I don't recommend adding any Faux Font Styles to your text.

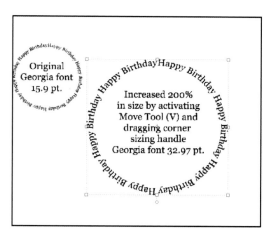

When you transform your Text Path by using the Move Tool (V) and dragging the corner sizing handle, you will probably have to resize the font. For example, my 4 inch circle is filled with text that is 15.9 pts in the regular Georgia font. If I transform my circle to approximately 200% of the original size, my font is now 32.97 pts, which may or may not be the look you want. If you want the circle bigger and want to change the font size, select the text and select the font size and change it. If you're making the text smaller, you'll need to type some more text.

Using The Polar Coordinates Filter to Write Words In A Circle

Open a new file Ctrl>N (File>New) that is 12 x 12 inches wide, 300 resolution, RGB color, on a transparent background. Activate the Text Tool (T). In my example, I used the Bookman Old Style Font, Regular Style, 23 pts. Start typing your text at the very edge of the left side and continue all the way to the right side. Click the checkmark to commit your text. If your text does not go to the edge of the page, activate the Move Tool (V), drag the right middle sizing corner and stretch it sideways just a tiny bit. If you drag it just a tiny bit you won't be able to notice the text is a little bit distorted. Check the checkmark to accept the transformation. To keep as a back-up in case you make a mistake, make a duplicate layer of your text and hide it by turning off the Eyeball icon. N,ext go to: Filter>Distort>Polar Coordinates, you will get a message that the text needs to be simplified; click OK. After simplifying your text, you will be unable to change the type, font, or font size.

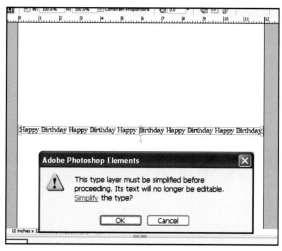

The Default for this filter is Rectangular to Polar which is what you want, so click OK. You will now have a 6 inch wide circle of your text exactly in the middle of your page. To move or transform the circle, use the Move Tool (V). For this example I placed my text circle on a white background so it could be seen esaily.

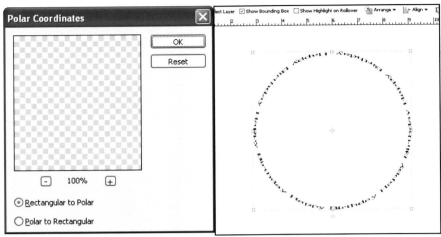

Save this file by itself for later use or make it directly on a scrapbook page.

Using Warped Text To Write Words In A Circle

This method isn't perfect, but it works. Type your text and check the check mark. Make a copy of your text layer to use for the bottom part of the circle. In case it's needed later because you make a mistake, it would be a good idea to make an additional copy and hide it by turning off the eyeball icon. Next, go to the Warped Text button on the Text Options Bar and slide the Bend % box until you get the amount of bend that you need for the top part of the circle and click OK. The % amount will vary with the amount and size of text that you have on your layer. Go to the second layer and also go to Arc, but put a – (minus) in the Bend % and use the same % that was used in the first layer box so that the arc bends down instead of up. Activate the Move Tool (V) to adjust the spacing between the upper and lower part of your circle. Link or merge the two warped text layers so that they don't get separated.

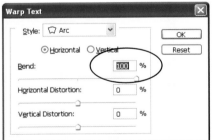

Personalized Fonts

There are several internet sites that offer to make a font from your own handwriting. Usually you have to download a template and fill it in with your handwriting, and then fax or upload the completed template to them. The templates have blocks for you to write upper and lower case letters, numbers, some symbols, and some punctuation marks.

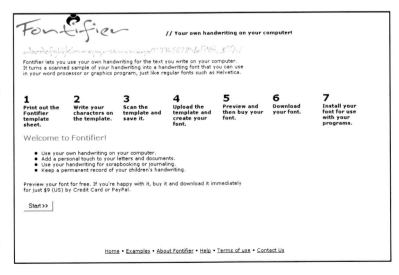

For $9 (at the time this book was written it may have changed by the time you read this), Fontifier.com will make you a personalized font in seconds. Follow their online directions and it's easy. When filling out their template they recommend using a felt pen, but I would recommend a Gel pen because my font came out a little bit fuzzy when I used a fine tip Sharpie pen. Pay attention to the marks on the template boxes so that your font lines up correctly. I wrote mine in crooked so the font came out a little crooked.

You have the opportunity to preview the font before you buy it and you're not obligated to buy it, so I'll fill out another template when I have five free minutes, probably when I finish this book!

How To Use Dingbats

Dingbats are fonts that have images instead of letters; sometimes they have letters and images combined. One of the popular dingbats that's installed on most computers is Wingdings. To use a dingbat in journaling, all you need to do is type your journaling in the regular font and then, switch your font to the dingbat font and type the image you want and then return to your regular font. If you are doing a lot of journaling and want to install the dingbats several times, it may be easier to figure out how much space you need for the dingbat and add to it after you finish the journaling.

The hardest part about using a dingbat is that you don't know which key to press to get the image you want. Many times you'll just end up typing all the different keys to find the one you want. If you'd like a little bit better method, I've got one. If you're using Windows XP this method should work for you.

Using a Character Map to display characters is easy once you know how to do it. To find the character map:

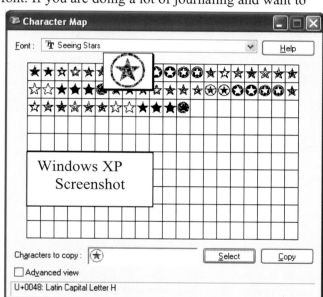

Short cut-Press your start button>Run and type charmap.

Long way-Press your Start button>Click on All Programs>Click on Accessories>Click on System Tools>Click on Character Map.

If your Character Map is not in this location, look around for it under Accessories, it is probably there.

The character map for fonts like Arial and Times New Roman are huge because they have all different kinds of symbols and characters, but for Dingbats, they are usually pretty small like this one for the Seeing Stars font downloaded from DaFont.com.

Click on the Character you want to use and then click on the Select Key. Go to your scrapbook page and type Ctrl>V to paste the dingbat on your page. It may take a few seconds to paste the dingbat. Notice in the Layers palette the Layer name is shown as the letter that was used for the character you typed. In the case of the Ding Bats title used in the beginning of this section, you can see that the stars I used were the a, b, & c keys.

Dingbats can be made into brushes or patterns easily.

Inserting Special Characters On Your Scrapbook Pages

If you're looking for some symbols other than what's shown on your keyboard, visit the Character Map. The examples shown here are in Windows XP.

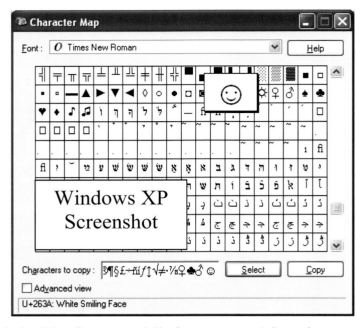

Using a Character Map to display characters is easy once you know how to do it. To find the character map:

Press your Start button
Click on All Programs
Click on Accessories
Click on System Tools
Click on Character Map

If your Character Map is not in this location, look around for it under Accessories, it is probably there.

The character map for Times New Roman is huge because they have all different kinds of symbols. Other fonts, especially free ones, won't have that many characters.

Click on the Character you want to use and then click on the Select Key. When you have all of the characters/symbols that you want, click on the Copy key.

Go to your scrapbook page and activate the Type Tool (T) and change the font selected to match the one on the Character map. Type Ctrl>V to paste the characters on your page. It may take a few seconds to paste the characters. If your type does not look like the characters you selected on the character map, check your fonts to make sure they are both the same. Not all fonts have the same characters, so changing a font is not advisable.

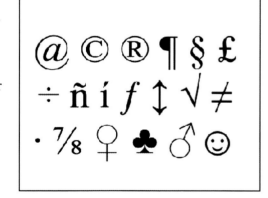

These are some of the characters available for the Times New Roman font.

Using Your Photos Or Scrapbook Paper To Write Words

As usual there are several ways that you can cut your photos or scrapbook paper into letters and words just like your own personal die cut machine. The only difference is that you don't have to buy all the different sets of letters in different sizes or store them!

In these examples photos and digital scrapbook paper do the same thing.

Open an image and select the Horizontal (or Vertical) Type Mask Tool (T). Use a "fat" font and a large size font. In my example, I'm using the Elephant font at 250 pts. Please note that methods using the Type Mask do not allow you to edit your text.

Start typing your text and the image will be covered with a red mask. The letters you type will show through the red mask to the color photo. Check the checkmark if your type is correct. As soon as you check the checkmark, the red disappears and your type is surrounded by a selection border (marching ants). If you want to move your selection to another spot on the photo (for example, because I want more of the butterfly included in the letters), use the arrow keys.

To move your title onto a scrapbook page, activate the Move Tool (V) and drag it onto your page in the Photo Bin. You can add a layer style such as a bevel or shadow and even a Stroke Outline to make the title stand out even more.

Dragging your photo onto your scrapbook page first and cutting out your type gives you another option of using the photo with the lettering cut out. At first it just appears that the photo has white type on it, but by adding a drop shadow, the look changes completely.

Open a new scrapbook page (Ctrl>N) and open your image. Drag your photo onto your scrapbook page with the Move Tool (V). Activate the Horizontal (or Vertical) Type Mask Tool (T). Use a "fat" font and a large size font. In my example I'm using the Elephant font at 250 pts. Start typing your text and the image will turn red. Check the checkmark if your type is correct. As soon as you check the checkmark, the red disappears and your type is surrounded by a selection border (marching ants). If you want to move your selection to another spot on the photo (for example because I want more of the butterfly included in the letters), use the Arrow keys.

Ctrl>J to make a copy of the selected cut out type layer.

Ctrl click on the layer thumbnail for the new cut out type layer so that the text is selected again. Go to the photo layer and tap the Delete key.

Activate the Move Tool (V) and drag the type off of the photo.

Tap the Esc key to remove the selection border (marching ants).

From the Special Effects Palette I added a Soft Edge Drop Shadow Layer Style to both the photo and the cut out type. On the cut out type I also added a Simple Sharp Inner Bevel Layer Style. Either one of these titles would work great on a page.

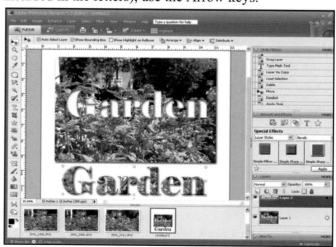

Open a new scrapbook page (Ctrl>N) and open your image. Drag your photo onto your scrapbook page with the Move Tool (V). Activate the Horizontal (or Vertical) Type Tool (T). Use a "fat" font and a large size font. In my example, I'm using the Elephant font at 250 pts of any color.

Type your text. If your image turns red, you still have the Mask Tool active so pick the first "T" icon on the Text Tool (T) option bar. Check the checkmark to commit your text.

Drag your text layer under your image layer. Ctrl>G to Group with Previous and your photo will now be cut into the letters.

Activate the Move Tool (V) and with the photo layer selected you can move the photo around to show different parts of the photo on the letters.

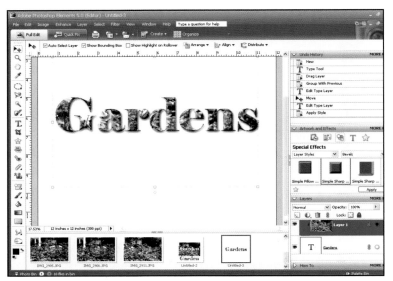

If you want to edit the text, double click on the text layer thumbnail and edit the text and it will automatically be cut out of the photo. In my example, I added an "s" to the end of the word garden.

From the Special Effects Palette I added a Soft Edge Drop Shadow Layer Style and a Simple Sharp Inner Bevel Layer Style to the type layer. To move the title around, select the type and photo layer together or better yet, link the layers by selecting them both and clicking on the link symbol in the Layers palette. In the example my layers are linked as shown by the link symbol on both layers. You can merge the layers, but after you merge them you'll be unable to edit your text or move the photo around in the letters.

Outlining Text

Photoshop Elements gives you an option for outlined Text in the Artworks and Effects Palette, but it leaves a lot to be desired. This method gives you lots of options for outlining your text.

Activate the Text Tool (T) and type your text. It is better to use a "fat" font in a large size. My example is using the font Cooper Black in 200 pt in the color black. You don't need to make your font that big. Ctrl click on the text layer thumbnail and you should have marching ants surrounding your text. Make a new layer by clicking on the New Layer icon in the Layers palette. Go to Edit>Stroke Outline and choose the Width, Color, and Location of your Stroke Outline. Since you are putting your Stroke Outline on its own layer, you can change the Blending Mode and Opacity any time so don't choose it here. Click Ok and your black text is outlined in red. Press Esc to remove the selection border (marching ants).

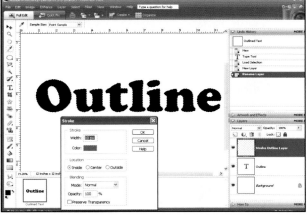

If you need to change your type, be aware that your outline will not change. All you have done is make an outline of the text, just as if you made an outline of a rectangle.

At this time you may be finished. If you don't plan on making any changes it is a good idea to link your layers, or merge them by selecting both layers in the Layers palette and typing Ctrl>E (Layer>Merge).

Another option is to turn off your original text layer and just use the Stroke Outline for your text which would look like this if you used black to make the outline.

By lowering the Opacity of your original text layer, you will have a look of outlined vellum. This example shows both the text and outline in white over a pink background. The opacity on the text layer has been reduced to 30% on the Layers palette which allows the pink background to show through. This effect works well on photographs too.

Embossing Words In A Photo

Open your photo and Ctrl>J to make a duplicate layer (Layer 1). Activate the Horizontal Type Tool (T).Type your text preferably in a large, "fat" font so that it will be seen. The color of the type does not matter. If you want to reposition your text, hold the Ctrl key and move the text (as shown in the example), before you check the checkmark. The text layer will be named whatever your text says, in my case the layer name is Paradise. Drag the text layer down in the Layers palette between the Background layer and Layer 1. Select Layer 1 and Ctrl>G (Layer>Group with Previous) and it will be grouped with the text layer. You will not notice any difference in the photo. Select the text layer and apply a drop shadow and bevel from the Artwork and Effects Palette in the Layer Styles menu.

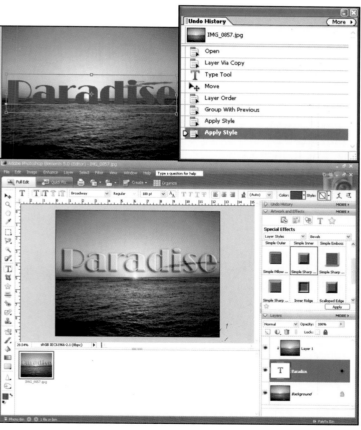

This image can be used on a card, scrapbook page, or by itself as a postcard.

Using these instructions with a shape instead of text will give an embossed look to scrapbook paper or to make your own stationary.

Text In Different Colors, Sizes, & Overlapping

To make your text overlap each other, the key is putting each letter on its own layer. In this example I have four layers of lettering, one for each letter (both of the p's are on the same layer). I've used two different fonts in varying sizes. With the letters on their own layer, you can use the Move Tool (V) to position them. Changing the size, font, and color is easy when the letters are on their own layer. I have also added a bevel to each layer of text.

The apple is actually 2 apples made with the Custom Shape Tool (U). I made the first apple green and then Ctrl>J to make an exact duplicate. Alt>Backspace to fill the top apple with your Foreground color (red from text). Use the Eraser Tool (E) to erase just the stem on the top red apple for the green stem to show through. You will be asked to Simplify the top apple to be able to erase-Click OK. Select both of the apple layers and Ctrl>E to merge them together. I also added a bevel and drop shadow to the apple.

Word Art

Adding your text in Word Art to a scrapbook page or card can make a bigger impact than if you just typed it out all in the same size font and color. Type your own journaling or add quotes from famous people to add emphasis to your project.

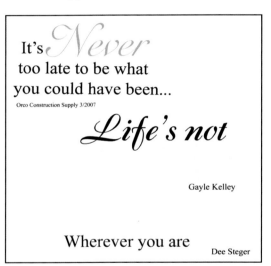

It's *Never* too late to be what you could have been...

Orco Construction Supply 3/2007

Life's not

Gayle Kelley

Wherever you are

Dee Steger

Word art is made essentially the same way. You overlap letters of different sizes, colors and fonts as explained in the preceding example. Type each portion of the text on its own layer in different font sizes and font styles. Vary the opacity on different words. Add drop shadows, bevels, or other layer styles to the text and you're done. Be aware that sometimes, when you add a layer style to type with a lower opacity, the opacity jumps back up to 100%. Adjust the opacity after you've applied the layer style.

Text Around The Edge of Your Project

Using your grid lines makes this project much easier. Go to Edit>Preferences>Grid and change Every Gridline to 50% with 1 Subdivision.

In my example I used Times New Roman font in a 29pt size. My page is 12 x 12. Depending on the text you type, this may or may not work.

Type the first line of text with the Type Tool (T) at the top of the page. Use the Move Tool (V) to center your text by lining up the center circle point exactly on top of the grid line (see arrow).

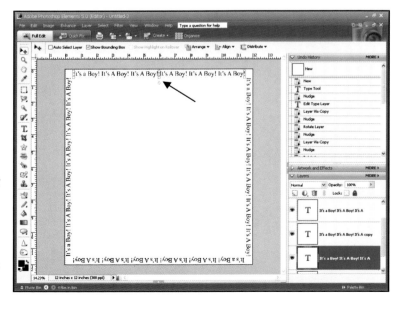

Make a duplicate copy of the text by Ctrl>J (Layer>New>Layer via Copy). Activate the Move Tool (V) and move the text down towards the bottom of the page. The text will have to be rotated. Remember, when you rotate a layer, you need to choose the layer options at the bottom of the list or you will rotate your whole page. Go to Image>Rotate>Layer 180°, move the text down to the bottom edge of the page lining up the center circle point with the grid line.

Go back to the top layer and make another duplicate copy and move it down. Go to Image>Rotate>Layer 90° Left. Move the text over to the left edge of the page. Repeat this step choosing Layer 90° Right.

This page can be saved as it is or as a transparent PNG file by deleting the white Background layer. By saving this as a transparent file you have the ability to use it as an overlay over your digital scrapbook papers. The color of the text can be changed easily.

Making Your Own Personalized Words Paper

I was recently at a scrapbook convention where one of the busiest booths there was one that was printing custom paper for about $3 a page. Here's a way to make your own for free!

Make a new scrapbook page 12 x 12 - 300 resolution with a white background. Make a new layer with the New Layer icon in the Layers palette. Fill the new layer with a color you choose for your Foreground color (Alt>Backspace). Activate the Type Tool (T) and type your first word and position it with the Move Tool (V). Adjust the opacity of the layer with the Opacity slider in the Layers palette. Type another word and rotate it by Image>Rotate>Layer 90° Right or Left. Be sure you are choosing the one that says "Layer" or your whole page will flip. Adjust the opacity, font size, and fonts on the different text layers, so they all look a little bit different. It's OK to move some of the words partly off the page. Moving a piece of digital scrapbook paper under the text layers will make this paper extra special.

This would make a great gift for a new mom who still scraps traditionally, or as a background for a baby's scrapbook page. Imagine the possibilities of the type of paper you can use this technique for. I always wanted paper that would match the schools my children went to, and this is an easy way to make it.

Make Patterns With Words

For this example, make a new file with the specifications as shown. Patterns can be made any size, however, remember that if you use a 2 x 2 pattern on an 8½ x 11 page part of the text in your pattern is going to be chopped off mid-sentence.

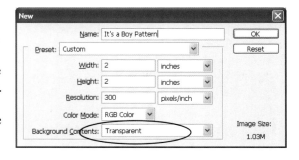

Make a new layer with the New Layer icon on the top of the Layers palette and fill it with white. You will discard this layer when you're done, but it makes it easier to see your text rather than looking at the checkerboard (transparent) pattern right now.

Activate the Type Tool (T) and type the text that you want to appear in the pattern. You can also add clip art or some of the custom shapes if you want to. Making a pattern with shapes is also covered in this section.

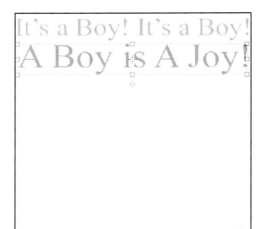

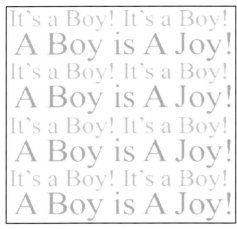

The key to making a pattern that doesn't have empty spaces in it is to make sure the text fills the canvas. This takes a little bit of sizing and nudging. Notice how my text in the example shown extends almost all the way to the side edges and top of the canvas. By adjusting your font size you can get pretty close to the edges. If you can't fill the canvas exactly by adjusting the font size, activate the Move Tool (V) and drag a side sizing handle to stretch (transform) it slightly. You will probably not notice that your text has been stretched. Both of my lines were stretched slightly.

It's best to have at least 2 different lines of text in the pattern to also avoid empty spaces.

Activate the Move Tool (V). With both of the text layers selected (click on one Ctrl click on the other one), hold the Ctrl, Alt, & Shift keys at the same time and drag down. Both type layers will be copied at the same time in a straight line. Do this 2 more times, and your canvas should look like the example above.

Delete the white fill layer so that your pattern has a transparent background. You want your pattern to have a transparent background so you can place it over other digital papers for more versatility. Your type will now be on top of a checkerboard pattern.

Go to Edit>Define Pattern. Type in a pattern name that you'll remember. Click OK. Your pattern will be added to the bottom of the pattern library that you last used. If you haven't ever used a pattern before, it will be at the bottom of the Default pattern list.

To try your pattern out, make a new scrapbook page (Ctrl>N) 12 x 12 with a white background 300 resolution. Make a new layer with the New Layer icon on the Layers palette.

Go to Edit>Fill Layer (Shift>Backspace) and choose Pattern. Click on the drop down arrow and your new pattern should be at the bottom of the list. Hover your cursor over the pattern thumbnail to make sure it has the same name as you named your pattern because they're difficult to see. Because our pattern has a transparent background, uncheck the Preserve Transparency box. Click OK and your blank layer is filled with your pattern.

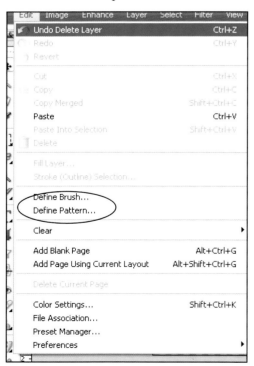

To save your pattern, click on the arrow (circled) and choose Save Pattern. By default this will be saved in the Patterns folder in Photoshop Elements 5. Type a name for your pattern and click Save. I also save my patterns in another folder in my Photoshop Elements Folder so that when the new version comes along, I can find it easily. The next time you start Photoshop Elements your new pattern will show on the drop down list.

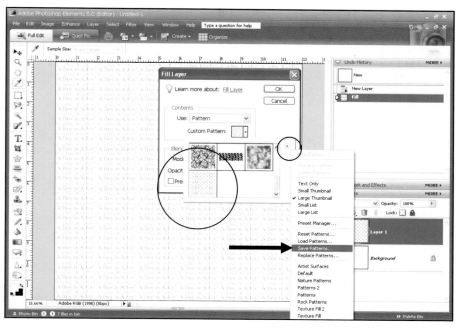

Make Patterns With Shapes, Brush Strokes, Ding Bats, Or Photos

To make a pattern with a shape, ding bats, or a brush stroke you will follow the same steps explained in the Pattern with Words, but will use a shape made with the Custom Shape Tool (U), or by stamping a brush. To make a pattern with a photo, simply crop the photo to the pattern size and then define the pattern as shown above. Making a pattern is the way a lot of traditional and digital scrapbook papers are made.

In this example, I made a new file (Ctrl>N) 4 x 4 inches, 300 resolution, transparent background. I made a new layer and filled it white, so I could see what I was doing because the checkerboard is distracting for me. I stamped the feet in different places in black only so I could see it better The pattern's color can easily be changed. To stamp the feet at different angles, use the More Options settings for the Brush Tool (B) and adjust the angle, or stamp each brush stroke on its own layer, and use the Move Tool (V) to rotate it by rotation point. This is easier for me. Delete the white blank layer. Go to Edit>Define Pattern and type a pattern name.

Make a new scrapbook page, go to Edit>Fill and choose the pattern as explained in the preceding example. Change your Foreground color to the color you want the pattern to be and Shift>Alt> Backspace. Adjust the opacity and put a piece of scrapbook paper underneath it or a sold color fill layer, and you have a nice piece of scrapbook paper you made yourself.

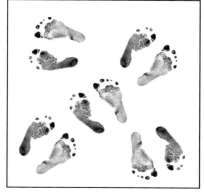

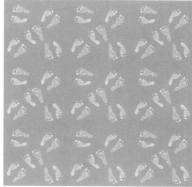

Gradient Filled Text

In the Text Effects section of the Artwork and Effects Palette are some Gradient Styles that can be added to text but can't be modified in any way. This method is quick and easy. Type your text with the Type Tool (T), using a "fat" font works best. This font is Cooper Black. Ctrl Click on the text layer thumbnail and you will have a selection border around your text. Make a new layer by clicking on the New Layer icon in the Layers palette. Activate the Gradient Tool (G) and choose the gradient you want from the drop down box and the pattern you want (linear, diamond, radial, etc.). Gradients are explained in detail in the Tools Section.

Click and drag the direction you want the gradient to go (top to bottom, diagonally, etc.) on the new blank layer and your selection border will fill with the gradient. In the top example (word-Gradient), I used the Spectrum Gradient from the default gradients set on a linear setting. In the bottom sample (word-Text), I used a custom gradient I made. The specifications for this gradient is in the Gradient Tool (G) section in the Tools section. In my example, each word was constructed separately.

If you want to add a stroke outline around your gradient, go to Edit>Stroke Outline and choose a size and color before you tap the Esc key to get rid of your marching ants. Hide your original text layer in case you want to change it later. Your type layer is editable, but you will need to redo the gradient and Stroke Outline. However, it sure beats redoing everything if you made a spelling mistake!

Gradient Filled Text Box

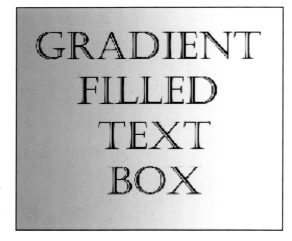

Adding a Gradient to a text box adds a finished professional look, and it's easy! Filling a text box is nothing more than filling a selection with a Gradient.

Activate the Type Tool (T) and drag a text box with your cursor and type your text. In my example I centered my text and used the Castellar font. Don't forget to commit your text by clicking the checkmark!

Click the Rectangular Marquee Tool (M) icon on the Toolbar and draw a selection around your text. If the Text Tool is still active and you type an M (shortcut for Marquee), you'll have an extra M in your text!

Next make a new layer under the text layer by Ctrl clicking the New Layer icon in the Layers palette.

Choose a color for your Foreground color by clicking in the Foreground color box located at the bottom of the Toolbar.

Activate the Gradient Tool (G) and choose a Gradient and a Gradient Pattern. Since I wanted my Gradient to fade out, I chose the Foreground to Transparent Gradient and the Linear Pattern. To fade the Gradient like my example, click on the far left side, drag across to the right side, and release your mouse. If you want to add an outline around your Gradient, go to Edit>Stroke Outline and choose a size and color and click OK before you tap the Esc key to get rid of the marching ants.

To make a gradient filled text box with a softer edge on it, feather your selection when you activate the Marquee Tool (M). Your edges will fade into your scrapbook page. You probably won't want to use a Stroke Outline when you feather the edges.

Instant Chipboard Effect

Included on the CD that came with your book is an Action graciously donated by AtomicCupcake.com. Instructions for installing actions are located in the Shopping, Downloading, & Installing Chapter. Once you see how this action works, you'll be speechless!

Open a 12 x 12 new file (Ctrl>N) 300 resolution, with a transparent background. Type a title, or make a shape or mat that you would like to add the chipboard effect to. In my example, I used the font Bondoni MT Black in a regular style in 150 pt. size. You'll want to use a "fat" font so that the effect shows up.

In the Artwork and Effects Palette, choose the Apply Effects, Filters, and Layer Styles button (circled). From there, choose Special Effects and choose Atomic_cupcake_chipboard. If you haven't installed this, it won't be there. Go to the Shopping, Downloading, & Installing Chapter and follow the instructions on how to install it.

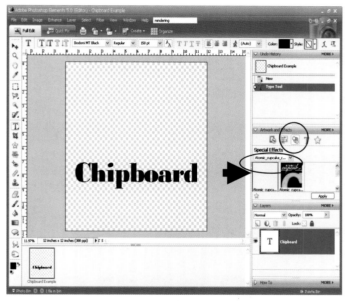

Double click in the blank square (to the right of the arrow) and the Action will start. If you've never seen an action work, you'll first think your computer is having a heart attack!

When the computer stops processing the action, you will notice that it has made another separate file with your words with the chipboard applied to it.

If you check your Undo History, you will see that it took about 50 steps for the Chipboard effect to be applied to your text which was done for you automatically and in this case, for FREE! Atomic Cupcake has many actions like this available on their website with very reasonable pricing.

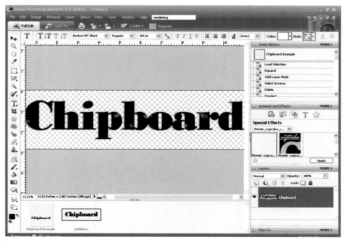

To use the word on your page, activate the Move Tool (V) and drag it onto your page and delete your original text layer (after you check your spelling, etc. on your chipboard copy). You cannot edit the Chipboard text, so if you made a mistake or want to add something to it, you'll have to start over. You can add the Chipboard effect to letters, mats or shapes that you've covered in scrapbook paper or photos. Your end result will vary with the type of digital papers or photos you use, so try it out!

Instant Chalked Edges Effect

You can spend a long time trying to get your edges to look like they were really chalked, or you can use the Chalked Edges Action by AtomicCupcake.com. I myself would rather buy a great product and get fast results than fool around trying to do it myself. Just like the Chipboard action shown in the preceding example, this action works like magic.

While the Chipboard action is a freebie available on their website and on your CD, you'll have to subscribe to their service to get this one. I know you don't believe that they aren't paying me to advertise for them, but they really aren't. I even had to buy my own subscription! One thing nice about their website is that you can subscribe for a month and download all of the actions and or scrapbook supplies you want, or you can sign up for a longer time period. When you sign up for a month, you don't have to remember to go back to their site and cancel your subscription if you only wanted one month's worth of time.

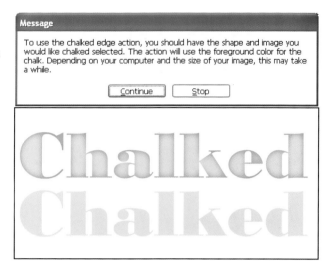

In this example I've followed all of the steps for the Chipboard example exactly, except that I've used the Chalked Edge action. To find this particular action on their website, it's identified as follows: Chalked Edges Action Added 2005-06-28.

I used a light pink for my text and then changed my Foreground color to a darker pink, which will be used as the chalking. Ctrl click on the text layer thumbnail to select the text; you should have marching ants around the text. Double click on the thumbnail for the Chalked edges and it's done faster than you can find a brush to do it yourself.
If you want a darker chalked edge, apply the action again or choose a darker Foreground color.

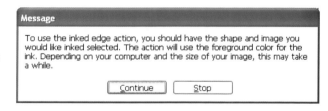

Instant Inked Edges Effect

Follow the directions for Chalking edges. This action is also made by AtomicCupcake.com and is available on their website. The action is identified on their website as: Inked Edges Action Added 2005-08-07

In this example I used a light grey for the text as show in the bottom example. My Foreground color was set to black. The middle example had the action applied to it one time, and the top example had the action applied three times.

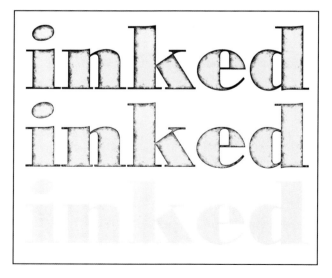

Instant Foam Stamp Effect

To make your text appear as if it was stamped by a foam stamp, use this FREE action by AtomicCupcake.com that's included on your CD. Follow the preceding instructions for the Chalked Edges action. This action requires your type to be 300 pixels high which, on a 300 resolution page, is only one inch (72 pts). Ctrl click to select the text and then press the Continue button. My original text is at the bottom of my example; the middle example had the action applied once, and the top example had the action applied two times.

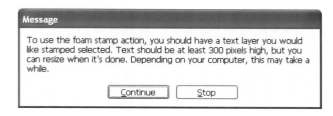

Realistic Stamped Effect

To make your stamped item look like it was really stamped on top of multiple layers of paper, follow these steps:

Type your text and run the Foam Stamp action. Position your text onto of a mat (or photo) as shown in the example above. Duplicate your foam text layer by Ctrl>J.

Ctrl click on the mat to select it. Go to the top foam text layer and tap the Delete key to delete the text inside the mat.

Shift>Ctrl>I (Select>Inverse) and select the bottom foam text layer and tap the Delete key to delete the text outside the mat.

With the top text layer active, activate the Move Tool (V) to very slightly move the text layer down so that a tiny space shows between the two text layers. Add a drop shadow (preferably the Mr. Scrap Pop Action drop shadow) to both layers of text and the mat.

This effect also works great with a rubber stamped type image. I explain how to make a rubber stamp image later on in this section.

Cool Things To Do With Brushes

Make Your Own Brushes

Making your own brushes is a lot of fun, and there are several different ways to make them. You can make an image using other brushes, shapes, or even photos and turn them into a brush. If you like to doodle you can doodle and scan the image to make a brush. Scan letters, newspaper articles, handwriting, or children's artwork. These brushes can be used as embellishments, frames, backgrounds, to erase areas, or anything else you can imagine.

Here are a few tips for making your own brushes:

If you're going to scan a doodle or something you've drawn for a brush use a dark Sharpie marker and draw it on white paper so there is a lot of contrast between the paper and doodle.

Remember that the maximum brush size is 2500 px (8.33 inches @ 300 resolution) by 2500 px. I once tried to make a brush out of an 8 x 10 inch photo. Because the original photo I scanned was bigger than 2500 px it just wouldn't work. Photoshop Elements gave me no explanation, it just wouldn't do it. Finally, I figured out the photo was too big and once I resized the photo it was easy!

How To Make A Brush From An Image

Open the image you want to make into a brush. This can be something you've constructed in Photoshop Elements from other brushes or shapes, a dingbat, a photo, or something you've scanned. The entire image or a selected area of the image can be made into a brush.

I scanned my grandson's feet stamped with an ink pad on a regular piece of paper. I saved this as a JPEG.

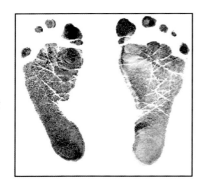

When you make a brush your image is changed to a black and white image. If you're using a color image, it's best to change it to black and white yourself to make sure you like how it will look. To change a color image to black and white go to Enhance>Adjust Color>Remove Color and your image will be black and white. If you're not happy with the contrast go to Enhance>Adjust Lighting>Brightness/Contrast (you may also want to adjust Shadows/Highlights and Levels under the same category) and adjust them too.

Next check the size of your image. Your image should be 300 resolution. Enlarge your image to 2500 px so that you can stamp it that size if you choose to. To resize your image go to Image>Resize>Image Size.

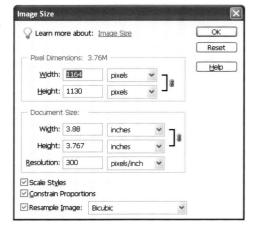

In my example my original image is 1164 px wide and I will change it to 2500 px. I did not change the height to 2500 px because it would have made the width too large for a brush because the height will enlarge in proportion to the width.

When you resize your image look at it and make sure that it looks OK. If it looks pixelated or blurry Undo the sizing change and make it smaller. My baby feet look fine at the bigger size.

Because my image is black and white only the black areas of the image will be the brush. If you are using a photo with a background and you want only a silhouette you will need to remove the unwanted areas by using one of the selection tools and deleting the background.

To make your brush go to Edit>Define Brush or if you are making a brush from a selection use Edit>Define Brush from Selection click and then name your brush.

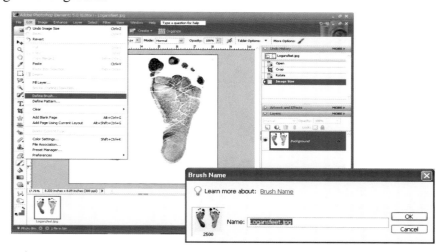

The new brush is now added to the bottom of the Default Brush drop down list. The brush can be used to stamp or erase now. Adjust the size by using the Bracket keys [or] or entering the size you want in the brush size box. Adjusting the brush Opacity, Blending Mode or color make a big difference in how the brush looks. Remember to always stamp on a new blank layer so you can go back and adjust it later.

Saving A Brush

To save your brush click on the brush drop down list and click on the small arrow on the far right side and select Preset Manager. Once the Preset Manager opens the Preset Type should be Brushes. Select the brushes you want to save in a set by Ctrl clicking on each one and then click on Save Set. The numbers on the brush thumbnails indicate the size in px that the brush was created in.

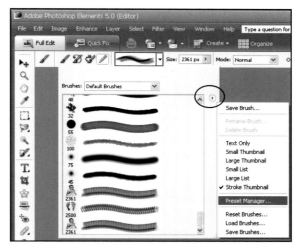

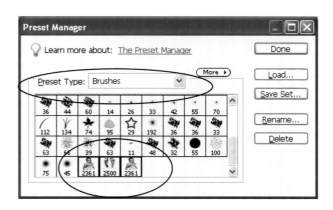

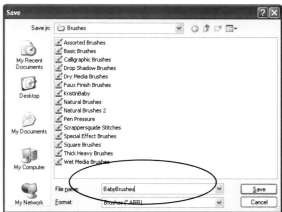

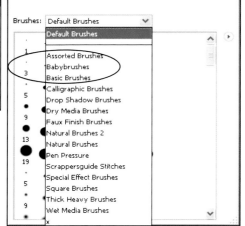

Type a file name for your brushes set and then click Save. The default location for brushes is located at: C>Program Files>Adobe>Photoshop Elements 5.0>Presets>Brushes.

After clicking Save you will be returned to the Preset Manager, once there click on Done. Restart Photoshop Elements and check the drop down list and your new brush set will show in the list. To keep your brush sets tidy up go back to the Default Brushes library and delete the brushes you saved to their own set by right clicking on the brush thumbnail and choosing Delete.

I also save a copy of my brushes in a folder called PSE Brushes that is in my My Documents folder. This way when Photoshop Elements 6 comes along I've got them all together. More important if I have to reinstall Photoshop Elements because of a computer problem, my brushes will be probably be deleted. This is my back-up copy for my brushes. Inside my PSE Brushes folder I have sub-folders for different kinds of brushes that I've bought or made. In this example these brushes are stored in the sub-folder BabyBrushes. In addition I save a copy of my brush as a PNG file, so I can view it in thumbnail view in my PSE brushes folder. This way I see what it actually looks like, because a brush is saved as an ABR file that does not display a thumbnail. Another reason to save this image as a PNG files is because not all digital scrapbook programs use brushes. If I wanted to give this to a friend or sell it I would need to have it saved in two different formats. Many companies that sell brushes also include a PNG file for the same reason. Installing a lot of brushes on your computer will slow it down so it's usually best not to install all of them that you have at one time.

Here is an example of two brushes that I made. The baby feet were made in the step by step directions. The photo was made the same way except that I deleted the photo background. I stamped both brushes (each on their own layer) on a white 12 x 12 scrapbook page. The baby feet are 100% opacity while the photo brush is 19% opacity.

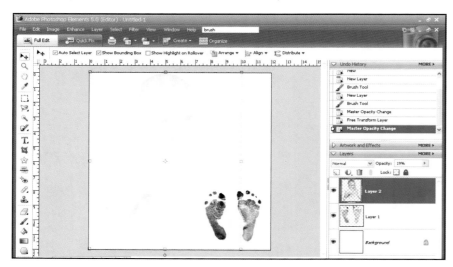

Remember the maximum size of a brush is 2500 px which is 8.33 inches but notice that the photo brush is now almost 12 inches. After I stamped the photo brush I activated the Move Tool (V) and I transformed the brush by dragging one of the corner sizing handles and enlarged it to fill my page. This is an effect you could use to make a background paper.

To stamp the baby feet brush at a different angle go to More Options on the Brush Options Bar and change the angle. Another quicker way for me is to stamp each brush stroke on its own layer and use the Move Tool (V) rotation handle to rotate them. See the Brush Tool (B) section for information on how to change the options and examples of the different options.

How To Make A Circle Brush

Circle brushes are a lot of fun and a good way to mark a scrapbook page with a date or other journaling information without being obvious. This example will show how to make a circle brush for the 4th of July. While this example uses a star brush you can use a circle, square, leaf, or other brush to make a different themed brush.

Ctrl>N to make a new document:
8 inches high and wide, 300 resolution, with a transparent background, in RGB color
Name the new document 4th of July Brush.

Turn on your grid lines by going to View>Grid, turn on your rulers by Shift>Ctrl>R or View>Rulers. Set your default colors to Black and white by typing the letter "D". Activate the Brush Tool (B) and go to Assorted Brushes and choose the star brush which is about 2/3's of the way down the list.

Go to Brush Options and make the following changes:

Set Spacing to 70%
Set Angle to 90°
Set Roundness to 33%

Set the size of the Star Brush to 200 px.

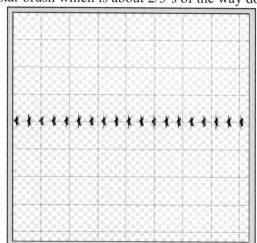

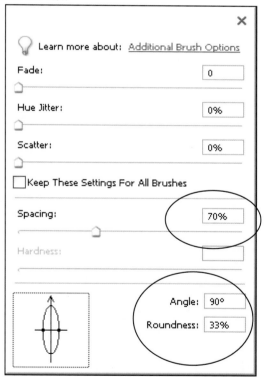

Starting at the middle horizontal grid line at the 4 inch mark hold the Shift key to draw a straight line across the page automatically, click and drag. The brush tool will automatically stamp the star brush. The star will look distorted and that's OK. Begin clicking right at the beginning of the line and stop before the end of the page. You want full stars, if you end up with partial stars Ctrl>Z to Undo. Your page should look like this example if it doesn't keep doing it until it does.

318

Once you get the spacing right on the brush go to Filter>Distort>Polar Coordinates and choose the default setting of Rectangular to polar. Click OK the filter may take a little while to work. When it's finished your stars will now be in a circle and their shape won't be distorted any more. This may take a few times to get this technique right just keep trying it. Once you use the Polar Coordinates filter it will be on the top of the Filter List so you won't need to make all the steps. You can even use the shortcut of Ctrl>F to apply the last filter you used.

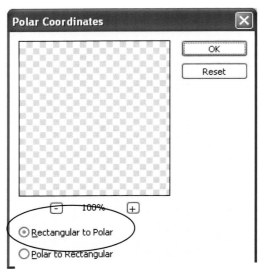

Depending on how elaborate you want your circle stamp to be, you can add text with the Type Tool (T) and/or add a circle frame around it. Use the Shape Tool (U) and drag a "Circle Thin Frame" around the stars which would make your brush look like this example. To add a circle of type around the stars (inside or outside) make a new blank layer and type the words you want on the 4 inch line. Be sure to fill from edge to edge and use the Polar Coordinates filter again just like you did with the stars.

In my example I wrote the word Independence Day 5 times in the Bookman Old Style Regular Font in 14 pt. size. If you use different words or font your spacing will be a little bit off. To even out my text I put two spaces after Independence Day.

To apply the filter type Ctrl>F if it's the last filter you used otherwise go to Filter>Distort>Polar Coordinates. Elements will tell you that you need to Simplify your text, click OK. Your text circle will be the same size as your star circle so activate the Move Tool (V) to size it. Hold the Alt key as you drag one of the sizing corners and it will size from the center to put it perfectly inside or outside of the star circle.

Once you're happy with your circle brush save it as a PSD file so you can make changes to it later on. Next save it as a PNG file and save it in your brushes folder. Finally go to Edit>Define Brush and save it as a brush, by default the brush name will be the file name. If you don't want the brush named the file name change it here. To save your brush set review the previous instructions under "Saving a brush".

Both of these 4th of July brushes are included on your CD in The Digital Scrapbook Teacher folder. The brushes are in PNG and ABR format as well as PSD format in case you want customize it for your own use. All layers are on the PSD file to make both brushes so you will have to hide/unhide layers to make the brush you want.

Distressing this brush with the Eraser Tool (E) or by using the next technique will give the brush a completely different look.

How to Make A Rubber Stamp Looking Brush

Make a new file with the following specifications:

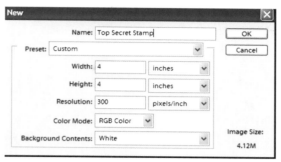

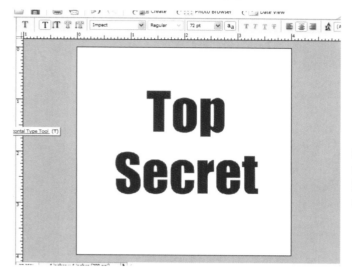

Change your foreground color to red, Impact 72 pt, Center. Type Top Secret and press and hold the Ctrl key (temporarily activates the Move Tool (V) to center the text on your Background layer.

Type U to activate the Shape Tool (U). Choose the Rounded Rectangle Tool (U) with a 30° radius with the same red color. Drag your mouse over the words "Top Secret" about the size shown by the grey outline mark in this example. When you let go of the mouse you will only have a red rectangle on your page. You will be able to see on your Layers palette the text layer underneath the rectangle layer.

Keep everything the same on the shape tool except change to "Remove from selection" or hold the Alt key and drag out a rectangle that is a little bit smaller than the first one. When you let go of the mouse the center part will be removed and you'll have an outline type shape. Merge the text and shape layer by selecting both layers in the Layers palette and choosing Ctrl>E (Layer>Merge Layers).

To add some grunge to this stamp, so that it looks imperfect like a rubber stamp does, you will need a photo of a rough texture. I've included a photo on the CD called RockyBeach that you can use to get the idea or you can use your own. Open the rocky beach photo and click on the Adjustment layer symbol in the Layers palette and choose >Threshold.

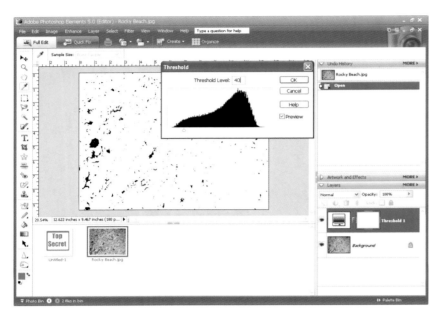

Slide the slider to the right and the photo turns to mostly white. In my example I have a threshold level of 40. Make sure preview is checked. Click OK

Zoom in on the spots by using your mouse wheel or the Zoom Tool (Z).

Select the Magic Wand Tool (W) and make sure that Contiguous is not checked. Click on one of the black spots. They should all be selected. With the Threshold Adjustment layer selected hold the Ctrl key and click on one of the larger spots and drag it down onto your Top Secret Stamp in the Photo Bin.

If you have trouble grabbing the spots try activating the Move Tool (V) and deselecting the Auto Select Layer option. The spots will be pasted onto your page in white not black like you originally copied. If you don't like where your spots have ended up on your words, use the Move tool to move the spots around.

Control click on the spots layer thumbnail which will select all of the spots, then click on the stamp layer and tap the delete key. Deselect to get rid of the marching ants. Now turn the Eyeball off on the spots layer. When you're happy with your results delete the spots layer.

You can change the background to any color you want now or turn it off completely to have a transparent stamp.

Drag this stamp onto your scrapbook page or photo. Delete the spots and Background layer and save this file as a PNG file. You can also make it into a brush. Be sure to read the preceding section on How to Make a Realist Stamped Effect.

Save a collection of photos like RockyBeach with tags in your Organizer to use for this purpose. The possibilities are endless!

Distressing With Brushes And Erasers

To distress an image you can use the technique in the preceding example of using a Threshold Adjustment layer with a photo. I take all kinds of photos now ranging from the side of my stucco home to the asphalt street in front of my house. I admit I sometimes get strange looks from my neighbors when I'm photographing the street but hey it's all about the scrapbook pages right?

Using a picture of a stucco wall, or concrete sidewalk with the Threshold Adjustment layer will produce a softer texture than using the RockyBeach photo in the preceding example.

Actions made by AtomicCupcake.com and others will produce distressed effects. Another way to distress is to use your Eraser Tool (E) and use different brushes to erase areas of your image. If you are erasing text or shapes they will need to be simplified first. Once you try to erase them you will be prompted to Simplify.

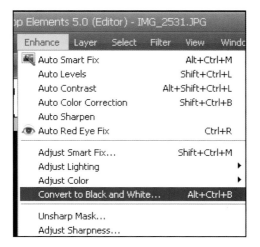

Try different brushes and erase areas to make it look like they're distressed. In this example I used a few different brushes that are included in Photoshop Elements. I changed the size and randomly erased areas. There are many digi-scrap sites that sell Grunge brushes. To also add to the distressed effect activate the Brush Tool (B) and paint on your layer with different brushes and colors. Play around with both tools with different brushes and find a technique you like.

Cool Stuff To Do With Color

Change A Color Photo To Black And White

Photoshop Elements makes it easy to convert your color photos to black and white. I'm sure the generation that was so excited when color photos became available are scratching their heads and asking themselves: "Why would you want to turn a color photo into a black and white one?"

Using the following methods to change your color photo to black and white keeps the photo as a RGB image. Saving as an RGB will allow color to be added in the future.

Convert To Black & White Method

This is a new feature of Photoshop Elements 5. If you have a lower version you will not have this Command, use one of the other methods.

Make a duplicate of your photo Ctrl J or Layer>Duplicate Layer.

Go to Enhance>Convert to Black and White or use the short cut Alt>Ctrl>B.

The Convert to Black and White dialog box will pop up and asks you to select a style. On my example I chose Portrait. The styles make a big difference in the end result. You are also given the option to increase or decrease the Adjustment Intensity.

To increase or decrease red, green, blue click on one of those squares. You are not actually increasing or decreasing these colors. These colors give you more information from the original color image in your new black and white image.

Click on the box to add more or less contrast. Normally I like to increase my contrast a little bit when changing a photo to black and white but the effect here was too much. See how to increase your contrast with a different method at the end of this section.

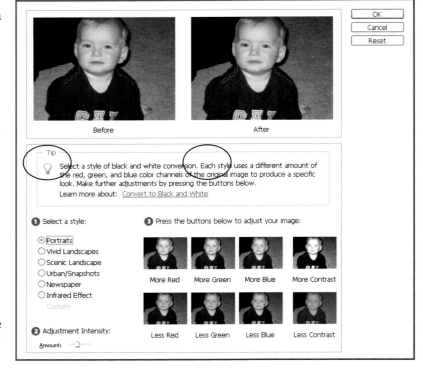

Click OK to accept your change.

Remove Color Method

Make a copy of your photo Ctrl>J or Layer>Duplicate Layer.

Go to Enhance>Adjust Color>Remove Color (Shift>Ctrl>U).

If you want to increase the contrast a little bit see the instructions at the end of this section.

Changing your photo to black and white with this method is the same as changing Saturation to -100 in the Hue and Saturation method.

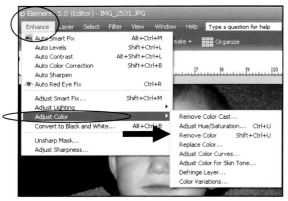

Hue And Saturation Method

Make a duplicate layer of your photo Ctrl>J or Layer>Duplicate Layer.

In the Layers palette Click on the Adjustment layer icon which is the half black half white circle and select Hue/Saturation.

Make sure that the Preview box is checked or you won't be able to see your results until you click OK.

The colorize box should <u>not</u> be checked.

Slide the Hue and Saturation sliders all the way to the left.

Experiment with your photo to see what you like the best.

Adjustment layers adjust <u>all</u> layers underneath them so if this is on a scrapbook page with other layers it's a good idea to Group the adjustment and photo layer by selecting the Adjustment layer and Ctrl>G or Layer>Group with Previous. Because you used an Adjustment layer you can double click on the layer thumbnail and adjust it at a later time even if you closed the file as long as you save it as a .PSD file.

Enhance>Adjust Color>Hue and Saturation (Ctrl>U) will also bring up the Hue and Saturation dialog box where you can change your photo to black and white. You won't have the option of adjusting the layer later that you do with the Adjustment layer.

Fine Tuning A Black and White Photo

If you're not thrilled with the final results of your black and white photo there are a few ways that you can adjust them. Use one or both methods on your photo.

My examples will show the Adjustment layer method. I believe it's important to be able to adjust your changes later on when you're working on your project, especially as a beginner. While the Adjustment layers look like more work, they aren't and they will save you time and work in the end.

Click on the Adjustment layer (half black, half white circle) icon on the Layers palette and select one of the following:

Levels Adjustment Layer

Click on the Adjustment layer icon on the Layers palette and select Levels. The Levels dialog box will open. My original dialog box is on the left. There are 3 sliders at the bottom of the histogram. Slide the white slider on the right towards the left where the histogram starts to increase. On the black slider on the left, slide it towards the right where the histogram starts to increase. When you slide the black and white sliders, the gray slider in the middle also moves. You can also move the gray slider by itself. Making this quick change improved my photograph immensely.

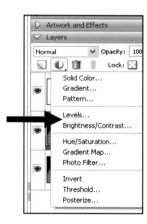

Original   Adjusted

This change could also be made without an Adjustment layer directly on the photo layer by going to Enhance> Adjust Lighting>Levels or with the shortcut Ctrl>L.

Brightness and Contrast Adjustment Layer

Click on the Adjustment layer icon on the Layers palette and select Brightness/Contrast. The Brightness/Contrast dialog box will open. Adjust one or both of the two sliders. Make sure that the Preview box is checked or you won't see your changes until you click OK. My original dialog box is on the left and my changes are shown on the right.

This change could also be made with out an Adjustment layer directly on the photo layer by going to Enhance>Adjust Lighting>Brightness/Contrast.

Black And White With Color Too

Everyone has seen a black and white photo that has just a little bit of color peeking through on it. Look at a wedding album and you're likely to see a black and white photo of the bride with her bouquet only in full color. There are lots of examples of this technique everywhere you look. People think this is a lot of work to do but isn't. Essentially what you need to do is duplicate your color photo so they are stacked on top of each other. Convert the top photo to black and white using one of the preceding methods. Adding a hole in the black and white layer allows you to see the color layer. I'll show you a couple of ways to do this.

For all methods do the following first:
1. Duplicate your color photo two times by Ctrl>J or Layer>New>Duplicate Layer

2. Convert the top layer to a black and white photo by one of the preceding methods.

3. Turn off the eyeball on the Background layer so you won't end up using it by mistake.

4. It is easiest if you make a selection (marching ants) with one of the selection tools (Lasso (L), Selection Brush (A), Marquee (M), or Magic Wand (W) tools) of the area that you want to be in color. Making a selection sometimes saves you time. You may or may not want to feather your selection to soften it depending on the end result you want.

Super Fast Delete Key Method (With A Selection)

Complete steps 1-4 above.
You will have marching ants on your photo to designate the area that you want to be in color.
On your top layer which is your black and white layer tap the Delete Key. You have now deleted the selection from your black and white layer only and the color layer is showing through. If you look on your Layers Palette or if you turn off your color layer you can see the black and white layer with a hole in it.

Tap Esc to remove the selection border (marching ants).

To go one step further, add a filter to the black and white layer. Make a duplicate layer of the black and white layer and then go to Filter>Blur>Gaussian Blur. The black and white background has a little bit of a blurred effect which makes the color selection stand out even more.
Merge your layers Ctrl>E to save your photo this way as long as you've made a duplicate.

Delete Key Method (With A Large Selection) & Stroke Outline #1

This effect can also be done with a larger not so exact selection like a circle or rectangle to draw attention to the focal point of your photo. Anyone who has children that play sports like football or soccer know that sometimes it's hard to pick your child out of an action shot. With this method there will be now question who is your focal point.

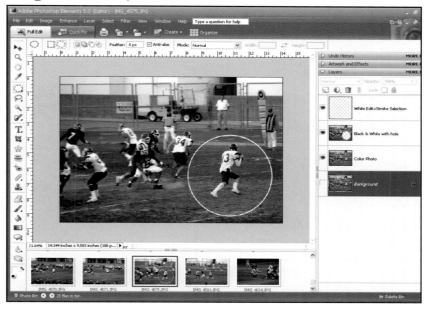

Complete steps 1-3 under Black and White and Color Too.

Make a selection with the Marquee Tool (M) of an oval, circle, square or rectangle. Remember to get a circle or square you need to hold the Shift key when you drag.

Go to the black and white top layer and tap the Delete key, my son is now in color. The other players are in black in white because I cut the selection out of the black and white layer. Keep your selection with the marching ants because you're going to use it to make a stroke outline around the shape you just cut out.

Make a new blank layer by clicking on the New Layer icon on the Layers Palette or Layer>New>Layer.

With your new blank layer active go to Edit>Stroke Selection. I chose an 8 pixel wide white stroke outline. If you are using a circle or oval you can choose any location. If you are using a shape with a square edge use inside location or you will end up with a strange little rounded corner on your stroke.

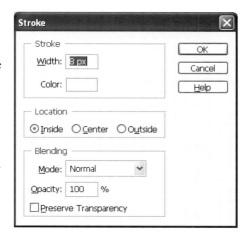

Tap the Esc key to remove your selction. There is now no question on which football player I was trying to highlight.

Delete Key Method (With A Large Selection) & Stroke Outline #2

This method will give you a similar effect but will keep your photo in color.

Duplicate your color photo two times by Ctrl>J or Layer>New>Duplicate Layer

Turn off the Eyeball on the Background layer so you won't end up using it by mistake.

In the Layers palette click on the Adjustment layer icon which is the half black half white circle and select Color Fill. Choose a color to fill the layer, in my example I chose white to give it a vellum type look but you can choose any color you want. Once you choose your color your layer will be filled with solid color and that will be all you see. Lower the Adjustment Layer Opacity with the opacity slider located on the Layers palette. I lowered my opacity to 38% on the Color Fill Adjustment layer.

With the Color Fill Layer the active layer make a selection with the Elliptical Marquee Tool (M) and draw a circle using the Shift key to make a circle shape as you drag it out. Tap the Delete key. Do not get rid of your selection (marching ants) yet.

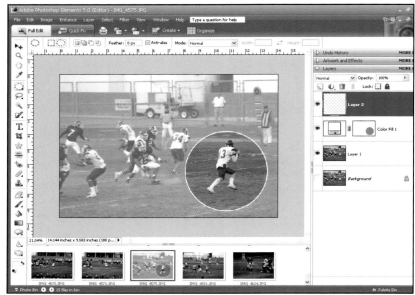

Make a new layer by clicking on the New Layer icon on the Layers Palette or Layer>New>Layer.

On the new blank layer go to Edit>Stroke Selection and add a stroke like in the preceding example. Tap the Delete key to get rid of your selection.

Fast Unforgiving Eraser Method (No Selection Made)

Complete steps 1-3 above under Black and White and Color Too. Activate your Eraser Tool (E) and choose a hard or fuzzy brush depending on the result you want.

With your top layer selected which is the black and white layer, begin erasing away the area that you want to be color. Erase and click often. If you make a mistake use Ctrl>Z to Undo. Every time you click you are erasing some of the black and white layer allowing more of the color layer to show through. Merge your layers Ctrl E to save your photo this way as long as you've saved a duplicate.

Adjustment Layer Method (Editable Later)

1. Duplicate your color photo two times by Ctrl>J or Layer>New>Duplicate Layer
2. Convert the top layer to a black and white photo by one of the preceding methods.
3. Turn off the eyeball on the Background layer so you don't end up using it by mistake.

Add a blank Adjustment layer under the black and white photo. To add a blank Adjustment layer click on the Adjustment layer icon in the Layers palette (half black/half white circle) and choose Hue and Saturation, Levels, or Brightness/Contrast and make no changes, just click OK.

Group the Black and White photo layer with the blank Adjustment layer by Ctrl>G or Layer>Group with Previous. It should look like the example above.

Activate the Brush Tool (B) and change your Foreground color to black (shortcut is D as long as your Text Tool (T) is not active). Paint on the Adjustment layer with black and when you release your mouse you will see the color come through. If you make a mistake you can click Ctrl>Z to Undo or paint white over the area and it will go back to the black and white photo.

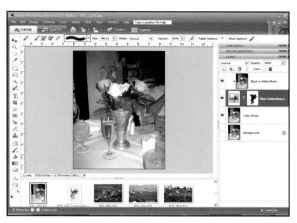

If you save this photo as a .PSD file with all of the layers intact you will be able to go back and change this at any time even if you've closed the file.

Change a Photo to Sepia Tones

Changing a color photo to a sepia tone can change the whole look of your scrapbook page. Color and black and white photos are nice but sepia photos have a warm feel that sets a different tone. There are probably 101 ways to change a photo to sepia in Photoshop Elements. I'll show you just a few! Each of the methods I show you give you a little bit different look. Try them all out and decide which method you like the best, and then mark it in your book so you remember next time! Two of the methods only work on color photos so don't try them on black and white.

Always make a duplicate of your photo!

Special Effects Layer Styles Sepia Method

Make a copy of your Background Layer by Ctrl>J or Layer>Duplicate Layer. If you get this warning when using this method you didn't make a copy of your Background Layer.

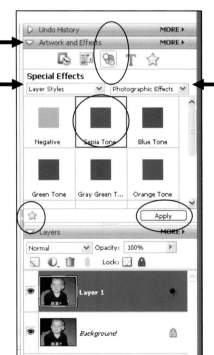

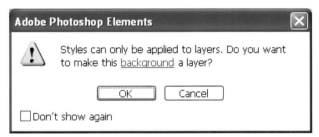

Select Sepia Tone from the Photographic Effects section of the Artwork and effects Special Effects Layer Styles.

Double click on the Sepia Tone box and your photo is now sepia, or click once on the Sepia Tone box and then click the apply box.

There are no adjustments for this Sepia Tone. What you see is what you get. If you don't like it try one of the other methods. If you do like it you might want to add it to one of your favorites by clicking on the star so it's added to your favorites and you don't have to remember where to find it anymore. The next time you want to use your Favorite layer styles click on the Start on the top left of the Layers palette and they'll be there without all of the other ones that you don't want to use.

Effects Filters-Photo Effects Sepia Method

This is quick and easy like the first method I showed you, but the results are a little bit different. You should still be in the Special Effects area of the Artwork and Effects Palette. Go to Photo Effects>Image Effects and select the Tint Sepia. Double click on the Tint Sepia box and your photo is now sepia, or click once on Tint Sepia and then click on the Apply button. You don't have any choice on the amount of the effect that is applied. However, if you forgot to make a duplicate copy this Sepia makes one for you and applies the tint to it automatically. If you like this effect click on the star and add it to your favorites.

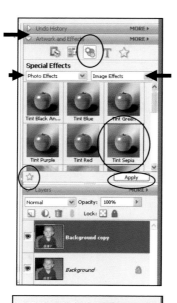

Adjustment Layer Photo Filter Sepia Method

Make a duplicate layer of your photo Ctrl>J or Layer>Duplicate.

In the Layers palette Click on the Adjustment layer icon which is the half black half white circle and select Photo Filter. From the Photo Filter drop down choose Sepia.

Make sure that the Preview box is checked or you won't be able to see your results until you click OK.

Slide the Density slider up or down according to how you want your photo to look.

Preserve Luminosity should be checked or your photo will get very dark.

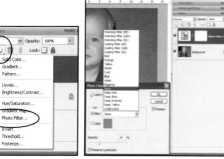

Adjustment layers adjust all layers underneath them so if this is on a scrapbook page with other layers it's a good idea to Group the Adjustment and photo layer by selecting the Adjustment layer and Ctrl>G or Layer>Group with Previous. Because you changed this with an Adjustment layer you can double click on the layer thumbnail and adjust it at a later time, even if you closed the file as long as you save it as a PSD file.

Adjustment Layer Hue and Saturation Sepia Method

This method only works with a color photo.

Make a duplicate layer of your photo Ctrl>J or Layer>Duplicate.

In the Layers palette Click on the Adjustment layer icon which is the half black half white circle and select Hue/Saturation.

Make sure that the Preview and Colorize boxes are checked or you won't be able to see your results until you click OK.

Slide the Hue, Saturation, and Lightness sliders up or down according to how you want your photo to look to achieve the desired Sepia effect.

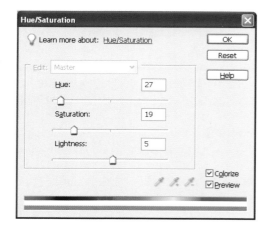

My settings on this photo are: Hue 27, Saturation 19, Lightness 5

You can also type the numbers directly in the boxes if you don't want to use the sliders. Experiment with your photo to see what you like the best.

Adjustment layers adjust all layers underneath them so if this is on a scrapbook page with other layers it's a good idea to Group the adjustment and photo layer by selecting the Adjustment layer and Ctrl>G or Layer>Group with Previous. Because you changed this with an Adjustment layer you can double click on the layer thumbnail and adjust it at a later time, even if you closed the file as long as you save it as a PSD file.

Enhance>Adjust Color>Hue and Saturation (Shortcut Ctrl>U) will also bring up the Hue and Saturation dialog box where you can change your photo to sepia. However, you won't have the option of adjusting the layer later like you do with the Adjustment layer.

Filter>Adjustments>Photo Filter Sepia Method

This method gives you the same photo filter but without an Adjustment layer. When you apply the filter, the only way to adjust the sepia affect would be to run the filter again on the layer or start over. I recommend the Adjustment layer method because you never know when you're going to want to make a change.

Make a copy of your photo layer Ctrl J (Layer>Duplicate Layer)

Go to Filter>Adjustments>Photo Filter.

Choose Sepia from the Filter list and set the Density by sliding the slider.

Make sure your preview box is checked.

Click OK.

As if you even need another method to turn your photos into Sepia here's the last one!

Adjust Color/Color Variation Sepia Method

<u>This method only works with a color photo.</u>

Make a copy of your photo, Ctrl>J or Layer>Duplicate Layer.

Go to Enhance>Adjust Color>Color Variations.

With the default of Midtones selected click on the Increase Red button two times and the Increase Green button one time. Your photo should be Sepia.

The Alt key changes the Cancel button to Reset. Click OK when you are happy with your effect.

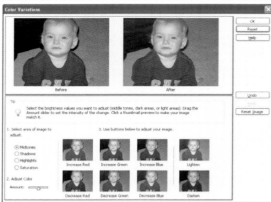

Tinting a Photo

Tinting a photo is fast and easy with this method. Ctrl>O (File>Open) a new photo. Duplicate the photo so you do not work on the original copy.

Choose Enhance>Adjust Color>Adjust Hue and Saturation (Ctrl>U). Move the Saturation slider to the left until you like the result.

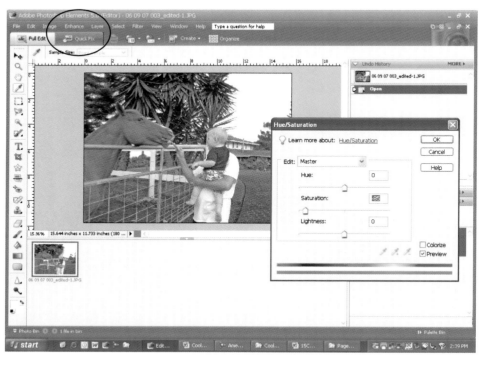

This can also be done by using an Adjustment layer. Using an Adjustment layer gives you the opportunity to make changes to the hue and saturation of your image at any time. To make an Adjustment layer click on the Adjustment layer icon on the top of the Layers palette shown circled. Choose Hue and Saturation from the drop down list and the same dialog box will appear. Move the Saturation slider to the left until you like the result.

Adding Color To A Black And White Photo

Ctrl>O (File>Open) a new photo. Duplicate the photo so you do not work on the original copy. Check to make sure that the photo is not a grayscale image by going to Image>Mode. RGB color should be checked. If it isn't, click on it so that a checkmark appears.

Make a selection with one of the selection tools around the area that you want to colorize. In my example I used the Magnetic Lasso Tool (L). I also feathered my selection by choosing Select>Feather, I chose a feather radius of 2 px.

Make a Hue and Saturation Adjustment layer by clicking on the Adjustment layer icon on the top of the Layers palette (shown circled).

Click on the Colorize box in the Hue and Saturation dialog box. Move the sliders for Hue, Saturation, and Lightness until you achieve the desired effect. Repeat for as many areas as you want to colorize.

The same effect could have been achieved by choosing Enhance>Adjust Color>Adjust Hue and Saturation (Ctrl>U), but you would not have had the opportunity to change the color of the image later without undoing all of the changes you'd made since you colorized the pumpkin.

Changing The Color Of Scrapbook Supplies

Hue And Saturation Method

In this example I'm using 2 papers from the Scrapgirls.com Refresh kit that is on the DVD that came with this book. Activate the Eyedropper Tool (I) and click on the color you want to use for your new element. This will change the Foreground color. In this example, I clicked on the dark purple of one of the flowers on the paper on the left side of the screen.

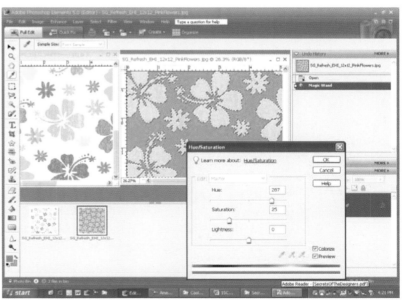

Activate the Magic Wand Tool (W) and click on the color that you want to change to the Foreground color. Contiguous should not be checked on the Magic Wand Option Bar. All of the color you want to change should be surrounded by marching ants. If you want to change the entire piece of paper to shades of purple do not make a selection.

Choose Enhance>Adjust Color>Hue and Saturation. Check the boxes for Colorize and Preview. Your selection will now be changed to the color in the Foreground color however, you may need to adjust the Saturation and Lightness. This method works best when the colors you are replacing are solid and not washed out looking colors.

A Hue and Saturation Adjustment layer can be used to do the same thing.

Replace Color Method

I will use the same flowered papers that I used in the preceding example.

Go to Enhance>Adjust Color>Replace Color. Click on the background of the paper on the right and the top color box will change to the pink from the background. Click in the bottom color box that says Result and then click on a purple flower on the paper on the right. The background will be changed to the purple color. You may have to adjust the Saturation and Lightness. Click OK.

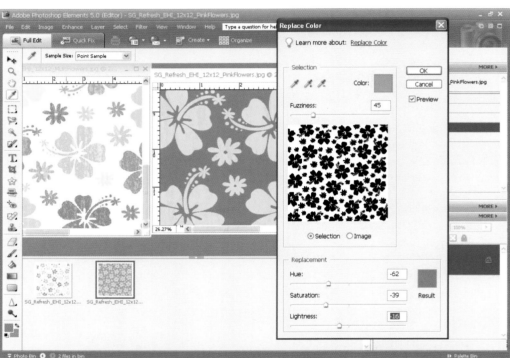

Cool Stuff To Do With Paper

Photoshop Elements gives you the ability to easily make realistic cardstock and vellum just like you'd purchase in a store.

Printing Digital Paper

You can also print out any of your digital papers or embellishments and use them for traditional scrapbooking or card projects. The big difference is that you can change the color and other things before you print it out. You can also print as many copies as you want, as long as you follow the designers Terms of Use policy. Try doing that with traditional paper!

Making Vellum

Vellum can be used to make a journaling block on a scrapbook page or to soften the look of a photo. To make a vellum effect on your scrapbook page, make a new blank layer and fill it with white. Make a new blank layer by clicking on the New Layer icon on the top of the Layers palette (shown circled). Type D to set your default Foreground/Background colors to black and white. Type Ctrl>Backspace to fill the layer with white. Adjust the Opacity on the white layer to achieve the look you want.

To make a smaller piece of Vellum, make a selection with the Marquee Tool (M). Make a new layer and fill the selection with white, adjust the Opacity on this layer. Add text and a drop shadow. If your Opacity reverts back to 100% when you apply the drop shadow, adjust it back down to where it was. This appears to be a glitch with the program.

Make Textured Cardstock

Make a new blank layer and fill it with any color. Make a new blank layer by clicking on the New Layer icon on the top of the Layers palette (shown circled above). Choose a new Foreground color by clicking in the Foreground color swatch. Type Ctrl>Backspace to fill the layer with the Foreground color. Duplicate this layer Ctrl>J. Go to Filter>Texture>Texturizer and choose one of the textures from the drop down list. Adjust the size of the pattern by sliding the Scaling slider. Adjust the height of the texture by sliding the Relief slider. Click OK and the filter will be applied to the top colored layer. If the effect is more than what you wanted, adjust the Opacity on the top layer.

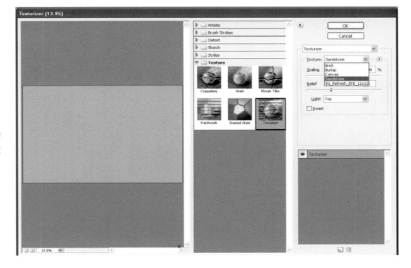

Cool Stuff to Do With Photos

Out of Bounds Photo

This is a great way to make your image look like it's popping right out of the photo. Photos with action work the best for this effect, but any kind of photo will do.

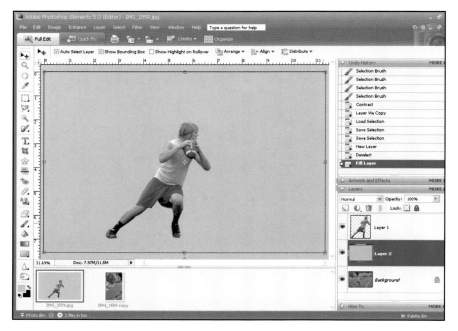

Ctrl>O (File>Open) a photo. Duplicate your image, choose File>Duplicate so you have two copies of the same photo open. Make a selection around your action figure. In my example, I used the Magnetic Lasso Tool (L) and then cleaned it up with the Selection Brush (A). I also contracted the selection by one pixel to clean up stray pixels by using Select>Modify>Contract 1 pixel. It would probably be a good idea to save your selection in case you need it again. Go to Select>Save Selection, name the selection and click OK. Make a copy of your selection on its own layer by Ctrl>J.

Make a new layer under the action figure by Ctrl clicking the New Layer icon. Fill the new layer with a color other than white; this will be temporary so you can see the effect. If you are doing this directly on a scrapbook page and the background is not white, you don't have to do this step

On the second photo, duplicate the layer by Ctrl>J. Crop the top layer so that it shows your action figure moving out of it. In my example I cropped my photo so that one of his legs is stepping out of the photo. Make a new layer with the New Layer icon on the Layers Palette and Ctrl click on the layer thumbnail to select the cropped photo. Go to Edit>Stroke Outline and add a white stroke outline about 40 px wide with an inside location. Select the cropped photo and the Stroke Outline and use the Move Tool (V) to drag the cropped photo onto the photo with the cut out action figure.

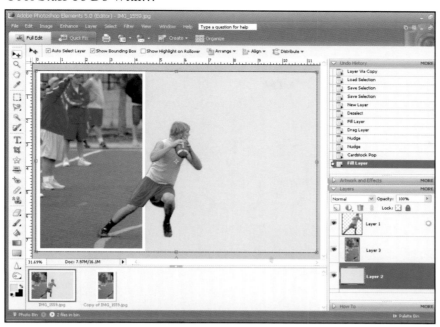

Move the cropped photo under the action figure by dragging it in the Layers Palette. Move the cropped photo so that it lines up with the action figure. Add a drop shadow on the action figure layer.

There are many different ways to get a different look for your out of bounds image.

Varying where you crop the photo and also distorting your Stroke Outline by using Image>Transform>Distort can make a big difference in your end result.

Change Your Photo Into A Puzzle

Using the Texturizer filter to turn your photo into a jigsaw puzzle is fun and easy. This example shows how to use this techinque on a scrapbook page but it can be used on a single photo or on any other kind of project.

Make a new scrapbook page by choosing Ctrl>N (File>New) with the specifications shown in the example.

Ctrl>O (File>Open) a photo that you want to turn into a puzzle.

With the Move Tool (V) activated, drag the photo onto your scrapbook page. Resize and position the photo on your blank scrapbook page. To center the photo horizontally on the scrapbook page, select both layers in the Layers palette as shown and choose Align>Horizontal Centers.

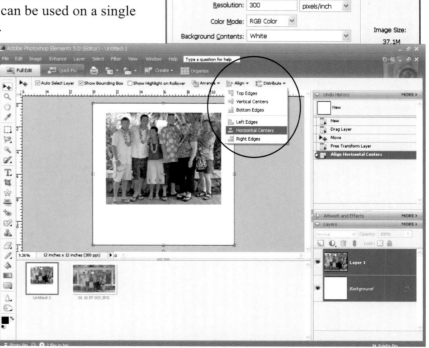

Select the photo layer only
(Layer 1) and go to Filter>
Texture and choose Texturizer.

Click the arrow to display the
options on the Texture list
shown circled. The puzzle
texture will probably not be on
the list. To load the puzzle
texture, click on the small arrow
to the left of the Texture box.
As soon as you click on the
arrow, the words Load
Texture… will appear, click on
the words.

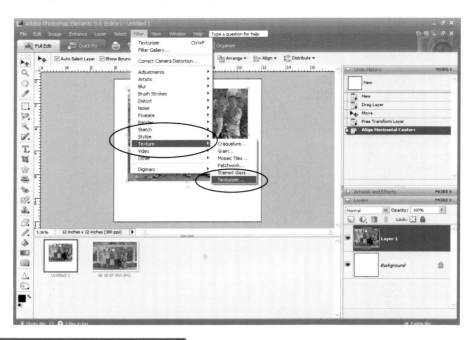

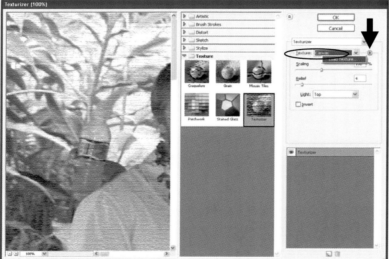

You may be lucky and Photoshop Elements
may open directly into the Texture folder as
shown. If it does, click on Puzzle and then
Open. If it doesn't, see the next example.

If Photoshop Elements does not open directly into the Textures
Folder, follow this path:
C:\Program Files\Adobe\Photoshop Elements 5.0\Presets\Textures,
choose Puzzle and click on Open.

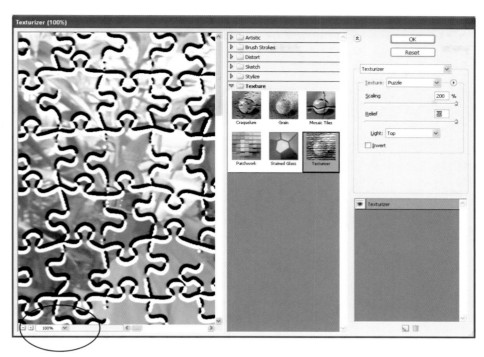

As soon as you click Open the puzzle texture will be applied to your photo.

Adjust the scaling to make the puzzle pieces larger or smaller. Adjust the Relief to make the cuts in between the pieces deeper. To better show the effect, I have my example set at the maximum for both settings.

The direction of the light source can also be changed.

Choose invert to make it appear that you're looking at the bottom side of the puzzle.

Hold the Alt key to change the Cancel key to Reset as shown. To change the size of your preview click on the drop down arrow circled. Click OK when you're happy with how your image appears in the preview window.

To select a few of the puzzle pieces and remove them from the puzzle, zoom in very close so that the puzzle pieces are very large on your screen like in the example. Use the Zoom Tool (Z) or the wheel on your mouse to do this. Activate the Magnetic Lasso Tool (L) and trace around the lines of the puzzle piece, click your mouse often to set anchoring points. Use the Backspace key if you need to remove an anchoring point. When you get back to your starting point, click on the starting point or, if you can't see it, Ctrl click and you will have a selection border of marching ants.

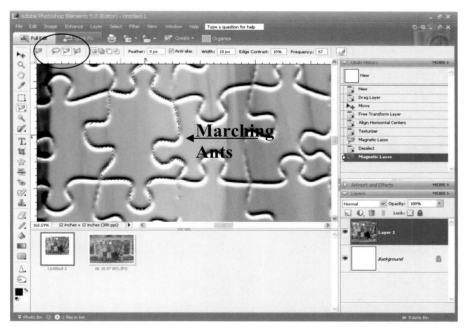

Use the Selection Brush Tool (A) to clean up your selection. Remember, holding the Alt key with the Selection Brush Tool (A) active allows you to work outside of the selection to push the selection border inward. You want your marching ants right in the crack of the puzzle piece.

Depending on the size of the photo, adding a Feather to the selection might make it look better. Choose Select>Feather (Alt>Ctrl>D). In my example, I chose a feather radius of 2 pixels.

With the puzzle piece still selected, Shift>Ctrl>J (Layer>New>Layer>Via Cut) to copy the puzzle piece onto its own layer. The puzzle piece will now be Layer 2.

Activate the Move Tool (V) and move the puzzle piece off of the photo. Rotate the pieces slightly by hovering over the corner sizing handle until the rounded two headed arrow appears.

With the photo layer (Layer 1 in my example) selected, repeat the steps of selecting and removing a puzzle piece several times.

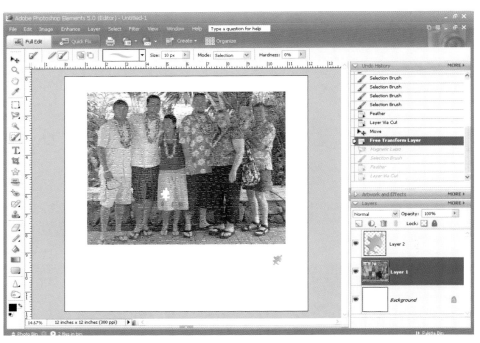

If you have problems getting the puzzle pieces on their own layer, check to make sure the photo layer is the selected layer. If you get a solid white puzzle piece, you had the Background layer selected. If you get this warning, you were probably on one of the puzzle piece layers.

After cutting out the puzzle pieces, if they have a rough edge or left over pieces that you don't want, to quickly clean them up, use the Eraser Tool (E).

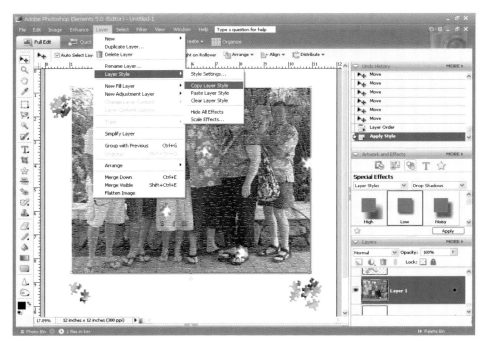

I cheated a little bit and duplicated a few of my puzzle pieces by clicking on the layer in the Layers palette and choosing Ctrl>J (Layer>New>Layer Via Copy). The new puzzle piece was placed directly over the original one.

Apply a drop shadow to the photo layer and go to Layer>Layer Style>Copy Layer Style. To save time, select all of the puzzle pieces in the Layers palette and go to Layer>Layer Style>Paste Layer Style to add drop shadows to all of the puzzle pieces at one time.

Add text with the Type Tool (T), a background paper if desired, and other embellishments and your page is done.

The puzzle texture can also be added to text that is typed with the Type Tool (T). A "fat" font like Impact works best. Text layers must be simplified before a filter can be applied to it. Photoshop Elements will tell you the layer must be simplified, choose OK. Follow the same steps after you Simplify the type to apply the filter and move the puzzle pieces.

To add a digital paper or photo to text with the puzzle texture, first drag the paper/photo over the text with the Move Tool (V). With the paper/photo layer selected, Ctrl>G (Layer>Group with Previous). The paper/photo will now be in the shape of the text. Apply the filter to the paper/photo layer. You will not have to Simplify the text layer. The paper shown is from the Scrapgirls.com Refresh kit on the DVD that came with this book.

Change A Photo Or Digital Paper Into A Texture

Ctrl>O (File>Open) a photo or digital paper that you want to use for a texture. Shift>Ctrl>S and save the image as a PSD file. Since the image is a JPEG it will automatically want to save it as another JPEG so you will need to click the drop down arrow and choose PSD. Save the PSD file in the Textures file located at:

C:\Program Files\Adobe\Photoshop Elements 5.0\Presets\Textures

I kept the file name the same as it was originally named by Scrapgirls.com.

Go to Filter>Texture>Texturizer and click on the side arrow as shown in the preceding section and load the Refresh PSD file as a texture.

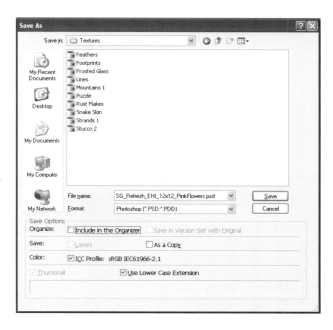

The paper I used to make the texture is shown at the left and is from the Scrapgirls.com Refresh kit and is on the DVD that came with this book.

The flower texture can also be added to text that is typed with the Type Tool (T). A "fat" font like Impact works best. Text layers must be simplified before a filter can be applied to it. Photoshop Elements will tell you the layer must be simplified, choose OK.

The texture can be added to a solid colored layer to make it appear that the pattern has been embossed into the layer.

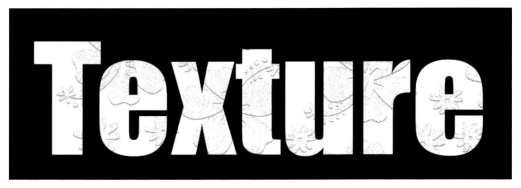

To make the texture pattern larger than the original design, adjust the Scaling slider larger than 100%. To increase the depth of the texture, increase the Relief slider to a higher number.

Choosing invert will make your paper look as if you are looking at the bottom side of an embossed paper.

This texture can also be added to the original paper or to other digital papers. If you want the texture to line up with the original paper, you will need to choose 100% for scaling.

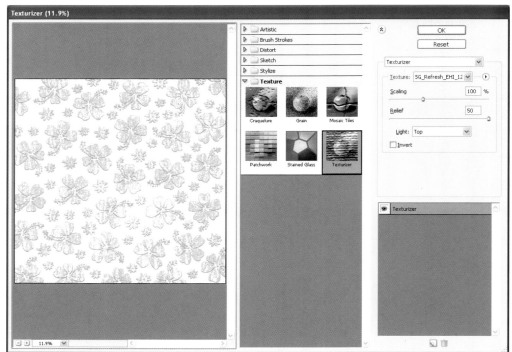

In the example on the left, I chose Scaling 200% and Relief 50, which are the maximum settings. In the example on the right, I chose Scaling 100% and Relief 50.

This technique can be used on photos too.

Use A Photo As A Background Paper

This is a very simple technique that students always ask about and when they realize how simple it is, they're amazed.

If you take a lot of photos, this is one way to use them all. This is also a great way to save money because your backgrounds are free. You'll quickly see that you start taking photos of all kinds of things that you normally never would, just so you can use them for your backgrounds.

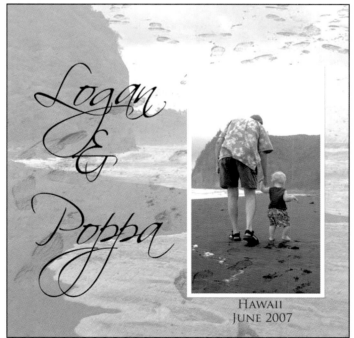

Ctrl>N (File>New) make a new file the size of your project. In my example I made a scrapbook page 12 x 12 inches, 300 resolution.

Ctrl>O (File>Open) the photo(s) that you want to use for your background. Activate the Crop Tool (C) and crop your photo(s) in the size of your project. In my example, I cropped two photos 12 x 12 inches at 300 resolution. Move your background photo(s) onto your blank scrapbook page. In my example, the mountain photo is below the footsteps in the sand photo. Adjust the Opacity on each layer. In the example, the mountain photo is 38% Opacity (Normal Blending Mode), the footsteps photo is 51% Opacity with a Hard Light Blending Mode.

Add other photos and text and you have a quick, fast, inexpensive page.

Montage

A Montage blends several photos together to make an image that blends together. This is a very popular technique with digi-scrappers. Several photos can be used at a time and the results are striking. There are several ways to make a montage.

For each method do the following:
Ctrl>N (File>New) a new blank white scrapbook page.

Duplicate any photos you will be using to make the Montage.

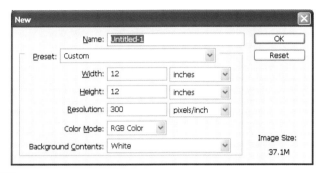

Using the Move Tool (V), drag the photos you will use for the Montage onto the blank scrapbook page. The photos should be overlapping each other a fair amount. I also like to crop a photo 12 x 12 inches, 300 resolution to cover my Background layer. This adds another photo to the Montage and also covers up any mistakes which might expose the white Background layer.

Temporarily, lower the Opacity on some of the photos slightly so you can see the photos below it. In my example, I have 5 photos overlapping each other. The 2 bottom photos I am using for my background paper. I lowered the Opacity on the top 3 photos so that you could see the photos that are underneath them.

Quick, But Unforgiving Eraser Montage Method

This is an unforgiving method because once you erase part of your image it's gone unless you Undo all of your steps. If the file has been saved, you cannot Undo all your steps.

Select the top photo layer and activate the Eraser Tool (E) and choose a Soft Round Brush or an Airbrush Soft Round. In my example I used an Airbrush Soft Round brush and used the Bracket key to increase the size to about 300 px. The size of your brush will depend on how big of an area you are erasing.

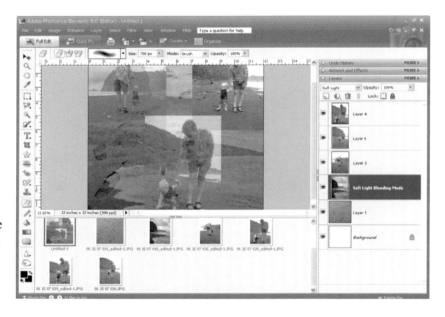

Begin erasing the top layer, the trick is to stay as far away from the edge of the photo as you can and just barely erase the edges so they feather into the next photo. This technique will take you time to learn. Try it and Undo if you're not happy with it. Click and release your mouse often. Adjust the size of your Eraser brush as needed by using the Bracket keys. As you start erasing, you will probably change your mind about the placement and size of the photos you chose. Resize your photos using the Move Tool (V). If you decide that you don't want to use a photo anymore, turn off the eyeball on the Layers palette next to the layer you want to turn off.

To see if you like the areas you've erased, increase the Opacity of the
layer you're working on to see how it blends into the photo below it.
Continue erasing each layer until you're happy with the effect.

Adjustment Layer Montage Method

By using an Adjustment layer you have the ability to go back and add
some of your photo back in after you erased it many steps before. In this
example, I'd like to add some of the green mountain back into my
image. Because I erased this part of the photo so many steps before, I
would have to almost start over to do it.

Make an Adjustment layer for each photo that you will use,
you do not have to make an Adjustment layer for the photos
you will use for the Background layers. To make an
Adjustment layer, click on the half black/half white circle at
the top of the Layers palette shown circled below. You can
use the Hue & Saturation, Brightness/Contrast, or Levels
Adjustment layers. Do not make any changes, just click OK.
We are only using the mask feature of the Adjustment layer.

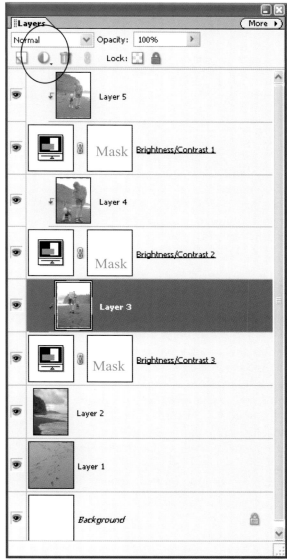

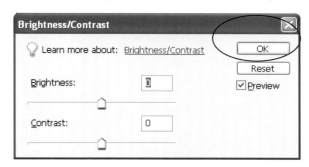

In my example on the right, Layers 1 and 2 are being used
for my Background paper. Layers 3, 4, and 5 are going to be
faded into the Montage like the example above.

Position the Adjustment layer under each of the photos you
are going to fade into the Montage. Next, group each photo
with the Adjustment layer by choosing Layer>Group with
Previous (Ctrl>G). When you do this you will have the
little crooked downward facing arrow coming out of the
side of the photo layer thumbnail. Do not proceed until each
of your photos is grouped with the Adjustment layer as
shown in my example.

Set your Foreground/Background colors to the defaults of
black and white by typing the letter D.

Activate your Brush Tool (B) and choose a Soft Round Brush or an Airbrush Soft Round. In my example I used
an Airbrush Soft Round brush and used the Bracket key to increase the size to about 300 px. The size of your
brush will depend on how big of an area you will be painting over, which will appear to be erased.

With the Adjustment layer selected, use your Brush Tool (B) to paint black on the mask. When you paint black on the mask, it's as if you are erasing the image that is grouped with the Adjustment layer. Do this on each Adjustment layer. If you see black painted on your page, you are painting on one of the photo layers and not the Adjustment layer. Undo and select the Adjustment layer.

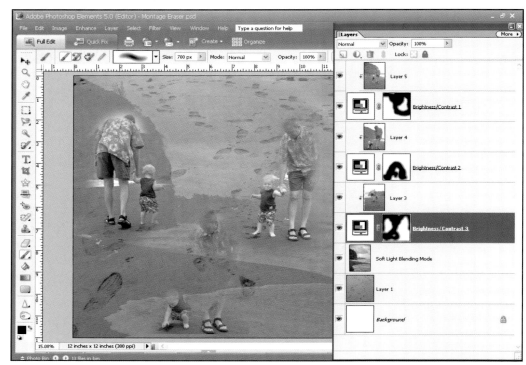

As you paint with black, you can see the black paint on the Adjustment layer mask. Everything that is painted black is no longer visible on your scrapbook page; think of it as being temporarily erased. Click and release your mouse often.

In my example, I quickly painted with black on the Adjustment layer just to see how I would like the way I arranged the photos. The really cool thing about using an Adjustment layer is that now I can go back and paint back in the areas I erased in error by painting white on the Adjustment layer. Type X to swap your Foreground and Background colors and now paint white on the Adjustment layer to paint back in your image. If you have white painted on your scrapbook page, you are not painting on the Adjustment layer.

To softly fade your image into the Background papers, paint with gray instead of black or white.

How To Make A Magazine Or Book Cover

Making a magazine cover is something you might not think you'd ever want to do, but they are a lot of fun and can be great gifts. I bought several cookbooks that were sold as a fundraiser for my son's football team. The cookbooks were in 3 ring binders with a plain cover inserted under the clear binder cover. I made individual covers for my friends and gave them as gifts. I used some very interesting photos of my friends and made up different article names to further personalize them. One of my friends made magazine covers for each table at the team's football banquet. She made a template with the personalized magazine header and writing and then added a photo for each player and coach. She inserted the magazine cover inside a clear plastic 8.5 x 11 inch frame and had a great, inexpensive centerpiece for each banquet table.

There are some great free magazine cover templates you can download to save time at: www.escrappers.com/magazine.html

To make a magazine cover Ctrl>N (File>New) using the specifications shown in the example. I am making this magazine cover 8.5 x 11 inches so that it will fit inside a binder cover or plastic frame.

Ctrl>O (File>Open) the photo that you want to use for the magazine cover. A portrait photo works best, but a landscape photo can be used.

Use the Move Tool (V) to move your photo onto your blank page. Depending on the style of magazine cover you are making you may want to completely cover the blank page or leave an empty spot at the top.

In my example I am going to leave a blank spot at the top for the title that I will fill with color.

Use the Type Tool (T) to print the title of your magazine and the titles for the stories that are supposed to be inside. Make each text section on its own layer. For the title of my magazine I used the Trajan Pro font, and for the articles I used the Times New Roman font.

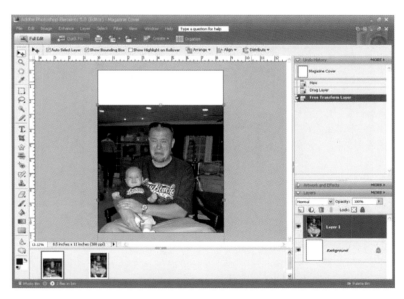

In my example I filled my background with black which filled in the top area. To fill the area with black make black your Foreground color and then Alt>Backspace.

To make this look like a real magazine, I added a price and a barcode on a white rectangle. To make the rectangle, activate the Marquee Tool (M) and drag out a rectangular shape. Make a new layer using the New layer icon on the top of the Layers palette. With white as your Background color Ctrl>Backspace to fill the rectangular selection with white.

Activate the Type Tool (T) and select a barcode font. The font I used is 2Peas Price Check that I purchased from twopeasinabucket.com. Dafont.com also has many free bar code fonts available. Some people get confused when they type the barcode because it looks funny. When you type the barcode it types the barcode line along with whatever letter you are typing at the base of the barcode line. If you don't see this, check to make sure that you are typing in black over the white rectangle. Highlight the font size and roll your mouse wheel to quickly size the type.

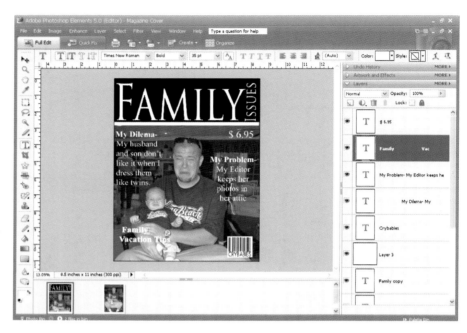

How To Put The Baby In The Bag

This section was going to be titled "My Head On The Body Of A Beauty Queen". However, I couldn't find anyone who would volunteer to let me use a photo of their beauty queen body. When I asked people on the street to volunteer they gave me strange looks. Unfortunately (for me and them), I didn't have any friends that qualified. The technique of putting the baby in a bag is similar to putting a head on another body.

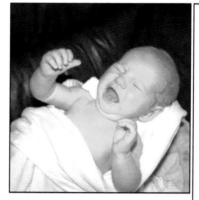

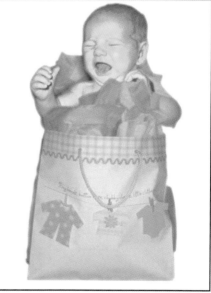

I have always admired Ann Geddes' photos of very young babies. After trying to take photos of an infant I realize that she is even more talented than I first believed. Originally, I tried to put the baby in the gift bag much to the dismay of his parents. I realized very quickly that he wasn't strong enough to hold his head up, so I improvised.

I began by taking a photo of the bag itself with the tissue paper in it. I used the Magnetic Lasso Tool (L) to cut out the bag and the tissue paper. Next I used the same tool to cut out the baby from the couch he was laying on as seen in the original photo. Work slowly and precisely to make good selections. Click often to set many anchor points. Use the Selection Brush (A) to help smooth out your selection border. When your selection is finished, click on the starting point or Ctrl Click to finish the selection. Marching ants will surround your selection.

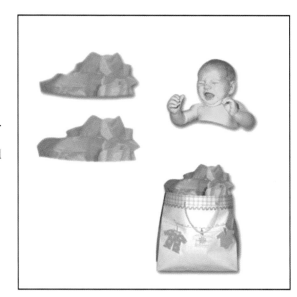

Feather your selection by choosing Select>Feather, Feather Radius 2 px. To delete the part of the photo you no longer need Shift>Ctrl>I to inverse your selection. Marching ants will now surround the unwanted area. Tap the Delete key. Tap the Esc key to remove the marching ants selection border.

Make a new file Ctrl>N (File>New). The size of the new file will depend on how you're going to use the final image. Choose 300 resolution and RGB Color.

Drag your selections onto the new blank page. In my example, this is the baby, the bag, and the tissue paper. I duplicated (Ctrl>J) the tissue paper layer so I could put some behind the baby to make it look more realistic.

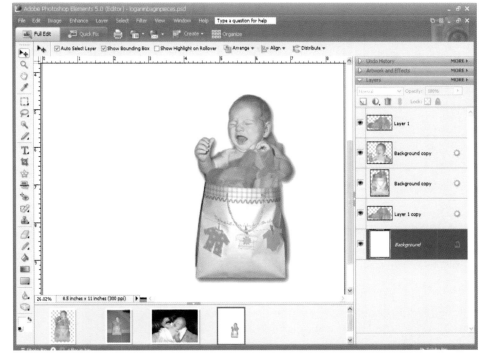

Use the Move Tool (V) to position everything in place. You might need to scale some of the layers to fit the image you're combining it with. To do this, drag one of the corner sizing handles with the Move Tool (V) activated.

Add drop shadows and you're done.

Quick And Easy Plastic Surgery Without Blood Or A Medical License

There are many things you can do to improve your appearance in a photo. It's a little discerning after you've spent a lot of time fixing a photo, only to catch a glimpse in the mirror to find that the changes only took place on the photo. The poor woman in this example has just been on the red eye to New York and even before she left she needed an extreme makeover!

Duplicate your image, because you would be very sad to ruin a photo of this quality. To begin with, in order to avoid a lawsuit, I cropped out the other woman in this photo, who also looked just as lovely. Use the Red Eye Tool (Y) to remove the red eyes.

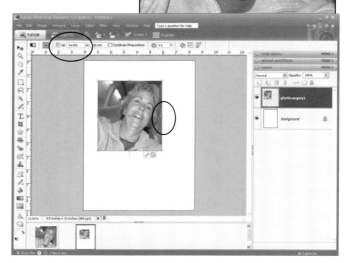

Duplicate the photo layer Ctrl>J or Layer>New>Layer Via Copy. On the top layer use the Healing Brush Tool (J) to tackle all of the wrinkles and other imperfections. This may take quite some time. Lower the Opacity on the top layer so that the two layers blend together nicely. Ctrl>E to merge the two layers.

One fast way to lose 5 lbs is to use the Move Tool (V). Grab one of the side sizing boxes (shown circled) and push in slightly. Once you start to move one of the side sizing boxes the transform option bar will be displayed as shown. It's not a good idea to change the width percentage (shown circled) to less than 95%.

Another way to shave off unwanted pounds is with the Pucker Tool. This can be found in the Distort Filter which is part of the Liquify Filter. Using the Bloat Tool in the same filter will open up a small eye. The Warp Tool can help you make someone smile by clicking on their cheek and ever so slightly pulling upward.

Use the Dodge Tool (O) to brighten up tea stained teeth. Set the exposure low so you don't over whiten them.

Lastly, using the Gaussian Blur filter at a low setting can also help smooth out wrinkles.

If you're still not happy with the results, buy a custom chick graphic from MatterofScrap.com.

Shopping, Downloading & Installing

How To Download A Free Scrapbook Kit

Many digital scrapbooking websites offer freebies, which can be full kits or individual elements. These sites also send newsletters that sometimes include freebies, or tell you where to download freebies from their site separately. At the time this book was written, Scrapgirls was sending a newsletter six days a week. This newsletter includes a freebie to download, instructional tips, interviews with people in the digital scrapbooking field, and product information. It's a great newsletter! To download a freebie at various sites you will probably need to set up an account. You don't need to provide any credit card information until you actually make a purchase. Most sites accept PayPal, which is nice for them and for you, because they never have to see your credit card information. If you pay by e-check, understand that you usually cannot download your purchase until your check clears your bank. Some websites will ask for your date of birth when you sign up for an account and they use this information to send you a coupon on your birthday.

Scrapgirls.com has graciously contributed the Refresh kit for the DVD that came with your book. To download another copy of this kit, go to Scrapgirls.com. Because websites change often, the front page will probably not look the same when you go to the website.

 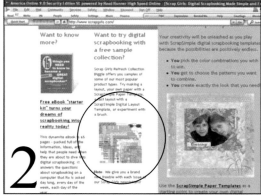

On the front page of the website (#1), scroll down until you see the Refresh Kit. Click on the Refresh Kit circled in example #2. When you get to the Refresh page (#3), do not enter in a quantity where it says "Add to Basket" (circled). Scroll down the page until you see the Download buttons (#4). Click on the first Download button, which is called 1Scrapgirls ReadMe. This is their Terms of Use (TOU), which explains what you are allowed to do with this free kit. Be sure to read the TOU's for all kits before you use them.

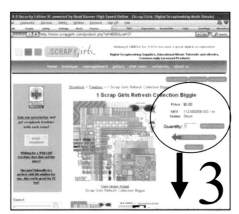 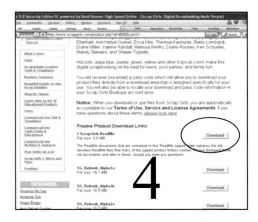

To learn how to Organize your scrapbook supplies so you can find them quickly, be sure to read the Organizing Your Photos, Digi-Kits, Ideas, Time, & Extras Section. Every second you spend organizing your digi-kits will pay off ten fold. Don't put it off! Start organizing from today forward and spend a little time each day organizing all of your old supplies.

All Screen Shots This Page Windows XP

After you click on the download button, you will be asked what you want to do with this file. Choose Save as circled (#5).

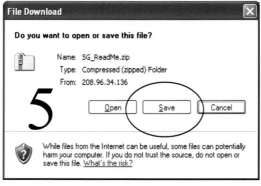

Choose the location that you want to save the file to. I am going to save this in My Documents (#6) in my !Scrapbook Supplies Folder (#7).

Since I do not have a folder for Scrapgirls.com, I will need to make one so that I practice good file management. Click on the New Folder Icon once and a new folder will be made with the name New Folder (#8).

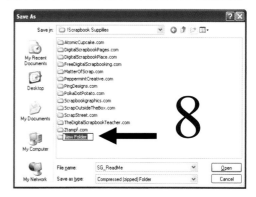

(#9) Immediately type Scrapgirls. Your file will now be named Scrapgirls. Double click on the folder or click on Open. Click on Save (#10).

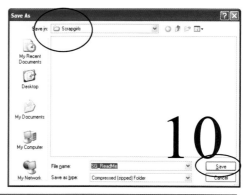

Once you see the screen that says Download Complete (#11), click the Close button and go back and download the rest of the files. Since there are a lot files, sometimes it's helpful to print the screen and then cross them off as you work down the list. Each of these files contains a different type of element, which is helpful when you bring the files into the Organizer to tag. Bring in one folder at a time and tag them all with that element type; like "Alphas" for example, along with the name of the kit and theme all at one time. I also tag by color.

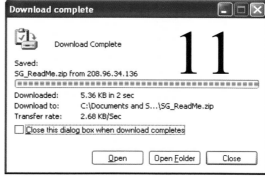

If you get confused and try to download a file twice, your computer will tell you that the file already exists, and ask you if you want to replace it. Click No and choose another file to download.

(#12) There are 16 files to download for the Refresh kit. Check and make sure that you have them all before you leave the website. This is especially important when you purchase a kit, because download links expire. If you try to go back later and download the file you missed, it won't be available.

If you are new at downloading kits, even though this kit is on the DVD that came with this book, it might be a good idea to practice by going to the Scrapgirls website and download it again yourself.

All Screen Shots This Page Windows XP

How To Unzip A Zip File

When you download digi-kit files, fonts, actions, etc., they are in zip files. You can easily tell if a file is zipped because of the little zipper on the folder. Data is compressed in Zip files, which saves time and space when you download them.

The easiest way to find your folders is to put a shortcut button to Windows Explorer on your desktop. This is explained in the Making New Folders in Windows XP section of the Organization Chapter, or check the index for Windows Explorer Shortcut. Unzipping files is so easy, after you do a few, you'll be able to do it in your sleep.

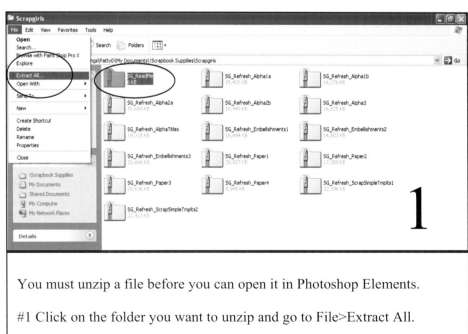

You must unzip a file before you can open it in Photoshop Elements.

#1 Click on the folder you want to unzip and go to File>Extract All.

All Screen Shots This Page Windows XP

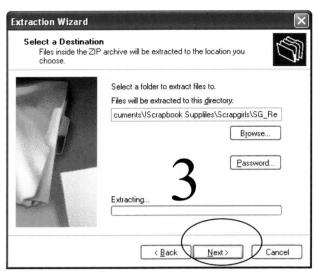

The Extraction Wizard dialog box will be automatically activated (#2). To continue, press the Next button. (#3) Select a folder that you want your files to be extracted to. Click inside the box and use your Arrow key to move to the right and you will see that it's extracting the file to the same folder that you are currently in. If you want to change where your file will be copied, click on the Browse button. Otherwise, click the Next button.

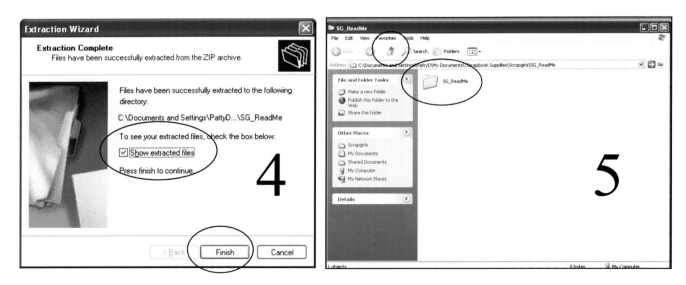

When your files are extracted, you will see the Extraction Complete dialog box (#4). With the Show extracted files box checked, you will be directed to a view of your extracted folder when you click on the Finish button (#5). Click on the Up One Level icon, and you will see all of the files in your Scrapgirls folder as shown on the next page in (#6).

(#6) This screen shows all of the folders inside your Scrapgirls folder. You now have an unzipped and zipped file of the SG_Read me file. Continue unzipping your files until all of them are unzipped.

If you encounter a problem, it is possible you have a corrupted zip file. Several times I have been asked to provide a password for a zip file. When I checked with the website where I purchased my kit, I was told that they don't use passwords. They said that the file was probably damaged when it was downloaded. Delete the corrupted file from your computer and download it again to a different location on your computer, and it should work. After you get it unzipped, move the folder back where you want it to be.

I've recently read about programs on some digi-scrapping message boards that will unzip multiple files at a time. I have not tried any of them yet, but I plan on checking them out when I have a chance. If I find a program that works great, I'll post this information on our website at TheDigitalScrapbookTeacher.com.

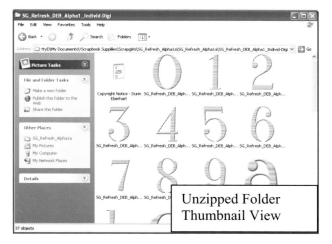

Unzipped Folder Thumbnail View

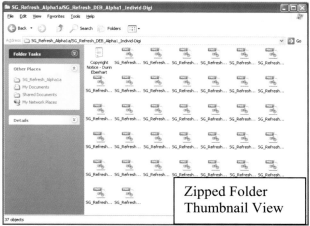

Zipped Folder Thumbnail View

If you attempt to view a thumbnail of your images in a zipped folder, you will be unable to see a preview of the image. You must unzip a file before you can open it in Photoshop Elements.

Shopping Tips

There are plenty of digital scrapbooking sites online where you can download freebies and purchase kits. Some of the websites have categories to search such as children, sports, holidays, etc., which is really nice. I wish they'd all add these categories because it would make shopping a lot quicker and I'd spend less money in the long run. All of the sites I've visited let you search by designer. You'll find after digi-scrapping awhile, that you like certain digital designers and can't live without their brand new kit.

PcCrafter.com not only lists their clip art and scrappables by theme, they also show on their website if you already own the kit, and if it's on your wish list. You must be signed in to your account for this feature to work. To create an account only requires your email address and a password. In addition, when you go to your account page, you can download any of the files you have previously purchased. You are given the option of downloading your files in Windows or Mac format along with JPEG or PNG files, when both are available. No, they didn't pay me to write this in here. I just think their website system is the best I've encountered so far. However, their file set up can be very confusing for a new customer.

While they didn't respond to my request for a digi-kit for the DVD that came with your book, you can go to their site and download a free sampler pack.

Most digital scrapbook sites have sales from time to time and will allow you to accumulate items in your shopping cart to purchase later. You must be signed into your account for this feature to work. Be aware that just because you put something in your virtual shopping cart and it's there when you check on it, there's a good chance that it can disappear later on. If you're going to place things in your cart and then wait for a sale, I'd also make a copy of your list as a back-up.

The perfect gift for your digital scrapping buddy is a gift certificate to a digital scrapbooking website. Different sites handle their gift certificates instantly, and others go through a verification process that may take a few hours. Your friend is notified by e-mail that you have sent them a gift certificate. If you want to print the gift certificate and hand it to your friend, enter in your email address to have the gift certificate emailed to you.

When I shop at digital scrapbooking sites, I usually buy kits because I like the examples they show. When I finally get around to scrapping, I can't remember what the example looked like. I used to print the example pages and stick them in binders, but now I copy the image (Ctrl>C) and paste it on a Word Document. If there are several examples, I save them all. I name this file whatever the kit name is with the word example after it. For example, if I saw a sample page for the Scrapgirls.com Refresh kit, I would name my file RefreshSamples. I save this file inside the kit file so I'll always know where to find it. This takes just seconds to do and is really helpful when I want to use the kit.

When you make a purchase of digital art, you are usually given a link to download your kit. This link will expire in a specified amount of time and you will only be able to access it prior to the expiration. Download and unzip your purchase as soon as possible. Tag your supplies in the Organizer, and you'll be all ready to scrap!

Downloading And Installing Fonts

There are many websites that offer free and for purchase fonts to compliment your projects. A few of my favorite free font sites are:

Dafont.com
MomsCorner4kids.com/fonts
1001freefonts.com
Fontica.com
TwoPeasInABucket.com

Fontseek.com and Identifont.com will help you locate a certain font that you are searching for.

All Screen Shots This Page Windows XP

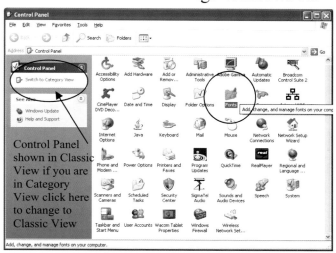

Downloading a font is exactly the same as downloading a scrapbook kit except that it's much quicker. To download a font, follow the instructions on how to download a scrapbook kit. I download my fonts into a Folder I added in My Documents named Fonts. This way, I always have a copy of my fonts available. Be aware that if you install a lot of fonts, it will slow down your computer. Unzip the font file as explained in the preceding example in this section. To install a font, after you've unzipped it, go to Start>Control Panel and choose Fonts (shown circled.) The icons in your Control Panel will be different than mine because I have different items installed on my computer than you do. If your Control Panel does not look like this example, click to Change to Classic View (shown circled). Double click on the Fonts Folder.

When your Fonts folder opens, you'll see all of the fonts that are installed on your computer. Choose File>Install New Font. The Add Fonts dialog box will appear. On the drop down list, I chose C Drive>Patty (user)>My Documents>Fonts. Once inside my Font folder in My Documents, I chose a folder that contained fonts I previously downloaded called digitalreadout. You can see the path I took to find my file in the dialog box under Folders (shown circled.) Make sure the Copy fonts to Fonts folder is checked. Click on the Select All button, and all of the fonts in the box will be hightlighted. Next, click the OK button. If you did not unzip your fonts, they will not show in the list and cannot be installed until they are unzipped.

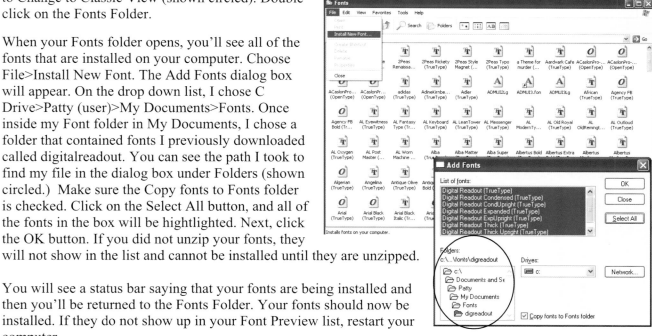

You will see a status bar saying that your fonts are being installed and then you'll be returned to the Fonts Folder. Your fonts should now be installed. If they do not show up in your Font Preview list, restart your computer.

Installing Actions, Layer Styles, Brushes, Patterns, Textures, And Custom Shapes

All kinds of extras that can add extra special effects to your projects can be found on the web and are free or for purchase.

I keep a copy of all of my extras in individual folders named PSE Brushes, PSE Layer Styles, etc. This way, if I ever have to reinstall Photoshop Elements or change computers, I have them all in one place. I also back-up these files regularly.

New in Photoshop Elements 5 are hidden files that you must display before you can install some of the extras that are available. Until you are aware of this, if you tried to install something with instructions from an earlier version of Photoshop Elements, you couldn't figure out what you were doing wrong. Some sites still have not updated their instructions for installing their products in Photoshop Elements 5. If you're having trouble installing an extra, follow these directions, and it's easy.

Before you install anything, close Photoshop Elements.

To Show Hidden Files, choose Start>My Computer>Go to Tools>Folder Options>View>Go to Hidden Files and Folders and be sure "Show Hidden Files and Folders is selected. Click OK.

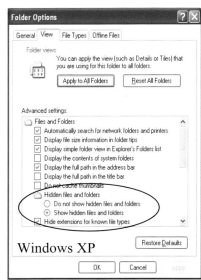

Copy the file of the item you are going to install by right clicking and choosing Copy (Ctrl>C) and then follow the paths below for each type of item you are going to install. Open the folder listed below and Paste (Ctrl>V) the item into the correct folder.

Brushes: C:\Program Files\Adobe\Photoshop Elements 5.0\Presets\Brushes

Patterns: C:\Program Files\Adobe\Photoshop Elements 5.0\Presets\Patterns

Textures: C:\Program Files\Adobe\Photoshop Elements 5.0\Presets\Textures

Custom Shapes: C:\Program Files\Adobe\Photoshop Elements 5.0\Presets\Custom Shapes

Color Swatches: C:\Program Files\Adobe\Photoshop Elements 5.0\Presets\Color Swatches

Gradients: C:\Program Files\Adobe\Photoshop Elements 5.0\Presets\Gradients

Actions (AtomicCupcake.com Actions included on CD): C:\Documents and Settings\All Users\Application Data\Adobe\Photoshop Elements\5.0\Photo Creations\special effects

Layer Styles: C:\Documents and Settings\All Users\Application Data\Adobe\Photoshop Elements\5.0\Photo Creations\special effects\layer styles

Photo Effects: C:\Documents and Settings\All Users\Application Data\Adobe\Photoshop Elements\5.0\Photo Creations\special effects\photo effects

Printing Your Pages & Cards

Printing At Home

Printing at home is the most convenient way to print, however everyone doesn't have room in their scrapping area or budget for a wide format (12 x 12) printer. 8½ x 11 scrappers have many more options. If you scrap in 12 x 12 format, you can always print your page 8 x 8 and use a standard color printer.

My directions will always tell you to save your project as a PSD because you will probably want to go back at some time and change it. When printing at home, you can print straight from the PSD file. You do not have to save your file first as a JPEG, which is the file format photo labs require. Not saving an additional JPEG copy of your file will save you space on your hard drive.

For best results when printing on your home printer, use the photo paper recommended by your printer manufacturer. I used to think this was just an advertising gimmick, but it's true. There is a huge difference between using the Epson scrapbook paper and high quality card stock. When I print I also get better results using Epson photo paper than the brand sold at the big membership store that everyone raved about. Do not refill your ink cartridges at a neighborhood store.

Even if you use the correct ink and paper, your page will probably not print exactly how you see it on your monitor screen. Calibrating monitors is very tricky and unfortunately, isn't covered in this book. If it were, this book would be 600 pages instead of almost 400! There are some tutorials online, but better yet, try to find a friend who's had luck calibrating their own monitor, and buy them lunch to do yours.

Before you print a 12 x 12 page, I recommend printing a smaller sample just to make sure that your colors are printing out OK and you don't have any errors on the page. Always, before printing your page, zoom way in to check for any errors because you almost always find one, and it's disappointing to print a page and have to throw it away.

If you're scrapping to preserve your memories, what good is it if you save a few dollars to have your pages fade and then disappear? Refilled ink cartridges are also known to break and spill inside your printer. If you're shopping for a new printer buy a printer, that has individual color cartridges. My old printer had a color cartridge and a black cartridge. When I printed pages for my son's football team, who had blue uniforms, I used up all of the blue but none of the other colors. I had to throw the cartridge away because it wouldn't work anymore. With my current printer, if I use up all my blue ink, I take it out and replace just the blue cartridge.

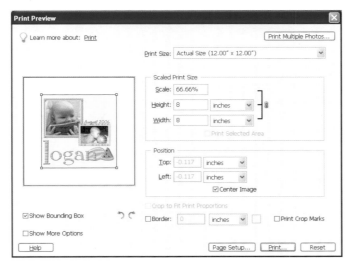

I am asked a lot of questions about printing pages on a 12 x 12 printer, so I am going to show some examples of problems you may encounter. These are the screens from my printer and my computer, so yours will probably not be the same, but hopefully they will show you what to look for on your set-up. The examples I'm showing are for an Epson R1800, which is a great printer that prints 12 x 12 scrapbook pages and larger sizes too. Chose File>P or Ctrl>P. On my computer this is the first screen I see. Notice that the actual size is 12 x 12 and I have entered that I want to print an 8 x 8 size, just by typing in an 8 in both fields. I did not have to figure out the percentage.

Notice that the preview screen on the preceding example looks like what my scrapbook page will print on a larger piece of paper. I will have to change this so I can print on smaller paper. If you are seeing something that doesn't look right, the paper size is probably set to the wrong setting.

If your print preview looks like this example, you will need to fix the problem before you push the print button. This example shows how my 12 x 12 page will look printed on an 8 ½ x 11 piece of paper. It's really important to check the preview window every time you print.

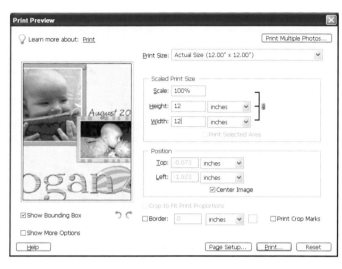

On my computer my default printer is set to my black and white printer that I use for work. To check your printer settings, go to Start>Control Panel>Printers and Faxes. Your default printer will have a ✓ by it shown circled below. To change your default printer, right click on one of the other printers and choose Set as Default Printer.

To correct the problem shown in the above example, click on the Page Setup button so you can make changes. If your preview looks fine, you can click on the Print button, but it doesn't hurt to go to Page Setup and check things out. Right away I can see that the size selected for the paper is letter and it should not be. When I click on the Size drop down arrow, there is no setting for 12 x 12 paper, so I click on the Printer button on the bottom of the box. I choose the R1800 from the list and click on Properties.

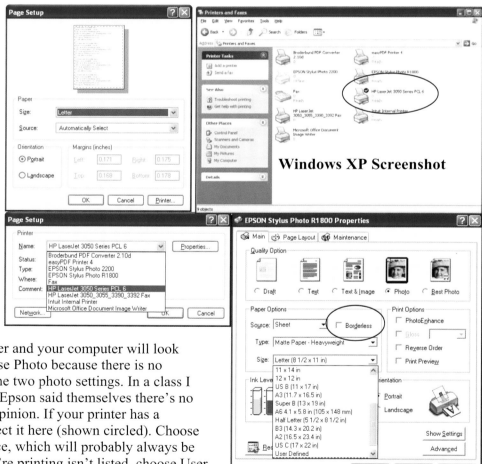

Remember, this is my computer and your computer will look different. In properties, I choose Photo because there is no difference I can see between the two photo settings. In a class I took the girls who worked for Epson said themselves there's no difference, so I go with their opinion. If your printer has a borderless option, you can select it here (shown circled). Choose the type of paper and the source, which will probably always be Sheet. For size, if the size you're printing isn't listed, choose User Defined, and set it up yourself.

Type a name for your paper. I've learned from experience that you should enter the dimensions first, and then a description. Previously I made some invitations and entered the description with names like Kristin's Shower Invite. When I choose paper sizes now, I have no idea what size I made that invitation years ago. Had I typed in something like 8.5 x 5.5 Invitation as a description, it would be a no brainer. Enter the Name, Width, and Height and check the Unit of measure, click on the Save button, and your Paper Size should show in the box like mine does.

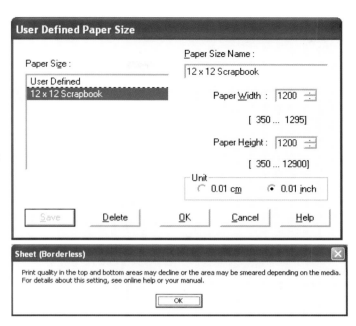

You may get a warning if you choose borderless printing that says it may smear. I've never had a problem with my ink smearing or being a poorer quality on the edges. Click OK, and print your page.

Commercial Printing

Polkadotpotato.com

My best prints have been printed at PolkaDotPotato.com. I order the prints through their website and they are shipped to me. Compared to others, the superior quality of these prints is noticeable. If you have been in any of my classes, you've seen quality of these prints. The prices for their prints are extremely competitive. On the DVD that came with this book is a coupon for printing, so you can try them out. PolkaDotPotato.com offers printing in the sizes scrappers want so that you don't have to crop off an extra few inches of unused photo paper. I only wish they were right next door, because sometimes I'm not organized enough to order my prints and have them shipped to me.

Costco

Even Hawaii has a few Costco's now, so there's probably one near you too. If you're not a member or have a friend who's a member, you can skip this section. If I need prints in a hurry, I can upload them through Costco.com, drive over to the store, and they're usually ready. I've found that I usually like their prints ordered with the Auto Correct feature turned off. They have recently added a feature to turn off Auto Correct permanently. At my Costco my photos were darker with the Auto Correct feature on, but try out your Costco yourself. Costco has just begun to offer 12 x 12 inch photos. They also offer 18 wide by 12 inch high prints for the same price. To stretch your budge you can make a new file (Ctrl>N) 18 wide x 12 high – 300 resolution, and move your 12 x 12 scrapbook page onto this file with the Move Tool (V). You will be left with an empty space, 6 inches wide by 12 inches high. In this space, three 4 x 6 photos will fit if you want to move them on your page. When you pick up your 18 x 12 print, you will need to use a paper cutter to cut the three photos and one scrapbook page apart.

I never seem to have enough time to do the things I want to do, and sending 4 x 6 inch photos to friends and family is one of them. With Costco it's easy and free too. I upload my photos and then choose the ones I want to print. I choose to have the photos sent to someone in my address book and Costco ships the photos to them free. I don't have to go to the store, place the order, pick them up, put them in an envelope, address them, and mail them, and it's all done for me, for free! Sometimes I even make a new 6 x 4 file (Ctrl>N) and use my Type Tool (T) to write a little note, add some clip art, and have it developed along with my photos in lieu of a note to the recipient.

Index

Photo Credit

Azurde Harris - Pages 149, 243
Chris Debowski - Pages 341-44
Kristin Boyd - Pages 17, 63-65, 121, 123, 145-46, 148, 218, 226, 322, 346

Nami Aoyagi - Page 263
Ryan Breska - Pages 223, 224
Sherrie Lodge - Pages 97, 105, 242
Unknown - (Heritage Photos) 228-31, 264

TheDigitalScrapbookTeacher.com
Check out our website for new products and special pricing.

The Digital Scrapbook Teacher specializes in digital scrapbook and card templates to save you time and money. Our templates are reasonably priced and easy to use.

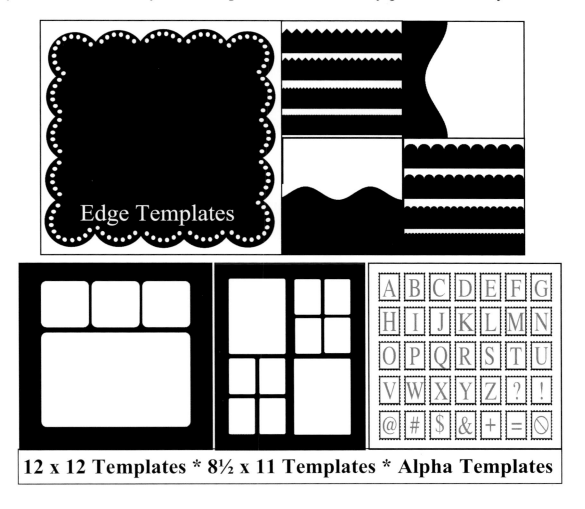

12 x 12 Templates * 8½ x 11 Templates * Alpha Templates

Also available:

- Card Templates

- Text Paths

- 24 by 12 inch high Double Scrapbook Page Layout Templates

- Desk Reference Card (8½ x 11- two sided) to keep by your desk to speed up your digi-scrapping

- Organizer Catalog Back-up* - All of the more than 1000 pieces of digi-scrapping elements included on the book DVE are pre-tagged for you. Save at least 10 hours of work yourself! *Book must be purchased now or previously to purchase this item.

THE DIGITAL SCRAPBOOK TEACHER
ORDER FORM

Please Print Legibly

NAME: _____

MAILING ADDRESS: _____

CITY: _____ STATE: _____ ZIP: _____

EMAIL ADDRESS: _____

TELEPHONE: _____ - _____ - _____ EXT. _____ FAX: _____ - _____ - _____

Advance payment required via check or money order
Please make payable to: Patty Debowski
Mail To:
The Digital Scrapbook Teacher
18837 Brookhurst St #201
Fountain Valley CA 92708-7302
For Credit Card orders and special offers visit:
THEDIGITALSCRAPBOOKTEACHER.COM
Orders shipped via USPS media mail, for faster shipping options please order from our website

SELECTION LIST	Qty	Unit Cost	Total
Book – Digital & Hybrid Scrapbooking & Card-Making by Patty Debowski		$39.99	
CD – (50) 12 x 12 Assorted Templates (Circle One A B C)		$19.99	
CD – (50) 8.5 x 11 Assorted Templates (Circle One A B C)		$19.99	
CD – (50) Total Templates – (25) 12 x 12 & (25) 8.5 x 11 (Circle One A B C)		$19.99	
CD - (25) 12 x 24 Double Wide Page Templates		$19.99	
CD – Card Templates (50)		$19.99	
CD – Edge Templates & Text Paths (50)		$19.99	
CD – Alpha Templates (10 sets upper and lower case letters & numbers)		$19.99	
New Scrapper Special choose 6 CDs from above		$99.99	
Desk Reference Card 8 ½ x 11 inch 2-sided card with everything you need to know about using Photoshop Elements to digi-scrap		$ 6.99	
Organizer Catalog Back-up – All of the more than 1000 pieces of digi-scrapping elements included on the book DVD pre-tagged for you. Save at least 10 hours of work yourself! *Book must be purchased now or previously to purchase this item.		$24.99*	
Shipping & Handling (USPS media rate)— Flat Rate per Order USA Only		$5.00	
Sub-Total			
California Only Residents add 7.75% Tax			
GRAND TOTAL ALL ITEMS			**$**